Modern
Peru

A Modern New Peru History

Paulo Drinot & Alberto Vergara, editors

DUKE UNIVERSITY PRESS *Durham and London* 2025

© 2025 DUKE UNIVERSITY PRESS
All rights reserved
Project Editor: Lisa Lawley
Designed by Matthew Tauch
Typeset in Garamond Premier Pro and General Sans
by Westchester Publishing Services

Library of Congress Cataloging-in-Publication Data
Names: Drinot, Paulo, editor. | Vergara, Alberto, editor.
Title: Modern Peru : a new history / Paulo Drinot and Alberto
Vergara, editors.
Description: Durham : Duke University Press, 2025. | Includes
bibliographical references and index.
Identifiers: LCCN 2024057279 (print)
LCCN 2024057280 (ebook)
ISBN 9781478032526 (paperback)
ISBN 9781478029175 (hardcover)
ISBN 9781478061380 (ebook)
Subjects: LCSH: Peru—History. | Peru—Politics and government. |
Peru—Economic conditions.
Classification: LCC F3444 .M556 2025 (print) | LCC F3444 (ebook)
LC record available at https://lccn.loc.gov/2024057279
LC ebook record available at https://lccn.loc.gov/2024057280

Cover art: Courtesy of *La República* Photographic Archive,
Lima, Peru.

Contents

The Curse of Freedom?

The French have an expression: "Ce n'est pas le Pérou!" (It's not Peru). Said of something unexceptional, mundane, the saying recalls a time when Peru was synonymous with unlimited riches thanks to silver flowing from Potosí. In Spanish, the phrase "¡Vale un Perú!" (It's worth a Peru) conveys much the same image. Today, for most, Peru evokes not unimaginable wealth but rather Machu Picchu, the Incas, or a plate of ceviche. Peruvian governments of late have welcomed this largely positive global image. It has fitted nicely into their promotion of the country as a destination for tourism and, increasingly, gastro-tourism. Not surprisingly, this simple image hides not only a far more complex contemporary reality but also a compelling, if not always palatable, history. This book, written in the run-up to Peru's bicentenary of independence in 2021, provides an up-to-date overview of Peru's history since the late colonial period that can help readers gain a better understanding of the country, past and present.

Peru shares some features with other Latin American countries but is also something of an outlier. Like Mexicans with the Aztecs, Peruvians can claim a past of civilizational greatness with the Incas and earlier pre-Inca cultures. Peru was one of the centers of Spanish rule in the Americas—a viceroyalty, no less. But the country also bucks regional trends: it became independent later than almost all its neighbors; it entered the export age early, when it became a global exporter of guano in the 1840s; it fought one of the major interstate wars in modern Latin America, the War of the Pacific (1879–83), which it lost to Chile, and saw its capital occupied by the enemy forces (something that only Mexico and Paraguay experienced); it developed a broad-based export sector in the late nineteenth and early twentieth centuries, when most countries in the region focused on a single export such as sugar, coffee, or bananas; when neighboring economies turned toward import-substitution strategies after the Great Depression, Peru stuck with laissez-faire; when those same countries fell to right-wing dictatorships, it was saddled with a peculiar left-wing one under Juan Velasco Alvarado; and when the region started to overcome the Cold War and democratize, it faced the violence of the Shining Path and a new authoritarianism under Alberto Fujimori.

In this book we set out to approach the history of Peru in the last 250 years in a broad way in order to account for, and explain, this historical trajectory. We set the chapter authors three objectives: First, to write novel and synthetic accounts of state-society relations in a designated period. In other words, not only to tell a story but also to put forward an argument. Second, to base that argument on the most recent scholarship. And third, to write chapters that could be read and enjoyed by a general audience, not only by academics. Thus, from the outset, we resisted imposing a theoretical framework on the authors, trusting, rather, that their experience would allow them to come up with the most effective strategy for narrating and explaining their periods of analysis. This is a volume, then, that can be read as an introduction to independent Peru but also as an introduction to the most recent scholarship on independent Peru.

This does not imply, however, that we are proposing a comprehensive, new national history, let alone an "official" history. Presidents Augusto B. Leguía and Juan Velasco Alvarado took advantage of the centenary of independence in 1921 and the sesquicentenary in 1971 to try to establish new narratives about the national past and, thus, about the country they sought to build. But today there is no comprehensive national project in Peru. In 2021, state efforts in relation to the bicentenary were modest and offered little by way of a grand reading of the past. The bicentenary arrived while, on the one hand, Peru was ravaged by the COVID-19 pandemic and, on the other, the country was in a deep political crisis (where it today remains). In other words, the bicentenary found a disoriented country and a state with little capacity for action in the cultural field.

In the last decade, Peru went from experiencing a period of national optimism, with a buoyant economy, to the current moment of pessimism, marked by a political, economic, and public health debacle—as chapter 6 shows, Peru's experience of the COVID-19 pandemic was one of the worst in the world and coincided with one of the deepest political crises the country has experienced since the turn of the twentieth century: Between 2016 and 2023 Peru had six presidents. In these circumstances, the temptation to explain the present crisis based on the presence or absence of certain isolated historical or sociological factors (the colonial legacy, the lack of a modernizing bourgeoisie, structural dualism, etc.) is understandable but not very useful. History cannot be reduced to a menu from which one chooses the factor that explains the present. At the same time, history undeniably contains elements that help to understand the present.

As the chapters show, these two hundred years of independence have been marked by the country's inability to flourish fully. Each new period generates new challenges that are added to earlier ones, making the country a puzzle of infinite dimensions that appears impossible to solve. Peru is a country in which the most stable feature seems to be instability. Each chapter in the country's history unintentionally ends up punctuated by recurring processes of construction and reconstruction, by feelings of expectation and disenchantment. It is a history marked by an endless back-and-forth between political, economic, and social options. Politically, the country has shifted between democracy and dictatorship dozens of times; in economic terms, it has oscillated between free trade and protectionism in both the nineteenth and twentieth centuries; structurally, it has been subject to centralizing and decentralizing efforts at various times.

The national projects that have shaped this history and which the different chapters explore in detail—the republican project of the early independence period, the guano state and the *pax castillista* of the mid-nineteenth century, *civilismo* from the mid-nineteenth to the early twentieth century, the *indigenismo* of the 1920s, the *aprismo* of the 1930s, the *acciopopulismo* of the early 1960s, Velasco's military reformism in the late 1960s and early 1970s, neoliberalism in the 1990s and onward—all evoke the famous myth of Sisyphus. The country seems condemned to carry the rock of each national project to the top of a mountain only to let it roll back down, and then to pick it up once more. Like Sisyphus, Peru seems cursed by freedom, with independence seemingly unleashing an endless repetition of national projects condemned to failure.

Because of this repetition of national projects that seem destined to fail, the mood of the citizenry fluctuates between affection for and rejection of the country. However, the Sisyphus metaphor serves not only to designate something that resembles a punishment as divine as it is inescapable; it also provides room for optimism and action. This is the other side of the curse of freedom. In Albert Camus's essay on the myth, Sisyphus becomes a rich and human character when he descends the mountain to pick up the rock. That moment of rest is the moment of consciousness. Sisyphus becomes a tragic character—and not just a puppet of destiny—when he recognizes the absurd condition in which he finds himself: "Crushing truths perish from being acknowledged" and then "He knows himself to be the master of his days."[1]

How Peru has dealt with the curse of freedom—that is, the extent to which it has been able to address the many challenges that its independent or postcolonial history has produced—is the subject of the seven chapters of this book. In the first chapter, Charles Walker covers the long transition from colony to republic between 1780 and 1840: from the Túpac Amaru rebellion and subsequent independence to the total defeat of the Peru-Bolivia Confederation. Although Peru was "born conservative," Walker argues, important movements challenged this system by defying social structures, slavery, and the status quo. Seeking alternatives, these heterogeneous projects contested continuities and extended into the nineteenth century (and into the present).

In the next chapter, Natalia Sobrevilla Perea explores the guano era (1840–80), which generated a prosperity that, rather than being illusory, as historian Jorge Basadre argued, was unequal. The enrichment of the state through guano exports made it possible to overcome some of the legacies of the colonial period and led to the construction of a new political system. Although the injection of money caused the economy to expand exponentially—making possible a certain "modernization" of society—this process was accompanied by immense corruption and clientelism that became the main characteristic of the guano system, which led to the country's bankruptcy and defeat by Chile.

José Luis Rénique, meanwhile, concentrates on the transition from the nineteenth to the twentieth century, the period that began with the War of the Pacific and the decades of reconstruction that followed (1883–1919). This was a "hinge" period, as Rénique calls it, in which economic recovery allowed for the challenge of building a viable political system in tune with the requirements of export growth and the country's emerging social and political complexity. Between oligarchy and democracy, equipped with a contradictory vision of "traditional modernization," the civilian elite took on the organization and direction of the state, which it did not succeed in maintaining.[2]

In chapter 4, Paulo Drinot focuses on the beginning of the Leguía dictatorship to the military regime of Velasco (1919–68), a period marked by the transformation of a mainly agrarian and sparsely populated country into an increasingly urban one that experienced significant demographic expansion. The chapter emphasizes how the emergence of mass politics and attempts to "integrate" the Indigenous population were embedded in processes of global change, such as the emergence of the United States as a global hegemon, the Russian Revolution, the Great Depression, the emergence of the "Third World" as a geopolitical category, and the Cold War.

Eduardo Dargent's chapter studies the period 1968 to 1994, beginning with the military government of Juan Velasco Alvarado, passing through the economic crisis and political violence of the 1980s, and concluding in the early years of Alberto Fujimori's rule, when the crisis waned. He proposes that in those years there was a significant increase in political participation and organization until the 1980s, but at the same time a series of processes (agrarian reform, political violence, economic crisis, and neoliberal reform), as well as the delegitimization of politics produced by the crisis, demobilized and dismantled these organizations, giving rise to a country with a very different political physiognomy.

In the sixth chapter, Alberto Vergara analyzes how political life gave priority to the imperative of governing over that of representing in contemporary Peru (1992–2021), in contrast to twentieth-century Peru, when representation was an objective in itself—and often at odds with the capacity to govern. The chapter also addresses another cycle of expectation and disenchantment, a trajectory that travels through the optimism of economic modernization to the demoralization of Peru during the COVID-19 pandemic.

Drawing on these chapters and drawing comparisons between Peru and other Latin American countries, Cynthia McClintock highlights in the last chapter of the book the exceptional scale of the challenges to inclusion, democracy, and development in Peru. However, she also highlights the progress that has been made in the twenty-first century, before the pandemic struck the country. In so doing, she assesses the extent to which classical theories of democracy help explain Peru's trajectory.

. . . .

While we began working on this book in 2017, the bulk of the writing was done in 2020 and 2021. The authors organized several workshops to discuss the chapters, and the editors are very grateful to Chuck Walker, Natalia Sobrevilla Perea, José Luis Rénique, Eduardo Dargent, and Cynthia McClintock for their willingness to participate. We would also like to thank Viviana Baraybar and Adrián Lerner, who participated in the meetings

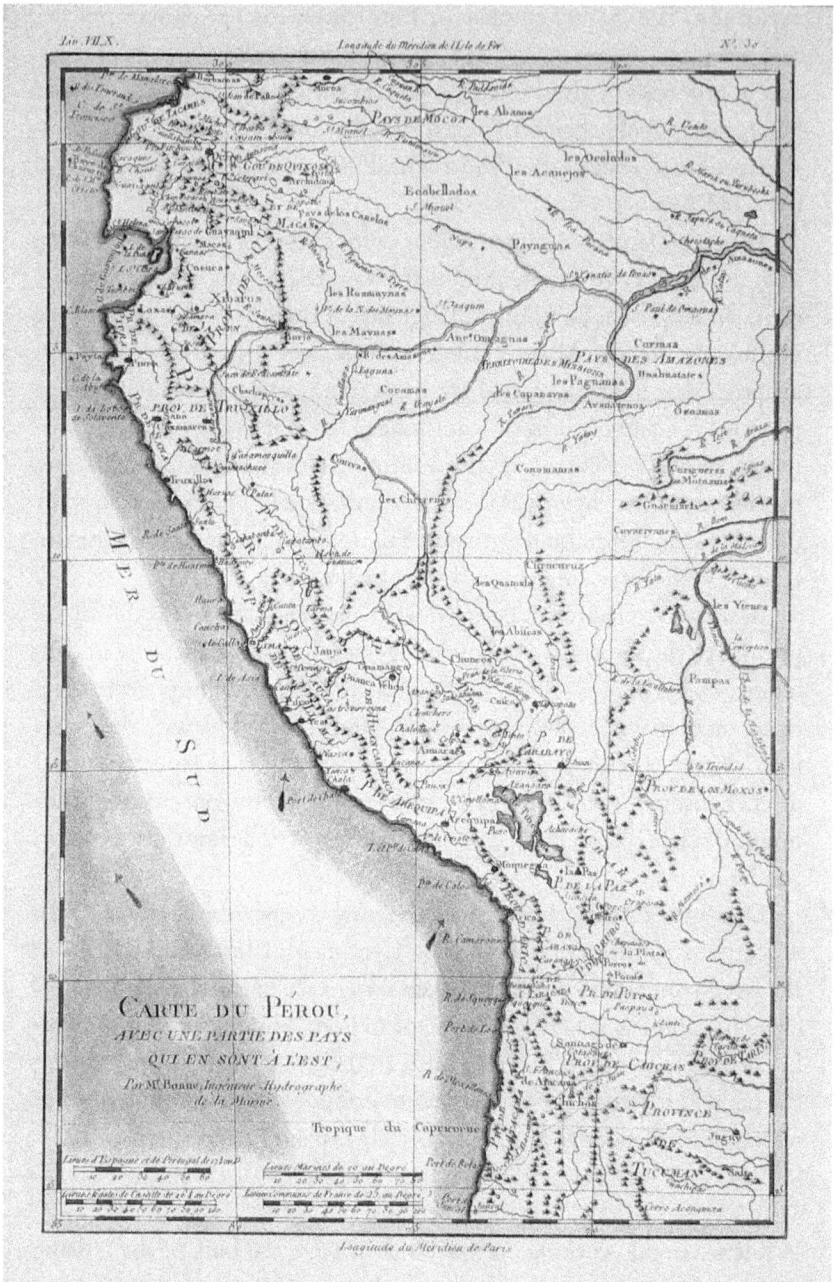

Figure I.1 Rigobert Bonne, *Carte du Pérou avec une partie des pays qui en sont à l'est* (map of Peru with some countries to the east), ca. 1780.

and were going to write a chapter with statistics, maps, and documents from independent Peru, an effort that, unfortunately, the pandemic thwarted. Likewise, a work of interpretative synthesis such as this would not be possible without the scholarship on which each of the chapters is based. The bibliographical notes at the end of each chapter give an account of the valuable contribution of historians, sociologists, anthropologists, archaeologists, journalists, economists, political scientists, and other specialists, both Peruvian and foreign, to our knowledge of the country. We would also like to thank Malena Romero at the Fondo Editorial of the Universidad del Pacífico and María Fernanda Castillo of Planeta for believing in this project, and Alessandra Miyagi, who displayed great care and attention to detail in editing the Spanish version of the book. We are particularly grateful to Gisela Fosado and her team at Duke University Press for agreeing to publish the English version of the book. Thanks too to Katia Villalobos for her work on the index. Finally, we want to acknowledge the institutions that gave us permission to reproduce various images: the newspapers *La República* and *El Comercio*, the Lima Museum of Art (MALI), and the Pontificia Universidad Católica del Perú.

Notes

1   Albert Camus, *The Myth of Sisyphus and Other Essays*, trans. Justin O'Brien (New York: Vintage Books, 1991), 122, 123.

2   See Fernando de Trazegnies, *La idea del derecho en el Perú republicano del siglo XIX*. Lima: Fondo editorial de la Pontificia Universidad Católica del Perú, 1992.

A Complex Destiny
Peru and the Difficult Transition from Colony to Republic (1780–1840)

Peru from 1780 to 1840 changed radically. A decades-long war of independence culminated in the defeat of the Spanish in the 1820s and the abrupt transformation from colony to republic.[1] These uprisings built from and contributed to the transatlantic age of revolutions, with the French occupation of Spain from 1808 to 1815 marking events in the Americas. Upon independence, democracy rather than the will of the king would be the ultimate arbiter, under constitutional rule. The old regime had ended, a republic created. The press flourished. And in 1820 the Inquisition was abolished. The nascent country was significantly smaller than the viceroyalty, with Bolivia and Chile to the south and Ecuador to the north gaining their independence. In terms of economic changes, Peru no longer counted the Potosí mines within its newly drawn borders (they were now part of Bolivia), and thousands of Spaniards, much of the dominant merchant class, departed. Peru was a vastly different entity by the middle of the nineteenth century.

Or was it? Many continuities stand out. While numerous countries emerged with new names, such as Colombia, Ecuador, and Bolivia, Peru remained Peru. More substantially, it maintained a rigid class or caste system, with severe stratification. African and Afro-American slavery persisted, and those deemed Indians continued to pay a head tax. Despite (timid) calls for egalitarianism and the partial dismantling of corporatism during the long war of independence, Indigenous people still constituted

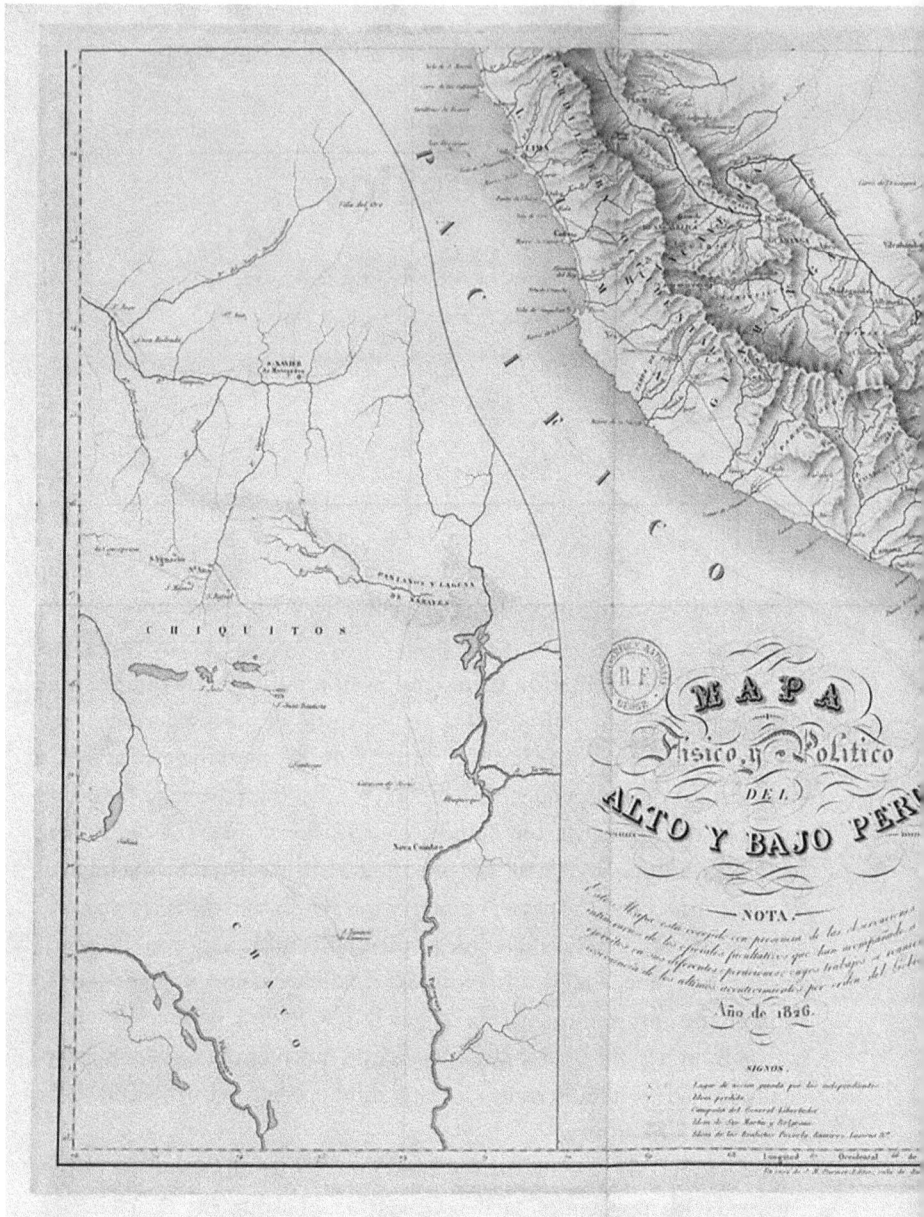

Figure 1.1 J. M. Darmet, *Mapa físico y político del alto y bajo Peru* (Physical and political map of upper and lower Peru), 1826. Source: Biblioteca Nacional de Chile.

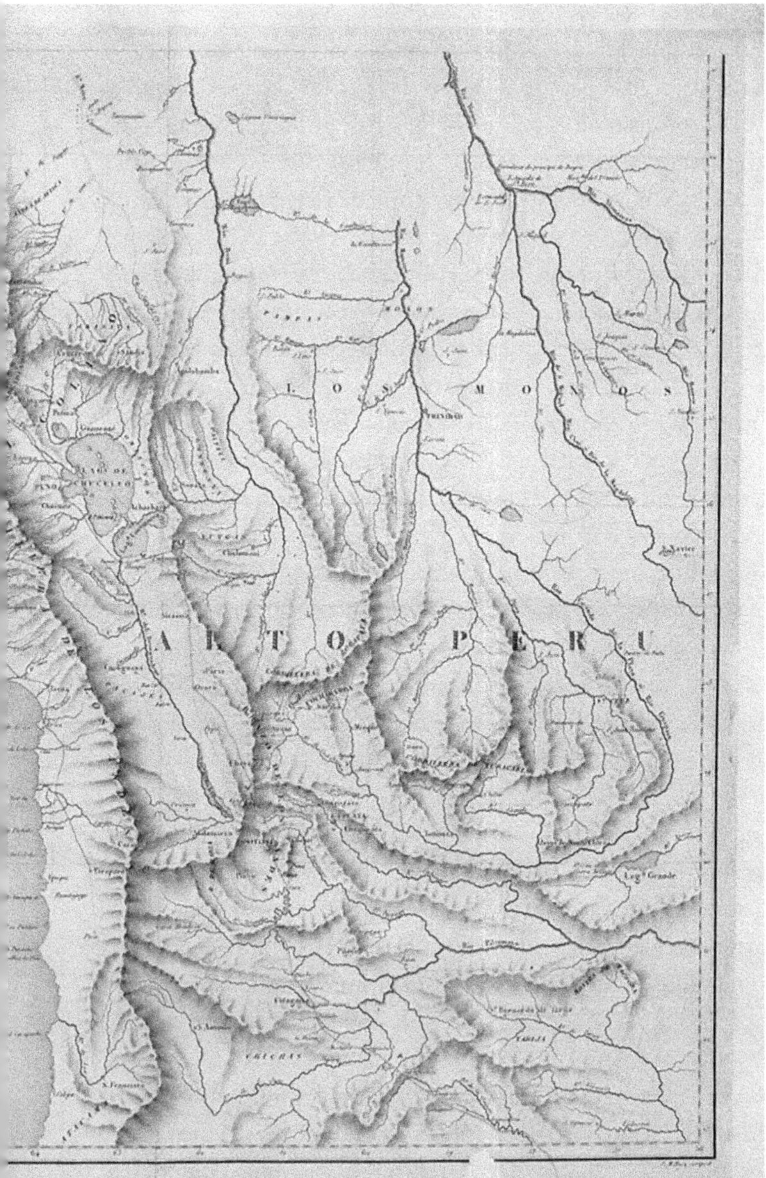
A L T O   P E R U
Lag.a Grande

a separate fiscal category, a distinct sociopolitical category. Although Lima lost some of its power vis-à-vis ports such as Buenos Aires or Guayaquil, it maintained its absolute dominance in Peru's political, economic, and cultural life. Furthermore, the Catholic Church also remained central in spiritual and daily life, intervening in politics as well. And although Potosí now belonged to Bolivia, mining continued to be the backbone of the Peruvian economy, with English merchants replacing the departed Spanish. Peru changed radically in these six decades but also stayed the same in many ways. It did so not because of the lack of political struggles or movements but because of a variety of confrontations and projects in which conservatives ultimately maintained the upper hand. Furthermore, below the chaotic decades of caudillo wars and seeming stasis brewed powerful demands for change, which would emerge in later decades. For example, enslaved people and other forces that challenged slavery, at the personal and institutional levels, succeeded in their challenges, but not until the 1850s.

This chapter probes Peru's meandering path to independence and the creation of a republic, from the mass Andean uprisings of the 1780s and the defeat of the Spanish in the Battle of Ayacucho in 1824 to the early caudillo regimes. While it outlines the events of these four decades, focusing on Peru but with an eye on events in Spain as well as elsewhere in Spanish America, it seeks to underline the richness or diversity of political projects that emerged. Peru was a royalist bastion in these decades, for reasons explored here, but also witnessed radical uprisings and a variety of political schemes or projects. Peru's bicentennial in 2021 fostered renewed attention on this period. This chapter stresses the need to examine the contingent nature of the war of independence, specifically the numerous outcomes that could have been—frustrated projects that nonetheless cast a shadow on republican Peru and cannot be subsumed under a royalist/patriot dichotomy. It also underlines the still unfinished agenda of the "new social history," the attempt to put the lower classes, subaltern groups, and women at the forefront of historiography. Despite the renaissance of "history from below," regional history, and other new currents in the 1970s and 1980s, we still focus on and have a clearer view of the upper classes and the elite, while our understanding of common people remains foggy.[2]

In terms of paths not taken, as we will see, Inca revivalism, the more radical strains of liberalism, and the diverse federalist dreams that questioned Lima's hegemony did not come to fruition but continue to represent tantalizing alternatives. They might not have prevailed in the 1820s, but they attracted followers and fertilized a variety of political projects.

Figure 1.2 Francisco "Pancho" Fierro, *Rabona en marcha* (Rabona marching), ca. 1800. Source: Museo de Arte de Lima.

Rabona en marcha

Furthermore, royalism deserves renewed attention—why did some remain so tied to the Spanish, not just the merchant elite that benefited from the Bourbon system but, during the long war of independence, subaltern groups as well? A return to these topics and the concomitant renewed attention to those written out of traditional history would greatly enrich our understanding of the war of independence, its long history and aftermath, and debates and discontent surrounding the bicentennial celebrations in 2021.[3]

This experimentation or search for alternatives continued after independence. Peru faced the great challenges the nascent Spanish American nations confronted. In the decades after independence, caudillos jostled for power; between 1821 and 1845 the average presidential term was barely a year and a half. Peru lost territory to the north, south, and east.[4] The uncertainty about Peru's new boundaries and the various plans to annex or unite with Bolivia prompted frequent border conflicts. Behind the facade of chaos and instability, however, lay a fissure between conservatives and liberals. These two groups struggled over the nature and organization of postcolonial Peru, creating complex and dynamic political alliances. These caudillo coalitions displayed the multiple tensions or divisions that marked Peru, the same ones that emerged during the long wars of independence: regionalism versus anti-Lima federalism, pro- versus anti-free-trade factions, elites wary of changes to the status quo versus subaltern groups searching for greater inclusion, and more. Caudillismo also displayed the tremendous challenges to state formation in Peru: the nation's vastness (for example, Iquitos still cannot be reached by road from the coast); its topography; its multiculturalism and multilingualism, so rarely recognized by the powers that be in Lima; and the legacy of Spanish colonialism. Although Peru was born conservative in the sense that the more radical schemes of the wars of independence waned and few deep-seated transformations took place in subsequent decades, it witnessed a fecund diversity of political projects and collective efforts to reshape the status quo. Many of these would persist.

Radical Change: From Túpac Amaru to Napoleon

In early November 1780, José Gabriel Condorcanqui, who also used the name Túpac Amaru to underline his ties to the Inca royal family, kidnapped a local authority, with whom he had had lunch earlier in the day: Antonio Arriaga, the *corregidor*, or chief magistrate, of the town of Tinta, near Cuzco. Túpac Amaru escorted him to his house in nearby Pampamarca, where he forced Arriaga to request money and arms. Túpac Amaru and his wife, Micaela Bastidas, called for Indigenous people of the area, the vast majority, to congregate. They held a "popular trial" of Arriaga, conducting much of the hearing in Quechua, and, to the shock of the thousands present, hanged him on November 10.

Thus began the largest rebellion in Spanish American colonial history. It spread rapidly to the south, as rebels ransacked haciendas and textile mills and pursued the odious *corregidores*. Túpac Amaru and Bastidas sought to limit the violence against non-Spaniards, often to no avail. Cuzco authorities sent the city's militia, but the rebels routed them. Túpac Amaru headed toward Lake Titicaca to recruit, haranguing locals with a call for rebellion in Quechua, and to ward off a royalist attack from Arequipa or even Buenos Aires. Bastidas oversaw logistics, wary that troops from Cuzco would overrun the rebel camp. Túpac Amaru returned to the base south of Cuzco in December but his forces, surging to over thirty thousand rebel troops, failed to take the city of Cuzco in late 1780 / early 1781.

Well-armed troops in battalions, including cavalry, reached Cuzco in early 1781. They tracked the rebels to the south, the heart of the uprising. The royalists captured Bastidas and Túpac Amaru, much of their family, and their inner circle in April. They marched them to Cuzco, tried them, and executed them in brutal fashion on May 18, 1781. Their youngest son, Fernando, was forced to watch as executioners strangled Bastidas with the garrote and quartered Túpac Amaru. Authorities displayed their body parts across the region. Yet the rebellion was far from over. Túpac Amaru's cousin Diego Cristóbal, their son Mariano, and a relative of Bastidas's, Andrés Mendigure, eluded the royalists and pushed the rebellion to the south. It became increasingly violent, as in some areas they targeted anyone who was not Indigenous; the royalists acted in kind, converting *Indian* and *rebel* into synonyms. The death count reached the tens of thousands, and by late 1782 the Spanish believed they could very likely lose control of the Andes from Cuzco to beyond Potosí. The exhausted rebels, however, accepted a ceasefire in January 1783. Months later, authorities claimed the rebels had broken the terms of the ceasefire and arrested them, executing them on July 18, 1783, in a manner just as brutal as the executions of Túpac Amaru, Micaela Bastidas, and others two years earlier. The Spanish had won, but at an enormous cost. Peru would never be the same.[5]

What did the rebellion seek? This is a surprisingly challenging question, one that has vexed scholars for many generations. Túpac Amaru and Micaela Bastidas sought a multiracial and multiclass coalition, striving to limit violence against creoles and other intermediary groups as well as the Catholic Church. In their discourse and action, multiple political currents emerged: Inca nationalism or the *utopía andina* (Andean utopianism), Habsburgian notions of *buen gobierno* or good government, and sweeping anti-Bourbon sentiments.[6] Their followers, particularly in the second phase, held much more radical views or at least took more violent measures, extending the definition of Spaniard or *puka kunka* (literally "red neck") to virtually everyone who did not speak Quechua. This eclecticism did not just reflect Túpac Amaru's ambiguity (the desire for revolutionary change that did not target the Catholic Church or affluent creoles) or tensions within the coalition—it was also a reflection of the period. The French and Haitian Revolutions had not taken place yet and the United States was just emerging as a republic. Túpac Amaru and Micaela Bastidas did not count on precedents for such a large undertaking.

This search for a platform or an ideology would continue in the coming decades as Peruvian dissidents considered alternative forms of monarchism, federalism, and republicanism. In this period, the late eighteenth and early nineteenth centuries, Spanish censorship sputtered and news from the Americas, the Caribbean, and Europe fostered hopes for alternatives to the ancien régime as well as fear. Peruvians learned about the Enlightenment and the rise of liberalism but also received a steady stream of reports, in the press but also from the pulpit, about the horrors of radical anticlericalism, slave uprisings, social disorder, and more. Peruvians in this period became aware of the possibility of freedom and broader rights, the cracks in the Spanish absolutist edifice, but also heard competing stories of alarming chaos and class violence.

The Túpac Amaru rebellion was certainly not the first uprising in the eighteenth-century Andes. The historian Scarlett O'Phelan Godoy uncovered more than one hundred, ranging from local mutinies to regional tax revolts; Juan Santos Atahualpa roared across the central Amazon and the *ceja* (the Andean piedmont) in the 1840s.[7] Nonetheless, the Túpac Amaru rebellion shattered the Spanish hold on the Andes. It demonstrated the fragility of Spanish rule and forced an odd combination of brutal repression and broad concessions. It ultimately destroyed the colonial pact that had held for two centuries, the relationship imposed by Viceroy Toledo in which Indigenous people paid a head tax and a labor tax (the odious *mita*) and maintained a degree of local autonomy overseen by *kurakas* (Indigenous leaders).[8] The Túpac Amaru and Katarista rebellions (the latter in Upper Peru, which became Bolivia) shattered this arrangement; it took decades or perhaps a century to find an alternative system.

Resentment against Spanish rule was not limited to the southern Andes, of course. The Bourbon reforms, a series of efforts implemented by the Spanish in the eighteenth century across the Americas to increase tax revenues, improve the military, modernize the state, control the masses, and impose state monopolies, had antagonized just about everyone. Creoles (people of European descent born in the Americas) understood that the system now favored Spaniards, while mestizos resented new taxes. Spain's frequent wars with Great Britain and France from the 1790s into the 1820s deepened the need for revenues, encouraging increased taxation (or more effective collection) and thus exacerbating tensions. Upper Peru and Potosí had been transferred to the control of the Rio de la Plata Viceroyalty, established in 1776. Furthermore, notions from the Enlightenment and revolutionary language or ideals crisscrossed the Atlantic: the French Revolution (1789–99) and the Haitian Revolution (1791–1804) demolished the status quo, weakening the old regime and broadening people's political repertoire. The Spanish censored the news of these events, but rumors and reports reached well into Peru.[9]

In the decades following the Túpac Amaru rebellion, Peru was the site of dozens of conspiracies, uprisings, and revolts, particularly after

1808. Most, at least until 1815, did not explicitly seek independence. Some framed their discontent in terms of *mal gobierno*, bad government, claiming they were acting within permitted practice by targeting authorities who did not fulfill the expectations of the Crown and the people.[10] And even the larger, more radical uprisings did not necessarily call for a republic. Some, such as those of Gabriel Aguilar and José Manuel de Ubalde in Cuzco in 1805, invoked the *utopia andina*, grounding their platform in the perceived superiority of Inca rule. A concerned judge wrote, "Indigenous people idolize Cuzco, where they revere the ashes of their ancient leaders, and they conserve the traits of the ancient nobility. The proclamation of an Inca would have provoked fatal consequences."[11] Other malcontents envisioned some sort of monarchy without the Bourbons. Some uprisings were local and others more regional, while discontent with Lima was found in many. But together they demonstrated growing discontent with Spanish rule and new aspirations by *el pueblo*, the people, demands that built from the Atlantic revolutions taking place in this period.

This mobilization should not be exaggerated. Many areas did not witness uprisings, and many residents in Peru of all statuses or classes remained steadfast royalists until or even through the 1820s. On the one hand, the status quo favored Peru in many ways. Lima had a commercial monopoly that benefited the city's merchants. Many coastal merchants and hacendados dreaded competition from Chile or beyond.[12] In addition, much of the elite feared lower-class sedition. The nightmare of enslaved people rising up or Indigenous people assaulting Lima weighed heavily on the upper classes.[13] On the other hand, the repressive capacity of the Spanish should not be underestimated. Since the Túpac Amaru rebellion they well understood the threat of insurgency in Peru. The Spanish reinforced the military, professionalizing the regular army and greatly expanding the militias. These forces proved capable of confronting uprisings across Peru, Upper Peru, and Rio de la Plata.[14]

Fear discouraged people from joining insurgents. As was the case with the Túpac Amaru rebellion, repression of these rebellions and uprisings was brutal, and people witnessed the extreme cost of subversion if defeated: death, destruction, or exile. The Spanish also adroitly used the power of the church to dissuade people from joining rebel movements. Although some priests and other men and women of the faith supported rebels and took leading roles, bishops and archbishops exhorted parishioners not to support the heretics, frequently alluding to the secularism and violence of the French Revolution.[15] This counterrevolutionary propaganda flourished. The historian Víctor Peralta underlines how the royalist press linked the autonomy movements with chaos. He gives the example of Guillermo del Río, who, in the 1817 *Gaceta del Gobierno de Lima*, "associated revolutions with the simultaneous triumph of anarchy, discord and sacrilege. . . . The editor concluded that only the protection of a monarch prevented these evils, and thus 'our calm, our well-being, our prosperity rely on remaining faithful to the King and his efforts to maintain order and legitimate authorities, and to make them obey and respect as before.'"[16]

Events in Europe in this period weakened Spain and encouraged dissidents in the Americas. Spain reacted to the French Revolution and to the slave uprisings in Saint-Domingue that developed into the Haitian Revolution by shifting allegiance to Britain, at least temporarily. The war against France (1793–95) became a costly stalemate, however, and by 1795 Spain realigned with France, at this point led by Napoleon. Spain ceded to France significant territory in North America and faced pressure from Britain, which negotiated with rebel ideologues such as Francisco de Miranda in Venezuela and attacked Buenos Aires and Montevideo in 1806 and 1807. (Buenos Aires inhabitants proved their loyalty to Spain by defeating the British, subsequently expecting and demanding increased political rights from Spain.) France commanded greater financial support from Spain, prompting an economic and political crisis. In 1807, protesters throughout Spain took to the streets against pro-Napoleon Prime Minister Manuel de Godoy. King Carlos IV and his son Prince Ferdinand dueled for power, the latter faction ousting Godoy and forcing King Carlos to abdicate in March 1808.

Napoleon, however, had other plans. He compelled Ferdinand to abdicate and placed his own brother on the throne as King Joseph I. The Spanish resisted massively, bolstering the political groups, old and new, most critical of the ancien régime. The Cortes de Cádiz (1810–14) served as a parliament and a shadow government. Liberals took charge in Cádiz and, after contentious deliberations, extended broader rights to Spain's American holdings, including Indigenous people. Many if not most uprisings across Spanish America in this period, particularly the juntas (councils or assemblies of local notables) that were established in cities and towns, did so in favor of Spain's efforts against the French invasion, in the name of the king or that of the Cortes. Even the more conservative reactions that defended the pre-1808 status quo ultimately demanded greater autonomy and political rights from Spain. From 1789 on but particularly after 1808, news of Spain's crisis and the emergence of alternative political systems and languages spread across the Americas, prompting debates about citizenship, monarchism, and autonomy. Spanish censorship sought to block the flow but failed.[17] Furthermore, Spain's lurching alliances and frequent wars prompted a constant economic crisis and thus increased demands for tax revenues from the Americas. In this context, *cabildos abiertos* (town councils) and juntas extended across the Americas, including Peru. Many of these defended Spain in its battle against Napoleon, refusing to recognize the regency. Nonetheless, the concepts of autonomy, independence, and an alternative monarchical system developed within these diverse movements, spreading across Peru.

Rebels in New Granada and Rio de la Plata refused to recognize the French but also demanded greater autonomy from Cádiz. These evolved into civil wars as different cities and regions fought for predominance and as divisions between royalists and rebels widened. In Rio de la Plata, insurgents from Buenos Aires led revolutionary efforts. They pushed into Upper Peru (Bolivia), seeking to once and for all put this mining-rich region under the hegemony of Rio de la Plata. The Peruvian Viceroy Abascal reannexed Upper Peru in July 1810, returning it back to his jurisdiction after its separation in 1776. At this point, the uprising confronted rebel Buenos Aires (which seethed at the commercial monopoly of Lima) versus royalists in Peru. The Porteño (i.e., Buenos Aires) rebels, led by Juan José Castelli, seized Potosí in November 1810. Nonetheless, a year later the royalists had expelled the rebels from Upper Peru. Most of the troops and the funding for these counterrevolutionary campaigns came from Peru. A mix of contesting political ideas spread with the military campaigns.

Southern Andean Foundations, the First Phase

From 1810 to 1814, insurgency extended in Mexico (with the rebellions led by the priests Miguel Hidalgo and José María Morelos), New Granada (under the "Libertador," Simón Bolívar), and Rio de la Plata. The 1810 May Revolution in Buenos Aires greatly influenced Peru, encouraging dissidents, and forcing royalists to battle over the control of Upper Peru.[18] "El Inca," as the rebel leader Juan José Castelli came to be known, led the Rio de la Plata insurgents' efforts to take Upper Peru, promoting different strands of Inca revivalism. Although Peru was a bulwark of royalism, it also was the site of several uprisings. Tacna rose in June 1811, in coordination with Castelli's efforts in Upper Peru. The Tacna economy aligned more with Potosí and other markets than with Lima, and the Rio de la Plata rebels sent emissaries to Tacna and Arequipa to gain followers and open a western front. On June 20, the creole and mint assayer Francisco Antonio de Zela led an assault on Tacna's military barracks, declaring the movement's support for the Buenos Aires junta. Zela counted on significant Indigenous allies such as the cacique Toribio Ara. That very day, however, Spanish forces crushed Castelli's at the Battle of Huaqui, news that dampened support for the Tacna uprising. The subdelegate of Arica arrested the rebels by the end of the month. The insurgency demonstrated the support for the autonomist juntas and the potential of creating multiclass fronts. Castelli's calls for uprisings and his plan to place a descendent of the Incas in power to bring justice found an audience. Conspiracies continued in Tacna as well as Arequipa and Tarapacá for several years.[19]

In 1811 and 1812 anti-Spanish lampoons appeared in many Peruvian towns and cities. In Huánuco, local people from the town itself and nearby villages revolted against corrupt local authorities and restrictions on tobacco production. The short-lived Huánuco uprising demonstrated deep hatred for Spanish rule and the threat of mass Indigenous insurrection. On February 22, 1812, Indians besieged Huánuco, counting on the support of local creoles (who were largely exempted from rebel violence) and priests. Rebels made their intentions quite clear, yelling "Death to *chapetones*" (a derogatory term for Spaniards) and "Viva el Ynga Castelli" and sacking the stores and houses of Spaniards (and some creoles) who had fled to Cerro de Pasco. The rebel leader and Augustinian friar Marcos Durán Martel wrote a letter on February 18, 1812: "Beloved brothers: Please notify without delay all the towns with this letter that everyone should come to Huánuco on Sunday at 4 A.M., ready to fight with loaded muskets, slings, arrows, sabers, pikes, daggers, knives, sticks, and stones to finish off the Spanish [*chapetones*] in one blow. . . . Your General, Fray Marcos Durán."[20] The rebels held a *cabildo abierto* and formed a junta, led by the creole Juan José Crespo and backed by several priests. The rebellion gained support in the surrounding area.

In early March, a group of Spaniards and creoles attacked the rebels in nearby Ambo. Indians armed with slings and a few muskets repelled them. The uprising continued to spread, but divisions emerged between a more radical vision and one that sought to protect creoles, the church, and middle sectors—the same division that had crippled the Túpac Amaru rebellion thirty years earlier. Reports calculated that the rebels counted on up to four thousand soldiers, overwhelmingly Indigenous. Royalists attacked again a week later and used their superior arms to defeat the rebels. They executed Crespo and other leaders in the Huánuco plaza, sending more fortunate prisoners to jail in Spain. The 1812 Huánuco rebellion showed how quickly a junta could become a mass Indigenous uprising.[21]

Wary of anti-Spanish and anti-Lima sentiments and conscious of the challenges of defeating rebels in the southern Andes, Spanish authorities had closely monitored Cuzco since the Túpac Amaru uprising. Creoles centered in the *cabildo* demanded the implementation of the 1812 liberal constitution, which royalists, clustered in the high court or audiencia, opposed. In 1814, the Angulo brothers (José, Vicente, and Mariano) created a Junta de Gobierno del Cuzco, gaining the support of the *kuraka* Mateo Pumacahua, who had aided in the defeat of Túpac Amaru decades earlier. The rebels (largely members of the creole middle class—professionals, small landowners, authorities, priests—and Indigenous allies) had a strong federalist component, demanding a larger role for Cuzco. They also invoked the Incas as a possible model, demonstrating the persistence and multidimensionality of the Andean utopia.[22] The Cuzco rebels organized expeditions to Puno, Huamanga, and Arequipa, recruiting massively in the early months. As was the case with the Túpac Amaru rebellion, rural insurgents showed their hatred for Spanish authorities as well as many estate and textile mill owners.

The Spanish repressed the movement, bringing troops from Lima but also from its Upper Peru forces, led by General Juan Ramírez. By March 1815 royalists had retaken Cuzco, and in another parallel to Túpac Amaru, they brutally executed the movement's leaders. In Sicuani, executioners decapitated Pumacahua, sending his head to Cuzco and an arm to Arequipa as bloody reminders of the defeat. They also exacted a punitive tax on Cuzco. General Ramírez sent Angulo's uniform and a banner seized from the rebels to Viceroy Abascal as war trophies. Local repression was gruesome.[23] Authorities and writers in Lima lambasted the Cuzco rebels. For example, Hipólito Unanue, a future *padre de la patria* (father of the homeland or national hero), called them, among other epithets, "a mob of bandits."[24]

These juntas demonstrated broad tensions in urban areas, particularly along the Spanish-creole fault line, as well as the potential for insurgency in the Indigenous countryside. Insurgents experimented with different ideologies and platforms, seeking to find an alternative to Spanish rule that could attract a large following among Peru's highly diverse population. More and more of Peru witnessed rebellion, received royalist and dissident propaganda, and suffered from higher taxes and demands for soldiers and supplies for the counterinsurgents; the seeds of subsequent subversion were planted.[25]

In March 1814, King Ferdinand returned to the throne in Spain, refusing to swear to the constitution and instead reimposing an absolutist monarchy. Although the French occupation and ensuing warfare had devastated Spain's economy, royalists continued with their military good fortune in late 1814, with important victories in Chile, Upper Peru, and, by early 1815, Cuzco. In Peru, Joaquín de la Pezuela replaced the militaristic Abascal as viceroy but faced a grave financial crisis. Lima merchants had financed much of the Upper Peru campaigns and showed increasing resistance against continued contributions. Furthermore, the war had weakened production, particularly in the all-important silver mines. Nonetheless, Pezuela sought to dislodge rebels completely from Upper Peru, reaching Salta by 1817. Spanish forces now confronted a mobile guerrilla war in which total victory was near impossible. Viceroy Pezuela and his top commander, José de La Serna, blamed each other for the stalemate. Peru remained relatively quiet in 1815 and 1816. This would change.[26]

San Martín, Bolívar, and Guerrillas, the Second Phase

Argentine military man José de San Martín had worked for the revolutionary government in Buenos Aires since 1812. In 1816, he changed the insurgents' tactics, eschewing Upper Peru and instead moving his forces across the Andes into Chile. El Ejército de los Andes (the Army of the Andes) had over five thousand soldiers, including many formerly enslaved people. Excellent planning and an element of surprise helped this relatively small force take Chile, particularly after the Battle of Chacabuco on February 12, 1817. San Martín engaged royalists throughout Chile, rejecting demands that he return to Buenos Aires to reinforce the Rio de la Plata insurgents. Instead, on August 19, 1820, "the largest amphibious military force ever assembled by patriot generals anywhere in Spanish America" left Valparaíso to attack Peru.[27] Not only had San Martín built an efficient army with a bold plan, but the warfare in Chile had further weakened Lima's economy.

The question about Lima's attitude toward and role in independence fascinated writers of the period and subsequent generations of historians. In his seminal study, Alberto Flores Galindo built on the argument that the merchant elite benefited from the Bourbon system, enjoying a variety of monopolies, and thus hesitated when faced with a possible break from the Spanish. He also underlined their deep fear of the lower classes, including the constant preoccupation with a lower-class (plebian, Indigenous, or enslaved people) uprising. As contemporary observer Basil Hall noted, the specter of the Haitian Revolution weighed heavily in Lima during the wars of independence.[28] But Flores Galindo also pointed out that the Lima upper classes did not have their own project and proved unable to create one. They chafed at Bourbon demands, particularly in wartime, but could not formulate an alternative. When the aristocrats José de la Riva Agüero and José Bernardo de Torre Tagle became Peru's first and second presidents in 1823, they involved themselves in inane internecine battles and quickly lost power and relevance. The Lima elite understood that the status quo had been shattered but feared rebellion. In the end, their nemeses, Bernardo Monteagudo, an Argentine rebel who had arrived in Peru with San Martín's Army of the Andes, and Simón Bolívar, had to push through radical reforms with totalitarian measures to defeat the Spanish.[29]

Change came not only from the battlegrounds across the Americas but once again from Europe. In 1820, a liberal revolution returned Spain to a constitutional monarchy, fostering a more conciliatory attitude toward rebels in the Americas. Viceroy Pezuela committed (unenthusiastically) to the liberal constitution in September 1820, just as San Martín's forces were close to landing in Pisco. After failed negotiations with the viceroy, San Martín sent his naval forces to Huacho, north of Lima, while Commander Juan Antonio Álvarez de Arenales took his troops to the Sierra Central, raising guerrilla support in Indigenous and peasant areas in the Valle de Mantaro. Pezuela did not attack San Martín, instead focusing on holding Lima, beset by an epidemic and food shortages. This tactic prompted much criticism, and a military coup deposed him in January 1821, with José de La Serna replacing Pezuela as viceroy. Internal divisions weakened the royalists. La Serna reversed strategy and evacuated Lima on July 6, leaving weapons and many ill soldiers and commanders at the Real Felipe Fortress in Callao. The royalists, including future president José de la Mar, faced a harrowing siege. On July 12, 1821, San Martín entered Lima, declaring independence on July 28 and taking the position of protector of Peru. The ceremony assumed all the characteristics of viceregal rituals, stressing continuity more than rupture. In the words of historian Pablo Ortemberg, "The traditional ritual of continuity allowed the elite to exorcize its fear of anarchy, slave uprisings, and the 'tumultuous plebe."[30] Even with the July 28 declaration, the war was far from over.

Commentators and analysts then and now wonder why San Martín did not pursue Pezuela's forces and instead remained in Lima. Some contend that his fear of a mass guerrilla war discouraged him from pursuit, while others believe he worried that Lima had been so isolated and was innately so conservative that he needed to ensure victory there first.[31] Bernardo Monteagudo, San Martín's minister of war, however, oversaw radical actions that infuriated Lima's ruling classes. Monteagudo, very likely a mulatto, implemented the *libertad de vientres*, which deemed the children of enslaved people free at birth; banned the *mita* (the forced labor draft); created a national library and teaching schools; and persecuted leading merchants and Spaniards. Approximately four thousand Spaniards abandoned Lima, including Lima's archbishop and the bishop of Huamanga. Monteagudo recognized that "I used all the means available to me to inflame hatred of Spaniards."[32] Unpopular for these actions as well as his monarchism, Monteagudo left Lima in 1822 but returned in 1824. He was assassinated on January 28, 1825, in the Plazoleto Micheo, what is today Plaza San Martín near Quilca Street.[33] Dismissed as a foreign extremist, Monteagudo attempted radical reforms that undermined the upper classes. The question of whether he gained mass support for his radical monarchist project remains unanswered.

La Serna consolidated royalist forces in the Andes, ultimately setting up a government in Cuzco. He hoped for naval support from Spain, which never arrived. Led by General José de Canterac, the royalists overwhelmed the rebel forces commanded by Domingo Tristán and Agustín Gamarra in Ica in 1822. Canterac believed that this stunning victory and the disarray of the patriots meant that viceregal forces would soon prevail.[34] Recently "liberated" Lima suffered food shortages and widespread malaria and typhoid; disgruntled patriot soldiers demanding pay added to the depressing scenario.[35] San Martín met with Simón Bolívar on July 26–27, 1822, in Guayaquil to discuss the dislodging of royalists from Peru. By the end of the year, San Martín had handed over power to Peru's nascent congress, effectively granting power to a three-person junta, and sailed for Chile and ultimately exile in Europe.[36] The royalists were reduced to the highlands in Peru, including Charcas.

The wars of independence cannot be understood without considering how Black, Indian, mestizo, and creole people participated, pushing local demands and aligning with broader forces. Despite a flurry of studies in the 1980s, we know far too little about the *montoneros* and guerrillas (two among many terms used for these heterogeneous fighters). They

Figure 1.3 Anonymous, *Death of Agustín Gamarra at the Battle of Ingavi*, ca. 1845. Source: Ministerio de Cultura, Museo Nacional de Arqueología, Antropología e Historia del Perú. Photograph by Atoq Ramón.

could serve alongside the formal army or act independently; they could focus on local issues or fight across broad areas in the name of the *patria*; and while most fought for the patriots, the royalists counted on them as well.[37] Women and the famous *soldaderas* barely appear.[38] We still have a telescopic view of the independence era: a clear image of the leadership, an adequate but less focused vision of the regional leadership, and a distant or unfocused impression of the guerrillas themselves.

These insurgents who were not formally part of the standing army were crucial in the independence era, particularly in the final years, after San Martín's arrival in 1820. The royalists and patriots largely fought to a standoff, with each side alternately taking and losing territory. Peru's geography, with the sheer Andes that loomed just east of Lima and the dry coast, favored smaller, more rapid forces that could mobilize local supporters. The royalist General José Carratalá captured this in two words: "damned mountains."[39] San Martín and Lord Cochrane, a Scottish naval commander who after his dismissal from the Royal Navy in 1814 helped command the Chilean, Peruvian, and Brazilian navies, recruited enslaved people while coastal bandits became politicized, many of them supporting the patriots and then the liberals. Their attacks against plantations and merchants weakened the economy and slavery itself. Both urban and rural enslaved people slipped away to join these popular movements.

With their hit-and-run attacks, constant pressure on supply lines, and calls for soldiers to desert, guerrillas in the central sierra, from Huarochirí, near Lima, to the Valle de Mantaro, in the central highlands, made life miserable for the royalists. Their motives varied, but in general they opposed tax increases, which the war had accelerated, and Spanish monopolies. Behind the anti-fiscal facade, however, lay broader social and economic demands and complex alliances. In military terms, the guerrillas' mobility, knowledge of the terrain, and local support made them a nightmare for the royalists.

Bolívar remained in Quito for much of 1822, entering Lima in September 1823. He sought a military solution as the rebel campaign stalled, suffering crippling losses to Canterac in the south in early 1823. Royalists counted on experienced commanders (Canterac, La Serna, Gerónimo Valdés, and Pedro Antonio Olañeta); a sense of desperation among those who feared a radical break from the status quo; and support from a heterogeneous coalition. Furthermore, as Bolívar well understood, the independence leadership was deeply divided, focusing on defeating one another rather than the Spanish. In the words of Timothy Anna, "From September 1822, when San Martín retired from Peru, to September 1823, when Bolívar arrived, the government of the independent regime was in the hands of the Peruvian aristocrats who had so long desired to hold power. They established three separate administrations, all of which failed to hold the government together or to strengthen independence."[40] Bolívar assumed dictatorial power and, as he had done in New Granada, improved the military, mobilized as large a force as he could, and sequestered money and goods needed for total war. He also demanded support from independent Chile and Rio de la Plata, but with little success, as they were mired in their own struggles. Absolutism had returned in Spain, and while Viceroy La Serna and his inner circle welcomed the abandonment of the liberal constitution, one key commander, Olañeta, switched to the rebels.

Bolívar pushed his advantage, using his beloved cavalry (many of them llaneros from Venezuela) in the Andean gorges and valleys. On August 6, 1824, patriot forces defeated the royalists in Junín, who lost hundreds of men and all-important horses. Canterac returned to Cuzco, while Commander Antonio José de Sucre pushed to the south. Bolívar retreated to Lima, assuming that any major battle would be delayed until after the rainy season. In early December, however, about nine thousand royalists confronted a rebel army of about six thousand outside the city of Huamanga (also known as Ayacucho). Curiously, the royalist army counted on a higher percentage of Peruvian troops, although the rebels had been recruiting successfully, adding locals to what had been largely a Colombian force.[41] The royalists coordinated their forces poorly, with the cavalry engaging battle only after the infantry had been rebuffed. In a battle that barely took two hours, patriot forces seized La Serna, and the viceroy and his top officers rapidly capitulated. Although a few royalist holdouts resisted, the war was largely over. Bolívar reportedly broke out into a dance when he heard the news.[42] Peru was an independent republic. Sucre and his forces moved to Upper Peru, and by April 1825, the Spanish had been defeated and the nation of Bolivia created.

Peru's bicentennial has provoked renewed discussion about the war of independence. Scholars debate whether 1821 is the correct date to be commemorated, proposing 1780 (Túpac Amaru), 1814 (Cuzco), or 1824 (Ayacucho) as alternatives. A more significant discussion focuses on questions about who fought for independence and what it signified. Too many historians have overlooked those earlier, Andean uprisings and reduced the struggle to the final years overseen by San Martín and Bolívar. They have failed to incorporate those influential projects, which, while not victorious, marked the period and shaped postcolonial Peru. This teleological view, which reviews what happened in an earlier period from the perspective of what happened subsequently, excludes the great diversity of political projects that characterized politics and insurgency from 1808 to 1825 and beyond, with federalism, Inca revivalism, radical liberalism, monarchism, and popular royalism being some key examples. Moreover, they have not followed the many leads of the new social history, which has explored the role of the popular classes in the insurgencies of the period.[43] Not only did these projects or currents impel movements as diverse as Cuzco in 1814 and that of Afro-Peruvian guerrillas, but they resurfaced after independence. As the following chapters by Sobrevilla Perea and Rénique indicate, federalist opposition to Lima centralism, the consideration of the Inca Empire as a model or inspiration, and conservative caudillismo were important parts of Peru well beyond 1821, in fact up until today. All have roots in the wars of independence. Furthermore, debates and armed struggles about the shape and nature of republicanism in Peru persisted for decades, if not longer.[44]

Exhaustion, wariness, and uncertainty more than unbridled glee marked Peru after the Battle of Ayacucho. A study of the coastal town of Huacho found that by the early 1820s, impatience with the patriot efforts and tedium over the seemingly endless war had taken hold.[45] The war had taken an enormous toll: Thousands had died while both armies as well as guerrillas expropriated goods and demanded emergency loans that would never be paid back. Ella Dunbar Temple uses one anecdote to highlight the devastation in a period when Lima and other urban areas suffered from food shortages: Spanish troops slashed the throats of more than a thousand sheep when fleeing toward the central highland town of Oroya. Countless similar acts characterized what had increasingly become a guerrilla war.[46] Diseases ravaged Lima in the final years of the conflict, and famine seemed a possibility. Peru was deeply in debt, virtually bankrupt. While the confrontations devastated infrastructure, increased debt, and depleted state resources, they could also be liberating: Many enslaved people used military service as a means to freedom, official or de facto, while in rural areas, landowners' control deteriorated.

A confluence of factors explains the weakening of social control in the early republic. Ideas about freedom and self-rule had crisscrossed Peru for decades; the disciplinary components of the state and Catholic Church had faded or in the case of the Inquisition been abolished; and oppressed groups had taken their future into their own hands. Thousands of mobilized guerrillas, the famous *montoneros*, imposed their notions of liberation and justice well after the end of the war. In 1825, a French official wrote that the Peruvian Indian, although "taciturn and unbusy in appearance . . . is now armed and knows how to use them, they were guerrillas or soldiers. They understand that important events have occurred that will shape their future. They remain hopeful."[47] Years of lower-class mobilization in many regions meant that a return to the status quo was nearly impossible.

Uncertainty reigned about what system would replace Spanish rule, although the path was much clearer than it had been a decade earlier. Inca revivalism, federalism, and constitutional monarchism had been important models throughout the long wars of independence but had lost impetus by 1824. The defeat of the 1814 rebellion in Cuzco weakened the presence of Cuzco as a potential political center and of the Incas as a model. While Aguilar and Ubalde in Cuzco in 1805, the Huánuco rebels of 1812, and the Angulo uprising of 1814 invoked the Incas, these invocations were less common after 1815, at least in mass movements.[48] The events of the early 1820s also eliminated or at least severely hampered other options. The deportation and murder of Monteagudo and the departure of San Martín as well as the 1820 victory of Spanish liberals had jettisoned the prospects of any type of constitutional monarchism in Peru. Although conservatives would remain powerful and nostalgic for Spanish rule for decades, Peru would not search for a king. On the other hand, Bolívar saw his vision of a great South American federation crumble with the opposition in Peru. Independent republics emerged rather than a confederation. While federalism was not dead (Andrés Santa Cruz would oversee the Peru-Bolivia Confederation in the late 1830s), the allure of both constitutional monarchism and federalism had weakened by 1827.[49]

Peru was born a republic and would remain so. After 1825, political struggles centered on the conflict between conservatives and liberals, those who focused on stability and social control versus those who believed in the constitution and broader freedoms. Battles between these two camps (also labeled authoritarians and constitutionalists), with important regional components, would characterize Peruvian politics for the first two decades after independence and, in many ways, into the twenty-first century.[50] These factions, usually led by a caudillo, would battle from 1826 until the 1840s over suffrage, centralism (Lima versus the interior), economic policy, and more. In general, conservatives counted on a strong base of support in Lima and the north, while liberals relied on the southern Andes, particularly Arequipa. This was only the most general of patterns, and countless exceptions can be found.[51]

For a caudillo who took power, oppositional forces must have felt like a persistent earthquake, one that did not stop after a short time. Nationwide, the ground shook from below as lower-class groups demanded greater inclusion and rights. Once residing in Lima, the caudillo felt lateral waves, pressure that frequently developed into full *temblores* (tremors), in the form of major challenges and coup attempts from Arequipa, Trujillo, and other regional centers. And pressure from within his coalition and above all from opponents could develop into a full-scale, destructive earthquake and tsunami. Coup attempts and civil wars meant that he lost control of much of the state (including revenues), had to focus on military struggles rather than policy, and was obliged to delay his projects and alliances. Violent transitions must have felt both to the loser and to much of society like a natural disaster, with chaos, economic ruin, and insecurity reigning. As seismologists stress, seismic waves come from many directions.

The caudillo wars included wide-ranging debates, often taken to the streets or the battlefield, over the content or applicability of the constitution, the breadth of voting rights, and the preeminence of the Catholic Church. Recent studies on caudillo politics have shown that they were not nonsensical battles of megalomaniac generals but instead policy and geopolitical wars. Behind them lay complex struggles over the nature of the postcolonial state, with important regional and local variations. The press was very active and relentlessly partisan, featuring policy debates, personal attacks, and mundane news stories.[52] Caudillos had to focus on the nitty-gritty of state formation and control: seizing power, paying the troops, overseeing the state, and watching over enemy factions. There was a strong correlation between political instability and economic crises—each caudillo was forced to raise money to rule, often to the great detriment of the economy, which weakened his hold on power. Instability weakened the economy; a frail economy hindered stability.[53] Moreover, virtually every president had to face conflicts on Peru's borders as nascent nations battled over boundaries.

Continuity rather than radical changes characterized the birth of republican Peru. The impetus of the more revolutionary programs such as those espoused in Huánuco in 1812 or by certain factions of the coastal guerrillas had waned by 1824. In the decades following independence, no president transformed social structures, and the status quo by and large persisted. Two pillars of social liberalism across the Americas were weak in Peru: secularization (specifically, efforts that challenged the power of the Catholic Church and sought to allow other religions) and abolitionism. Secularization did not gain a foothold in any of the early republican constitutions; Jeffrey Klaiber showed that "the liberal attack on the church was relatively gentle [*suave*]."[54] The 1823 constitution declared, "The Republic's religion is Catholic, Apostolic, Roman, and excludes the practice of any other." The issue only resurfaced in the late nineteenth century when the lack of religious freedom—that is, the Catholic Church's monopoly, as stipulated by the constitution—impeded efforts to attract European immigrants.[55]

Abolitionism, an international movement, had few followers among the early republican intelligentsia and politicians. The role of slavery in the Peruvian economy was formidable. While not a slave society centered around the plantation, like Cuba, Haiti, and much of Brazil, Peru counted on plantations that generated vast fortunes and cemented social hierarchies. In cities, particularly Lima, enslaved people worked as artisans, domestic servants, day laborers, and more. Approximately a hundred thousand enslaved people were imported into Peru. At the time of independence, free Black people made up 20 percent of Lima's population. Despite the importance of slavery to the Peruvian economy and the multidimensional efforts by enslaved people to gain freedom, the abolition of slavery was a largely muted subject in the era, not nearly as prevalent in the press or in the streets as was the case in other republics.[56] In the years immediately after independence, authorities pocketed promises of freedom made to enslaved people, and estate owners oversaw the passage of laws to reinforce slavery. For example, the 1825 Reglamento Interior de las Haciendas de la Costa stipulated that slavery would not be abolished.[57] To quote historian Jorge Basadre:

> At the beginning of the republic, in first place, caste divisions survived. Although some Spaniards returned to Europe, their Peruvian children were alongside the descendants of the nobility fully criollo, and comprised the leaders of the salons; the family regimen continued without alteration; the Indian continued as the "vile mud from which the social edifice is constructed," blacks continued as appendages of the old mansions and the great coastal haciendas. The clergy conserved its role as owners of the spiritual life of both the affluent and the popular classes, protected by privileges and laws; although their missionary passion in the Amazon region and the roar of the convents diminished.[58]

Many historians would quibble about some of these assertions from 1931, but by and large Lima remained the center of Peru, the church maintained its power, Indians continued to pay a head tax, and legislators reinforced slavery, although enslaved people certainly knew how to seek freedom on their own. English and French merchants became important economic figures, replacing those Spanish who departed and overseeing trade with a larger part of Europe. They did not bring vast amounts of capital for investment but instead sought to market their nation's exports in Peru and benefit from exports.[59] Radical liberalism remained weak in postcolonial Peru.

Peru was thus born conservative. The more far-reaching programs that challenged Lima's centralism or evoked the Inca Empire lost traction in the long wars of independence and the status quo more or less prevailed. When searching for its history, the young republic did not harken back to the mass Túpac Amaru rebellion or even the more recent uprisings in Tacna, Cuzco, and Huánuco but instead focused on the last, coastal phase of the wars of independence. If nineteenth-century intellectuals romanticized, they looked to the "distant" past, the Incas, contrasting them with contemporary Indians. Túpac Amaru did not become a national hero until the second half of the twentieth century.[60] Even novel and potentially radical transformations such as elections were watered down and controlled from above. The less democratic indirect election system prevailed, and only about 10 percent of the population voted in much of the nineteenth century.[61] The Franco-Peruvian Flora Tristán captured this conservativism in her heated conversation in 1834 with Juan Bautista Lavalle, owner of the Hacienda Villa in Chorrillos, near Lima. As they toured his sugar plantation, Lavalle defended slavery and decried the Haitian Revolution and other uprisings. Tristán described the "old planter" as "deaf."[62]

But the maintenance of colonial structures and mentalities is not synonymous with the absence of social struggles and an easy path for conservatives: Women demanded greater rights; the urban lower classes resisted efforts to discipline and contain them; enslaved people sought freedom; regions battled against centralism; and people struggled against oppression and inequality in infinite ways. The "tension between equality and hierarchy" that Jürgen Osterhammel posits as a central characteristic of the nineteenth century certainly animated sociopolitical struggles in Peru, taking on earthquake-like dimensions from time to time.[63] The nationwide caudillo struggles brought new (and old) political currents to the countryside, and elections and constitutions proved to be important experiments in republicanism. Artists presented a variety of images of Peru past and present, sparking contentious debates about the *patria*'s symbolism and essence.[64] Nonetheless, change came slowly.

Peru faced great economic challenges. Peter Klarén summarizes Peru's dire fiscal situation: "Initial foreign loans totaling 1,816,000 pounds sterling were contracted during the first half of the 1820s from British bondholders. . . . By the late 1820s, the foreign debt was five times the government's annual revenues, and by 1848, it had grown to an estimated 4,380,530 pounds sterling. The internal debt likewise grew to an estimated 6,646,344 pesos by 1845."[65] The war had destroyed much infrastructure and prompted foreign and internal debt, while the departure of thousands of Spaniards meant a loss of capital. Spanish America could not count on an economic partner willing to invest massively in infrastructure until well into the second half of the century. The creation of Bolivia as an independent republic in 1826 and the decline of the Potosí silver mines ravaged the trans-Andean economic circuit that stretched from Cuzco into northern Argentina.

Not only had mines and Peru's already poor road system been damaged by the war, but the price of silver languished during the long nineteenth century as gold and currencies replaced it as the favored international commodity for trade.[66] The nineteenth-century expansion of maritime trade, particularly with the development of the steam engine and ironclad ships, challenged Andean producers due to the high cost of transporting goods to Callao, Ilo, or Peru's other ports. Increased shipping along the Pacific weakened but did not eliminate the trans-Andean networks of exchange. In fact, many scholars have shown how the disruption of traditional colonial markets and of mechanisms used to control peasants offered Andean peasants renewed economic opportunities. Carlos Contreras deemed this process "less silver, more potatoes."[67] These broad tendencies, the decline of the centrality of silver and the rise of maritime trade to the detriment of Andean producers, only began to emerge in the decades after independence.[68] In these years, trade policy was at the center of political and economic disputes, prompting curious alliances.

Conservatives, Liberals, and Caudillos

In general, conservatives favored protectionism, whereas liberals sought greater free trade. Producers in Lima, Cuzco, and elsewhere worried about the arrival of cheaper European goods, while liberals lobbied for the advantages of greater internal and international trade. Thus, the conservative caudillo Agustín Gamarra created an unusual Cuzco-Lima alliance based on his nationalist and protectionist vision and his ties in his native Cuzco and the capital. Liberals such as José de la Mar and Luis José de Orbegoso saw expanding international trade as the solution to Peru's stagnation and instability, even if it hurt some producers. Regional economies varied, and some new exports blossomed, such as wool in the southern Andes.[69]

The timeline shows patterns in the dizzying changes in the presidency from independence into the 1840s. First, all were generals except for the two central caudillos of the period, Andrés Santa Cruz and Agustín Gamarra, who both ascended to the post of *mariscal* (marshal) during these years. Second, liberals and conservatives alternated power. Gamarra and Santa Cruz marked the period and epitomize early republican caudillismo. Well-educated mestizos who abandoned the royalists in the early 1820s, they were men of action who fought for their beliefs and sought to anchor their movements within the republican system. They were childhood friends who became fierce enemies; neither accumulated great wealth. Andrés de Santa Cruz departs from the conservative-liberal division, as he began as a conservative yet became the architect of the most

Table 1.1 Peruvian Rulers, 1821–1841

Ruler	Years
José de San Martín	1821–22
Junta de Gobierno: General José de la Mar Manuel Salazar y Baquíjano Felipe A. Alvarado	1822–23
Mariscal José de la Riva Agüero	1823
Mariscal José Bernardo de Torre Tagle	1823
Libertador Simón Bolívar	1823–26
General Andrés Santa Cruz	1826–27
General José de la Mar	1827–29
General Agustín Gamarra	1829–33
General Luis José de Orbegoso	1833–34
General Pablo Bermúdez	1834
General Luis José de Orbegoso	1834–35
General Felipe Salaverry	1835–36
Mariscal Andrés Santa Cruz	1836–39
Mariscal Agustín Gamarra	1838–41

Source: Jorge Basadre, *Historia de la república peruana* (Lima: Editorial Historia, 1961).

ambitious project of the period, the federalist Peru-Bolivia Confederation, supported by liberals and despised by conservatives.

Coups and conspiracies marked politics, as no liberal president finished out his term. Even Gamarra's seemingly stable 1829–33 presidency confronted more than a dozen revolts, coup attempts, conspiracies, and putsches.[70] This was followed by a particularly chaotic several years: civil war between Gamarra and the liberal Orbegoso in 1833, with Orbegoso becoming president but facing implacable opposition from Salaverry,

Santa Cruz, and, in exile, Gamarra; Salaverry formed a conservative government in early 1835; in August 1835 Santa Cruz defeated his old friend Gamarra in the Battle of Yanacocha, and six months later he defeated and executed Salaverry. Thus began the Peru-Bolivia Confederation, the most interesting geopolitical experiment in the early republic.

The Peru-Bolivia Confederation revived Bolívar's dream of a confederation and southern Peru's desire to have autonomy with strong links with both Bolivia and Peru. It reorganized Peru and Bolivia into three sovereign states: Northern Peru, Southern Peru, and Bolivia. Each had extensive autonomy, at least in theory, while a supreme protector, a position that Andrés de Santa Cruz assumed, managed military, economic policy, and foreign affairs. The project reunited the region stretching from Cuzco to Potosí and south, the heartland of the Incan Empire, an important economic trade zone during the colonial period. It also reunified the core area of those who spoke Quechua and Aymara, the predominant Indigenous languages in South America.

In general, the confederation found broad support in Bolivia, where it was seen as a way to maintain close ties to Peru while preventing the annexation or "return to Peru" projects espoused by Conservatives such as Gamarra. In addition, Santa Cruz had been an effective president since 1830 and had created an extensive alliance of supporters, although he also counted on influential enemies. Cuzco, Tacna, and Arequipa saw the confederation as a guarantee of greater local control in that it shifted administrative duties outside of Lima. In the words of Natalia Sobrevilla, the confederation "responded to a wish the southern provinces of Peru had cherished for a long time: to become, on the one hand, more autonomous and, on the other, to maintain their links with Bolivia, particularly the department of La Paz."[71]

Northern Peru looked at the project warily. They saw it as dangerous decentralization and even as Bolivian interference in Peru. The conservative press attacked Santa Cruz in racist fashion, ridiculing his predilection for France and calling him "the thick-lipped *cholo*" (*el cholo jetón*) and "Monsieur Alphonse Chunga Capac."[72] Internationally, the battle lines were clearly drawn as well. The United States, France, and Britain championed the free trade policies espoused by Santa Cruz and the seeming stability that the confederation would offer. Argentina and Chile, where many Peruvian politicians hostile to Santa Cruz had gone into exile, despised the project, disliking the prospect of a significantly larger and more powerful neighbor to the north. Diego Portales of Chile and Juan Manuel Rosas of Argentina proved to be formidable enemies.[73]

The Peru-Bolivia Confederation faced strong opposition from the outset, and Santa Cruz had to focus on military defense more than statebuilding. On August 21, 1836, the Chilean navy seized the Peruvian navy's only three ships in Callao. Diplomatic discussions delayed military hostilities, so in 1835 and 1836 supporters and defenders of the Peru-Bolivia Confederation battled in the press.[74] Hostilities began in September 1837 when a Chilean contingent with 2,792 Chilean troops and 402 Peruvian exiles set sail from Valparaíso. They attacked via Arequipa, a bastion of the confederation, and struggled to find provisions, gain territory, and win over hearts and minds. Nonetheless, Santa Cruz also faced mutinies in Bolivia as well as the deep opposition of Rosas in Argentina and an alliance of groups in Peru. In 1838, Gamarra joined the military campaigns and led efforts in Peru, ultimately creating a "Restoration Government" in Lima. The confederation was at this point reduced to southern Peru and Bolivia. Former supporters bristled at the cost of the war and what many saw as Santa Cruz's dictatorial tendencies. On January 30, 1839, the Restoration Army under the leadership of General Ramón Castilla defeated Santa Cruz in the Battle of Yungay, signifying the virtual defeat of his project. After months of negotiations, Santa Cruz accepted exile in Guayaquil, Ecuador. Gamarra seemed to have a clear path to impose the Lima-based, authoritarian, and anti-free-trade vision that inspired the Santa Cruz opposition in Peru. He, however, also found himself mired in conspiracies, uprisings, and foreign opposition. Gamarra led his forces into Bolivia in 1841 and was killed in the Battle of Ingavi on November 18, as seen below. Some contend that he was likely killed by one of his own troops.[75]

Caudillismo prevailed in postcolonial Peru. Generals led complex coalitions divided along the liberal-conservative axis while also battling over Peru's borders and its relationships with its neighboring nations. How did those outside the Peruvian military experience the caudillo wars, and what was their ultimate legacy? Regional and local political developments, of course, varied widely in this period. The war of independence experience, the economic situation, and the concomitant change in political culture and power relations (the well-stocked arsenal of political platforms or ideologies) varied greatly between, for example, Puno in the south and Trujillo in the north. A spate of caudillo studies has highlighted these diverse experiences.[76] So, what occurred in these decades in the countryside and what changed or remained the same?

Figure 1.4 Johann Moritz Rugendas, study for *La plaza mayor de Lima*, ca. 1843.
Source: Museo de Arte de Lima.

City and Countryside

Scholars have found a variety of *campesinado*-caudillo relations. Some rural groups supported certain caudillos, while others sought to avoid the potentially dangerous and costly conflicts. Rural people had numerous tools at their disposal to negotiate with the state, with the payment of the Indigenous head tax at the core of these negotiations. The so-called *contribución* constituted a shockingly high portion of state revenues in the early republic, about 40 percent.[77] What is clear in this period is a remarkable resurgence of the Indian population, both relative and total, and a parallel expansion of the Quechua language. The "liberal onslaught" against Indian land and autonomy that some scholars detected, the alliance between the state and the landed elite, often with the collusion of the local priest, did not occur until much later in the nineteenth century.

Why? The state was too weak and too dependent on the head tax to oversee any effective attack on community resources. In this period of incessant caudillo warfare, presidents and their officers had to focus on holding on to power more than implementing policy, particularly within rural society. Caudillos needed the Indian head tax to rule; Indigenous people used this as an important tool in negotiations. Moreover, the stagnant economy gave little incentive for landowners to infringe on community land. Indigenous producers and traders took advantage of the situation to seize an important market share of the wool economy, building on their experience and low overhead. Furthermore, Indigenous peoples and other subaltern groups resisted and negotiated, as the turbulent politics of the era often increased their opportunities—caudillos and the state needed their support, as fighters and as taxpayers. The state and the landed elite failed to usurp community land and autonomy, in part because the state did not have sufficient will or resources to do so and the landed elite did not have the economic incentive needed either, but also because Indigenous people and other rural dwellers used a variety of resources to defend themselves.

The demographic data underline a remarkable increase in the relative Indian population, halting the decline due to death and assimilation that had been seen since the sixteenth-century arrival of the Spanish. On the one hand, this reflects the weakness of the Peruvian state, which despite anticorporate and anti-Indigenous rhetoric from both liberals (egalitarianism meant the abolition of Indian community rights) and conservatives (who underlined the Indians' "backward" nature) could not enforce its largely force-based assimilationist policies. In economic terms, haciendas and other large estates did not expand massively until the latter half of the nineteenth century, when internal and external demand increased, infrastructure improved, and relative stability returned. Not only did the Indian population increase in the period stretching from the late colonial era (the 1790 census is an important benchmark) into the second half of the nineteenth century, but also the percentage of people who spoke Quechua as their primary language grew. Simply put, the state could not effectively impose assimilation projects, and the stimulus for *mestizaje* (urbanization, market expansion, and mass media) would come much later, in the late nineteenth and twentieth centuries.[78]

The republican state had a physical presence throughout Peru, collecting the all-important Indian head tax and providing some basic services. But this presence was faint, focused on fiscal and military matters and the most basic administrative issues. For example, the defeat of the Spanish did not translate into an increase in public education. The number of schools, already abysmally low in the colonial period, barely increased. The best data are from Lima, where primary school enrollment was a stunningly low 1,350 in 1826 and had increased only to 1,756 a decade later even though Lima had a population of over 50,000.[79] Education constituted the quintessential form of nation-building in the nineteenth century. It was in schools that children learned about the *patria*, national history, and commonalities, and where the national language, in this case Spanish, was imposed. These changes would only come much later, in the twentieth century. Rural ties to the nation via the public school system remained weak into the late twentieth century.

Caudillo civil wars crisscrossed the country, ruralizing political conflict in the early republic.[80] Lima was more the objective than the epicenter of political struggles. Nonetheless, it retained its absolute hegemony in this period, continuing as the capital and economic center. Even though people from Arequipa, Cuzco, Trujillo, and other cities and towns well understood the disadvantages of centralism and fantasized about replacing Lima, the failed Peru-Bolivia Confederation was the only real threat to the centrality of the City of Kings. And the status quo more than radical change marked the city in the transition from colony to republic. Conservatives (and many liberals) continued to decry lower-class truculence, women's freedom, and the lack of effective social control over the multiethnic plebian groups. Travelers and others continued to comment on the city's multiracial nature and dynamic street life. Lima looked like and felt very much the way it had under the Bourbons; its dominance within Peru would only increase in the coming decades and skyrocket in the twentieth century, as seen in the other chapters in this book.[81]

Conclusion

The conservatives' euphoria over the overthrow of the Peru-Bolivia Confederation did not last long. Gamarra was killed on the battlefield and a new generation of caudillos fought for power. As the following chapter shows, one general, Ramón Castilla, and—more importantly—one curious export product, guano, would bring stability. The guano boom finally provided the state with steady revenue. Although historians maintain that much of the windfall was wasted via corruption (from the crass pocketing of funds to the more subtle overpayment of plantation owners for their enslaved people when abolition came in 1854), the period witnessed the

Figure 1.5 Francisco "Pancho" Fierro, *"Negros chalas" on Corpus Christi Day*, 1836. Source: Museo de Arte de Lima.

Figure 1.6 Léonce Angrand, *Cake and Flower Sellers*, 1837. Source: Museo de Arte de Lima.

Figure 1.7 J. Huyot, *A Procession of the Lord of Earthquakes at Cuzco, Peru*, 1873. Wood engraving after Édouard Riou. Source: Museo de Arte de Lima.

strengthening of the state, improved infrastructure, and relative political peace, at least in contrast to the 1820s and 1830s.[82]

The early decades of the republic were not mere chaos, a frustrating delay of nation-state formation. Instead, important ideological battles undergirded the caudillo wars as Peruvians battled over the shape and nature of the postcolonial state and society. These struggles can, in turn, only be understood in light of the uprisings and *inquietud* (uneasiness) that convulsed Peru after Túpac Amaru in the 1780s. However, the democratic essence of these postindependence battles should not be exaggerated. Elections were limited; both factions, even the liberals, frequently disregarded the constitution; a military elite ruled; and few intellectuals or policymakers addressed deeper questions of nation-state formation in a country so richly diverse as Peru. The Lima merchant elite retained an enormous amount of power, and the Catholic Church continued to oversee daily life, the domestic sphere, and often political struggles. Reindigenization—or, more simply, relative Indigenous autonomy vis-à-vis the republican creole state—was de facto rather than de jure, emerging not from any policy or enlightened views about the role of the Indigenous majority but instead as a result of the weakness of the state and economic instability.

Yet below or to the side of the caudillo wars and this seeming continuity lay fascinating struggles by groups to defend their notion of newly granted rights, to claim a role in the nation, to participate in the creation of a postcolonial Peru. Most of these efforts were local and often barely appear in historical records, yet those in power felt these tremors. When large-scale uprisings or mass organization were deemed impossible or suicidal, subaltern groups often used "quieter," less confrontational tactics, which prove more elusive to historians. For example, the absence of a large-scale abolitionist movement in no way means that enslaved people did not resist slavery or that Afro-Peruvians did not question racist paradigms. Studying these subtle forms of resistance is much more difficult than organized movements. This chapter has insisted that comprehending the nature and role of these smaller, often defeated struggles, those that stood outside the bright light of the major battles and wars outlined here, remains the missing link in our understanding of the creation of the Peruvian nation-state. This includes seemingly paradoxical matters such as Indigenous support for conservatives or certain plantation owners' preference for protectionism.

In sum, from the time of the Túpac Amaru rebellion until the 1840s, numerous crises beset Peru, often prompted by broader tensions at the colonial or global level. Peruvians responded with a variety of proposals and alternative ideas, but internal divisions and larger hemispheric challenges derailed the more innovative projects. Peru saw momentous change but failed to create a new nation-state, or more just and inclusive structures. The key themes or tensions reviewed here continue to resonate today, more than two hundred years after independence.

Some of them are obvious. Debates about the advantages and disadvantages of authoritarian rule and about how fully Peru should immerse itself in the global economy (protectionism versus liberalism) raged in the 2021 elections. But the other social and political issues underlined here and developed in each of the following chapters also persist. Enduring disagreements about the dominance of Lima and the search, by many, for decentralized alternatives animate political discussions and projects. In the 1820s and the 2020s, many people question the explicit or implicit placement of Indigenous people as secondary citizens. As will be seen in the following chapters, all of these have deep, complex historical roots that lead us to Peru today.

Notes

Chapter title: "What a Complex Destiny" echoes the eminent Peruvian historian Jorge Basadre in reference to republican Cuzco. It captures well his ideas and concerns regarding early republican Peru in its entirety. Jorge Basadre, "Prólogo," in José Tamayo Herrera, *Historia social del Perú republicano* (Lima: Editorial Universo, 1981), 16.

1   I use both *viceroyalty* and *colony* to refer to Peru under Spanish control. Good (and not-so-good) historians have questioned the applicability of the concept of colonialism for Spanish America. I believe, however, that it is germane, particularly when reading about *la mita*, the *reparto*, and other hyperexploitative institutions mentioned in this chapter. For a broader discussion, see Juan Carlos Garavaglia, "La cuestión colonial," *Nuevo Mundo Mundos Nuevos*, sec. "Debates," 2004.

2   I want to thank Carlos Aguirre, Ruth Borja Santa Cruz, Antonio Espinoza, Javiera Fermandoy, Alvaro Grompone, Zoila Mendoza, Carlos Paredes, Víctor Peralta, and José Ragas for their help, and also two excellent readers for Duke University Press. I also want to acknowledge *el equipo* for doing the near impossible: making several years of Zoom meetings productive and entertaining. *Gracias* Alberto, Cynthia, Eduardo, José Luis, Natalia, and Paulo. Kique Bossio translated this chapter from English into Spanish and provided great feedback and suggestions.

3   I use the terms *return* and *renewed* because the 1970s and 1980s saw a blossoming of social history in and about "forgotten" Peru, tendencies that have unfortunately faded.

4   The parallels with Mexico, the other core viceroyalty established in the sixteenth century, are clear. Mexico lost roughly 50 percent of its territory in the War of 1848 with the United States. See Peter Guardino, *The Dead March: A History of the Mexican-American War* (Cambridge, MA: Harvard University Press, 2017).

5   Sergio Serulnikov, *Revolution in the Andes: The Time of Túpac Amaru* (Durham, NC: Duke University Press, 2013); Charles F. Walker, *The Tupac Amaru Rebellion* (Cambridge, MA: Harvard University Press, 2014).

6   Alberto Flores Galindo, *In Search of an Inca* (Cambridge: Cambridge University Press, 2010); Manuel Burga, *Nacimiento de una utopía: Muerte y resurrección de los Incas* (Lima: Instituto de Apoyo Agrario, 1988).

7   Scarlett O'Phelan Godoy, *Un siglo de rebeliones anticoloniales* (Cuzco: Centro de Estudios Regionales Andinos Bartolomé de Las Casas, 1988).

8   O'Phelan Godoy, *Un siglo de rebeliones*; Serulnikov, *Revolution*; Walker, *The Rebellion*.

9   See Víctor Peralta, *La independencia y la cultura política peruana (1808–1821)* (Lima: IEP, Fundación M. J. Bustamante de la Fuente, 2010); and Claudia Rosas, *Del trono a la guillotina: El impacto de la Revolución francesa en el Perú (1789–1808)* (Lima: Instituto Francés de Estudios Andinos, Embajada de Francia, Fondo Editorial PUCP, 2006).

10 For an important reframing of neo-scholasticism and natural rights, see Hilda Sábato, *Republics of the New World: The Revolutionary Political Experiment in Nineteenth-Century Latin America* (Princeton, NJ: Princeton University Press, 2018), 27–28.

11 Charles F. Walker, *Smoldering Ashes: Cusco and the Creation of Republican Peru, 1780–1840* (Durham, NC: Duke University Press, 1999), 87. On Aguilar y Ubalde, see Flores Galindo, *In Search*, chap. 6.

12 Alberto Flores Galindo, *Aristocracia y plebe: Lima, 1760–1830 (Estructura de clases y sociedad colonial)* (Lima: Mosca Azul Editores, 1984); Elizabeth Hernández García, "Un espacio regional fragmentado: El proceso de independencia y el norte del Virreinato del Perú, 1780–1824," in *El Perú en revolución: Independencia y guerra: Un proceso, 1780–1826*, ed. Manuel Chust and Claudia Rosas (Zamora, Mexico: Universidad de Michoacán, 2017).

13 Flores Galindo, *Aristocracia y plebe*; on a possible enslaved people's uprising near Chincha in 1820–21, see Jorge Basadre, *El azar en la historia y sus límites: Con un apéndice, La serie de probabilidades dentro de la emancipación peruana* (Lima: Ediciones P.L.V., 1973), 101; Maribel Arrelucea Barrantes, *Sobreviviendo a la esclavitud: Negociación y honor en las prácticas cotidianas de los africanos y afrodescendientes: Lima, 1750–1820* (Lima: Instituto de Estudios Peruanos, 2018).

14 Anthony McFarlane, *War and Independence in Spanish America* (New York: Routledge, 2014); Mónica Ricketts, *Who Should Rule? Men of Arms, the Republic of Letters, and the Fall of the Spanish Empire* (New York: Oxford University Press, 2017); Leon Campbell, *The Military and Society in Colonial Peru, 1750–1810* (Philadelphia: American Philosophical Society, 1978).

15 Rosas, *Del trono a la guillotina*.

16 Peralta, *La independencia y la cultura*, 280.

17 Peralta, *La independencia y la cultura*. On the press, see the many works of Daniel Morán—for example, "El mundo de los impresos y los discursos políticos en el Perú: La prensa en la experiencia de las Cortes de Cádiz y el ciclo revolucionario en América," in Chust and Rosas, *El Perú en revolución*.

18 Víctor Peralta Ruíz, "Las resonancias de la Revolución de Mayo en la independencia del Perú (1810–1821)," in *España en Perú (1796–1824): Ensayos sobre los últimos gobiernos virreinales*, ed. Víctor Peralta Ruíz and Dionisio de Haro (Madrid: Marcial Pons Ediciones Jurídicas y Sociales, 2019).

19 Ella Dunbar Temple, *Conspiraciones y rebeliones en el siglo XIX: La revolución de Huánuco, Panatahuas y Huamalíes de 1812*, vol. 2, *Colección Documental de la Independencia del Perú 2* (Lima: Comisión Nacional del Sesquicentenario de la Independencia del Perú, 1971); Lizardo Seiner L., "Una rebelión a la deriva: Fisuras y represión realista en Tacna, 1811," in *Abascal y la contra-independencia de América del Sur*, ed. Scarlett O'Phelan Godoy and Georges Lomné (Lima: Instituto Francés de Estudios Andinos y Pontificia Universidad Católica del Perú, 2013); Alejandro

Rabinovich, *Anatomía del pánico: La batalla de Huaqui, o la derrota de la revolución (1811)* (Buenos Aires: Sudamericana, 2017).

20 Dunbar Temple, *Conspiraciones y rebeliones*, 2:65, document from February 18, 1812.

21 On Huánuco, see Dunbar Temple, *Conspiraciones y rebeliones*, vol. 2; Marissa Bazán, "El impacto de los panfletos y los rumores en la rebelión de Huánuco, 1812: Los Incas y la interpretación hecha en el caso de Juan de Dios Guillermo," in Chust and Rosas, *El Perú en revolución.*

22 McFarlane, *War and Independence*, 207–9; *La revolución de 1814 en la ciudad del Cuzco* (Cuzco: Dirección Desconcentrada de Cultura del Cusco, 2015); Colectivo por el Bicentenario de la Revolución del Cusco, *El Cusco insurrecto: La revolución de 1814, doscientos años después* (Cuzco: Ministerio de Cultura, Dirección Desconcentrada de Cultura del Cusco, 2016). On Inca revivalism, see Luis Miguel Glave, "Una perspectiva histórico-cultural de la revolución del Cuzco en 1814," *Revista de las Américas* 1 (2003): 29–30.

23 Luis Antonio Eguiguren, *La revolución de 1814* (Lima: La Opinión Nacional, 1914), 166–70.

24 El Pensador del Perú, *Al Rey, Nuestro Señor*, 1815. Scholars believe Unanue was the author.

25 Historians have downplayed the importance of these juntas. As Carlos Contreras wrote, for example: "The fact that juntas were not formed in Peru or if attempted were not consolidated expressed the lack of consensus regarding their necessity and who should integrate and lead them." Carlos Contreras, *El aprendizaje de la libertad: Historia del Perú en el siglo de su independencia* (Lima: Pontificia Universidad Católica del Perú, 2016), 32. Historians need to pay attention to movements that did not gain consensus.

26 Gabriel Di Meglio, *1816: La trama de la independencia* (Buenos Aires: Planeta, 2016).

27 McFarlane, *War and Independence*, 360.

28 Cited in Marcos Cueto and Carlos Contreras, *Historia del Perú contemporáneo* (Lima: IEP, 2018), 42.

29 Flores Galindo, *Aristocracia y plebe.*

30 Pablo Ortemberg, *Rituales de poder en Lima (1735–1828): De la monarquía a la república* (Lima: Fondo Editorial PUCP, 2014), 248.

31 The generally laconic William Miller blamed indolence: "But, unfortunately, the pleasures of a luxurious capital had taken such a firm hold on the minds of the chiefs and others, that, when the march of some battalions had been determined upon, obstacles were raised, and pretences fabricated for delay." William Miller, *Memoirs of General Miller in the Service of the Republic of Peru* (London: Longman, Rees, Orme, Brown & Green, 1829), 410.

32 Quoted in Scarlett O'Phelan Godoy, "Campaña antipeninsular y exilio en la independencia del Perú: El testimonio de los viajeros," in *Viajeros e independencia: La mirada del otro*, ed. Scarlett O'Phelan Godoy and

Georges Lomné (Lima: Fondo Editorial del Congreso del Perú, 2017), 307. See also Scarlett O'Phelan Godoy, *El general Don José de San Martín y su paso por el Perú* (Lima: Fondo Editorial del Congreso del Perú, 2017); and Carmen McEvoy, "De la comunidad retórica al estado-nación: Bernardo Monteagudo y los dilemas del republicanismo en 'América del Sud' 1811–1822," in *Convivencia y buen gobierno: Nación, nacionalismo y democracia en América Latina*, ed. José Nun and Alejandro Grimson (Buenos Aires: EDHASA, 2006).

33 Scarlett O'Phelan Godoy, "Sucre en el Perú: Entre Riva Agüero y Torre Tagle," in *La independencia del Perú: De los Borbones a Bolívar*, ed. Scarlett O'Phelan Godoy (Lima: Instituto Riva-Agüero y Pontificia Universidad Católica del Perú, 2001); Pablo Ortemberg, "La entrada de José de San Martín en Lima y la proclamación del 28 de julio: La negociación simbólica de la transición," *Histórica* 33, no. 2 (2009): 65–108.

34 Letter from Canterac to Viceroy La Serna, cited in McFarlane, *War and Independence*, 381.

35 On epidemics and health, see Susy Sánchez Rodríguez, "Clima, hambre, y enfermedad en Lima," in Godoy, *La independencia del Perú*, esp. 249–53; and José Manuel Valdés, *Memorias sobre las enfermedades epidémicas que se padecieron en Lima el año de 1821 estando sitiada por el ejercito libertador* (Lima: Imprenta de la Libertad, 1827).

36 McFarlane, *War and Independence*, 392–94.

37 On royalists, see Cecilia Méndez, *La república plebeya: Huanta y la formacion del estado peruano 1820–1850* (Lima: Instituto de Estudios Peruanos, 2014).

38 On the different terms, see Ella Dunbar Temple, *La acción patriótica del pueblo en la emancipación: Guerrillas y montoneras*, vol. 1, *Colección Documental de la Independencia del Perú* (Lima: Comisión Nacional del Sesquicentenario de la Independencia del Perú, 1971). On women and insurgency, see Claudia Rosas Laura, *Mujeres de armas tomar: La participación femenina en las guerras del Perú republicano* (Lima: Ministerio de Defensa, 2021). On the *montoneros*, see Flores Galindo, *In Search*; Peter Guardino, "Las guerrillas y la independencia peruana: Un ensayo de interpretación," *Pasado y Presente* 2–3 (1989): and 101–17; Christine Hünefeldt, "Cimarrones, bandoleros y milicianos: 1821," *Histórica* 3, no. 2 (1979): 71–88; Raúl Rivera Serna, *Los guerrilleros del Centro en la Emancipación Peruana* (Lima: P. L. Villanueva, 1958); and Gustavo Vergara, *Montoneros y guerrillas en la etapa de la emancipacion del Perú, 1820–1825* (Lima: Editorial Salesiana, 1974). For a reconsideration of the topic, see Silvia Escanilla Huerta Kosovych, "A Fragmented Sovereignty: Indigenous Peoples, War and Political Changes in the Process of Independence in the Central and Southern Andes (1783–1825)" (PhD dissertation, University of Illinois at Urbana-Champaign, 2022); for a bibliographical overview, see Carlos Aguirre and Charles Walker, "Nota a la segunda edición," in *Bandoleros, abigeos y montoneros: Criminalidad y violencia en*

el Perú, siglos XVIII–XX, ed. Carlos Aguirre and Charles Walker (Lima: La Siniestra, 2019), 11–20; and Víctor Espinal Enciso, "Guerra y guerrillas en los Andes Central: Perú 1820–1824" (bachelor's thesis, Universidad Nacional Mayor de San Marcos, 2020).

39 Dunbar Temple, *La acción patriótica*, 1:xxiv.

40 Timothy Anna, *The Fall of the Royal Government in Peru* (Lincoln: University of Nebraska Press, 1979), 215.

41 On numbers of combatants, see Natalia Sobrevilla, *The Caudillo of the Andes: Andrés de Santa Cruz* (Cambridge: Cambridge University Press, 2011), 81–83; Méndez, *La república plebeya*; and Nelson Pereyra Chávez, "La batalla de Ayacucho: Cultura guerrera y memoria de un hecho histórico," in Chust and Rosas, *El Perú en revolución*.

42 Pereyra Chávez, "La batalla de Ayacucho"; David Quichua Chaico, *Derrotados beneficiados: Sectores realistas de Huamanga en la independencia del Perú* (Ayacucho: Fondo Editorial Universidad Nacional de San Cristóbal de Huamanga, 2021).

43 I develop these points in Charles Walker, "'Más de una alternativa': Flores Galindo y la independencia," in Carlos Aguirre and Charles Walker, *Alberto Flores Galindo: Utopía, historia y revolución* (Lima: La Siniestra, 2020).

44 Chust and Rosas make this point well, particularly regarding liberalism and the "Cádiz moment." I disagree, however, with their rosy portrait of recent Peruvian historiography. Chust and Rosas, "Una independencia sin adjetivos, un proceso histórico de guerra y revolución," in Chust and Rosas, *El Perú en revolución*. On radical liberalism, see Florencia Mallon, *Peasant and Nation: The Making of Postcolonial Mexico and Peru* (Berkeley: University of California Press, 1995).

45 Luis Alberto Rosado Loarte uses the terms *disenchantment* and *indignation* regarding corruption among rebel leaders in Huacho in the early 1820s. Luis Alberto Rosado Loarte, "Infieles al rey: El pueblo de San Bartolomé de Huacho durante el proceso de Independencia, 1812–1822," in *Narra la independencia desde tu pueblo: Huacho, Arequipa, Tarapacá*, ed. Juan Carlos Estensoro and Cecilia Méndez (Lima: Instituto Francés de Estudios Andinos and IEP, 2018), 99.

46 Dunbar Temple, *La acción patriótica*, 1:xxxi.

47 Pascal Riviale, "Los informes oficiales de la Marina Francesa sobre el Perú en el momento de la independencia," in O'Phelan Godoy and Lomné, *Viajeros e independencia*, 387, quoting Alphonse de Moges.

48 On the invocation of the Incas, see Flores Galindo, *In Search*; Bazán, "El impacto de los panfletos"; and Fabio Wasserman, *Juan José Castelli: De súbdito de la corona a líder revolucionario* (Buenos Aires: EDHASA, 2011), 187–203.

49 In the words of Jorge Basadre, "Bolivar's caudillismo, which sought to create a hierarchical peace and an Andean federation, was replaced by secondary caudillos, who fought in the name of a limited nationalism." Jorge Basadre, *Perú, problema y posibilidad* (Lima: F. and E. Rosay, 1931), 20.

50 "Over the years and despite the incongruencies of political life, the perennial struggle between two ideas stands out: the idea of a strong government and that of freedom, the former defended by authoritarians and the latter liberals." Basadre, *Perú, problema y posibilidad*, 53.

51 Peter F. Klarén, *Peru: Society and Nationhood in the Andes* (New York: Oxford University Press, 2000), 154–47; Walker, *Smoldering Ashes*.

52 Luis Miguel Glave, *La república instalada: Formación nacional y prensa en el Cuzco 1825–1939* (Lima: Instituto de Estudios Peruanos, 2004); Cecilia Méndez, *Incas sí, indios no: Apuntes para el estudio del nacionalismo criollo en el Perú* (Lima: Instituto de Estudios Peruanos, 1993); Luis Daniel Morán, *Batallas por la legitimidad: La prensa de Lima y de Buenos Aires durante las guerras de independencia* (Lima: Universidad de Ciencias y Humanidades, 2013); Charles Walker, "'La orgía periodística': Prensa y cultura política en el Cuzco durante la joven república," *Revista de Indias* 61, no. 221 (2001): 7–26; Claudia Huerta, "La palabra impresa durante la guerra de independencia peruana," in Peralta and de Hara, *España en Perú*.

53 This point is covered well in Paul Gootenberg, *Between Silver and Guano: Commercial Policy and the State in Postindependence Peru* (Princeton, NJ: Princeton University Press, 1989), 101; and Paul Gootenberg, "Paying for Caudillos: The Politics of Emergency Finance in Peru, 1820–1845," in *Liberals, Politics and Power: State Formation in Nineteenth-Century Latin America*, ed. Vincent Peloso and Barbara Tennenbaum (Athens: University of Georgia Press, 1996).

54 Jeffrey Klaiber, *La iglesia en el Perú: Su historia social desde la independencia* (Lima: Pontificia Universidad Católica del Perú, 1988), 35. See also Gabriella Chiaramonti, *Ciudadanía y representación en el Perú (1808–1860): Los itinerarios de la soberanía* (Lima: UNMSM, SEPS, and ONPE, 2005), 85.

55 Quoted in Joëlle Chassin, "Opinión pública 1750–1850," in *Las voces de la modernidad: Perú, 1750–1870*, ed. Cristóbal Aljovín de Losada and Marcel Velásquez Castro (Lima: Fondo Editorial del Congreso del Perú, 2017), 311–12.

56 Carlos Aguirre, *Agentes de su propia libertad: Los esclavos de Lima y la desintegración de la esclavitud 1821–1854* (Lima: Pontificia Universidad Católica del Perú, 1993), 20 percent figure from 89; Peter Blanchard, *Slavery and Abolition in Early Republican Peru* (Wilmington, DE: Scholarly Resources, 1992).

57 Carlos Aguirre, *Breve historia de la esclavitud en el Perú: Una herida que no deja de sangrar* (Lima: Fondo Editorial del Congreso del Perú, 2005), 165–68, example from 167.

58 Basadre, *Perú, problema y posibilidad*, 21.

59 Cristina Mazzeo, "El comercio colonial a la largo del siglo XVIII y su transformación frente a las coyunturas del cambio," in *Compendio de historia económica del Perú*, vol. 3, *Economía del período colonial tardío*, ed. Carlos Contreras (Lima: Banco Central de Reserva del Perú e Instituto de Estudios Peruanos, 2020). For a personal account of this process, see

Heinrich Witt, *The Diary of Heinrich Witt* (Leiden: Brill, 2015), particularly 1:77–84. On the lack of investments, see Tulio Halperin Donghi, *Historia contemporánea de América Latina* (Madrid: Alianza Editorial, 1969), chap. 3, "Una larga espera."

60 Méndez, *Incas sí, indios no*; Charles Walker, "El general y su héroe: Juan Velasco Alvarado y la reinvención de Túpac Amaru II," in *La revolución peculiar: Repensando el gobierno militar de Velasco*, ed. Carlos Aguirre and Paulo Drinot (Lima: Instituto de Estudios Peruanos, 2018). See also Colectivo por el Bicentenario, *El Cuzco insurrecto*, on reflections about how Cuzco has been marginalized. For a fascinating analysis of the creation of new symbols and emblems, see Natalia Majluf, "Los fabricantes de emblemas: Los símbolos nacionales en la transición republicana: Perú, 1820–1825," in *Visión y símbolos: Del virreinato criollo a la república peruana*, ed. Ramón Mujica (Lima: Banco de Crédito del Perú, 2006).

61 Chiaramonti, *Ciudadanía y representación*, 276–341; for percentages, see Cristóbal Aljovín de Losada, "Sufragio y participación política: Perú, 1808–1896," in *Historia de las elecciones en el Perú: Estudios sobre el gobierno representativo*, ed. Cristóbal Aljovín de Losada and Sinesio López (Lima: Instituto de Estudios Peruanos, 2005), 50–51.

62 Flora Tristán, *Ensayos escogidos* (Lima: PEISA, 1974), 58.

63 Jürgen Osterhammel, *Transformation of the World: A Global History of the Nineteenth Century* (Princeton, NJ: Princeton University Press, 2014), 914–15.

64 Majluf, "Los fabricantes de emblemas."

65 Klarén, *Peru*, 144. See also Cristina Mazzeo, "Pagando por la guerra: Comercio y finanzas: Entre la independencia y la guerra de la confederación," in *Tiempo de guerra: Estado, nación y conflicto armado en el Perú, siglos XVII–XIX*, ed. Carmen McEvoy and Alejandro Rabinovich (Lima: Instituto de Estudios Peruanos, 2018).

66 John Tutino, "The Americas in the Rise of Industrial Capitalism," in *New Countries in the Americas: Diverging Routes to the World of Nations and Industrial Capitalism*, ed. John Tutino (Durham, NC: Duke University Press, 2016), 48. For different perspectives, see Carlos Contreras, "Menos plata pero más papas: Consecuencias económicas de la independencia del Perú," in *La independencia del Perú: ¿Concedida, conseguida, concebida?*, ed. Carlos Contreras and Luis Miguel Glave (Lima: Instituto de Estudios Peruanos, 2016), 452–82; and José Deústua, *La minería peruana y la iniciación de la república, 1820–1840* (Lima: Instituto de Estudios Peruanos, 1986).

67 Contreras, "Menos plata"; Nils Jacobsen, "Ciclos cambiantes de materias primas, internacionalización limitada y productividad restringida: La economía del sur peruano, 1821–1932," in *Historia económica del sur peruano: Lanas, minas y aguardiente en el espacio regional*, ed. Martín Monsalve Zanatti (Lima: Banco Central de Reserva del Perú, Instituto de Estudios Peruanos, 2019); Magdalena Chocano, "Población, producción agraria y mercado interno, 1700–1824," in Contreras, *Economía del*

período colonial tardío. For important arguments and data, see Bruno Seminario, *El desarrollo de la economía peruana en la era moderna: Precios, población, demanda y producción desde 1700* (Lima: Universidad del Pacífico, 2015).

68 Klarén, *Peru*, 139–42; Sarah Chambers, *From Subjects to Citizens: Honor, Gender, and Politics in Arequipa, Peru, 1780–1854* (University Park: Penn State University Press, 1999); Martín Monsalve, "Industria y mercado interno, 1821–1930," in *Compendio de historia económica del Perú*, vol. 4, *Economía de la primera centuria independiente*, ed. Carlos Contreras (Lima: Banco Central de Reserva del Perú and Instituto de Estudios Peruanos, 2020).

69 Gootenberg, *From Silver*; Heraclio Bonilla, *Gran Bretaña y el Perú: Informes de los cónsules británicos, 1826–1900* (Lima: Instituto de Estudios Peruanos, 1975); Jaime Urrutia F., "La feria de Vilque: Entre mulas, lanas y timba," *Historia y Cultura* 30 (2019): 135–62.

70 Dante Herrera Alarcón, "Las rebeliones durante el primer gobierno del Mariscal Gamarra," *Revista Histórica* 23 (1957–58): 246–77.

71 Sobrevilla, *Caudillo*, 155.

72 Jorge Basadre, *La iniciación de la república: Contribución al estudio de la evolución política del Perú*, Vol. 2. (Lima: F. y E. Rosay, 1929), 43.

73 Sobrevilla, *Caudillo*.

74 The press in this period was brutally pugnacious. For example, *Nueva historia natural de la tiranía en el Perú*, an eight-page pamphlet published in Cuzco in 1834, called Gamarra "a four-footed Indian and animal," his wife "a hyena so ferocious that she cannot be domesticated," and his two main followers "pig" and "elephant."

75 Walker, *Smoldering Ashes*, 222.

76 Innovative studies on caudillos and the early republic include María Isabel Remy, "La sociedad local al inicio de la República: Cusco: 1824–1850," *Revista Andina* 6, no. 2 (1988): 451–84 (with valuable comments by a range of scholars); Cristóbal Aljovín de Losada, *Caudillo y constituciones: Perú 1821–1845* (Lima: Pontificia Universidad Católica del Perú, Instituto Riva-Agüero y Fondo de Cultura Económica, 2000); Julio Pinto Vallejos, *Caudillos y plebeyos: La construcción social del estado en América del Sur (Argentina, Perú, Chile) 1830–1860* (Santiago: LOM, 2019); Méndez, *La república plebeya*; Núria Sala i Vila, *Y llegó el Tole-Tole: Tributo indígena y movimientos sociales en el virreinato del Perú, 1784–1814* (Lima: IER José María Arguedas, 1996); Sobrevilla, *Caudillo*; Mark Thurner, *From Two Republics to One Divided: Contradictions of Postcolonial Nation-Making in Andean Peru* (Durham, NC: Duke University Press, 1996). For an excellent synthesis, see Brooke Larson, *Indígenas, elites y estado en la formación de las repúblicas andinas* (Lima: Pontificia Universidad Católica del Perú e Instituto de Estudios Peruanos, 2002).

77 Gootenberg, "Paying for Caudillos"; Walker, *Smoldering Ashes*, 188–93.

78 Paul Gootenberg, "Population and Ethnicity in Early Republic Peru: Some Revisions," *Latin American Research Review* 26, no. 3 (1991): 109–57; Adrian Pearce, "Reindigenzation and Native Languages in Peru's Long Nineteenth Century (1795–1940)," in *History and Language in the Andes,* ed. Paul Heggarty and Adrian Pearce (New York: Palgrave Macmillan, 2011); Tristán Platt, *Estado boliviano y ayllu andino: Tierra y tributo en el norte de Potosí* (Lima: Instituto de Estudios Peruanos, 1982).

79 Antonio Espinoza, *Education and the State in Modern Peru: Primary School in Lima, 1821–c. 1921* (New York: Palgrave Macmillan, 2013), 27. See the report by the Ayacucho prefect in 1829, Domingo Tristán, about the difficulty of opening and maintaining schools. Domingo Tristán, "Noticia posible del estado en que se halla la instrucción primaria y científica en el departamento de Ayacucho" (1829). I thank Antonio Espinoza for sharing this document.

80 Halperín, *Historia contemporánea.* For a vivid testimony of the national (i.e., not just Lima) nature of politics, see Félix Denegri Luna, ed., *José María Blanco, diario del viaje del Presidente Orbegoso al sur del Perú* (Lima: Pontificia Universidad Católica del Perú e Instituto Riva-Agüero, 1974).

81 Flores Galindo, *Aristocracia*; Gabriel Ramón Joffré, "Urbe y orden: Evidencias del reformismo borbónico en el tejido limeño," in *El Perú en el siglo XVIII: La era borbónica*, ed. Scarlett O'Phelan Godoy (Lima: Instituto Riva-Agüero y Pontificia Universidad Católica del Perú, 1999); Carlos Aguirre and Charles Walker, *The Lima Reader: History, Culture, Politics* (Durham, NC: Duke University Press, 2017).

82 Alfonso Quiroz, *Historia de la corrupción en el Perú* (Lima: Instituto de Estudios Peruanos, 2013).

How Illusory Was Prosperity?

The Rise and Fall of the Guano State in Peru (1840–1880)

Revolutions and coups are followed by
fraudulent elections, the embezzling,
rapacious and tyrannical government
returns to the same revolution,
the same coup, to the same elections,
and the same government.
Our national life can be exactly
symbolized by an endless belt divided
in three pieces: red, black and yellow
representing blood, fraud and excess.

—MANUEL GONZÁLEZ PRADA, "LA ELECCIÓN DE DON JOSÉ PARDO" (1933)

Between 1840 and 1880, Peru became extremely wealthy thanks to a peculiar commodity: guano. However, by the end of the period the country
was more indebted than before. And the economic crisis turned into a
national debacle when the country was defeated by Chile in the War of
the Pacific (1879–83). This chapter looks into the way these resources were
used and how the prosperity guano brought to Peru was more unequal
than illusory. To do so, it focuses on four main aspects: the debates over a
colonial-style state monopoly of guano versus a more free-market export

model; whether the military or civilians should control the state; who would be able to participate as citizens in the new republican government under construction; and how best to use the funds created by guano.

The contracts signed with British merchant houses in the 1840s refinanced the debt incurred during the wars of independence, placing the country's finances on a more even keel and allowing the Peruvian state to increase its expenditures exponentially, but this short-lived economic cycle had profound consequences. The money generated by guano was used to pay internal and external debts, increase bureaucracy, and build ambitious railway projects. The state grew, the economy was modernized, education was prioritized, some liberal measures were implemented, and the church's grip on society began to loosen. However, ambivalences that would go on to characterize Peru appeared during this period: The state grew, but corruption consolidated; liberal measures were implemented, but inequality increased; and the state tried to centralize like never before, but autonomies and local power remained, even if impoverished in relation to a Lima elite strengthened by guano wealth.

In the nearly 140 years since the defeat in the War of the Pacific, one question has dominated Peruvian historiography: Were opportunities wasted? In the years that followed the war, Manuel González Prada described the nineteenth-century state as a "robber's cave." Years later, historian Jorge Basadre coined the phrase "illusory prosperity" to describe the period between 1845 and 1872, thus helping to establish the prevailing view of this period.[1] In the 1970s, in his classic book *Guano y burguesía*, historian Heraclio Bonilla argued that the main problem in this period was the lack of a national project. More recently, however, historian Carmen McEvoy has rejected this view and argued instead that a national project had existed and consisted of a "republican utopia" where elites sought to create a functioning state.[2] Whether guano income produced actual wealth or not, there is little doubt that the revenue generated by the export of this fertilizer transformed society.

As I show below, some institutional holdovers from the colonial period finally came to an end when the state became wealthy and a new political system was established. The cash injection resulted in exponential economic growth. Society modernized, and the banking system and communications were transformed by the arrival of railways, the telegraph, and steamships; the church no longer controlled as many aspects of daily life; and primary education expanded. But immense corruption accompanied this growth, and patronage systems became the most important characteristic

Figure 2.1 Artist unknown, *View of the Plaza de Armas and Cathedral de Lima,* ca. 1825–40. Source: Museo de Arte de Lima.

of the guano system. Sudden enrichment ended direct collection of taxes, making the state extremely dependent on guano income. Liberals found it problematic to separate the category of taxpayer from that of citizen, so they tried to constitutionally link them. Another consequence was that guano transferred funds to an emergent plutocracy who invested in export agriculture, trade, banking, and railroads. Regional economies also grew, in Arequipa thanks to wool exports and along the northern coast because of rice, cotton, and sugar production.

At the start of the republic, Peru, like other emerging nations in the continent, first had to resolve its political organization. And even if—in contrast to Argentina, Colombia, and Venezuela—the civil wars that characterized the early republican period were not fought between those wanting to impose a unitarian or a federal system and those against such a move, confrontation between the provinces and the center was recurrent. As we will see, guano made centralization in Peru possible, to a large degree because it funded state growth in Lima. The 1839 constitution ended regional autonomy, and after the abolition of the Indian head tax that had been imposed in the highlands, the central government went on to control most of the country's income. Paradoxically, municipal governments would go on to gain more power and autonomy, thanks to a process started by President Ramón Castilla in 1846. Therefore, even though state capacity grew, this growth was gradual and many services, such as education, remained under municipal control.

Confrontation between liberals and conservatives, and even radicals who struggled to abolish institutions and practices inherited from the colonial period, characterized the second half of the nineteenth century, just as in the rest of the continent, as I discuss below. A heavily disputed issue was who should have the right to vote and why. Guano wealth and liberal reforms favored the economic elites, who received compensation after the abolition of slavery and bought land from Indigenous communities or the state, or land that originally had been gifted to the church. Even if the idea of funding the state by selling natural resources and collecting customs taxes came from the colonial period and was not restricted to Peru, the failure to establish a relationship between taxation and citizenship eventually led to economic collapse. At the time, liberals warned about the risk of not having tax income, not just because the country's finances depended on a single resource but also because it weakened the connection between citizens and the state.

Caudillismo

After military defeat ended the dream of creating a political union with Bolivia, the enactment of the conservative and militarist constitution of 1839 appeared to finally put an end to the efforts liberals had been making since independence to shape national institutions. Municipalities and departmental juntas were abolished, as was the position of vice president, who typically was the candidate who had received the second-largest number of votes in the election and thus tended to compete with the president. The constitution established that prefects were to be selected from among the army officers and that Congress would meet only every two years, which meant that, in effect, the president governed with a state council made up of fifteen men. However, after Agustín Gamarra's death in 1841, during the failed invasion of Bolivia, this governmental structure wobbled.[3] An intense conflict over power erupted, leading to a series of interim presidents who succeeded each other at dizzying speed. The situation was so fraught that interim president Justo Figuerola asked his daughter to throw the ceremonial presidential sash out of the window to the people in the street shouting a caudillo's name.

As Walker's chapter shows, in the first years of the republic the caudillos who had emerged during the wars of independence were involved in a seemingly unending struggle for power. These conflicts brought great instability and reflected tensions between the cities and the countryside and between protectionism and free trade. The anarchy experienced after Gamarra's death, however, was due not only to military leaders' ambition to replace him but also to the efforts organized in the regions, particularly in the south, to combat the centralism imposed by the Chilean-inspired conservative constitution of 1839. The national guards created in different provinces after the fall of the confederation provided Gamarra's principal lieutenants, as well as their enemies, enough mobilized men to challenge one another.[4] This fight for control of the state underlines how significant regions were but mostly highlights the role national guards, organized in each locality, played in Peruvian politics.

Lack of resources fueled further instability, as many fought for a faction that would give them access to economic compensation. A noteworthy event that illustrates how these conflicts were fought was the so-called Battle of Agua Santa (1842), when two caudillos, each with two or three hundred men, arrived ready to fight, but once on the field of combat both decided to run away even while claiming victory. During these struggles over power, Ramón Castilla emerged as the principal caudillo, supported by the national guards from the southern provinces of Tacna and Moquegua, with whom he took the city of Arequipa at the Battle of Carmen Alto (1843), after which he and his troops victoriously marched to Lima. Between 1841 and 1845 more than a dozen caudillos fought to gain power but managed to control only the city where they were located. Some succeeded in getting to Lima, but only Castilla was able to break the cycle of anarchy. Once he arrived in the capital, however, he did not take power until elections confirmed his position.

Guano exports began during this cycle of political confrontation when Peruvian merchant Francisco Quiroz signed a contract with his French associates.[5] But large-scale guano exploitation really began only in 1842, when the Anthony Gibbs merchant house agreed with the provisional government of Manuel Menéndez to export 120,000 tons over four years. Gibbs doubted the Peruvian government's capacity to meet its end of the bargain, as it was constantly on the verge of collapse, but nevertheless agreed to advance most of the money.[6] Men transported mountains of excrement to chutes connected directly to boats anchored at the edge of the desertic guano islands off the Peruvian coast. When the guano was moved, some of its nitrates were liberated, producing the characteristic smell.[7] When the first shipment of guano arrived in Liverpool, according to contemporary accounts, the whole city was shrouded in a strong smell of excrement that lasted for weeks.

Guano exports allowed Castilla to implement a series of measures that consolidated the state and radically changed its funding structure. Previously, it had been haphazardly financed by loans from the Tribunal del Consulado (Merchants' Guild) and by funds raised by provincial tax offices. Because there was no centralized fiscal authority, and because only the Indigenous population was subject to direct taxation (the *contribución*, or Indigenous head tax) after Gamarra abolished taxes for the other ethnic groups, known as *castas*, the provinces of Cuzco, Puno, Arequipa, and Ayacucho, where most of these Indigenous taxpayers lived, supplied the bulk of state revenues and, as such, enjoyed a degree of fiscal autonomy.[8] Since there was no centralized collection structure, the colonial tax farming system, where private individuals extracted tribute for the state in exchange for an advance payment, persisted. Between that and the money retained in the provincial capitals, only a fraction of the income actually reached the central government. Similarly, taxes on silver production were collected in the highlands, and Lima controlled only the revenue from the customs house.

Guano changed all that. Between 1845 and 1850, Castilla's government received 5 million pesos, of which 2 million came from the actual sale of guano, and the rest from loans secured by future sales.[9] This financial bonanza created its own distortions, but initially it allowed for a certain stability. It funded pension payments to army veterans without regard to which side they had fought for, transforming early nineteenth-century caudillismo into a patronage system and, in effect, paying for peace. Indeed, some members of the military groups previously aligned with various caudillos were incorporated into the national guards and into the middle echelons of the state, through salaries, perks, job appointments, and the payment of outstanding debts. These debts included salary arrears and money lent during the wars of independence to finance the campaigns.

A veteran of the wars of independence who had begun his career fighting for the king of Spain, Castilla was in one sense a typical traditional conservative caudillo. He made guano into a state monopoly, not unlike the resource monopolies of the colonial period. But in contrast with other contemporary leaders in the region, such as Antonio López de Santa Ana in Mexico or Juan Manuel de Rosas in the province of Buenos Aires, Castilla considered it important to govern under constitutional rule. He came to power in defense of the 1839 conservative constitution, but he did not take office until he was confirmed by election. Once in office he went on to implement some liberal policies, such as decentralizing power to municipalities, by following legal channels and leading discussions in Congress. He also opened up the economy, allowing free trade with foreign powers. However, many of his policies ended up further entrenching inequality.

Despite guano's preeminence, mining never ceased to be a cornerstone of the national economy.[10] In contrast with other countries in the region such as Mexico, Chile, and Bolivia, until at least 1890 mining exploitation in Peru was small-scale and continued to depend on pure veins of gold and silver. Some regional economies continued to depend on mining, which articulated large areas of the economy such as local and regional trade, the minting of coin, and muleteers, who transported goods.[11] Indeed, the internal economy remained varied, and deep connections existed between mining, agriculture, and trade. In southern Peru, the wool economy generated a regional trade that continued to gain prominence in the following half century. On the coast, meanwhile, the production of rice, cotton, and sugar started to undergo a process of modernization, through the incorporation of new machinery and know-how, thanks to new sources of investment, new sources of labor, and technological developments.

From the beginning of the guano era, Castilla sought to favor the "children of the country" (*hijos del país*)—that is, Peruvians rather than foreigners. But local capitalists could not lend the Peruvian state enough in exchange for future sales of guano. They were unable to compete with the foreign merchant houses.[12] An attempt to renegotiate the guano contract had failed in 1849. A year later, the Guano Consignee Society—organized by the main Peruvian traders—obtained the monopoly to sell guano for a decade in Spain, France, the Antilles, and the United States. But despite the initial enthusiasm, the "children of the country" had to abandon all these markets except for North America because they lacked sufficient capital.[13]

Nevertheless, this period witnessed the development of a national merchant class that benefited from an economy fueled by guano exports. National merchants invested in railways, hoping to enter commodity trading, while the government guaranteed these merchants' access to capital by paying back the national debt it had acquired since independence. But this led to a vicious cycle, because to finance debt repayment the Peruvian state acquired new debt. The process was known as the internal debt consolidation, because old bills of payment were brought together into newly issued bonds that most benefited those merchants close to the government.[14] As the guano trade grew, more national *consignatarios* or consignees, those granted the right to extract guano from the islands in exchange for a proportion of the revenues, appeared, while others developed import and export businesses; as a result, certain groups were notably enriched.

Slaves remained the main coastal workforce, even though during the wars of independence the trade had been abolished and "free womb" laws—laws declaring that any child born to an enslaved person was free at birth—were implemented. In 1846 and 1847, Castilla briefly reopened slave trading with New Granada but was forced to close it because of strong opposition. Enslavers argued that their humane treatment civilized the enslaved and that without them they could not produce anything. They succeeded in having the age of majority for *libertos* born after 1821 raised from eighteen to fifty, meaning that those who in theory had been born free had to serve their parents' owners for most of their life.[15] Some of the enslaved bought their freedom through manumission or escaped in search of a better life, thus challenging slavery as an institution. Nevertheless, slavery continued to be important in the department of Lima.[16]

However, as abolitionism gained ground across the Americas and in Europe, enslavers started to look for alternative sources of labor and eventually turned to indentured Chinese workers. Liberal politician, landowner, enslaver, and merchant Domingo Elías, one of the first consignees, brought Chinese workers to labor in coastal haciendas, extract guano from the islands, and build railways.[17] Between 1849 and 1874 some 100,000 men and 150 women arrived and quickly mixed with the local population.[18] The Chinese greatly impacted Peruvian society: Hacienda capitalist expansion was made possible by the productivity gains resulting from the mechanization of sugar, rice, and cotton production, and the labor provided by so-called coolies, which lowered the cost of guano extraction and were key to the construction of railways in this period.[19] In the long term their presence dynamized the economy and helped transform Peruvian society. Once they had served their contracts, many of the Chinese moved into trade and agriculture, while others introduced new forms of healing and foodways to Peru.

During this period the country's Indigenous population continued its demographic recovery, in a process that Adrian Pearce has called "reindigenization," which resulted in a degree of autonomy vis-à-vis the national state.[20] The Indigenous *contribución*, the only form of direct taxation, represented an important source of national revenue, as the central government was unable to impose new taxes. The first official republican census

Figure 2.2 Francisco "Pancho" Fierro, *Chinese Fisherman*, ca. 1858. Source: Museo de Arte de Lima.

of 1876 indicated that the Indigenous population represented 60 percent of the national population. At the same time, Indigenous men had the right to vote, a right they used to preserve their interests, exchanging ballots for patronage.[21] Moreover, Indigenous people were not considered suitable for labor in the guano islands or on coastal haciendas. The highlands and the coast were not really integrated, and after independence commercial large-scale agricultural production in the highlands ceased to be viable. This also contributed to Indigenous autonomy.

With guano, support for free trade grew as Lima elites realized they could obtain greater revenues by freely trading in international markets and abandoning protectionist agreements, most notably the exchange of Peruvian sugar for Chilean flour.[22] The merchants' embrace of free trade, and the resulting influx of cheap imports, was a blow to local artisans, who responded by becoming involved in midcentury politics. Cigarmaker José María García voiced artisans' opposition to free trade in Congress, arguing it represented a threat to the "industrious class" and the "children of the country."[23] But ultimately artisans could not compete with a free trade coalition made up of "the national traders, lenders turned into *consolidados*, regional oligarchs, domesticated caudillos, anxious and responsible

Figure 2.3 Anonymous, *Indigenous Woman on Her Way to the Market*, ca. 1835–40. Source: Museo de Arte de Lima.

functionaries. They were joined by recently accepted southern proto-exporters and foreign houses."[24] Vague promises to support national industry aside, guano helped free trade win the argument that had raged since independence.

Between 1845 and 1850, guano funds allowed Castilla to reorganize the army by forcing many officers to retire with a generous pension. Others were transferred to the recently created police, and the salaries of those who remained in service were paid punctually.[25] A new law regarding municipalities ended the centralist vision imposed by Gamarra in 1839, and local authorities recovered a degree of autonomy. As Antonio Espinoza shows, municipalities organized and managed public schools, even as the central government continued to subsidize them with guano funds.[26] The first educational code was issued in 1850. School reforms were supposed to follow it, but most retained patronage systems and the new curriculum rarely reached rural areas. Authoritarian methods therefore prevailed in the classroom, as did teaching materials that expressed and promoted traditional hierarchies, including respect for the church.[27]

Debate on the electoral law, unchanged since the Cádiz constitution of 1812, was rife in Congress in this period. The indirect electoral system in place meant that large numbers of men could vote, but only for electors, who would then cast ballots.[28] Voting rights for the illiterate had at first been considered a temporary measure; the colonial system had denied many the opportunity to learn to read and write, but it was thought that national educational policy would correct this situation. In 1847, Castilla and his minister Domingo Elías sought to extend the literacy exception so that all the men who paid tax could continue to vote until 1860.[29] This dynamized the debate over who should have this right. Bartolomé Herrera, the conservative director of the College of San Carlos and a congressman, defended the idea of "sovereignty of intelligence"—that only those who could read and write should have the right to vote. Liberals, like Benito Laso and the brothers Pedro and José Gálvez, meanwhile, considered that all men should be allowed to vote because the people were sovereign. Despite opposition from Herrera, liberals led by José Gálvez won the debate easily, and a large majority of men retained the right to vote.[30]

In short, as we have seen, Castilla endeavored to build a more functional state with the guano income. He balanced the centralism of the 1839 constitution with a recognition of regional sentiment by passing the municipalities law. He achieved a degree of pacification in the country, since the newly acquired funds provided many with a pension or a military post that reduced the incentives for mobilized men to organize uprisings. This cemented patronage systems, which characterized all institutions from the army to the public primary schools, and in those institutions employment continued to be for life. Parliamentary victories during this period strengthened liberals, who passed free trade legislation and maintained the right of illiterate people to vote.

Liberalism

Scholars who study liberalism in nineteenth-century Peru have tended to focus exclusively on liberals' role in promoting free trade.[31] In Peru the deep rifts that characterized early republican instability elsewhere in Latin America, such as Mexico, New Granada, and what would later become Argentina, were not as common. The divide between federalists and centralists was resolved early with a compromise that meant that the country would always remain united, as there were strong fears that otherwise it could unravel. Despite this centralism, municipal governments were given a degree of autonomy. Also absent was the conflict between church and state that led to the War of the Supremes in New Granada in the 1830s and to the War of the Reforma in midcentury Mexico. In Peru, as in Chile and Argentina, the relationship between the state and the church did not become a major bone of contention, and by the 1860s the church had lost most of the battles over control of its land. What did galvanize Peruvian liberals, just as it did their peers elsewhere in the region, was the issue of slavery and the desire to abolish this institution, as I discuss below.[32]

The 1850–51 presidential campaign marked the end of the first constitutionally mandated presidential term. Liberals supported businessman Domingo Elías, but despite all their efforts they were defeated at the ballot box by General José Rufino Echenique, who replaced Castilla. Soon after taking power in 1852, Echenique passed a new civil code superseding colonial-era legislation and creating a legal framework for private transactions. Legal modernization accompanied the economic modernization already in progress. That same year the first civil procedural code regulating trials came into force, and a year later the first trade code followed.[33]

The implications of this legal modernization were mixed. While certain crimes that had been considered private matters in the colonial period, including robbery and serious physical attacks, were now perceived as public issues, matters related to matrimony, family, and sexuality ceased to fall under canon law and were referred to the legal system only if they called into question a patriarch's authority to control his dependents in the domestic space.[34] Still, such cases were now subject to a liberal and secular legal code rather than a religious one. Women remained subordinate to patriarchal authority, but they used the law to challenge their subordination.[35] Even in relatively remote provinces such as Cajamarca, women turned to the law to challenge patriarchy, with female domestic servants using the law to seek autonomy from abusive patrons.[36]

In the mid-nineteenth century in Peru, like in the rest of the continent, some liberals concluded that guano was a providential resource that should be used to abolish slavery and Indian tribute.[37] Men such as Francisco Bilbao, a Chilean radical settled in Lima, the brothers Pedro and José Gálvez, who had intervened in the debates on the right to vote, and younger radical men like José Simeon Tejada strongly believed that equality was a most precious good, and that instead of spending the income generated by guano to further enrich those who already had the most, it should be used to dismantle the remnants of the colonial order. As José Casimiro Ulloa, a doctor, put it, "Guano is [an] immense flow that providence has given us so that we can realize its designs; it guarantees the freedom of slaves, the extinction of Indian servitude, the education of the people, the progress of our industry, the advancement of our science, and the creation of art."[38]

The bonanza originated by guano accelerated Lima's modernization. The first railway in the continent joined the capital with the port of Callao in 1851; in order to make way for the construction of the "iron road," a symbol of modernity, convents had to be demolished. And the injection of funds transformed what had hitherto been a peaceful colonial city, with new buildings constructed and streets broadened. These changes registered also in how men and women socialized. Women radically changed the way they dressed: they stopped wearing their traditional pleated skirt and the *tapada*, a mantle that largely covered the face and left only one eye in view. It became much more common to see them wearing crinolines and French fashion. Beginning in the mid-1840s, the importation of English clothes increased, and by 1852, foreign products were subject to a tax of only 20 percent. As a result, sumptuary consumption grew and served to reinforce patriarchal notions of women as the "weaker sex," who sought to dress fashionably because their interests were limited to such matters.[39]

Along with adapting this new style of clothing, elite women followed bourgeois convention of the time and abandoned the public sphere, where they had previously participated as *tapadas* (the anonymity provided by traditional dress, with its concealing mantle, had made it possible for "decent" women to walk freely in the streets of the city, thus escaping the confines of their homes). An episode narrated by contemporary writer Ricardo Palma in his *tradition* (short story) "The Dance of Victoria" shows how Lima had become a cosmopolitan city where issues of dress mattered. In October 1853, Victoria Tristán, President Echenique's wife, gave a party where some 1,000 men met 289 richly attired ladies. According to the writer, jewelry marked the difference between new money and old, as women from traditional families wore silver pieces, while the nouveau riche were covered in diamonds, rudely flaunting their newly acquired wealth.[40]

At the party, Echenique's wife wore only silver. She was a member of one of the most important Arequipa families, after all. However, her husband was regarded with distrust. Echenique had continued with Castilla's policy of debt repayment and added an even more problematic element: He converted what had been internal debt into external debt. In 1853 he transferred

Figure 2.4 Francisco "Pancho" Fierro, *Priest Begging for Alms from a Tapada*, ca. 1850–60. Source: Museo de Arte de Lima.

46 percent of the country's internal debt to the London capital markets, transforming it into a different kind of liability. Historian Alfonso Quiroz considers that he did this to "launder funds tainted by their corrupt origin in the internal debt consolidation."[41] Echenique was accused of favoring those close to him and accepting falsified bonds. The president finally ended the process of debt consolidation in October 1852 because he believed that "it had brought terrible greed, wealth gained by three or four people who knew how to take advantage of the situation with the true creditors."[42]

Despite having been one of the main beneficiaries of consolidation payments and external debt conversion, Elías, Echenique's rival in the presidential campaign of 1850–51, headed the opposition to the president.[43] When Echenique asked for extraordinary powers from Congress, to deal with threats on the Bolivian border, the reaction was immediate: Elías accused him of trying to establish a dictatorship.[44] In his letters published in *El Comercio* in 1853, the merchant from Ica accused Echenique of corruption. In turn, Echenique claimed that Elías had tried to bribe him and was orchestrating a campaign to destroy him as a reprisal for canceling his guano-exporting contract, as well as his monopoly to import

Chinese workers. The president alleged that even though he had been one of the greatest beneficiaries of consolidation, Elías was unhappy because he had not reaped as much from debt conversion as he had wanted to.[45]

Elías was not, however, the only powerful figure to attack the president. Fernando Casós, who had supported Echenique in 1850, was employed at the Ministry of Finance in 1852, and in 1853 was elected as deputy for Jaen, took the time to investigate irregularities in governmental function. In 1854 he declared that even though the government had been installed with the best of intentions, once in power "there was no more discussion, only force, favor, gold and coercion."[46] Years later, from his Parisian exile, Casós, who has been described as a "*zambo* (a [Black-Indian] half-caste) from the provinces," who, perhaps because of his access to education, rose up the social ladder, portrayed Lima's upper class in his novels, presenting it as venal and vain: It thought itself "decent" but lacked social sensitivity because of what Casós described as the "dammed guano."[47]

Quiroz has shown how Peruvian economic elites took advantage of the legislative vacuum and lack of oversight that resulted from Echenique's gaining of extraordinary powers, both with respect to the process of consolidation and regarding the conversion of national to foreign debt, to ensure that "the long-term bonds would be turned into high-yielding short-term ones."[48] In this context, capitalists like Elías took advantage of the consolidation process, buying debt bonds for very little and claiming repayment at a much higher value. This is one of the reasons debt grew from 5 million pesos in 1852 to 24 million in just one year.[49] Of course, if the uprising that inevitably took place against Echenique was largely organized in reaction to the question of debt, other factors—such as continuous currency devaluation due to the constant influx of low-grade Bolivian coin, and the impact this had on ordinary people—also contributed.[50]

The 1853–54 armed uprising erupted to topple Echenique. When Elías's leadership abilities were found wanting, the liberals decided to support Castilla, who still coveted the presidency. Although the former president had never shown any interest in the abolition of slavery, even briefly reopening the trade with New Granada, during the rebellion he saw how ending slavery would result in popular support.[51] It was then that Castilla spoke about "recovering the rights of man, guarantees for citizens and the nation's sovereignty." José Gálvez, one of the main backers of the uprising, abolished Indigenous tribute in Junín on February 8, 1854, but Castilla did not extend the measure to the entire country until July 5, when his secretary Pedro Gálvez convinced him to sign legislation to that effect while fighting in Ayacucho.[52] As for the abolition of slavery, Castilla's attitude was also reactive: He conceded liberty to all and economic compensation to enslavers only after Echenique offered to free any enslaved people who enlisted in the army.[53]

The abolition of slavery and Indian tribute during the 1854 revolution had profound economic repercussions. President Castilla and Elías, as minister of finance, believed that doing away with all sources of state income save the revenues from guano exports was problematic. They believed the government should collect a head tax, but even though they advocated for this, they did not manage to convince the members of the national convention (an extraordinary Congress) elected in 1855 to vote to implement such a tax.[54] Elías created the Junta for Fiscal Examination to review all the debt owed by the Peruvian state, as well as the redeemable bonds created by the provisional government to fund the revolution and pay enslavers 300 pesos for each of their enslaved people who were required to be freed.[55] As Quiroz has shown, manumission bonds were plagued by inexactitudes and favoritism, as Castilla and Elías used every opportunity to benefit their acolytes, further strengthening political patronage. To a large degree this was possible because the Junta for Fiscal Examination was made up of people close to Elías. "Former slave owners received approximately 2.8 million [pesos] in cash and some 5.2 million pesos in bonds valued in total at around 8 million pesos."[56] Elías, the third-largest landowner in the country, received 110,000 pesos in bonds for his 370 slaves and left the ministry soon after. In 1855, Francisco Bilbao, the Chilean radical who had encouraged the uprising, disappointedly wrote: "There has never been a more just revolution, and after triumph there has never been a more fruitless revolution."[57]

To consolidate change, Castilla called an election in 1855, so that a national convention would ratify him as provisional president, write a new constitution, and work as a parliament. The greatest innovation was that for the first time the elections would be direct, meaning that men would not choose electors but instead vote directly for their representatives. Anyone who had not been part of Echenique's army or government had the right to cast a ballot.[58] The liberals and radicals blamed the indirect electoral system for all the ills experienced by Peruvian democracy. The new system was not, however, uncontroversial, as many, seeing their privileges challenged by the new radical measures, complained that men who had until very recently been enslaved could vote while the members of Echenique's government and army could not.[59]

Authors such as Felipe Barriga y Álvarez claimed that giving the right to vote to "the black slave whose soul and body had been marked with deep ignorance, with instincts for robbery and assassination, and their whip scars" was an affront to the nation.[60] Manuel Atanasio Fuentes, a journalist known as "El Murcielago" (the bat), called Castilla's government "such a harsh dictatorship that it seemed like the government of the *conquistadores*; his ministers wanted to rule through terror."[61] But this disquiet with the radical character of the government was not limited to the opposition. Castilla began to distance himself from his own liberal ministers, and by August 1855, not a single one remained in his post.

The reforms introduced in this period were substantial. After the revolution, the provinces demanded more autonomy. In response, the 1856 constitution reestablished the departmental juntas abolished in 1839. Prefects would be elected locally instead of designated by the executive.[62] The presidential term was reduced to four years instead of six, while the legislative gained the prerogative to declare the presidency vacant and oversee military appointments.[63] In 1855 the judiciary was reformed and internal customs houses abolished. The following year a new law for municipalities was passed, increasing their prerogatives. In 1857 a new law for internal organization "determined the jurisdiction and power of local authorities (prefects and subprefects)."[64]

Reforms extended to military and religious matters. Military and ecclesiastical courts of justice, known as *fueros*, were abolished, thus ending the existence of separate legal orders. This enraged the military, which did not want to lose access to its own parallel courts, while the church wholeheartedly rejected the move and took advantage of the popular support it had garnered to oppose the possible imposition of freedom of worship. Bartolomé Herrera organized the conservative reaction from his newspaper *El Católico*. He encouraged women to go out to protest the attacks on the church.[65] In this period, women's political participation mostly aligned with conservative politics. Priests convinced them to sign petitions and temporarily leave the private sphere to defend religion in public.

In short, the 1856 constitution liberalized the country: It introduced direct elections; decreed the end of slavery, Indian tribute, and the death penalty; eliminated the life tenure of jobs, a practice inherited from colonial times; and abolished military and ecclesiastical courts. Although liberals welcomed these radical measures, they were not universally popular. The granting of regional autonomy through departmental juntas did not prevent opposition to the 1856 charter from beginning in the provinces. In Arequipa, Castilla was accused of "having sanctioned an anomalous, anti-religious, inopportune constitution, opposed to national sentiment," and on October 31 an armed uprising broke out, giving way to a new revolution.[66] The provinces of Ayacucho, Moquegua, and Piura joined together with sections of the navy led by Miguel Grau and Lizardo Montero, which handed rebels control over the guano-producing Chincha Islands.[67] Castilla's government, however, could count on popular sectors, as was evident in the defense of Callao in April 1857, when the revolutionaries' advances by sea were repelled by locals. In recognition of their support the government designated such areas "constitutional provinces."

For six months the war was concentrated in the north and center of the country. When nearly all the provincial uprisings had been defeated, the people of Arequipa continued to fight for another year. Congress was suspended during the civil war (1856–58). The total cost of the conflict was estimated at ten thousand lives and "more than 20 million pesos that came from the treasury, without counting the dilapidation the revolutionaries brought on to state revenues and private interests."[68]

The revolution may have been defeated, but the 1856 constitution was repealed, and Castilla called general elections, as set out by a law passed in 1857. The elections were direct, and voting was limited to those who could read and write, along with artisans, property owners, and army veterans, which still allowed for wide access to the ballot. Municipalities were tasked with creating the civil register of voters and taking over from parish priests to organize local and provincial electoral juries.[69] Artisan participation in these elections was key, and many of the candidates, including those from the governing party, did everything they could to gain their support, promising to limit free trade policies in exchange for their votes.[70] This election thus marked the emergence of a new social group, urban artisans, an as important political force. Particularly in Lima and Callao, they would continue to play an important role in Peruvian politics well into the first half of the twentieth century.

During extensive parliamentary discussions in 1858, the artisans of Callao protested against the importation of materials to build the Lima–Chorrillos railway. They had hoped goods that competed with national products would be prohibited, as had been promised during the electoral campaign.[71] Artisans from the carpenters guild presented themselves to the press as "peaceful citizens and industrious and republican patriots" and used public petitions to seek support from President Castilla and from the general public.[72] The situation was much graver than in the previous decade, when artisans had participated in debates over protection of their industries. However, support in Congress for free trade meant that the artisans' demands were ignored and their protests heavily repressed.

The parliamentary representatives in 1858 were, however, much more liberal than the government, and in November they voted to reject the closure of the national convention during an uprising in Arequipa, thus challenging the authority of the president. This resulted in such a deterioration in the relationship between the executive and the legislative that in April 1859 the members of Congress proposed declaring that the country was in peril and the presidency vacant. However, facing the risk of war with Ecuador and Bolivia, this did not come to pass, and the representatives agreed to close the extraordinary session so that a regular Congress could meet.[73] This prompted a rebellion in Cuzco, with rebels accusing the national legislators of having prostituted themselves.[74]

The 1858 Congress tried to meet again as an ordinary one, but Castilla managed to call new elections after mobilizing thousands of people to write petitions asking for a fresh vote, which was held in December 1859. His agents worked indefatigably, using the sturdy patronage system to ensure the people closest to the government would be elected, and setting up coalitions with former enemies of the administration with whom they shared conservative views.[75] The conservative Bartolomé Herrera presided over the new legislature, and after much discussion a consensus was achieved. Some of the changes introduced in the 1856 charter were maintained, including the abolition of military and ecclesiastical corporate courts, the *fueros*. The abolition of Indian tribute and of slavery were enshrined in law. The death penalty, however, was reinstated for homicide, and there was no further talk of ending life tenure of jobs or reintroducing departmental juntas. Moreover, a new electoral regulation put forward in 1861 ended direct elections.[76]

Little was done, however, to address the rampant corruption. In 1858 the foreign minister, Manuel Ortiz de Zevallos, was involved in a scandal linked to restitution of the debt consolidation and conversion process. He was accused of receiving 70 million pesos from a French company, an amount apparently distributed among several legislators.[77] The guano exploitation model showed its limitations in this web of corruption and political instability. In 1860, five years after the abolition of Indian tribute, the Peruvian state depended almost exclusively on the advances paid on the future sales of guano, while the provinces no longer managed their own fiscal affairs. Meanwhile, the consolidation and conversion of the in-

Figure 2.5 Francisco "Pancho" Fierro, *Montonero*, ca. 1858. Source: Museo de Arte de Lima.

ternal debt, as well as the payment to former enslavers for manumission, produced a large cash injection to the economy that primarily benefited the elites. Liberalism achieved important victories, but guano money also generously oiled the patronage system. Guano wealth, in short, brought about important social changes accompanied by great corruption.

As we have seen, Peruvian liberals shared with their contemporaries in the region a desire to modernize politics and have more inclusive representation with direct elections. Civil wars were not uncommon at midcentury in the region, as liberals fought to ensure that their policies were implemented. In Peru, just as in New Granada, liberals tried to widen the franchise at the same time as they abolished slavery. The confrontations in the Argentine Confederation that led to the toppling of Juan Manuel de Rosas at the Battle of Caseros in 1852 shared similarities with these liberal civil wars in Peru, as Argentina's new 1853 constitution enshrined the abolition of slavery and sought to implement other liberal reforms. However, in contrast to what happened in Mexico, in Peru the conflict between church and state was not as intense as the War of the Reforma, which led to the passing of the 1857 Mexican constitution. In Peru there was some conflict with the church, but it was limited to the abolition of *fueros* and to land disentailment.

The new constitution that inaugurated the 1860s in Peru coincided with the end of the guano boom and intensifying political instability. In fact, contrary to what had been expected, the sudden wealth created by the advances procured from guano sales led not to a sturdier political system but to a more volatile one.

When the Gibbs contract (first signed in 1842) expired in 1861, the concession passed to the National Company of Guano Consignees, and large-scale railway-building schemes began.[78] Economic growth allowed for the development of a banking sector based on abundant capital, and in 1863 a series of guano consignees, including future president Manuel Pardo, created a bank.[79] In 1852, before the abolition of tribute, only 27 percent of the national budget was dependent on guano income; by 1861 this share had grown to 79 percent, but by 1879 it had dropped to 50 percent.[80] The Peruvian state operated with an extremely high deficit that became ever more pronounced after the 1860s. To cover state expenditures, a new international market-rate loan was negotiated, doubling the external debt. Part of those funds was used to build railways. Most were intended to transport export commodities to the coast. During Marino Ignacio Prado's dictatorship (1865–67), a fifth of the guano income was used to build railways, and Peru accumulated a debt of 35 million pounds sterling, the second-highest for a nonindustrialized country.[81] To shore up state finances, Prado tried to reintroduce a head tax, but rejection was so widespread that it led to his downfall.[82]

During this period, Lima became the national economy's center and growth engine: The city's colonial-era walls were destroyed to allow for the city's expansion into the suburbs and modernization following the building of the Callao and Chorrillos railways.[83] But alongside this development came an inflationary process that resulted in currency devaluation and subsequently penury for many.[84] Banks, operating a system of deposit, issuance of currency, and discount, had issued more money than they could guarantee, causing the depreciation of paper money.[85] The situation became even more precarious for the least wealthy sectors of society in 1864 when the government converted low-grade Bolivian coin circulating in Peru to general use. That currency immediately lost 20 percent of its face value, and to recoup the losses caused by the devaluation, merchants raised their prices by 20 percent.[86] This deepened the gulf between the rich and the poor. The pensions paid to army veterans, as well as their widows and daughters, and the salaries of those who worked for the state bureaucracy—from schoolteachers to judges and prosecutors—were devalued in such a precipitous manner that large sectors of society faced financial ruin.

In 1866 Spain, in a quixotic naval venture, attempted to retake its former colonies in the Pacific and attacked both Callao and Valparaíso, but it was swiftly defeated by a united Peru and Chile. After the victory on May 2, Prado's leadership gained strength (Prado had overthrown President Juan Antonio Pezet in 1865 after the latter surrendered the Chincha Islands to the Spanish).[87] Prado called for direct elections after abolishing the 1861 electoral law.[88] His administration sought to renew the liberal ideals that had been abandoned by previous governments, and the new Congress passed a new constitution in 1867. Nearly identical to the 1856 one, it also gave the vote to all men age twenty-one and over.[89] This constitution, like Prado's government, was short-lived. But regardless of the instability that reigned between 1864 and 1868, some parliamentary groups could already be identified through their voting patterns: the conservatives, led by Echenique, and the liberals, headed by Castilla and the governing party.[90]

The 1860s began with a truce as ideological confrontations diminished with the passing of the moderate 1860 constitution. Still, the slow process of reforming the political, social, and economic order inherited from the colonial period continued, even if there were at times temporary reversals. Judicial reforms became more entrenched with more regular publication of judicial decisions. In 1860 Toribio Pacheco published his first treatise on civil law, which presented a detailed liberal analysis of the role that the state should have in society: guaranteeing freedom and individual rights regarding the family and property, ensuring that citizens would also fulfill their legal obligations.[91] The penal code passed in 1862 was influenced by the Spanish one. In terms of honor and patriarchal power, however, it presented innovations first seen in the courts of Arequipa, from where the men who passed the new legislation hailed—namely, treating those convicted of theft, murder, or assault more harshly than they had been under colonial practice.[92]

In the period that followed Castilla's second government (1858–62), liberal economic reforms continued to gain ground with the passage in 1864 of a law that ended ecclesiastical entailments. Its aim was to free the land held by the church in what was known as mortmain; under this system, church land could not be bought, sold, or transferred, as it remained bound to chaplaincies and bequests left expressly to fund masses to be said in the benefactors' honor in perpetuity. These entailments had been a target for liberals since 1829, but after forty years of economic and juridical modernization they remained in place.[93] Liberals considered their dismantling a necessary step to loosen the church's grip over land tenure. During that decade, too, Indigenous communities started to sell land, leading to the consolidation of large landholdings in the highlands. Although this was not dissimilar to what had been done in the War of the Reforma in midcentury Mexico, it did not cause as much disruption in Peru.

While these reforms had far-reaching consequences in terms of land tenure, in the short term they did little to alter the increasingly somber economic situation that Peru faced. After the fall of Prado's dictatorial regime in 1867 (following yet another military uprising that began in Arequipa), all the agreements with the guano consignees were once again revised, and in 1868 President José Balta and his ministers established a leasing procedure to cover the fiscal deficit, which reached 16 percent that year. Finance Minister Nicolás de Piérola obtained congressional permission to negotiate a new agreement, and in July 1869 a contract was signed with the French merchant house of Dreyfus, signing away the monopoly of guano sales in Europe in exchange for a loan to finance regular expenditures.[94] This measure proved deeply unpopular and led to Piérola being branded a traitor.

National consignees opposed the Dreyfus contract, alleging it infringed the law stipulating that such agreements had to be approved by Congress. In the Congress, opposition representatives voted against the contract, while all those supporting the government voted in favor.[95] According to what was said at the time, the contract was approved because Dreyfus bribed members of Congress, and once the contract was in place the borrowed money was used for new railway projects. In 1870 the French merchant house provided the government a new loan of 12 million pounds sterling.[96] This coincided with the sharp fall in guano sales due to the exhaustion of the reserves and competition from other fertilizers, resulting in the collapse of guano income, which by 1872 was only enough to service the external debt.[97]

Financial volatility accompanied the 1871–72 elections, when President Balta supported former President Echenique, who ran against Manuel Pardo. A merchant, landowner, and guano consignee, Pardo had been Prado's minister of finance and Lima's mayor (1869–70). His supporters established the Society for Electoral Independence, out of which would emerge the Partido Civil (Civil Party).[98] These highly contested elections were marked by physical battles for control of the ballot boxes.[99] Political operators used patronage networks, as well as the offer of pisco and the typical ham sandwiches called *butifarras*, to appeal to voters.[100] After the War of the Pacific, this electoral system came under scrutiny, and it was finally reformed in 1896, when the right to vote was limited to men who could read and write.

Some historians see Manuel Pardo, the first civilian president of Peru, as representing a decisive break in the history of Peruvian politics. Pardo, they claim, presented a new vision of Peru, a national project no less, which revived the promise of republicanism of the independence years and was expressed in his notion of a *república práctica* (practical republic), which incorporated many of the ideals of liberal developmentalism shared with other contemporary leaders in Latin America, from Porfirio Díaz in Mexico to Domingo Sarmiento in Argentina. For Pardo, progress was achievable as long as the resources of the country were put to use through the application of technology (such as railways) and know-how, as well as through the promotion of European immigration to address the "moral backwardness" of the Peruvian population, a process that enlightened men like him were well placed to lead. Historians even view his project as enhancing a form of democratic politics, given that he sought to incorporate non-elite actors, such as artisans, into his Partido Civil. Yet, though he was critical of the easy money of the guano years and of the state it had created, Pardo's own fortune as well as those of other members of the Society for Electoral Independence stemmed from the "white gold" of guano (and before that from slave-based plantations), while, as we have seen, he owed his electoral success to questionable electoral practices.[101]

Once in power Pardo found himself in a desperate situation. Before he started his political career he had argued that railways would bring much-needed development. But he was now president of a nation bankrupt due to overinvestment in railway projects. Pardo declared total war on Dreyfus and did not rest until, in 1874, he renegotiated the guano contract, revaluing its price and ensuring external debt service. According to the French merchant, this was an act of revenge because the Peruvian consignees had lost out on the guano contract.[102]

Looking for ways to shore up the country's ailing economy, Pardo saw an opportunity to raise more income for the state coffers in the emerging nitrate industry and introduced a 50 percent tax rate on sales of the commodity.[103] To reduce public expenditures, Pardo made cuts to the army and ended subventions given to primary schools, which were now to be funded solely by municipalities. These changes in the patronage system meant that he made powerful enemies, who resented losing control over the income generated by guano. Two attempts were made on his life.[104] Pardo began losing parliamentary support, even from those who had helped him gain power in 1872.

Pardo wanted Prado, whom he had asked to renegotiate the debt with Great Britain, to be his party's candidate in the 1875–76 presidential elections, but internal divisions within the party led to Lizardo Montero being named the candidate instead. In spite of this, and thanks to Pardo's support, Prado prevailed.[105] Once Prado took office, the situation he found was desperate, because the banks had lent the government important amounts of money in exchange for the extremely depreciated bills that they had issued to be circulated as de facto currency. This added to a mountain of bad debt that led to the collapse of the banking system.[106]

In 1876, Prado signed an agreement with the Raphael trading house and the members of the Peruvian Guano Corporation to end Dreyfus's monopoly and service the external debt.[107] In response, Auguste Dreyfus drew on his political connections to undermine Pardo and Prado, and even though Pardo was not directly implicated in the move, he was forced into exile in Chile. It was at that moment that the members of his political movement, the Partido Civil, organized themselves for the 1877 congressional campaign.[108] Despite his absence from the country, Manuel Pardo was elected to preside over the Senate; he took his seat in 1878. Some weeks later, however, he was shot dead by a soldier who feared that a law then being debated would prevent his promotion.[109]

Pardo's death was the preamble to disaster. Mariano Ignacio Prado's government had invested in developing nitrate fields in the south of the country in the hope that once they controlled this resource they could mortgage it, as they had done with guano. They managed to buy two-thirds of the deposits, and those belonging to individuals who did not want to sell were expropriated. But this was only enough to cover 36 percent of the state's fiscal expenditures.[110] As nitrate became an increasingly important source of income, the southern border's economic potential increased exponentially. Chile and Bolivia fought over control of that resource, and Peru was forced into that conflict, the War of the Pacific, because it had signed a secret treaty of mutual defense with Bolivia in 1873, during the Pardo administration.

When the war with Chile was declared in 1879, Peru was bankrupt and the guano income could not even service the debt.[111] The war was disastrous: Prado fled to Europe, and Piérola took over as dictator; by the end of 1879 Chile occupied the southern provinces of Tacna and Arica, and in January 1881 it occupied Lima. The Chileans occupied the Peruvian coast until 1883 but never managed to subdue the population in the highlands, where Andrés Avelino Cáceres led the resistance. Even so, defeat and territorial loss left Peru in a deep abyss. In the final balance, guano had brought debt and an increased bureaucracy, enriched an extremely wealthy minority, and encouraged the development of railways that focused on transporting exports but did not create the connections needed to bring real progress to the country.

Guano allowed Peru to embark on a series of projects that neighboring countries could not have even dreamed of at the time. The funds obtained through its commercialization were used to organize the state, pay military pensions, build schools, modernize Lima and the coast, and support important merchants, who in turn became the motors of the economy. From the beginning the aim was for the "children of the country" to become the state's financiers, but this was not possible until the independence-era debt was consolidated and repaid and the compensation for enslaved people's manumission was paid. All these measures led to the creation of a plutocracy that invested in trade, railroads, and coastal haciendas.

Corruption was, however, an important feature of the system created with guano money. Favored groups were close to power, and the economic elites helped create and sustain a patronage system. The economic bonanza also prevented the creation of a tax system that would permit citizens to contribute to the financing of the state. The many attempts in the 1850s and 1860s to introduce new taxes all failed. In the long run, this was one of the greatest weaknesses of the guano system, as that income was exhausted in a little more than twenty years. The millions that entered the economy weakened the state while strengthening the elites. Guano wealth was transferred to private hands, making it possible for a new economic elite to eventually take control of political power, but once it did, it found the country bankrupt.

Conclusion

The guano system helped centralize power, although some regional autonomy was maintained as municipal authorities were reinforced. This was much harder to achieve in Colombia, Venezuela, and Argentina, where the struggle over federalism persisted until the 1860s. In Peru, like in Chile, a centralist state was created much sooner, even if in the Peruvian version municipalities maintained more autonomy. Guano funds allowed for this centralization: Without the Indian head tax, provincial authorities could no longer raise their own income, making them dependent on the money sent from the center. Guano wealth prevented the development of a more solid fiscal system even though several attempts were made to implement one.

Just like their peers in Colombia, Chile, and Venezuela, mid-nineteenth-century Peruvian liberals, inspired by the liberal movements of 1848 in Europe, sought to create a more egalitarian society. To achieve this, they put all their energies into abolishing slavery and widening the franchise. Castilla, who was more of a pragmatist than a convinced liberal and sought power for his own aims, helped liberals achieve many of their goals. Liberalism was also characterized by the ideas of free trade and the goal of opening markets to international trade. Politicians sacrificed artisans (whose livelihoods depended on protection from the influx of cheap goods) to pass free trade policies even before midcentury, despite needing their electoral support as an organized and mobilized sector of civil society.

The modernization Peruvian liberals imagined was mainly linked to legislative changes, which is why the writing of constitutions and preserving ample access to the ballot box were among their greatest aims. The conflict with the church was focused on ending its control over land linked to entailments. Liberals also wanted to strip the church of its control over legal procedures involving its own members through the ecclesiastical *fuero*. Even though these were important liberal victories, these politicians did not manage to impose freedom of worship, due to the strong and organized conservative opposition. And just as the church controlled some aspects of society, so the military maintained its grasp over the state, and in particular the presidency, which its members held until 1871. This was partly because the caudillos of the beginning of the republic had represented regional interests, but later it was linked to the caudillismo patronage system they developed.

The economic gains from guano allowed some merchants such as Pardo to compete in politics. The so-called *civilistas* began to attempt to take control of the state beginning at midcentury, but they achieved their goal only in the 1870s, when Pardo was elected president. His election signaled the beginning of political control by a new elite of guano plutocrats.

When Manuel González Prada described national life as an endless belt divided into three pieces, "blood, fraud, and excess," he did so from a position of absolute disenchantment, marked by defeat in the War of the Pacific. After independence, revolutions and coups were frequent. Though their frequency diminished during the guano years, their intensity did not. The revolutions of 1853–54 and 1856–57 as well as the uprisings in 1859 and 1872 show that conflict was a feature of the guano boom. During this period, civilians blamed the military for instability, but Manuel Pardo's administration (1872–76) showed that a civilian in the presidency was no guarantee of change. This became evident with his assassination and the disastrous war with Chile that once again led the military to power.

Another characteristic of the political system based on the "illusory prosperity" of guano was that uprisings were often either preceded or followed by elections, which, according to González Prada, were always fraudulent. Electoral corruption was not, however, as extensive as González Prada believed. And all political actors considered that legitimacy was gained only through the ballot box or public endorsements in a kind of direct democracy. Elections in nineteenth-century Peru were competitive, and many more men voted in them than in the first half of the twentieth century. Liberals wanted a more representative electoral system, first by ensuring that illiterate individuals could continue to vote and then by passing laws to end indirect voting. Even though they managed to maintain ample access to the ballot box, direct voting lasted for less than a decade. At midcentury this stance was abandoned by those who were in power and wanted to keep it, and found it hard to control electoral results when elections were direct.

Manuel González Prada reserves his sharpest criticism, however, for the guano state, which he described as "embezzling, rapacious and tyrannical." This was to a large degree because a small elite enriched itself by preying on the state—benefiting from the payment of the independence-era debts, the conversion of the internal debt into foreign debt, the compensation for manumission, and the possibility of purchasing land recently disentailed from the church and from Indigenous people who no longer paid tribute and who had thus lost the protection for their land it had provided. Therefore, the most important consequence of guano enrichment was that wealth was transferred from the state to the new elites, cementing

Figure 2.6 Mariano Felipe Paz Soldán, map of Peru, 1862. Source: Bibliothèque Nationale de France.

great fortunes and increasing the distance between them and the rest of the population. The guano boom had very long-term consequences. More than illusory, the prosperity generated by this resource was extremely unequal, establishing the basis for a financial recovery that after the War of the Pacific benefited those who already had the most.

But guano also made it possible to attain a certain level of modernity, to strengthen centralism, and to consolidate Lima as the political and economic center of the country. Thanks to guano resources, liberals were able to abolish slavery and the Indian tribute. The problem was that their good intentions clashed with the ambitions of the powerful. The Peruvian state carried out a process of manumission by paying owners for each enslaved person, in a process rampant with corruption that once again transferred capital to those who had the most. The freed people gained the right to vote for a short period but were forced to continue working for their former bosses and remained in poverty, while former enslavers received an important injection of cash, allowing them to amass great fortunes. The payment of the internal debt and its conversion into external debt made it possible for the beneficiaries to establish banks and eventually become guano consignees. All this created a plutocracy that was impacted by the banking collapse, the end of the guano boom, and the defeat in the war, but which managed to recompose itself during the period known as "National Reconstruction," cementing the basis for the "Aristocratic Republic" that resulted from the restriction of the vote to literate individuals in 1896. In the end, the guano state was centralist while paradoxically municipal. It was liberal to a degree, embracing some of modernization's goals.

To summarize, guano prosperity was more unequal than illusory; it was not a question of lies or deception. Instead, it served to consolidate the economic and symbolic power of a minority.

Notes

Epigraph: Manuel González Prada, "La elección de don José Pardo," in *Bajo el oprobio* (Paris: Tipografía de Louis Bellenade et Fils, 1933), 183. Translation mine.

1   Manuel González Prada, *Pájinas libres* (Paris: Tipografía de P. Dupont, 1894); Manuel González Prada, *Horas de lucha* (Lima: Tipografía El Progreso Literario, 1908); Jorge Basadre, *Historia de la república peruana* (Lima: Editorial Historia, 1961).

2   Heraclio Bonilla, *Guano y burguesía* (Lima: IEP, 1974); Carmen McEvoy, *La utopía republicana: Ideales y realidades en la formación de la cultura peruana* (Lima: Fondo Editorial PUCP, 1997).

3   Natalia Sobrevilla Perea, "Batallas por la legitimidad: Constitucionalismo y conflicto político en el Perú del siglo XIX (1812–1860)," *Revista de Indias* 69, no. 246 (2009): 101–28.

4   The national guards were civil-military institutions made up of citizens directly committed to the defense of their locality. Until 1834 they were called militias, and all men between the ages of fifteen and fifty were required to join them, with certain exceptions. See Natalia Sobrevilla Perea, "Del imperio a la república: Las milicias peruanas de la primera mitad del siglo XIX," in *Milices et gardes nationales latino-américaines: Dans une perspective atlantique (au XIX siècle)*, ed. Flavia Macías and Véronique Hébrad (Rennes: Les Perséides, 2022).

5   Alfonso Quiroz, *Historia de la corrupción en el Perú* (Lima: IEP, 2013).

6   Natalia Sobrevilla Perea, "Entre el contrato Gibbs y el contrato Grace: La participación británica en la economía peruana (1842–1890)," *Histórica* 27, no. 2 (2003): 389.

7   William Mitchell Mathew, *The House of Gibbs and the Peruvian Guano Monopoly* (London: Royal Historical Society, 1981), 69.

8   The colonial caste system imposed by the Spanish administration classified people according to "purity of blood" criteria in order to organize society in a stratified manner. Among the established castes were the descendants of free Africans and the Indians and mestizos who had migrated to the city, who paid a head tax until the 1830s.

9   Juan Maiguashca, "A Reinterpretation of the Guano Age, 1840–1900" (PhD dissertation, Oxford University, 1967), 39.

10 José Deustua, *The Bewitchment of Silver: The Social Economy of Mining in Nineteenth-Century Peru* (Athens: Ohio University Press, 2000), 7.

11 Deustua, *The Bewitchment of Silver*, 12–13.

12 Sobrevilla Perea, "Entre el contrato Gibbs y el contrato Grace," 393.

13 Bonilla, *Guano y burguesía*, 25–26.

14 José Deustua, "Salitre, guano, minería y petróleo en la economía peruana, 1820–1930," in *Compendio de historia económica del Perú*, vol. 4, *Economía de la primera centuria independiente*, ed. Carlos Contreras (Lima: BCRP and IEP, 2011), 179.

15 Peter Blanchard, *Slavery and Abolition in Early Republican Peru* (Wilmington, DE: Scholarly Resources, 1992), 39–42.

16 Carlos Aguirre, *Agentes de su propia libertad: Los esclavos de Lima y la desintegración de la esclavitud, 1821–1854* (Lima: Fondo Editorial PUCP, 1993); Christine Hünefeldt, *Paying the Price of Freedom: Family and Labor Among Lima's Slaves, 1800–1854* (Berkeley: University of California Press, 1994).

17 Peter Blanchard, "The 'Transitional Man' in Nineteenth-Century Latin America: The Case of Domingo Elías of Peru," *Bulletin of Latin American Research* 15, no. 2 (1996): 157–76.

18   Humberto Rodríguez Pastor, *Chinos culíes: Bibliografía y fuentes, docu-mentos y ensayos*, Serie Historia 2 (Lima: Instituto de Apoyo Agrario and Instituto de Historia Rural Andina, 1984), 183.

19   Eugenio Chang-Rodríguez, *Diásporas chinas a las Américas* (Lima: Fondo Editorial PUCP, 2015), 182

20   Adrian Pearce, "Reindigenización y economía en los Andes, c. 1820–1870, desde la mirada europea," *Historia Mexicana* 67, no. 1 (2017): 233–93.

21   Natalia Sobrevilla Perea, "The Enduring Power of Patronage in Peruvian Elections: Quispicanchis 1860," *The Americas* 67, no. 1 (2010): 31–55.

22   Paul Gootenberg, "Los liberales asediados: La fracasada primera gener-ación de librecambistas en el Perú 1820–1850," *Revista Andina* 6, no. 2 (1988): 403–50.

23   Iñigo García-Bryce, *República con ciudadanos: Los artesanos de Lima, 1821–1879* (Lima: IEP, 2008), 102.

24   Gootenberg, "Los liberales asediados," 430.

25   Natalia Sobrevilla Perea, "Ciudadanos en armas: El ejército y la creación del estado, Perú (1821–1860)," in *Las fuerzas de guerra en la construc-ción del estado: América Latina, siglo XIX*, ed. Juan Carlos Garavaglia, Juan Pro Ruíz, and Eduardo Zimmermann (Rosario: Prohistoria, 2012), 161–82.

26   G. Antonio Espinoza, *Education and the State in Modern Peru: Pri-mary Schooling in Lima, 1821–c. 1921* (New York: Palgrave Macmillan, 2013), 16.

27   Espinoza, *Education and the State in Modern Peru*, chap. 3.

28   On elections in Peru, see Natalia Sobrevilla Perea, "Elecciones y conflicto en la historia del Perú (1812–1980)," *Elecciones* 10, no. 11 (2011).

29   Vincent Peloso, "Liberals, Electoral Reform and the Popular Vote in Mid-Nineteenth-Century Peru," in *Liberals, Politics, and Power: State Forma-tion in Nineteenth-Century Latin America*, ed. Vincent Peloso and Barbara Tenenbaum (Athens: University of Georgia Press, 1996), 194.

30   Natalia Sobrevilla Perea, "The Influence of the European 1848 Revolu-tions in Peru," in *The Influence of the 1848 Revolutions in Latin America*, ed. Eduardo Posada-Carbó and Guy Thompson (London: Institute of Latin American Studies, 2002).

31   Paul Gootenberg has been one of the main exponents of this trend, and most of his work concentrates on understanding liberals through their economic policies.

32   Natalia Sobrevilla Perea, "The Abolition of Slavery in the South Ameri-can Republics," *Slavery and Abolition* 44, no. 1 (2023): 90–108.

33   Fernando de Trazegnies, *La idea del derecho en el Perú republicano del siglo XIX* (Lima: Fondo Editorial PUCP, 1992), 162.

34   Sarah C. Chambers, "Private Crimes, Public Order: Honor, Gender, and the Law in Early Republican Peru," in *Honor, Status, and the Law in Mod-ern Latin America*, ed. Sueann Caulfield, Sarah C. Chambers, and Lara Putnam (Durham, NC: Duke University Press, 2005), 28.

35 Christine Hünefeldt, *Liberalism in the Bedroom: Quarreling Spouses in Nineteenth-Century Lima* (University Park: Penn State University Press, 2000), 14.

36 Tanja Christiansen, "Sirvientes, dependientes e hijas adoptadas: Los distintos nombres de las trabajadoras domésticas: Cajamarca siglo XIX," in *Más allá de la dominación y la dependencia*, ed. Paulo Drinot and Leo Garofalo (Lima: IEP, 2005).

37 Natalia Sobrevilla Perea, "El proyecto liberal, la revolución de 1854 y la convención de 1855," in *La experiencia burguesa*, ed. Carmen McEvoy (Madrid: Veuvert Iberamericana, 2004), 231.

38 José Casimiro Ulloa, *El Perú en 1853* (Lima, 1854), 24.

39 Alicia del Águila, *Los velos y las pieles: Cuerpo, género y reordenamiento social en el Perú republicano (Lima, 1822–1872)* (Lima: IEP, 2003), 87–100.

40 Ricardo Palma, "El baile de la Victoria," in *Tradiciones peruanas completas* (Lima: Aguilar, 1967), 1124–25.

41 Quiroz, *Historia de la corrupción*, 238.

42 José Rufino Echenique, *El general Echenique, presidente despojado del Perú en su vindicación* (Lima: Tipografía El Heraldo, 1855), 11.

43 Alfonso Quiroz, *La deuda defraudada: La consolidación de 1850 y dominio económico en el Perú* (Lima: Museo de la Nación, 1987), 58.

44 Sobrevilla Perea, "El proyecto liberal," 231–32.

45 Sobrevilla Perea, "El proyecto liberal," 232.

46 Fernando Casós, *Para la historia del Perú: Revolución de 1854* (Cuzco: Imprenta Republicana, 1854), 3.

47 Very useful reflections on Casós can be found in Pablo Whipple, *La gente decente de Lima y su resistencia al orden republicano* (Lima: IEP, 2013), 15–20.

48 See Quiroz, *La deuda defraudada* and *Historia de la corrupción*.

49 Quiroz, *Historia de la corrupción*, chap. 2.

50 For more than a decade, Bolivian President Manuel Belzú allowed the country's currency to be devalued by combining silver with lower-grade metals in coins. The use of this practice in Peru increased inflation, and in 1853 tensions escalated to such a degree that Belzú mobilized his troops to the Peruvian border. Basadre, *Historia de la república peruana*, 3:1029–30.

51 Julio Pinto, "La construcción social del Estado en el Perú: El régimen de Castilla y el mundo popular 1845–1856," *Historia* 49, no. 2 (2016): 555.

52 Sobrevilla Perea, "El proyecto liberal," 232–34.

53 Blanchard, *Slavery and Abolition*, 40.

54 The proposal can be found as an appendix in Domingo Elías, *Memoria que presenta el ministro de hacienda de la república del Perú a la Convención Nacional de 1855* (Lima: Imprenta Masías, 1855), 38–41.

55 Sobrevilla Perea, "El proyecto liberal," 238.

56 Quiroz, *Historia de la corrupción*, chap. 2.

57 Francisco Bilbao, *El gobierno de la libertad* (Lima: Imprenta El Comercio, 1855), iv.

58 Sobrevilla Perea, "The Influence of the European 1848 Revolutions," 213.

59 César Gamboa, "Los filtros electorales decimonónicos: Los órganos y los procedimientos electorales en el Perú, 1822–1896," in *Historia de las elecciones en el Perú: Estudio sobre el gobierno representativo,* ed. Cristóbal Aljovín de Losada and Sinesio López (Lima: IEP, 2005), 201–3.

60 Felipe Barriga y Álvarez, *El Perú y los gobiernos del general Echenique y de la revolución por Timoleón* (Lima: Imprenta Monterola, 1855), 69.

61 Manuel Atanasio Fuentes, *Aletazos del Murciélago* (Paris: Imprenta Lainé y Havard, 1866), 8.

62 Sobrevilla Perea, "Batallas por la legitimidad," 121.

63 Natalia Sobrevilla Perea, "Caudillismo in the Age of Guano: A Study in the Political Culture of Mid-Nineteenth-Century Peru (1840–1860)" (PhD dissertation, University of London, 2005), 208–10.

64 Trazegnies, *La idea del derecho en el Perú republicano,* 161.

65 Sobrevilla Perea, "El proyecto liberal," 237–38.

66 *Registro oficial del Departamento del Cusco,* November 8, 1856.

67 Sobrevilla Perea, "El proyecto liberal," 240–41.

68 Letter from Ramón Castilla to Manuel Ortiz de Zevallos, Carmen Alto, March 9, 1858, *Archivo Castilla,* 3:257.

69 This regulation was less generous in providing the right to vote than the preceding one of 1855. See César Gamboa, "La periodificación electoral y las elecciones directas en el Perú decimonónico: Tras las huellas de Basadre," *Revista de la Asociación Ius et Veritas* 27 (2004): 372.

70 Martín Monsalve, "Del sufragio a la sociedad civil: Pánicos morales, utopías liberales y las campañas electorales limeñas, 1850–1858," in Drinot and Garofalo, *Más allá de la dominación y la dependencia,* 224–25.

71 Francisco Quiroz Chueca, *La protesta de los artesanos: Lima-Callao, 1858* (Lima: Fondo Editorial de la UNMSM, 1988), 44–45.

72 García-Bryce, *República con ciudadanos,* 106.

73 Between 1858 and 1860 the Peruvian-Ecuadorian War took place; it ended with the signing of the Treaty of Mapasingue on January 25, 1860. In those same years there was also a threat of war with Bolivia, but it did not materialize.

74 Natalia Sobrevilla Perea, "Power of the Law or Power of the Sword: The Conflictive Relationship Between the Executive and the Legislative in Nineteenth-Century Peru," *Parliaments, Estates and Representation* 37, no. 2 (2017): 231.

75 For a detailed example of how this took place in a province, see Sobrevilla Perea, "The Enduring Power of Patronage in Peruvian Elections," 31–55.

76 Sobrevilla Perea, "Batallas por la legitimidad," 124–25.

77 Quiroz, *Historia de la corrupción,* chap. 2.

78 Sobrevilla Perea, "Entre el contrato Gibbs y el contrato Grace," 398.

79 Basadre, *Historia de la república peruana,* 3:281.

80 Alejandro Salinas, "Las finanzas públicas entre 1831 y 1930," in *Compendio de historia económica del Perú,* vol. 4, *Economía de la primera centuria independiente,* ed. Carlos Contreras (Lima: BCRP and IEP, 2011), 351.

81 Paul Gootenberg, *Imagining Development: Economic Ideas in Peru's "Ficti-tious Prosperity" of Guano, 1840–1880* (Berkeley: University of California Press, 1993), 7.

82 Bonilla, *Guano y burguesía*, 31–32.

83 Deustua, "Salitre, guano, minería y petróleo," 179.

84 Nelson Manrique, *Mercado moderno y región: La sierra central, 1820–1930* (Lima: Desco, 1987), 93–94.

85 Deustua, "Salitre, guano, minería y petróleo," 180.

86 Bonilla, *Guano y burguesía*, 29.

87 In the 1860s, Spain sought to reclaim payment of independence debts and attacked several of the Pacific republics, including Ecuador, Peru, Bolivia, and Chile. In April 1866, Spaniards seized the islands of Chincha and bombarded Valparaíso and Callao; they then withdrew and claimed victory, although they had achieved nothing.

88 Bonilla, *Guano y burguesía*, 29.

89 Basadre, *Historia de la república peruana*, 5:19–58.

90 Ulrich Mücke, "Los patrones de votación y el surgimiento de los partidos parlamentarios en el Congreso del Perú, 1860–1879," *Investigaciones Sociales* 8, no. 13 (2004): 119–21.

91 Carlos Ramos Núñez, *Toribio Pacheco: Jurista peruano del siglo XIX* (Lima: Fondo Editorial PUCP, 1993), 194.

92 Chambers, "Private Crimes, Public Order," 42, 148.

93 Fernando Armas Asín, *Iglesia: Bienes y rentas: Secularización liberal y reorganización patrimonial en Lima 1820–1950* (Lima: IEP and Instituto Riva Agüero, 2007), 65.

94 Salinas, "Las finanzas públicas," 356.

95 Mücke, "Los patrones de votación," 121.

96 Quiroz, *Historia de la corrupción*, 210–11.

97 Bonilla, *Guano y burguesía*, 94–95.

98 Carmen McEvoy studies the details of this electoral campaign in "Estampillas y votos: El rol del correo político en una campaña electoral decimonónica," *Histórica* 18, no. 1 (1994): 99–101.

99 Ulrich Mücke, "Elecciones y participación política en el Perú siglo XIX: La campaña presidencial de 1871–1872," *Investigaciones Sociales* 8 (2004): 139.

100 Manuel Vicente Villarán, "Costumbres electorales," *Mercurio Peruano* 1, no. 1 (1918): 11–19.

101 See Carmen McEvoy, *Un proyecto nacional en el siglo XIX: Manuel Pardo y su visión del Perú* (Lima: Pontificia Universidad Católica del Perú, 1994); Ulrich Muecke, *Political Culture in Nineteenth-Century Peru: The Rise of the Partido Civil* (Pittsburgh: University of Pittsburgh Press, 2004). See also Carlos Forment, *Democracy in Latin America, 1760–1900*, vol. 1, *Civic Selfhood and Public Life in Mexico and Peru* (Chicago: University of Chicago Press, 2003).

102 Bonilla, *Guano y burguesía*, 96.

103 Salinas, "Las finanzas públicas," 360.

104 Quiroz, *Historia de la corrupción*, 222–23.

105 Mücke, "Los patrones de votación," 124.

106 Quiroz, *Historia de la corrupción*, 225.

107 Quiroz, *Historia de la corrupción*, 224.

108 Mücke, "Los patrones de votación," 125.

109 Quiroz, *Historia de la corrupción*, 225.

110 Salinas, "Las finanzas públicas," 365.

111 Sobrevilla Perea, "Entre el contrato Gibbs y el contrato Grace," 401.

"We Want a Homeland!"

The Struggle for a Technical State (1879–1919)

Between 1879 and 1919, Peru experienced defeat in one of Latin America's major international wars, the War of the Pacific (1879–83), losing not only control over valuable nitrate deposits but also a significant part of its national territory; lived through a brief second period of military rule that shaped the character of postwar national reconstruction; and eventually transitioned, around the turn of the century, to a relatively long period of political stability under civilian rule and economic growth fueled by a renewed and much-expanded export sector. However, at the end of this period, which has come to be known as the "Aristocratic Republic," the politics had become unstable and the growth anemic while social tensions in the cities and in the countryside, along with a certain cultural effervescence, expressed a growing challenge to the economic and political order that had been established at the dawn of the twentieth century.

Coming to power in 1895, following the brief civil war of 1894–95, in alliance with an old foe—the caudillo Nicolás de Piérola—the Partido Civil sought to establish a new order, integrating Peru into world markets as an exporter of a range of commodities, including sugar, cotton, oil, minerals, rubber, and wool, and attracting foreign capital. The *civilistas* attempted to "modernize" the country, promoting infrastructural development as well as improvements in public health and education. But they proved reluctant to integrate the popular sectors in the cities and the countryside into their project of rule—or perhaps were incapable of doing so. This created opportunities for now civilian caudillos to emerge and take advantage of the tensions that resulted—first, briefly, in 1912–14, with Guillermo Billnghurst, and then in 1919, when a former *civilista*, Augusto B. Leguía, returned to unwind the order that he had helped to create. This chapter provides an account of these major transformations.

The War of the Pacific

The War of the Pacific divided the country's history in two, becoming an open wound that would take a long time to heal. When Chile occupied the port of Tarapacá in protest at attempts by Bolivia to impose a tax on nitrate production on largely Chilean-run *salitreras*, Bolivia declared war. Peru was drawn into the conflict by a secret pact it had signed with Bolivia. After a brief naval campaign and Bolivia's withdrawal from the war in May 1880, Chile invaded Peru, occupying Lima in January 1881. Although a war of resistance to the occupying forces was waged in the highlands, Peru's defeat in the war was finally acknowledged with the signing of the Treaty of Ancón in October 1883.

In making sense of defeat, Peruvians could point to a number of factors. Beyond the traumatic events—the Lynch expedition (a campaign led by Chilean naval officer Patricio Lynch, whose objective was to destroy the agricultural estates of the northern coast), the razing of towns in the central highlands, the gratuitous burning of the Chorrillos district in Lima, or the looting of educational and cultural institutions—the very fact of being defeated by an old colonial province of the Peruvian viceroyalty, with resources clearly inferior to those of Peru, was deeply humiliating.

From the trip that President Mariano Ignacio Prado (1876–79) made to Europe to purchase armaments, only to not return, to the inept "defense of Lima" organized by the dictator Nicolás de Piérola, who took power in a coup in 1879 and fled to the southern highland city of Ayacucho after the capital fell to Chilean forces, the war experience was a strong blow to national morale. In turn, it prompted a heartbreaking collective introspection to which the maverick intellectual Manuel González Prada would put words. He urged the youth to despise the elites who, after drinking the "generous wine" in the guano "orgy"—leaving behind only "feces"—had led them to a fight that they lost due in part to the effects of "their enemy's weapons" but primarily because of their own "ignorance and spirit of servitude."[1]

Added to this, of course, was the doubt about the cohesion of Peruvian society, the vast majority of which—as the writer Ricardo Palma observed in a private letter to Piérola—was made up of an "abject and degraded" Indigenous race unable to distinguish between a "white man from the [Peruvian] coast" and a Chilean or a Turk.[2] Not forgetting, of course, the evidence of corruption that reached its highest point during the administrations of José Balta (1868–72) and Nicolás de Piérola (1879–81),[3] and the "pathetic tears" of the elite that were reflected in phrases such as "[We will side with] Chileans rather than Piérola," attributed to a *civilista* leader during the power vacuum that occurred at the end of the occupation.[4]

Through the figures of Miguel Grau, the "Gentleman of the Seas" who led the naval campaign and died heroically at the Battle of Angamos (where his ship, the *Huáscar*, was captured by the Chilean navy), and Francisco Bolognesi, who died defending the city of Arica against numerically superior Chilean forces, Peru would develop a narrative of heroic resistance that stood alongside—and, when necessary, obscured—the more damning reckonings of defeat produced by González Prada and others.

The historian William F. Sater has elaborated an explanatory framework of the structural factors that favored Chile's victory in the war: (1) the geopolitical location of Chile, which allowed it to receive war supplies via the Strait of Magellan, compared to the much more complicated situation in Peru, which depended on the goodwill of the Colombian authorities to facilitate the transport of these resources through the Panamanian isthmus; (2) the superior Chilean civil infrastructure, in particular the existence of a railway system that connected Santiago to the south of the country and Valparaíso, thus facilitating the accumulation of supplies and men and their shipment to the north; (3) Chilean political stability between 1830 and 1859, versus the chaotic Peruvian panorama, a situation that would prevent Peru from having a well-established military hierarchy at the time of the war; and, derived from the third factor, (4) the intellectual superiority and greater experience of the Chilean military forces, demonstrated by the fact that around 1870 the majority of Chilean officers went through a military school where the Prussian model was taught.[5]

Overall, the war was catastrophic for Peru: It resulted in a large death toll (estimates suggest 25,000 military and civilian casualties), economic devastation resulting from the destruction of agricultural estates and infrastructure during the Chilean occupation, and the loss of territory as a consequence of the Treaty of Ancón. According to the treaty, the province of Tarapacá would pass into Chilean hands permanently, and Chile would also receive the provinces of Tacna and Arica for ten years, until a plebiscite decided their fate. And yet for Peruvians the outcome of the war was more than a military defeat, with many perceiving it as the dissolution of the homeland. While the elites raised foreign flags as a form of protection during the occupation of Lima, chaos spread as a result of the looting of Chinese stores (and the killing of Chinese shopkeepers), with the violence threatening to spread to large local businesses.[6] So much so that the mayor of Lima—with the support of the diplomatic corps—had to request that the leader of the Chilean invasion rush his entry into the city, in order to restore order.

Militarism and Reconstruction

Both Miguel Iglesias and Andrés Avelino Cáceres, seasoned military officers, had heroically fought the invader. The latter's exploits, as head of an army made up of Indigenous guerrillas who resisted the advance of the Chilean army in the central highlands, would remain one of the great episodes of the war.[7] Both Iglesias and Cáceres staged an agonizing resistance, finally cut short as a result of the so-called Grito de Montán in August 1882, when Iglesias declared his willingness to accept the signing of a peace treaty—as the Chilean forces demanded—that included territorial cession.

Desperate to conclude an occupation that was beginning to seem overwhelming, the Chilean forces sought to provide Iglesias with the necessary legitimacy to become an effective party to the Treaty of Ancón, signed on October 20, 1883.[8] The consequent confrontation that took place between the two Peruvian generals then turned into a civil war that—against the background of a social and ethnic eruption in the highlands—added yet another level of destruction. It also became the framework of an "arrangement" to end the war in which Peru's creditors had the upper hand.

The Iglesias-Cáceres contest lasted two years and nine months. After the victory of the latter at the end of 1885 (legitimized half a year later in indirect elections without any opposition), the *cacerista* officers were the only ones who could establish a semblance of order in a country in which politics had become "ruralized" at the same time that "the traditional framing of the Indigenous peoples in the existing structures of domination" was relaxed because of the debt of gratitude that Cáceres owed his Indigenous backers.[9] With the veterans of the La Breña campaign, as the campaign of resistance to the Chilean army in the central highlands came to be known, a second period of militarism, as historian Jorge Basadre

notes, emerged from the fog of war (the first period of militarism had occurred after independence during the rule of caudillos).

Possessing strong ties to family networks, many of them landowners,
the *breñeros* of Cáceres became the political authorities who laid the foundations for a postwar order much more similar to the times of Ramón
Castilla than to those of Manuel Pardo.[10] The reimposition of the Indigenous *contribución* (a head tax) and the creation of departmental boards
in charge of managing the funds raised by the tax sealed the alliance between *cacerista* authorities and local power holders.[11] This was the ultimate
foundation of the *pax* imposed by the "organizing dictatorship" of the
hero of la Breña.[12] This was a relative pacification—as Peter Klarén calls
it—in that the distribution of "significant local funds" gave rise to "intense
fights between different factions of landowners and their followers." In
fact, the proliferation of banditry was the inevitable consequence of these
provincial commotions.[13] Founded in 1882 by Cáceres, the Constitutional
Party became the vehicle in which, for a time, the agendas of *breñeros* and
plutocrats reached a modus vivendi.

The five-year period 1885–90 was the climactic moment of export
growth throughout South America based on strong foreign investment,
which Peru could not attract.[14] Recovering access to external credit was,
therefore, the top priority of the business sector, represented by a *civilismo*
that, according to González Prada, had suffered a "cadaverous disaggrega-
tion," as a consequence of the war, that led them to resign themselves to
being "accessory parties" in the "political combinations," becoming experts
in "eating from any table" and in "putting their hands in all pockets"—a
reference to their momentary subordinate, even dependent, status vis-à-
vis the Constitutional Party of Cáceres.[15]

While export earnings in Peru were falling to a quarter of their prewar
level, the larger region was in the midst of a golden age of trade expansion.
"We are among ruins," said the president of Congress, Francisco Rosas,
but the war, he emphasized, "had not exhausted the proverbial riches of
Peru."[16] Matters had to be sorted out in order to reinsert Peru in the continental export boom, and the Irish businessman Michael P. Grace became
the main architect of this process.

It took three years to reach a final agreement, the so-called Grace contract.
This, Klarén argues, reflecting a widespread view, was "probably the best deal
that Peru could achieve under those circumstances."[17] As Rory Miller con-
firms, though the chief beneficiary was Grace himself, the contract did allow
Peru to regain access to international capital markets, which indirectly con-

tributed to the development of its diversified export economy from the 1890s onward.[18] At the time, however, many described the Grace contract as one that, among other negative elements, ceded control of the country's rail system for sixty-six years, as well as assigning exports of the remaining guano to creditors, who were also paid a sum of £80,000 a year for thirty-three years. The newspaper *El Comercio* described it as "treason against the homeland," reflecting the sentiment of a sector of *civilismo*. Despite everything, the prevailing opinion was that in order to recover the lost years, a "surgical operation" was required—that is, a "comprehensive solution."[19]

Beyond the technical aspects of this negotiation, historian Alfonso Quiroz has drawn attention to its personal dimensions. Like Auguste Dreyfus (whose merchant house, Dreyfus Frères, had been granted a monopoly over guano exports in the late 1860s) and Henry Meiggs (builder of Peru's railways) before him, Grace actively "courted" those in power. Thus, a year and a half after his overthrow, Iglesias could be seen "pleasantly enjoying Grace's hospitality" in one of the businessman's residences in Paris. Quiroz makes a similar observation about the "notorious private wealth" exhibited by Cáceres himself, despite having arrived "with nothing to the presidency."[20] Were the key figures of the second militarism "for rent," as Quiroz proposes? More than finding the "smoking gun" of a supposed "purchase" of Cáceres, Quiroz's work allows us to appreciate the continuity of the patterns of corruption established in previous decades, an ecosystem in which "heroism," "patriotism," and "bribery" (in money or in kind) had been naturalized within the framework of the Peruvian state's distinctive lack of autonomy. In this environment, stealing from the public treasury had become a "national habit."[21]

Absent a state with the vision and the will to direct and regulate the course of economic growth, the reconstruction that occurred in the late nineteenth and early twentieth centuries took the form of an uneven mercantile penetration with little integrating impact. Thus, when the War of the Pacific swept away even the most modest economic achievements of the guano boom, underdevelopment became the inevitable companion of the "open economy."[22] The increase in the state's spending on the civil and military bureaucracies and on railway construction meant that there was little left for the development of an incipient consumer goods industry in Lima and in the valleys of Ancash and Cuzco, where the Lucre textile factory (in the province of Quispicanchis) became a solitary symbol of what could have been: the development of regional manufacturing aimed at supplying the internal market.[23]

On the other hand, it proved impossible to use the tax structure to impose even a minimal coordination of economic activity when neither censuses nor surveys were available.[24] In any case, in many parts of the country, towns resisted paying tax.[25] Faced with this situation, the business elite's agenda was quite precise: attract foreign capital to promote the modernization of their businesses with minimal state intervention, developing their own security and coordination structures through organizations such as the National Agrarian Society and the National Society of Industries. In so doing, they produced an "oligarchic centralist model" for the reconstruction of the tax system. This was a model that, in the "traditionalist modernizing" worldview of the business elite, relied initially on the restoration of colonial-era practices such as the Indigenous *contribución* under Cáceres and on indirect taxes such as the salt tax under Piérola (on whom more below), for which a state monopoly was created in 1896.[26] Inevitably, this pattern of reconstruction generated resentment in the country, particularly in the Andean region—including Ancash, where resistance to the *contribución* resulted in an Indigenous rebellion led by the local "cacique," Pedro Atusparia, in the mid-1880s and in Huanta, in Ayacucho, where the salt tax produced an Indigenous uprising in the mid-1890s. In both cases, however, the revolts had as much to do with the interplay of local political conflicts as with the fiscal demands of the central state.[27]

In these circumstances, local market economies came to depend on what might trickle down from the large investments in the coastal agro-export enclaves. Only toward the end of the century did exceptional conditions make possible the brief but intense industrial cycle in the capital symbolized by the conversion of Vitarte—a small town neighboring Lima—into a vibrant manufacturing center where the founders of the modern Peruvian labor movement were forged. Indeed, in this later period, even though it never witnessed the sort of industrialization seen in Argentina or parts of Brazil, Peru nevertheless experienced an important diversification of investment within the export elite, beyond traditional export sectors (such as sugar, cotton, and minerals) and into industrial manufacturing as well as banking and insurance. Moreover, certain family business groups (such as the Prados) focused on financial services to service the expanding export economy, with little connection to landed property.

As historian Nelson Manrique argues, in looking at the Peruvian economy at the end of the nineteenth century it is possible to discern the existence of several "markedly differentiated regional logics,"[28] delimited by the complex geography of the country:[29] (1) the Andean south, articulated around the export of sheep wool and fibers from Andean camelids; (2) the central sierra, which had experienced at least three different economic cycles (silver, cattle raising in the high Andes, and sugarcane brandy production in the tropical valleys of the neighboring jungle area); (3) Lima and the central and northern coast, articulated around the exploitation of guano and the development of export agriculture focused on sugarcane and cotton production; and (4) the Amazon region, with its boom in rubber exploitation (a classic example of a boom-and-bust pattern in the face of sudden demand in a distant market, here the emerging US automotive industry).

Piérola's Cavalcade to the New Peru

On March 17, 1895, a force made up of *montoneras* (armed groups) from various parts of the national territory, led by Nicolás de Piérola, entered Lima. It was the culmination of perhaps the most important civil confrontation among the many that occurred during the first republican century. In the following forty-eight hours, the immediate objective of the uprising was achieved: an end to the regime of General Andrés Avelino Cáceres. The most famous of the country's civil conspirators thus displaced one of its most distinguished military commanders, thereby ending a prolonged dispute over the leadership of Peru. This was also the starting point of an unprecedented cycle of political stability, evidenced in the succession of various civilian governments that came to power through the ballot box. This period, the ambiguous nature of which Jorge Basadre described with the phrase "Aristocratic Republic," would last until 1919.

According to Basadre, between 1895 and 1899—the time that Piérola's presidency lasted—Peru was able to build a modern state, "with a clean administrative function, with solid social roots, engendered by a large mass movement and represented by a beloved caudillo leader"—a caudillo who, "faithful to the principle of legal succession in government, complied with vacating the presidency at the end of his constitutional term."[30] The painter Juan Lepiani sought to capture this spirit in an oil painting that was reproduced ad infinitum in Peruvian school textbooks for decades to come.

Lepiani celebrated the entry of the Peruvian nation into its maturity: The people and their leader, in short, were riding toward a different future, leaving behind a long era presided over by a disastrous "empirical state" that emerged from the struggle for independence. This had been a fragile

Figure 3.1 Juan Lepiani, *Piérola's Entrance to Lima Through the Cocharcas Gate, During the Civil War of 1894–95*, ca. 1890–1900. Source: Museo Nacional de Arqueología, Antropología e Historia del Perú.

"inauthentic state" headed by unstable leaders, the product of often rigged elections and Congresses of questionable origin, both of which conspired in supporting a "false democracy."[31]

In the end, however, Lepiani's work was a portrait of a missed opportunity rather than of the beginning of a virtuous process. Why didn't the *pierolista* movement manage to function as an effective transition toward the long-awaited "state in order"—in other words, a "technical state"? Why did it instead end up being a mere hinge for the consolidation of a plutocracy that originated in the guano boom but was temporarily displaced from power by a combination of financial bankruptcy, war, and militarism toward the end of the 1870s?

In Lima, a city of just over 100,000 inhabitants, the thousand casualties and hundreds of wounded that the combat of March 1895 left behind were unparalleled. The carnage stopped only after a truce was negotiated following the intervention of the diplomatic corps, headed by the papal nuncio. Then, understanding the futility of continuing the fight, Cáceres agreed to cede power to a government junta headed by Manuel Candamo, the historical leader of *civilismo* and a key piece of the coalition with the Democratic Party that had made possible the unusual victory of an irregular force of *montoneros* over the national army—an event never again to be repeated. Although Piérola's cavalcade remained as a fundamental reference to discourage "military pronouncements," it was quickly absorbed by the beginning of a "new era of growth with external financing." This was a cycle that initially entailed (as has already been said) an exceptional growth of manufacturing centered in the capital, within the framework of an "open economy."[32] The figures are compelling: Between 1895 and 1900, the value of Peruvian exports grew by 137 percent.[33]

Both phenomena—the ceding of power to the governing junta and the growth of manufacturing—promoted the creation of a financial system capable of channeling export revenues toward the process of import substitution. This was clearly reflected in a decrease in the percentage of manufactured products as part of Peruvian imports: from 58 percent between 1891 and 1892 to 39 percent in 1907.[34] Thus, centralism was accentuated as the central state channeled the gains from the reinvigorated export economy. Meanwhile, regional economies developed their own dynamics: on the coast, a capital-intensive agro-export sector dependent on an increasingly proletarianized workforce; in the central highlands, variations in the prices of minerals continued to set the pace of regional economic life; in the south, the contradiction between capitalist penetration and "archaic" methods in the collection of wool continued; and in the Amazon, rubber production generated a boom that was as intense as it was brief and controversial—particularly beginning in 1904, when the Casa J. C. Arana & Brothers, the most important rubber company, "absolutely dominated the Putumayo and its tributaries."[35]

The social consequences of this dynamic soon became evident: the formation in the mines, plantations, and factories of a new working class with an unprecedented capacity for mobilization, new expressions of rural protest in the southern Andes,[36] and, of course, denunciations of the abuses committed by the Peruvian *caucheros*, or rubber barons, against the Amazonian communities. These expressions of discontent came to be known as the "social question"—a question that eventually the political elites would need to reckon with.

Piérola reentered the political arena in the mid-1890s with the prestige of having dealt "a mortal blow to the speculation and usury" that overwhelmed the Peruvian state during the peak of the guano bonanza: It was he who in 1869, as minister of finance, had negotiated the Dreyfus contract, which ended the consignment system (and made him persona non grata to those who would coalesce in the Partido Civil).[37] Encouraged by his charisma, what came to be called *pierolismo* took the form of a sort of mestizo messianistic alternative to the *civilista* regime of Manuel Pardo that promoted—perhaps in spite of Piérola himself—a rudimentary proto-populist classism of previously unsuspected proportions: "Down with *la argolla* [a reference to cronyism]! Long live Piérola, damn it!" his followers exclaimed, airing their resentment toward the rich. Piérola's willingness to take power in the most unfortunate circumstances for the republic—following President Prado's trip out of the country in December 1879, in the midst of the War of the Pacific, a trip that, as previously noted, he would not return from—further increased his prestige. Such was his political capital that not even his significant errors in the defense of Lima and his flight to Ayacucho after the defeat in the Battles of San Juan and Miraflores were able to erase it. In 1884 he reappeared in Lima, as popular as ever. Upon his return, he founded the Democratic Party, betting on an "enduring" organization focused on the "political education" of the people rather than on an immediate victory.[38]

Piérola aimed to stop the civil war that "military leaders" and "special interests" had imposed on the country. In 1886, he abstained from participating in an election that, in his opinion, led to the consolidation—with the backing of *civilismo*—of a second militarism under Cáceres. His collaborators asked how the Democratic Party could confront the *civilista-cacerista* "marriage of interest." Pierola responded by telling them to be patient and by sharing with them reports of the emergence of a powerful social reaction to military rule. He described what was to come as the unstoppable course toward the forging of a "new people," a process his party was prepared to lead.[39] The scenario that led to the uprising of 1895 thus began to take shape.

In 1890, because of the constitutional mandate that prevented him from being reelected—and convinced that his prestige would allow him to return without major problems in four years—Cáceres was preparing to leave power, temporarily, in the hands of one of his comrades from the La Breña campaign, Colonel Remigio Morales Bermúdez. Meanwhile, *pierolismo* unleashed a formidable mobilization: a crowd that marched from Lima's Alameda de los Descalzos to the Palacio de la Exposición. It was said the throng was such as "the capital had never seen": ten thousand *demócratas* marching as part of their respective neighborhood committees, shouting "Down with *la argolla*!" But afterward Piérola himself became a victim of *cacerista* repression, arrested for disorderly conduct and prosecuted for irregularities committed during his years as dictator. After escaping from prison, he fled to Europe, from where he went to Chile in the months prior to the final phase of the 1895 uprising. Due to his legendary ability to flee from his pursuers, he earned the nickname "the Caliph."

At this point, Piérola lectured his followers about the inconvenience of Peru being seen to have "scandals" before the "world" if it aspired to be taken seriously by the "great nations." Therefore, he promised not to use force to gain power, as long as it was possible to "save Peru" by legal means.[40] His main concern at that time was how to raise massive support without disturbing the establishment. This was a political style that anticipated the populist politics of the following century. In this way, according to the historian Nils Jacobsen, it reaped the fruits of "decades of strengthening civil society."[41] *Civilismo*, on the other hand, sought to regroup around its own candidate, Francisco Rosas, bringing to an end its pragmatic alliance with Cáceres.

At the beginning of 1894, Cáceres returned to Lima to launch his presidential race. Supported by a combination of former military officers, lawyers, and landowners from the country's interior, Cáceres's Constitutional Party appeared as an alternative to the *civilistas*. Its power derived, according to Jorge Basadre, from its efficient manipulation of Congress and its handling of electoral campaigns. The party "used intrigue and money as their favorite weapons in political action" and had the best *capítuleros* (political operators). The latter were critical to winning elections because of their ability to dominate—usually by force—polling stations during elections and, then, their expertise in manipulating the vote count, allowing them to obtain a parliamentary majority.[42] Everything seemed to be going smoothly in early 1894. However, the sudden death of President Remigio Morales Bermúdez forced a change of plans. As first vice president, the lawyer Pedro A. del Solar was supposed to assume power as Morales Bermúdez's replacement. But the *cacerista* leadership did not trust him to ensure an effective transition. They decided to impose the second vice president, General Justiniano Borgoña, who was one of their own. As a consequence, *montoneras* rose up throughout the country.

It was the beginning of the great reaction anticipated by Piérola, who was in exile at that time in northern Chile. Jacobsen has managed to identify more than one hundred *montoneras*, each with between a dozen and 1,500 troops. This turnout is evidence of a phenomenon of local origin that escalated to produce the broadest social mobilization that the country had seen in several decades. When the *montoneras* attacked a city, Jacobsen explains, hundreds of citizens "came out to support the coalition forces in any way they could."[43] Regional and local conditions determined their character: from mobilizations of a traditional nature—large landowners and their private armies—to those composed of middle sectors resentful of the excesses committed by the *cacerista* authorities. *Pierolistas* like Alberto Ulloa praised the multiclass nature of the phenomenon. In sharp contrast to the ragged clothes of the precariously armed *montoneros*, wrote Ulloa, was the imposing presence of leaders such as Augusto Durand (the founder of the ephemeral Liberal Party, about whom more below), who wore a French-style uniform and often carried "his right hand on his chest so that they would call him the Napoleon of Huánuco."[44] Whether the *montoneros* were referred to as "armed citizens" or "groups of peons," the mobilization of 1895 was the last time that a decentralized campaign of irregular forces succeeded in overthrowing a formally established government.

The pact between *civilista* and democratic elites that formed the National Coalition—a pact that was signed on March 30, 1894, two days before the death of President Morales Bermúdez—finally granted legitimacy and "national" projection to a movement with local roots.[45] This decision led, in April 1895, to the electoral victory of Piérola, who won 4,150 of the 4,310 votes cast under the electoral college format. In the midst of the enthusiasm for the victory, Manuel Candamo—head of the transitional government established after Cáceres was ousted—absolved his former adversary Piérola for his "past mistakes," recognizing him as the great leader of the consolidation of the civilian regime.[46]

From being old foes, Piérola and the *civilistas* had found a common cause: preventing Cáceres from further entrenching the power of the military and, crucially, a project of rule that refocused power in the highlands and away from Lima. However, if, as many Peruvians believed, there were no differences between *civilismo* and *pierolismo*, the question then was how Piérola was going to maintain his relevance with his *civilista* partners. He sought to become the political guarantor of the emerging "technical state," acting as an intermediary between the authorities and those who had put their blood quota into the insurrection: regional middle sectors, artisan organizations, and, of course, urban masses. But how to do this when the reality was that Piérola—in the words of Basadre—"lacked any ties to social or economic demands"? Was it his inevitable destiny to be absorbed by *civilismo*?

Two measures were, according to Piérola, essential to celebrate a clean electoral process: direct suffrage (thus eliminating the confrontation for control of the "electoral tables") and the creation of an autonomous body, the National Electoral Board, to oversee the entire process through departmental and provincial electoral boards subordinate to it (thus suppressing confrontations between local factions as well as the subsequent congressional dispute over the certification of disputed candidacies). By centralizing and circumscribing the electoral universe, excluding the great Indigenous majorities (by imposing literacy as a requirement to vote), and, above all, consolidating the electoral predominance of the wealthiest, Piérola aimed to banish old vices from the system. Thus, the Peruvian electoral establishment went from "absolute decentralization" to "the greatest centralism"—an arrangement that worked as long as "harmony" prevailed between the coalition partners. Eventually, according to Basadre, the Democrats understood that with this arrangement, they had simply put "the noose around their necks."[47]

Centralization was also the key to the other strategic measure of the new order under construction: military reform. The aim was to transform military officers from potential allies of local powers in the interior into integrating agents loyal to the central state. This objective was supported by measures that helped to convert a military career into an attractive professional option. The abolition of the Indigenous *contribución* or head tax—a substitute for the colonial-era Indigenous *contribución*— simultaneously aimed at extending the state presence in the interior of the country and extracting the political authorities from a collection process that produced dangerous "indigenous uprisings."[48] On these bases the long-awaited "technical state" was to be erected, and it was thought that the creation of a Ministry of Development and Public Works would be the mainstay of such a state. The goal was to create a new order in which "roads take precedence over the temple and the school" and "over governmental presence, the rule of law, and industries" because they are an essential condition "for all the rest to happen," as Piérola had said in 1889.[49] This strategy ended up accentuating Lima's monopoly over the regions and its role as the bridge to the rest of the world.[50]

As a consequence—according to José Frisancho, a lawyer from *Puno* writing in 1928—if for the coastal region the revolution of 1895 had meant an "advance toward democracy," for the departments of the southern sierra it was a "total debacle."[51] In fact, measures such as the imposition of a state monopoly on salt production or a new property tax—seen from Lima as perfectly adequate to replace the old-fashioned personal *contribución*— confirmed this negative perception. To this was now added an electoral reform that gave all the advantages to the "largest taxpayers," while excluding the main protagonists of the wool boom in progress in that region of the country: the Indigenous peasantry.[52] The long-lasting resentment that was produced in the sierra region of Peru by this new era of centralization—which came right after a vigorous regional insurrection—became very significant for the future of the *civilista* experiment, particularly in the "remote" southernmost border region of the republic.

In a newly dominant and centralizing Lima, however, a relative ideological consensus consolidated around positivism, the philosophy, developed by thinkers including Auguste Comte and Herbert Spencer, that society could be ordered successfully and progress achieved by the application of supposedly scientific principles; a notion with influence in Peru dating to the prewar years.[53] To national reconstruction, positivism brought optimism and an overall vision: the promise of a prompt insertion of Peru into the economic boom sparked by the second industrial revolution.[54] The opening speech of the 1904 academic year at the University of San Marcos, by the young professor Javier Prado y Ugarteche—"The Social State of Peru During Spanish Domination (Historical-Sociological Study)"—is a good example of that vision. In a highly critical tone, Prado y Ugarteche offered in his speech a crude assessment of the colonial legacy: from the inveterate government corruption to its policy of benevolence toward and marginalization of its subordinates, which in the long run translated into a "degeneration almost impossible to remove from the indigenous race." This was a diagnosis, by implication, of the obstacles to be overcome to achieve the development of Peru.

At that time, opposition to the agro-export consensus was practically reduced to Manuel González Prada and a small group of his followers. In 1891 he had founded the political party Unión Nacional (UN), although his true objective had been to form a radical party. Soon after, however, he left for Europe, leaving that organization without effective leadership. When he returned to Lima in May 1898, he distanced himself from the UN, criticizing its multiple concessions to the establishment that emerged from the 1895 revolution. His disillusionment with reformists and liberals was almost total.[55] He opted for a "solitary apostolate," a pamphleteering campaign sustained by libertarian ideas that had significant influence among workers, students, and intellectual circles.[56] Thus, *gonzalespradismo*—a set of "propaganda and attack" essays that had more of a strong literary nature than a cohesive doctrine—was born. Future generations would see this as the founding moment of a radical tradition that they used as the basis to launch themselves into a fully revolutionary praxis.[57]

Uncertainty surrounded the final months of the Piérola administration. There were those who encouraged him to become the Peruvian Porfirio Díaz and stay in office, and there were those who saw Vice President Guillermo Billinghurst as Piérola's natural successor. But to succeed him the president opted instead for his former minister of public works, Eduardo López de Romaña. In this engineer without significant political background Piérola saw the best choice to complete his work toward the construction of a "technical state." This was good news for the *civilistas*, who saw López de Romaña as someone they could control. Not so much for his working-class followers, for whom the Caliph's passage through power had meant little to nothing. In a publication called *El Montonero*, Piérola was accused of having "turned his back" on the "Democratic *pueblo*." One of the conclusions drawn in that piece was that the "disguised gendarme, the salaried employee and the secret servant" were his new supporters.[58]

His most combative adherents asked themselves if it was possible that the astute Caliph did not perceive the hegemonic intentions of the *civilistas*—that he continued to believe that they were really interested in a bipartisan alternation of the presidency as the National Coalition pact between *demócratas* and *civilistas* had originally intended. Pretending to complete his own transition from caudillo to civilian politician, Piérola became a candidate for mayor of Lima in 1900. For his rivals, that was a golden opportunity to inflict a painful humiliation on him. Piérola announced his retirement from politics as a result. For the *civilistas*, this symbolic victory was complemented by some critical facts: that they had taken over the National Electoral Board, and that they had control of Congress, where they had a new ally, the Constitutional Party of General Cáceres, which Cáceres himself now led. The former dictator had returned from Europe seven years after his overthrow. With its ties to *pierolismo* broken, *civilismo* resorted to the network of *cacerista* officers to ensure order in the interior, thus proceeding to rebuild the alliance of the years prior to the 1895 revolution. For *pierolismo*, meanwhile, the small Liberal Party, founded in 1902,was the only ally available. From then on, Basadre noted, "the entire history of the Democratic Party was nothing more than one long gasp for air from a drowning man."[59]

When Augusto Durand founded the Liberal Party, a relative enthusiasm for the new party was generated among the mesocratic sectors in the interior, which, when considering the best way to confront the rise of the oligarchy, vacillated between the *montonera*, a journalistic platform, and the Congress. Representatives of that mesocratic sector from the country's interior, including the lawyer and writer Enrique López Albújar, the future leader of Cuzco *indigenismo*, Luis E. Valcárcel, and the celebrated journalist Abelardo Gamarra, joined the party. Gamarra hoped, at the time, to bring together the various liberal nuclei existing throughout the country, with a view to creating a force capable of filling the void left by the decline of *pierolismo*. By contrast, the constitutionalism of Cáceres, in its new incarnation, had nothing to offer. It was an entity that one observer described as an "old patronage" dressed in a "partisan suit"—united around the cult of its leader, dedicated to achieving support in Congress for the hegemony of *civilismo* in exchange for some perks.[60]

Aware of his weakness, Piérola proposed that an assembly of five hundred individuals choose, by consensus, the most suitable presidential candidate. However, disagreements about the number of representatives for each party frustrated the realization of this plan. In this situation, the old partners in the 1895 revolution, the *demócratas* and *civilistas*, now organized into two competing blocs, were preparing to confront each other. However, on the eve of the vote, Piérola withdrew his candidacy, citing a lack of guarantees for a clean process. Thus, he left the way clear for the victory of the *civilista* Manuel Candamo, with 99 percent of the votes cast. With all the power in their hands, the *civilistas*, with all their hegemonic and corrupt tendencies and despite their shakiness, were able to run the country with little opposition.

Civilismo in Power (1904–1912)

If the election of Manuel Candamo represented—as Justo Tovar has observed—a new opportunity for a "reunion of the elite" around an agreement on "alternation of government" between the relevant political forces, his death eight months after taking office left José Pardo, the son of the founder of *civilismo*, as the only option for the ruling party.[61] With Pardo's election, according to Basadre, it was clearer than ever that power was "in the hands of the rich"—a control that only the "popular fascination with the caudillos" and the "political interference of the military" had been able to challenge. In 1904, however, neither of those last two forces was a threat. The first had evaporated with the retirement of Piérola, and the second was neutralized by the ongoing process of the professionalization of the military.[62]

The *civilistas'* wielding of power displayed a style that combined legalism and strong elements of "arbitrariness, capriciousness, or a narrow spirit," although without becoming an "unbridled tyranny."[63] The seats of Congress, meanwhile, served as a conduit to link gentlemen from the capital with the landowners of the interior, on whom the governability of the nation ultimately depended, given their vast power in those extensive areas of the country where the state did not reach. This was the profile of the supposed "class dictatorship" that, according to Sinesio López, the "oligarchic state" imposed with the relative collaboration of the middle classes and the passivity of the "undifferentiated masses."[64] But how durable could this "aristocratic" mise-en-scène be?

Building a state suited to the requirements of export growth was the great objective of the Partido Civil, which preferred to do so in a manner that would bring modernization without causing major alterations to the social order, producing a manageable "traditionalist modernization."[65] Thus, insertion in the global process of capitalist expansion occurred at the same time as the systematic exclusion of the majority, mostly Indigenous rural masses, from that process. Peru, like other Latin American countries undergoing similar processes at the time, were republics that benefited 20 percent of the national population, bringing modernization for some and relegating others to tradition, according to Pedro Planas.[66] Time would define the rates of change of that basic equation. From this dynamic, likewise, would derive the multiple debates that agitated *civilismo*.

Was the country prepared to receive "the torrent of capital and labor" that was already beginning to "overflow into this country"? wondered Isaac Alzamora, head of the Partido Civil beginning in 1904. Though Peru did not receive a large influx of migrants in this period compared to Argentina or Brazil, both European (particularly Italian) and Asian (particularly Japanese) migrants arrived to provide labor, and capital, for the expanding export sectors and the equally expanding service sector. Though small, these migrant communities would go on to play key economic, cultural, and even political roles in the twentieth century.

One either forged a nation or ran the risk of being devastated by the forces of capital, added Víctor Maúrtua, a diplomat and parliamentarian. How far could one go in granting rights to companies like the Cerro de Pasco Corporation? The company, founded in 1901 by J. P. Morgan and the Vanderbilt family, among others, gained full control of mining in the central region by buying up smaller concerns. In other sectors, too, such as petroleum, sugar, cotton, and wool, foreign capital started to displace local capital in this period, resulting in an important "denationalization" of key economic sectors.

Likewise, what should be the role of the state with respect to the expansion of coastal agriculture and the social problems that its growth entailed? If Piérola had provided "good administration" and López de Romaña offered "order and peace," Candamo could not limit himself to simply maintaining what he had found. The question was—according to an editorial in *La Ley*, directed by Maúrtua—how to continue governing the republic with a budget of only 14 million soles. How would it be possible to pay for the railways and the roads but also for the schools that were required to build the nation?

Governing effectively, on the other hand, required addressing the increasingly complex "social question." For this it was necessary, according to José Matías Manzanilla, a lawyer, academic, and member of Congress, to undertake a "doctrinal renewal" of the Partido Civil, "inscribing" in its "flags" the "urgency" of carrying out "social reforms," such as the Work Accidents Law of 1911, one of the first such laws in the Americas, to give an example. The distinguished *civilista* Luis Miró Quesada de la Guerra contributed bills on employment contracts and other labor issues; later, as mayor of Lima between 1916 and 1918, he promoted the first school refectories and a number of hygiene- and sanitation-related modernizations in the Peruvian capital.[67]

Regarding educational policy, there were clearly different generational approaches. We can see them in, for example, the objections of the philosopher Alejandro Deústua to the Organic Law of 1901, which aimed to extend the scope of public education; for Deústua, there could be no point in teaching reading, writing, or arithmetic to those who "still were not people" (that is, Peru's Indigenous population). It would be much more practical, in his opinion, to concentrate resources on the formation of an intellectual elite, on which the "improvement" of the nation truly depended.[68]

In fact, various testimonies show that the racism of Deústua was not the predominant vision in *civilismo*. For example, Don Pedro Ignacio Cisneros, president of the superior court of Ancash, maintained in 1901 that studies on the development of the social organism "have not yet demonstrated the inability of any group of the human family to enter into the role of civilization." And Jorge Polar, minister of justice, education, charity, and worship, pronounced in the same vein in 1905: "Fortunately it has been proven that there is no ineducable race," hence "the legend that the Indian does not want to leave his miserable condition" was "rapidly discredited."[69]

For the "young Turk" Mariano H. Cornejo, a lawyer and academic, educating the Indian and incorporating him, through the vote, into national life was the best way to take away from caudillismo its great base of support.[70] Similarly, lawyer and academic Manuel Vicente Villarán's proposal for legal protection for Indigenous communities noted that their "insignificant productivity" was due neither to "the lack of encouragement from private property" nor to the "appreciated semi-barbarism and ignorance of the Indians" but to "the impossibility of giving lucrative use to their lands due to the lack of roads and places of consumption for their products."[71] In short, there would be no way forward without a national education program that linked the broader population to the great task of economic progress.[72]

Such views were shared by those outside *civilismo*, such as Joaquín Capelo, a *demócrata*. Capelo was an engineer with a notable service record, from his participation in the construction of the fortifications for the defense of Lima (1880–81) to the layout of penetration routes into the eastern Amazon. He was a sensitive man who was deeply touched by the miserable conditions in which his compatriots in the interior of the country lived. From criticism of the wasteful management of public funds to his concern for the "Indian problem," this interest led him to the public arena as a senator for Junín (1901–12) in the ranks of *pierolismo* and, moreover, to join Pedro Zulen and Dora Mayer, an academic and an activist, respectively, to found the paradigmatic Pro-Indigenous Association in 1914, a precursor of the nongovernmental organizations of the future.[73]

In this way, Capelo, Zulen, and Mayer moved into the political sphere a discourse about "the Indian" that had earlier emerged in the cultural sphere in the work of painters such as Francisco Laso and writers such as Clorinda Matto de Turner. Laso and Matto de Turner's paintings and novels pioneered a particularly Peruvian version of the broader *indigenista* movements of the twentieth century, which simultaneously critiqued the exploitation of Indigenous populations and proposed policies, often of a paternalistic nature, to morally and culturally uplift them.

Capelo's participation in the Pro-Indigenous Association was fundamental to the metamorphosis of Teodomiro Gutiérrez Cuevas—a veteran of the La Breña campaign, subprefect in the provinces of the southern sierra and center of the country, and activist of the Methodist Church—who, influenced by the Association's message, went from public official to agrarian insurgent in the context of a series of peasant uprisings in response to the growing encroachment of haciendas on the lands of peasant communities and the growing exploitation of peasants residing on haciendas by *gamonales* (local white or mestizo power holders) as a result of the wool boom. In fact, under the name of General Rumi Maqui Ccori Zoncco (in Quechua, "hand of stone and heart of gold"), in 1916 we find him leading an attack on one of the largest highland haciendas.

In this context of emerging social reformism and new perspectives on the "Indian question," José Pardo's presidential candidacy seemed to many to be the best way to ensure a harmonious generational transition, trusting in the unifying power of his lineage. But for those who feared the proximity of the "dauphin" to the "young Turks" of the party and, by extension, his susceptibility to their overly radical goals, Ántero Aspíllaga—a man trained in "the sugarcane fields" and in the "capital law firms"—was the best alternative.[74] For Pardo to overcome the obstacles that the old guard of *civilismo* put in his way, he would need the backing of Augusto B. Leguía, who at that point was still at the beginning of his political career.

Those who have studied the first administration of José Pardo, from 1904 to 1908, point to three key elements: (1) the continuity of the institutionalizing impulse initiated by Piérola as a contributing factor to the revitalization of export growth; (2) his concern for education and social legislation; and (3) public peace, internal order, and an unprecedented freedom of the press. This was the relatively progressive face of a regime that, on the other hand, continued to depend for its survival on pacts with the traditional local powers—and even more so in the absence of *pierolismo*, which had been *civilismo*'s connection to and buffer against the country's interior. Moreover, these pacts meant supporting the access to Congress of a group without any interest in reform. In this sense, the *civilista-constitutionalista* pact adequately fulfilled its role.[75]

Within this framework, a dynamic finance minister like Leguía (1904–7) found a way to secure funds to resume railway construction, promote port modernization and the building of telegraph lines, and facilitate establishment of shipping companies such as the Compañía Peruana de Vapores. At the same time, two cruisers—the *Grau* and the *Bolognesi*—were acquired, along with other military equipment. To do this, the administration relied on the irreplaceable "sanity of the people," which had allowed it to raise taxes without causing major riots.[76] Thus, in a country in which the leaders had previously left the capital only "to defend their threatened authority," in an unprecedented move President Pardo visited several regions of the country. Would his successor be capable of reproducing the aristocratic halo of the "dauphin" of *civilismo*?

The Rise of Leguía

With the endorsement of José Pardo, the outgoing president, Leguía's nomination to be the next president went smoothly. His reputation as a modern man, his international connections, and his financial success made up for his lack of pedigree. Augusto B. Leguía was, according to Basadre, the typical parvenu: a "young and seductive" man who "had no prominent classmates in Lima" (he had been educated in Chile, at the famous Goldfinch and Bluhm school in Valparaíso) but was "innately gifted" in a way that allowed him to enter the circles of power of the Peruvian capital.[77] At the age of seventeen, he had participated in the defense of Lima, fighting in Battalion No. 2, "constituted by the most select youth of Lima."[78] He received praise for his effective appearances in Congress as minister of finance. He challenged the opposition to authorize the public works that would make Peru great. But this expected too much from an opposition whose only philosophy was survival and that—devoid of popular support—increasingly resorted to threats of legal challenges or *montonera* uprisings to try to obstruct the approval of the loans that Leguía was hoping to obtain.

In fact, on May 1, 1908, Durand made real such a threat, with an uprising that bore all the hallmarks of the *pierolista* style. It was no more than a mere skirmish, and all the leaders except Durand were captured—apparently the "Napoleon from *Huánuco*" aspired to be the new Caliph. The resulting repression would extend beyond the Liberal Party to members of the Democratic Party, relatives of the Caliph, and even the director of the *Pierolista* newspaper *La Prensa*, Alberto Ulloa. However, as soon as he came to power, in September 1908, Leguía decreed an amnesty for those accused of the uprising. Establishing a modus vivendi for the National Coalition was, at that time, the challenge facing the largest parties.

The decisive test came in May of the following year when elections were held for a third of the seats in Congress. Taking a "deferential" attitude toward the *pierolistas*, the coalition in power—the leaders of the *civilistas* and *constitucionalistas*—offered not to put forth candidates in some localities, leaving those seats to the opposition alliance, composed of *demócratas* and *liberales*. However, Piérola intervened to reject any such agreement, reaffirming his conviction about the moral value of abstention as a complaint against arbitrariness. Around that time, the newspapers reported on a popular demonstration organized to receive the amnestied Durand upon his return from exile, after which a "large group" of demonstrators went to the home of José Pardo with the aim of attacking it, expressing a "deaf anger" that "has broken out" at the first opportunity. The ferment became more bitter in light of the humiliating electoral results three months later, which further reduced the presence of *pierolismo* in Congress—while there had previously been eight representatives in both chambers of Congress, after the election only six remained (compared to 129 *civilistas*, 29 constitutionalists, and 2 liberals). "Everything, absolutely everything" had been tried to "reconcile the Peruvian family," a *leguiísta* report would later say, but they had been unable to prevent their adversaries from clinging to the "stubborn path of resistance," thus becoming "the most terrible enemies that human history has recorded."[79] Between the "abstentionism" of its leader and the humiliations the *pierolistas* had suffered, the question was when the *montonero* instinct of *pierolismo* would reappear.

On May 29, 1909, the *pierolistas* decided to act. In contrast to the insurrection of 1895—which consisted of a movement, literally, from the countryside to the city—this time the coup targeted the highest echelon of power, with the participation of a group of twenty-five individuals, commanded by two sons and the brother of the Caliph. This was an operation that Jorge Basadre considered to be without parallel in the history of the country. Its success was based on simplicity and surprise: seizing the president in an act of such daring that "its very audacity made it implausible."[80] The objective was to force him to resign from the presidency. But Leguía refused to resign. Then, for a couple of hours, Lima witnessed the president's *via crucis.* Why "had no defenders of the president appeared when his captors did not reach fifty" and were "almost completely unarmed"? "A music band would have been enough to rescue him!" a witness exclaimed.[81]

An inevitable "hunt for the regime's enemies" followed the attempted coup. *La Prensa*—the unofficial mouthpiece for *pierolismo*—and Liberal Party leaders, such as Durand himself, who had no connection with the coup attempt, were targeted. From then on, the idea of conciliation as the basis of good government would be replaced by a legalistic point of view, according to which public order was of "supreme national necessity" and thus took precedence over the constitution. Beyond the authoritarian gesture, however, the regime's lack of a clear project of government had been exposed. Leguía's problem, according to the weekly periodical *Variedades,*

Figure 3.2 Pierolista coup against Leguía, Plaza de Armas, Lima, May 1909. Source: Congreso de la República del Perú.

was that he had appointed a "purely administrative cabinet" incapable of handling the demands and concerns emerging from "domestic politics." Consequently, the remaining years of his presidential term proved to be particularly conflict-ridden.

Facing conspiracies and *montoneras*, the Partido Civil divided into a *leguiísta* wing and a "bloc" of *pardistas*. At the same time, long-standing border problems were intensifying. In these circumstances, Leguía sought to control Congress regardless of the means to which he had to resort: arrests and persecution of "hostile" members of the different boards that monitored the electoral process, bribery, intimidation, resurrection of forgotten trials, and so on. Meanwhile, the *"bloquista"* contenders—who controlled the National Electoral Board—used their power to block government initiatives. Eventually, the government decided to dissolve the National Electoral Board, arguing that it had exceeded its powers by replacing several members of its provincial boards.

With the founding of the Partido Civil Independiente, in November 1912, the division of *civilismo* became official. In Paris, José Pardo was quick to express his support for the dissidents.[82] Leguía found himself on his own. Soon, like his former boss Pardo, he would follow the path of self-exile. It was logical that, after being disappointed by an outsider, the leadership of a republic tailored to agro-export interests would revert to Pardo or to one of the "sugar barons" like Ántero Aspíllaga at the head of the Partido Civil. Nobody in mid-1912 could have imagined that, on the contrary, a new and more radical outsider would become the next president of Peru.

The Billinghurst Government

At the beginning of 1912, while the details of the presidential succession were being discussed in the elitist National Club or in the residences of the *civilista* leaders, a spirit of anger and rebellion prevailed among the ordinary people of the capital. There was no reason, however, to think that this fifth change of government since the revolution of 1895 was going to be special, and even less to predict that—with the support of an unusual mass mobilization—a last-minute candidacy would prevail.

If Leguía was a provincial parvenu, Guillermo Billinghurst was a "frontiersman": born in Arica and educated in Valparaíso, he had spent his adult life in Iquique, in the province of Tarapacá, which Peru had lost to Chile.[83] Following in his father's footsteps, he had made his fortune in the nitrate trade. The sociologist Osmar Gonzales views him as a prototype of a "national bourgeois."[84] His irrigation project for the Pampa del Tamarugal, as part of a plan for the economic advancement of his region, is testimony to his vision.[85] The fact that his economic base remained abroad (Tarapacá) simply reinforced his autonomy with respect to the Lima elite, for whom he felt enormous disdain. The Caliph himself feared that aspect of his character. The Democratic Party had rewarded Billinghurst with the vice presidency of the republic during Piérola's term (1895–99) for his contribution to the victory of 1895. Billinghurst would later be denied the presidential candidacy in 1899, which led him to break with his former leader. This situation, paradoxically, led him to discover workers as a political resource.

Thus, while the Democratic Party leadership insisted on turning the initial coalition formula into a bipartisan scheme—an option that entailed lowering the tone of its original anti-elitism—Billinghurst aimed to represent the most populist version of *pierolismo*. Billinghurst's greater objective was to overcome the great bottleneck that the party's alliance with the landowners of the interior represented when it came to effective modernization of the country.

Between 1909 and 1910, as mayor of Lima, Billinghurst had the opportunity to demonstrate that different vision. He did so with a series of public works in health, hygiene, transportation, housing, and food that had a positive impact on the living conditions of the popular sectors. As long as more than 90 percent of the city's "living capital" continued to live in "filthy alleys and lots," he argued in his 1910 municipal report, "we have no right to call ourselves a cultured people." The national context maximized his political capital. In 1912, various factors—the extreme wear and tear suffered by the *leguiísta* regime, a persistent financial crisis, and conflicts within *civilismo*—generated favorable conditions for "an important political change."[86] Hence, based on an accurate reading of the situation, Billinghurst and a small circle of collaborators from the Democratic and Liberal Parties chose to initiate a cautious propaganda effort. This was a test balloon that immediately took flight, and which took by surprise a *civilismo* worn down by routine and tied to a candidate with no experience in the emerging mass politics.

Ántero Aspíllaga, the candidate of the Partido Civil, had been minister of finance in the Cáceres government at the end of the 1880s, and beginning in 1892 he was a senator from Lima. He was appointed mayor of the capital in 1910 but resigned very soon after. His career, in truth, was based on business success—he had transformed the Cayaltí hacienda into "one of the first sugar businesses" in the country.[87] His trips to Europe to buy machinery would make him one of the great protagonists of the modernization of the agro-export sector.[88] As such, Aspíllaga had developed an intense suspicion of the "politicians," as they controlled the appointments of local authorities, who in turn put up "obstacles" when it came to key issues related to the accumulation of land, distribution of water, and recruitment of labor. Hence, the *civilistas* were forced to enter a political arena that was much more fluid and contested than generally assumed, as Rory Miller notes. They came with the perspective that they represented the "general interest"—that what was good for them was good for the country. Thus Aspíllaga held that the exploitation of the "great natural wealth" of the country was the "fundamental objective," the "primordial" task around which the other aspects of government were organized.[89]

The role of the government was to "remove" the country from a "sterile political life," opening up "broad horizons" for a "happy and fruitful existence through order and work." A key factor was the development of "human, collective and individual energies." This framework was an expansion, one could say, of what had been done in Cayaltí to guarantee productivity: sanitation, hygienic housing, technical education, and so on. But Aspíllaga privileged the coast, considering that it presented "greater facilities than other regions for immediate and remunerative exploitation and prosperity." In other words, the coast was to be Peru's showcase, so that the country could attract investment and immigration, particularly from Europe. The opening of the Panama Canal, moreover, made it urgent to prepare to take advantage of the opportunities that direct communication with "the American and European countries of the North Atlantic" would produce. In addition to supporting the agro-export expansion, Aspíllaga's proposal for communication and transportation routes revealed some aspiration toward national integration: he favored "national roads, of fast and cheap employment, mainly in the inter-Andean region," and a railway scheme in which the lines penetrating into the Amazon had priority over "coastal longitudinal" ones.[90]

Regarding the Indigenous population, Aspíllaga's proposal drew attention to the important services that could be expected from them, by virtue of their great physical resistance, their capacity for "intelligent imitation," their "admirable perseverance," and their habits of "discipline and obedience" that qualified them as good soldiers. Hence, the priority was to save them from the "great scourges that plague the *braceros* of the sierra": malaria and tuberculosis. Likewise, efforts had to be made to promote "habits of temperance" that would "contain suicide or the decline of the race" and support the moral improvement and "instruction" that would result from "contact with superior races." Only then would the gradual "resurgence" of the Indigenous population become evident, allowing it "to start acting as the greatest free and conscious factor of national prosperity."[91]

Billinghurst's candidacy challenged this vision, which was dependent on the aforementioned "traditional modernization" model and was impossible to translate into a popular discourse. Billinghurst's career allowed him to articulate what became the most advanced populist discourse in almost a century of republican history. That discourse found willing ears in a young and resentful working class, conscious enough to resist the paternalistic and tutelary approaches of the "Lord of Cayaltí." Never before had anything like this been seen: an open confrontation between a hardcore member of the ruling *argolla* and an upstart from a region that, at the time, was not fully considered an integral part of the country.

With the eight-hour working day as its banner, a class-based trade union movement was taking shape at the beginning of the century. Influenced by anarcho-syndicalism, this movement relied more on direct action than on negotiation with the bosses. Neither *pierolismo* with its early populist discourse nor the reformist *civilismo* of the "young Turks" had been able to channel this social effervescence. Luis Torrejón has shown how a multitude with a distinctive mobilization capacity, which emerged from the spontaneous organization of artisans and workers, supported political parties with diverse motivations—nationalist, patriotic, *pierolista, anticivilista*, and anarcho-syndicalist.[92]

This was where the labor movement was when Billinghurst emerged as a presidential candidate. They needed each other: a leader who was willing to confront the "oligarchy" and who recognized the rights of the working people, and a grassroots movement that would support a dissident who understood that "civic protest" could be his vehicle to gain power.

On May 19, 1912, the authorities were forced to divide the center of the capital into two large zones in preparation for the mobilizations that were to take place. They used the Government Palace as the central reference point. From there to the east, where the working-class Rímac neighborhood was located, would be for the *billinghuristas*. The area to the south, by the upper-class neighborhood surrounding the Palacio de la Exposición, would be for the *aspillaguistas*. According to press reports, only 1,500 people gathered in support of Aspíllaga, in contrast to some 20,000 who turned out for Billinghurst.

The pro-Billinghurst march featured banners depicting two loaves of bread: a tiny one, which represented what the two-cent loaf would be like if Aspíllaga was in power, and another that was several times larger, representing what the loaf would be like if Billinghurst was in charge. It attracted so much attention that the opposition campaign began to be called "big bread."

There, in the very center of national power—after giving Leguía a document denouncing the maneuvers of the National Electoral Board, which was deemed responsible for the marginalization of "nine-tenths" of the citizenry—the protesters announced the decision made by an assembly of sixty *billinghurista* clubs: to declare a general strike during the days designated for the election. The "social question," the future president Manuel Prado Ugarteche observed, "had completely absorbed the political question, leaving electoral officials without guarantees." Never before, according

Figure 3.3 The "big bread" mobilization, Lima, 1912. Source: Biblioteca Nacional del Perú.

to Osmar Gonzales, "had the crowd occupied the streets and squares in favor of a politician who was not even officially a candidate."[93]

The Lima mobilization was only the tip of the iceberg of a much greater agitation. In the sugar enclaves, for example, the working conditions themselves began to generate large-scale protests.[94] In mid-1912, a Trujillo newspaper described the wave of strikes that occurred in the northern Chicama valley—which would leave hundreds dead and injured—as "the largest and most violent recorded in the workers' annals of the area." In the capital, meanwhile, the electoral boycott was a complete success. By becoming the "axis" of the movement of "reaction against the electoral farce," *Variedades* commented, in the span of just twenty days Billinghurst had managed to block the fundamental mechanism of the oligarchic state. The installation of Congress became, in these circumstances, the moment of truth. It would taste like victory for Leguía to see Aspíllaga denied a victory in the election, even more so because, in the negotiation in which Leguía granted Billinghurst the presidency, he had managed to impose his brother Roberto as vice president.[95]

The new president promised to continue the modernizing drive without repeating the "wasteful" style of his predecessor. As Basadre observed, despite the novelty that Billinghurst's path to power entailed, the new president's proposal was not far from the "practical republic" of Manuel Pardo. What Porfirio Díaz said of Francisco Madero when the former left the presidency of Mexico in 1911 could be applied to Billinghurst: A tiger had been released, and it remained to be seen if it could be returned to its cage. The tiger, of course, was an emboldened labor movement that felt its time for redemption had come.

Spurred by the rising cost of living, the *billinghurista* electoral clubs made demands that the government was unable to capitalize on to its own advantage. The libertarian—that is, markedly anti-political—affiliation of the government's leaders was, in this regard, a serious obstacle. Thus, instead of appeasing the *billinghuristas*, the concessions granted by the government seemed to encourage mobilization. Calls for repression ensued, particularly following the granting of the eight-hour day for the workers of Callao. Only in February 1913, with the promulgation of a decree regulating strikes—which would be followed by other specific measures such as the creation of a General Labor Inspectorate—did the "epidemic of strikes," as Basadre called them, begin to subside. The cost, however, was a significant reduction in support for the regime among the workers.

Without its own congressional bench, the incoming regime was beholden to the political groups that had elected it. In these circumstances, Billinghurst had two options: either he could enter the fight for the parliamentary vote using the same tools as his peers, or he could call for the dissolution of Congress and a new vote to elect its members. If reaching "electoral truth" had been the great motto of the *pierolista* revolution of 1895, the reality was that what had been imposed in the subsequent eighteen years was a vast repertoire of tricks—illegal extension of expired congressional terms, postponement of electoral deadlines, transformation of substitutes for elected members into actual representatives, or the simple resource of "incorporating representatives with bullets" (that is, using intimidation in the electoral process)—used to convert the seats into "the patrimony of a few families selected by the central power."[96]

Following Piérola's death on June 23, 1913, conditions existed for a reconciliation of the regime with *pierolismo* that would put an end to its "abstention policy." Toward this end, Billinghurst named a *pierolista* cabinet headed by Aurelio Sousa y Matute. It didn't work. Nothing seemed to be enough at that point to avoid a head-on clash between the president and *civilismo*. His program, writes Víctor Andrés Belaúnde, was "a documented and overwhelming indictment of the economic policy of the old *civilismo*," and in his first address to Congress, Billinghurst had carried out a "'ruthless dissection' of the financial policy of his predecessor." But engaging in a direct confrontation was far beyond what his political capital allowed him to do. He resorted, therefore, to a "dissolution of parliament" and "a constitutional reform carried out by a referendum."[97] His opponents later claimed that he did not "know the country, nor its homes, nor its desires," and they advised him "to retire immediately and return to Chile to live in peace."[98] In this way, the system expelled an outsider who seemed not to understand the implications of touching the heart of a system made up of pacts and alliances on which the mediocre *pax civilista* was based. Billinghurst thought he could isolate *civilismo*, but he was the one who ended up isolated.

His detractors spread the image of a neurotic and revengeful president searching day and night for a way out of the impasse, with his star adviser—Mariano Cornejo, from Arequipa—at his side. How to develop a "national policy" above the "game of fights and alliances" orchestrated by the *limeño* elites? This was the question that Cornejo wanted desperately to answer. His proposal included a constitutional reform that would introduce plebiscite consultation, the elimination of the system in which a third of congressional seats came up for election at any one time and its replacement by one in which all seats of Congress would be voted on at once, making it coincide with the presidential election. This would require the radical measure of dissolving Congress to allow its regeneration.[99] This, in turn, meant reactivating mass support for the regime. Another member of the palace group, Justo Cassaretto, a worker from the mutualist movement and organizer of the Public Health Committee, took on this charge, forming an institution that—it was said—had the aim of harassing opponents of the regime. Nearly nine hundred workers repatriated from Chile the previous year had been assigned to this task, thus filling the void left by the withdrawal of the labor movement on which *billinghurismo* had initially relied.

With these elements, what was cooking in the palace was "a revolution made by the government itself"—a movement "equivalent" to that of Porfirio Díaz in Mexico, a regime of "violence and beneficial tyrannies" that "remakes national life." How would the opposition react to this challenge? Several groups constituted the opposition: (1) a parliamentary group of diverse origin; (3) a group consisting of the Prado family and close friends; (3) a journalistic front, including several outlets that, like *La*

Prensa, had initially supported Billinghurst; and (4) a group of military officers. Would they be able to forge a joint response? Two days before the military coup, *El Sur,* from Arequipa, published a kind of early epitaph of the *billinghurista* biennium:

> He wants a Congress that is at the same moral level as the people around him to carry out his crazy projects. To settle with Chile in the ignominious way that he intends to do it, to raise a loan of 60 million soles and all those that he later decides to carry out, so that nobody asks him for accounts or finds out about his mismanagement. In no country in the world, not even in the tribes of Africa, has it ever been seen that the underworld rules. The ignominy of the Cassaretto government will never be a reality.[100]

In Colonel Óscar R. Benavides, who at that time was well known for his outstanding performance in response to the border disputes with Colombia in the Leticia area, the conspirators found a leader for the operation that would be launched early in the morning of February 4, 1914.

If, as *Variedades* affirmed, Billinghurst wanted "to make us a French revolution in the Creole way," it was quite possible to declare the "homeland in danger," as the National Assembly of France had done in 1792.[101] The extreme accusations against Billinghurst are striking. The unparalleled verbal avalanche reveals the level of anguish at the time. And not only in Lima—this was what *El Comercio* from Cuzco said, hours after the overthrow:

> Our reason is disturbed when contemplating the degree of relaxation we had reached here in Cuzco, where we felt dizzy when perceiving the political dunghill in which they wanted to suffocate us. . . . We had a supreme ruler who was nothing more than a human beast, thrown with all his vanities and with all his miseries on a path that seemed to have no fences or obstacles. Dignity was lost in a sea of mud and arrogance and independence sold at public auction to a few imbeciles, who splashed our faces with the filthy drool of their mediocrity. During the 16 months that he has been in power, Billinghurst had displayed the worst sides of his country, enough to be excluded from the concert of nations.[102]

Even those who aimed for a somewhat more moderate interpretation issued harsh judgments of the overthrown president. From the newspaper *El Callao*:

> Perhaps the former president's thought was not so brutal and malevolent, perhaps he did have a sincere desire to rebuild and do good work: but the

projected path was so senseless, so beyond all logic and every political concept, that the entire nation has revolted, and has preferred not to expose itself to the success of the experiments of a madman. Only in this way, considering that man as foolish as impulsive, in the quality of an abnormal person, is it that he can be generously granted ostracism instead of the prison cell of the criminal.[103]

The reappearance of the military, then, was inevitable. This was not the same army of the "barracks riots" of the nineteenth century; rather, it was one that "defended territorial integrity in the legendary Caquetá," a reference to recent conflict with Colombia, acting in defense of the homeland and constitutionality. The genesis of this new army dated back to 1895, a time when it had ceased to be "mercenary" and "praetorian" and instead took on "true patriotic and guardianship mission that corresponded to it in national life." No longer was it an "unconscious phalanx"; now it was an institution capable of listening to the "cry" of the "entire nation" and then taking action. The nation and its army, as Benavides said in a speech delivered at the National Club, appeared in "an intimate communion of souls before the same altar, and in action, before the same danger."[104]

However, the country was far from being able to transform the ephemeral anti-Billinghurst unity into the long-awaited "national harmony." Given the rampant divisions that were present, Benavides would be appointed provisional president three months after the coup, against the wishes of an important sector of the political class. Over the years, as Peter Klarén observes, it would become clear that the 1914 intervention foreshadowed "the future role of the armed forces in national politics."[105]

The serious economic problems generated by the First World War had a calming effect on local politics and on *leguiísmo*, in particular, which, by reconciling with Benavides, made possible a relatively peaceful ordinary legislature. In the same sense, those events contributed to the return to Peru in November 1914 of former President José Pardo, who played a crucial role in appeasing the factions that divided his party.

From Arica, Billinghurst responded to the charges that had justified his overthrow. He had been caught between two forces, he said—the "bureaucratic party," which governed Peru with such "great damage," and the "feudal lords" of the Andean provinces—and his reformist program had aimed at transcending constitutional formalities to do what hitherto no one had ever tried: to create citizens, something much more important than "introducing innovations in our usual laws."[106] From that perspective, his goal had been neither to call a constituent assembly nor to dissolve Congress. Rather, his objective had been to obtain recognition of the referendum as a constitutional mechanism to resolve conflicts between the legislative and the executive. Under this logic, to submit to the "plebiscite verdict" the great issues of the running of the state meant strengthening that very state, providing it with a "more solid popular base."[107]

Billinghurst claimed he had been a victim of a parliamentary majority that resorted to the "old and unpatriotic tactic of sterilizing government work" via obstructionist maneuvers until it ended up cornering the executive. Thus, Billinghurst emphasized, he had been removed not because of his political and administrative acts but rather because of the "truly non-partisan and popular origin of my mandate." His removal had been accomplished by appealing to his enemies, to an "oligarchic and despotic militarism," in order to "get rid of a regime that could not last beyond the constitutional period." But his big mistake, he confessed, had been to "deny the people rifles," which would have allowed him to "defend myself against the uprising," thus saving his administration "with the armed intervention of the citizens."[108]

On June 28, 1915, Guillermo Billinghurst died in Iquique. A couple of months before, José Pardo had assumed the presidency of the republic for the second time. He was at that time the most representative element of the "privileged caste" that, according to the ousted president, had orchestrated his departure from power.

The Second Pardo Government

Against a backdrop of strong economic deterioration, with steep inflation produced first by the disruptions of the war and later by planters switching their production from foodstuffs to export crops such as sugar and cotton, new voices joined the political debate, at the precise moment when *civilista* elitism reached its highest point.[109] To save Peru from the threat of mass politics and to avoid the appearance of a new Billinghurst, a final attempt was made to consolidate the oligarchic management of the mechanisms of power. This was an uphill fight against the growing politicization of workers and students. There was a rebellious atmosphere in which, paradoxically, the possibility of Leguía's return sounded as threatening to the establishment as that of the man with the "big bread." The return of a recharged Leguía was feared because this time he managed to overcome the barriers that had blocked his modernizing plans in his previous administration. Hence, in a brief electoral campaign and a new civic-military coup that took place on July 4, 1919, which confirmed his ascent to power, Leguía managed to defeat Pardo's *civilista* republic. Like the chronicle of a death foretold, one can view the final years of the republican experiment—one that, as discussed below, Víctor Andrés Belaúnde had proposed to defend five years earlier—as uniting the most lucid elements of the Democratic and Civil Parties.

Could the so-called *novecentistas*, as a handful of intellectuals linked to the *civilista* project of rule came to be known, save the *civilista* republic? As children of the postwar national reconstruction, they had begun their public life optimistically, convinced that, with a combination of *civilista* business muscle and the leadership of the Caliph, the dream of a "republic in order" was within reach. Not surprisingly, *Le Pérou contémporain* (1907), by Francisco García Calderón—published in French, since attracting European investment to that resurgent South American "Latin republic" was its main objective—would become its symbolic text. It outlined a nation that, under the leadership of an enlightened oligarchy and by recycling methods of colonial management of its population, had managed to rise to the demands of an expanding world economy. Its author maintained that the war with Chile had ended political Caesarism and had stimulated "individualism" and "associative" zeal. Peruvians had learned hard "lessons of work and examples of stoicism" in that terrible era, which they could now apply to strengthen their country.[110]

However, sustaining that same optimism seven years later proved difficult. Hence, when commissioned to deliver the inaugural speech of the 1914 academic year in San Marcos, a young professor from Arequipa, Víctor Andrés Belaúnde, chose "the serious situation" the country was going through as his central theme. Several of his *novecentista* colleagues—Manuel Vicente Villarán, Alejandro Deústua, and Mariano Cornejo, among others—had already criticized diverse aspects of the republican model in force since 1895. Belaúnde himself, under the influence of authors such as Joaquín Costa, Ricardo Macías Picavea, Ramiro de Maeztu, and other exponents of Spanish "regenerationism"—had explored the roots of the "national incapacity" for "joint action," as well as the damaging "incoherence" of its elites.[111] Three recent events gave his speech a distinctive tone of urgency: (1) Leguía's shady dealings to ensure a parliamentary majority in 1911 and the danger of "presidential absolutism" that this represented; (2) the "demagogic" incursion of Billinghurst in 1912;

and, finally, (3) the death of Piérola in 1913 and the subsequent disappearance, in practice, of the Democratic Party.

In light of these events, another trio of problems appeared as the true "cause of evil" in the current political order: (1) the critical situation of a "bureaucratized and cacique" parliament that, by virtue of the "provincialist election," functioned as the perfect counterpart to the centralism of the capital; (2) the conformism of the ruling classes, manifested in their reluctance to reform a system that they had become accustomed to parasitizing; and (3) the economic crisis of the middle class, which condemned it to "bureaucratism and *empleocracia*" (jobs for the "boys").

Even so, Belaúnde did not believe that there was an "original vice" in the model that had been in force since 1895. The moral crisis of the ruling class was, in his opinion, the underlying problem. Hence, absent the "generous idealism" of a Nicolás de Piérola toward "pure oligarchy"—a regime "worse than *caudillaje*"—the republican model born of the 1895 revolution had gradually eroded. That was the key to the "absolute disorientation" that involved "all spirits." Such a situation could be reversed only with a "sincere return to the idealism of the early years of the Republic." Hence the final phrase of his speech: "*¡Queremos patria!*" (We want a homeland)!"—a melancholic call to return to the original demand of Peruvian identity: the desire for freedom and sovereignty, the historical mission of building a national community. However, almost a century later, that commitment was quite weakened by the traffic of selfish and base politics, often violent, and perfidiously far from the original "idealism."

In this spirit, in 1915, with the leadership of José de la Riva Agüero, the most aristocratic of all of them, the *novecentistas* would found the National Democratic Party, with the hope that it would bring together "the elite of the *civilista* youth and the *pierolista* youth" in a project of a "nobly restorative rather than conservative nature."[112] The hope was to build a force that would capitalize on what Piérola had done in terms of building a "technical and modern" administration—for example, by betting on irrigation that would "double coastal workable land," thus increasing the ability to attract European settlers.[113] Backed by the intellectual prestige and lineage of their leader, the great-grandson of a president and the grandson of a founder of the Partido Civil, the National Democratic Party was, like the original *civilismo*, born as an "intellectual party" that aspired to generate a relative national structure from academic contacts in various departmental capitals. Urban in nature, it was far from the pacts that had articulated the center with the periphery in the classic oligarchic model.[114]

It would not be long before the "futurists"—as Luis Fernán Cisneros called them, ridiculing their reformist claims—came to understand the futility of their project. They understood that the "conformism" of the ruling classes also included the rejection of any proposal that questioned the privileges of *pardismo*. And, despite their organizational efforts, they did not have the weapons to penetrate the "bureaucratized" and "cacique" network that Belaúnde had identified as the great pillar of the system. With Piérola's Democratic Party gone and the civilian project exhausted, did it make sense to go ahead with a project that was intended to be a rejection of those involved in the events of 1895? What chance of success did they have at a time when "the discontent of public opinion," to quote Basadre, gravitated toward those who "spoke in a cruder, stronger, more passionate, more everyday language"?

At the end of 1915 Belaúnde wrote to his friend Riva Agüero some very eloquent lines: "We are not the Quixotes that nobly crash against windmills, but the failed Sanchos exposed to universal laughter." The world in which the *novecentistas* had been born into public life was in the process of dissolution, engulfed by a "crisis of civilization," of which the First World War and the Mexican and Russian Revolutions were maximum expressions. Thus, stranded in a "historic bankruptcy," their expectations would end, with their brilliance extinguished by being out of step with their own time.[115]

In January 1915, five months before the general elections—with the country still experiencing the serious economic effects of the Great War, and after an intense debate on presidential succession centering around the call to elevate Roberto Leguía to the presidency of the republic—the possibility emerged of a return to militarism, via an operation promoted from the palace in conjunction with the Constitutional Party to bring General Pedro Muñiz to power. According to this plan, a convention of political parties would consecrate his candidacy as representative of a true "national harmony."

In agreement with Durand's Liberal Party (their civilian cover), three generals—Benavides, Muñiz, and Cáceres—designed a strategy whose objective was to impose General Muñiz as the "official candidate." In order to ratify his candidacy, one hundred delegates from each of the Civil, Constitutional, and Liberal Parties would meet at the end of March 1915. This meeting, in the session room of the Chamber of Deputies, brought together some two hundred deputies and senators and around a hundred ex-ministers (who had held office from 1885 onward).

Faced with this threat from the military wing of the national political class, the Partido Civil rediscovered its lost unity. In fact, it was the resignation of Javier Prado y Ugarteche, president of the Partido Civil, from any candidacy that made it possible to restore party unity. Consequently, a final appeal was made to the dynastic halo represented by the "son of the founder," José Pardo, whose absence from the country since 1908 had put him "above recent disputes."[116] It would not, however, be an easy victory. Three rounds were necessary to define a winner—and this was achieved only when the Liberal Party put to one side its old enmity with *civilismo* and endorsed José Pardo to bring him over the required threshold of 85 percent of the vote.

If Pardo's victory was not easy, neither was his government, which did little to address the growing economic and social problems that the country faced, and which proved unpopular with the increasingly politically active popular sectors. "History will exalt me!" With that pompous phrase, written more than a decade after his overthrow, José Pardo summarized his frustration at the poor evaluation of his work as a civil servant by a public opinion that, far from appreciating the "righteousness" of his performance, favored "those who shout, slanderers, and agitators." That was a typical characteristic, in his opinion, of countries with a "formless institutional life." Behind his image of "righteousness," his detractors saw a timorous leader, self-absorbed and lacking in vision, the eternal dauphin of *civilismo*.[117]

In this sense, as a chronicle of the growing gap between the Partido Civil and Peruvian reality, one can read the editorials that the writer Clemente Palma—a confessed *pierolista*—published in *Variedades*, a weekly aimed primarily at Lima's upper classes, during the forty-six months that José Pardo held power in his second administration (1915–19). The son of the founder of *civilismo* was seen as a statesman who, despite his knowledge of the world, was on his way to being "another creole-style ruler," reflected in the "cynical and shameless policy of placements" that—responding to his pacts with the "feudal" powers of the interior—his party deployed to ensure control of the legislature.

Three themes reinforce the image of the Pardo regime as a sellout: (1) its passivity about demanding the transfer of a significant amount of gold that had been received as payment for Peruvian exports but which had been retained by the United States with the excuse of the world war; (2) the assignment to the London Pacific Petroleum Company—for a "little less than in perpetuity," according to *Variedades*—of the La Brea and Pariñas oil fields; and (3) the designation of Aspíllaga as the *civilista* candidate for the presidential elections of 1919, to round out the portrait of *civilismo* as an oligarchic entity. These shortcomings accentuated the belief that only Leguía would be able to get the country out of the morass in which it found itself.

In these circumstances, in view of the "inferior psychological state" in which the country found itself—locked in the "petty fight of base ambitions" instead of facing the "more arduous problems" of the nation's progress—even a conservative like Clemente Palma would dare to say that in 1919 the only alternative for Peru was a revolution. Palma defined this event as a "social cataclysm" that, like the one that occurred in Mexico, would bloodily shake the country "to its deepest foundations." Only in this way, he concluded, could a "new Peru" emerge from the current "rot." By then, Leguía had already returned from London to Peru. With this, the *civilista* republic entered into a regressive countdown.

In their own way, between fantasy and transgression, between the classrooms of the University of San Marcos and the famous café Palais Concert, in the manner of an "anti-*novecentista* heresy," another contingent of intellectuals also aspired to revolutionize the country in the 1910s in order to build a strong homeland.[118] This group had become known through magazines such as *Colónida*. The trajectory of its director, Abraham Valdelomar, from Ica, illustrates the contradictory course of that intellectual current: He was assigned to a consular post in Italy during the brief presidency of Billinghurst, was made secretary to José de la Riva Agüero later, and finally became an adherent of Leguía. Because of his dandy-like eccentricities—he called himself the "Count of Lemos"—many did not take him seriously. He and his entire group were seen as mere snobs, fans of "tourism" in the "artificial paradises" of "opium and chloroethyl."[119] His style was actually a strategy to draw attention to a new character, that of the writer—neither a scholar nor a "thinker" of the elite, but an individual of a different origin, although not exactly from the lower classes either. At a time when the "middle class" had a rather virtual existence—in a country where a common goal of aspiring but disadvantaged people was to reach the category of *gente decente*[120]—the so-called *colónidos* made their way on the basis of their education, creativity, and critical spirit, in a context in which the universe of readers was expanding and, with it, the relevance of the written word.[121] These were the unmistakable signs of an intellectual revolt that the *leguiísta* operators were quick to pick up on.

Valdelomar aspired to create a "sort of intellectual federation, with the best elements from all of Peru," whose objective would be to create a *patria nueva* (a new homeland). To that end, he undertook an unprecedented eighteen-month tour across the country. His presence caused "true delirium" in the cities he visited. His aspirations, however, were cut short by his early death, in 1919, four months after the start of the *leguiísta* regime he had helped inspire. "The *patria nueva*—Valdelomar had written—whose silhouette already appears on the misty horizon . . . that does not perish, that is immortal."[122]

His legacy would be carried on by young people who, like Valdelomar, were searching for a political alternative, drawing on literature and journalism, including Luis E. Valcárcel in Cuzco, Gamaliel Churata in Puno, Antenor Orrego in Trujillo, Enrique López Albújar in Piura, and Francisco Mostajo in Arequipa. In Lima, José Carlos Mariátegui, César Falcón, and Félix del Valle went vertiginously from being bohemian chroniclers to being founders of left-wing journalism in Peru, in a context shaped by social mobilization driven by the growing economic deterioration. Together, these *colónidos* developed an alternative vision of the country that bore fruit in the following decade. None of the already existing parties could accommodate this intellectual ferment.

Their appreciation of the masses, and of their Andean or African ancestors, is an essential element of their vision of the country. Ranging from a discussion of Rumi Maqui to the procession of the Lord of Miracles, the chronicles of Juan Croniqueur—the pseudonym of José Carlos Mariátegui—appear as the seed of a different perspective, one that the magazine *Amauta* tried to articulate in the 1920s.[123] Those chronicles were also the basis for a critique of the present that gradually shifted from humor to ideology. It was inevitable that links with the worker and student mobilizations that had punctuated the Aristocratic Republic would emerge. This dynamic brought about a convergence of old radicals, veterans of the *billinghurista* movement, sympathizers of anarcho-syndicalism, progressive lawyers, and defenders of the Indigenous cause.

Catapulted by his participation as an intermediary between the labor movement and the government in the fight for the eight-hour day, the student delegate Víctor Raúl Haya de la Torre activated the Universidad Populares González Prada, a program of night classes for workers organized by the Federation of Peruvian Students. In the magazine *Germinal*, individuals such as Hildebrando Castro Pozo, Erasmo Roca, and

Jorge Guillermo Leguía outlined a kind of left-wing *leguiísmo*, headed by German Leguía y Martínez, a former member of the *gonzalespradista* circle and cousin of Augusto B. Leguía. From the 1914 exclamation "We want a homeland!" to the *patria nueva* slogan of 1919, an anti-oligarchic stance had displaced the "regenerationism" of the *novecentistas*, opening a still formless space that the *leguiístas* would seek to use in their favor: convincing, co-opting, and many times intimidating.

In 1917, Leguía was feared or respected, but he was not seen as a presidential alternative. The mediocrity of the José Pardo administration and the appointment of Aspíllaga as a candidate, however, helped to make Leguía's candidacy viable. As early as 1914, José Matías Manzanilla had indicated two reasons *civilismo* could not be perceived as a valid electoral option for 1919: its reluctance to incorporate "fresh elements" into its ranks and a policy of alliances that confined it to amalgamating with "deteriorated political elements." This was in sharp contrast to the pragmatic Leguía, who, from London, seemed to read the local reality better than his competitors in Peru. Distance also did not prevent him from making his presence felt in Peru. For example, he was named by the student union as a "Master of the Youth" (*maestro de la juventud*) in February 1919. What intellectual merits did the businessman from Lambayeque have to deserve that distinction?

It is possible to trace the process by which the *leguiístas* sought to give their candidate a progressive or center-left image by reading *El Tiempo*, the voice of *leguiísmo* during 1918. With the invaluable help of Mariátegui, Falcón, and Del Valle, the newspaper portrayed the critical situation in the country: the quasi-insurgent violence in the rural areas, the weakness of government authorities in the face of the power exercised by the landlord or *gamonal*, and the growing convergence of the popular movement and the political-intellectual vanguard. A new axis of political action and a new consensus around the need for a "very radical change" was emerging, according to *Variedades*. It was clear that a "simple change of buttocks in the government seat" was not going to be enough to "substantially modify national life."[124]

Although the Great War, and the disruptions to global trade that it initially caused, had initially hobbled Peru's increasingly export-oriented economy, demand for its export commodities produced a significant war dividend for Peru's elites. By contrast, war-induced inflation (some imported, some a product of the reassignment of land previously used for domestic-use agriculture to export production) and stagnating wages contributed to growing social tension and, eventually, open social conflict, including a general strike in late 1918. President Pardo responded with concessions in the shape of new social legislation, including a law regulating work by women and children, and eventually the granting of the eight-hour day, a major demand of the nascent organized working class. But government repression of a mass movement calling for measures to address the cost of living did little to change the dominant perception that neither Pardo nor the *civilistas* could deliver for this sector of the population.

Thus, the arrival of Leguía before a "fresh" electorate allowed him to compensate for his well-known personal "hatefulness" and gave "massive heat" to his candidacy. Aspíllaga, the candidate of the Partido Civil, meanwhile, was losing support even among his friends of "the highest social category." It was the opinion of *Variedades* that "even if he achieved a high percentage of the votes, Aspíllaga could not succeed," because such a victory would be the expression of an unacceptable "political lie."[125]

As early as 1918, as Jorge Basadre points out, the signs of Leguía's "imminent and sensational political resurrection" had started "to become evident."[126] Hence, his status as the incarnation of anti-*civilismo* outweighed the memory of the outrages of his first government. This was a sentiment clearly expressed by an anonymous writer in a letter sent from London in 1917: "We need a man who leads a bloody reaction that destroys everything that currently exists," including *civilismo*.[127] This was the same anger evident in the *pierolista* demonstrations—when passing by the residences of the *civilista* leaders, they chanted "Montoya! Montoya!," the name of the sergeant who had murdered Manuel Pardo in November 1878—which the Democratic Party had been unable to channel into an effective political alternative. Others preferred to blame nothing less than "the country itself, debased, rotten, already lost the notion of a homeland, without a collective ideal and with no more dynamism than the interest and prosperity of each one."[128]

It is also highly probable that those who perceived the growing labor activism as a threat saw in Leguía's character a guarantee of firmness, an alternative to the infiltration of "nihilistic purulence" from Russia, as it was put by *Variedades*.[129] They trusted, that is to say, in his capacity as a leader, the only one capable of stepping into Piérola's shoes, and in his ability to fight the left, to co-opt activists and absorb the "resentment" of the middle classes even as he relaunched the agro-export program with greater breadth and zeal. By contrast, his competitor, Aspíllaga, was "politically educated within the somewhat contemptuous concepts of his party regarding the value of public opinion."[130]

Thus, the ex-president was received by "enthusiastic crowds" on his stops in Paita, Lambayeque, and Trujillo. Some ten thousand people were there for his arrival in Callao, in addition to the "immense crowd" that awaited him when he got off the train in Lima. But, knowing the traps that could still undermine his victory, and counting on sufficient military support, on July 4, 1919, after all the ballots had been cast, he promoted a preventive coup with which he would manage to attack the nerve center of the system: the Congress of the Republic. The following September, a brand-new Constituent Assembly allowed him to establish the rules of the game, allowing him to govern without major setbacks throughout the next decade. In this way, Leguía accomplished what Billinghurst had been unable to do.

Conclusion

Without needing *montoneras*, instead deploying a political apparatus capable of operating on the new critical sectors of society—the subaltern sectors and the middle classes—Leguía canceled the republican experiment that had emerged from the 1895 uprising. With the support of US capital—which had eluded him in his first administration—he would undertake an important reformulation of the role of the state vis-à-vis society: because of its repressive capacity, it could function as a source of conflict resolution or as a source of perks. Thus, Leguía deployed an unprecedented co-optative capacity aimed at the mobilized middle and lower sectors, at the same time as he reorganized the police force, which he renamed the Guardia Civil del Perú.

Recycled in this way, the Peruvian political system could better face the transition from oligarchic politics to mass politics that the *civilistas* feared so much. In this context, in the absence of parties capable of organizing mass demands, Leguía would find enough space to establish himself as a new brand of caudillo, to make his own the path that Piérola had categorically ruled out in 1899: to be a Peruvian version of the Mexican Porfirio Díaz. And, of course, he was also a less romantic and more purely modernized version of what Piérola himself had claimed to be: President Wiracocha (the name of an Andean divinity that was used as the equivalent of "my lord" in modern times) for consumption in the interior, the "Giant of the Pacific" (the nickname widely used by the pro-*leguiísta* press) in Lima and abroad.

Figure 3.4 Geographical Society of Lima, map of Peru, 1913, published by the government of Guillermo Billinghurst. Source: Sociedad Geográfica de Lima.

Notes

This chapter was translated by Inés Rénique.

1   Manuel González Prada, "Discurso en el Politeama" (1888), in *Pájinas Libres* (Lima: Librería Studium, 1987), 44, 60–67.

2   Ricardo Palma, *Cartas a Piérola sobre la ocupación chilena de Lima* (Lima: Editorial Milla Batres, 1979).

3   Alfonso Quiroz, *Historia de la corrupción en el Perú* (Lima: IEP, 2015), 154.

4   Jorge Basadre, *Perú: Problema y posibilidad* (Lima: Fundación M. J. Bustamente de la Fuente, 2014), 145.

5   William F. Sater, *Andean Tragedy: Fighting the War of the Pacific, 1879–1884* (Lincoln: University of Nebraska Press, 2007), 347.

6   Elsewhere, anti-Chinese violence flared up in areas where the Chilean forces had sacked haciendas, such as in Cañete, where contemporary reports indicate that up to 1,400 Chinese workers were killed.

7   Nelson Manrique, *Campesinado y nación: Las guerrillas indígenas en la guerra con Chile* (Lima: Centro de Investigación y Capacitación, 1981).

8   Carmen McEvoy, "Chile en el Perú: Guerra y construcción estatal en Sudamérica, 1881–1884," *Revista de Indias* 236 (2006): 195–216.

9   Nelson Manrique, *Yawar mayu: Sociedades terratenientes serranas: 1879–1910* (Lima: Instituto Francés de Estudios Andinos and DESCO, 1988), 32.

10 For more information about the *civilista* project, see the chapter by Natalia Sobrevilla Perea in this book.

11 Manrique, *Yawar mayu*, 9; Jorge Basadre, *Historia de la República del Perú* (Lima: Producciones Cantabria S.A.C., 2005), 10:118.

12 Carmen McEvoy, *La utopía republicana: Ideales y realidades en la formación de la culture política peruana (1871–1919)* (Lima: Fondo Editorial PUCP, 1997), 260.

13 Peter F. Klarén, *Nación y sociedad en la historia del Perú* (Lima: IEP, 2004), 248.

14 Rory Miller, "The Making of the Grace Contract: British Bondholders and the Peruvian Government, 1885–1890," *Journal of Latin American Studies* 8, no. 1 (1976): 73–100.

15 Manuel González Prada, "Los partidos y la Unión Nacional (conferencia dada el 21 de agosto de 1898)," in *Horas de lucha* (Lima: PEISA, 1969), 9–38.

16 Basadre, *Historia de la República del Perú*, 10:70.

17 Klarén, *Nación y sociedad en la historia del Perú*, 248.

18 Miller, "The Making of the Grace Contract."

19 Basadre, *Historia de la República del Perú*, 10:93, 100.

20 Quiroz, *Historia de la corrupción en el Perú*, 198.

21 González Prada, "Los partidos y la Unión Nacional," 17.

22 Rosemary Thorp and Geoffrey Bertram, *Perú 1890–1977: Crecimiento y políticas en una economía abierta* (Lima: Fondo Editorial de la Universidad del Pacífico, 2013), 14.

23 Martín Monsalve, "Industria y mercado interno, 1821–1930," in *Compendio de historia económica del Perú*, vol. 4, *Economía de la primera centuria independiente*, ed. Carlos Contreras (Lima: BCRP and IEP, 2020).

24 Manuel Osores, *Conferencia dada en el Ateneo de Lima: Causas económicas de la decadencia de la república y medidas que podían adoptarse para mejorar la situación* (Lima: Imprenta Liberal de F. Masías y Compañía, 1886).

25 Alejandro Salinas, "Las finanzas públicas entre 1821 y 1930," in *Compendio de historia económica del Perú*, vol. 4, *Economía de la primera centuria independiente*, ed. Carlos Contreras (Lima: BCRP and IEP, 2020), 398.

26 Salinas, "Las finanzas públicas entre 1821 y 1930," 399.

27 Salinas, "Las finanzas públicas entre 1821 y 1930," 399. On the Atusparia rebellion, see Mark Thurner, *From Two Republics to One Divided: Contradictions of Postcolonial Nationmaking in Andean Peru* (Durham, NC: Duke University Press, 1997). On the salt "war" in Huanta, see Patrick Husson, *De la guerra a la rebellion (Huanta, siglo XIX)* (Lima: Institut Français d'Études Andines, Centro de Estudios Regionales Andinos Bartolomé de Las Casas, 1992).

28 Nelson Manrique, *Historia de la república* (Lima: Fondo Editorial de Cofide, 1995), 77–78.

29 Paulo Drinot, "Peru 1884–1930: A Beggar Sitting on a Bench of Gold?," in *An Economic History of Twentieth-Century Latin America*, vol. 1, *The Export Age: The Latin American Economies in the Late Nineteenth and Early Twentieth Centuries*, ed. Enrique Cárdenas, José Antonio Ocampo, and Rosemary Thorp (London: Palgrave Macmillan, 2000).

30 Jorge Basadre, "Crónica nacional: En torno al Perú de 1900 a 1939," in *Apertura: Textos sobre temas de historia, educación, cultura y política, escritos entre 1924 y 1977* (Lima: Ediciones Taller, 1978), 477.

31 Basadre, *Historia de la República del Perú*, 8:256.

32 Thorp and Bertram, *Perú 1890–1977*, 46.

33 Drinot, "Peru 1884–1930," 155.

34 Drinot, "Peru 1884–1930," 156.

35 Demetrio Salamanca, *Cuestión peruana: Para la historia* (Bogotá: Editorial de El Republicano, 1912), 31–32.

36 Thorp and Bertram, *Perú 1890–1977*, 47.

37 Jorge Dulanto Pinillos, *Nicolás de Piérola* (Lima: Cia. de Impresiones y Publicidad, 1947), 56.

38 Partido Demócrata, *Declaración de principios y otros documentos* (Lima: Imprenta y Librerías de B. Gil, 1889).

39 Dulanto Pinillos, *Nicolás de Piérola*, 351.

40 Dulanto Pinillos, *Nicolás de Piérola*, 350.

41 Nils Jacobsen, "Populism Avant La Lettre in Peru: Rebuilding Power in Nicolás de Piérola's Mid-Career, 1884–1895," *Jahrbuch für Geschichte Lateinamerikas / Anuario de Historia de América Latina* 51, no. 1 (2014): 36.

42 Basadre, *Historia de la República del Perú*, 10:151.

43 Nils Jacobsen, "La guerra de la Coalición Nacional, 1894–1895: De las guerras civiles de la etapa caudillista a los movimientos de la sociedad civil," in *Tiempo de guerra: Estado, nación y conflicto armado, siglos XVI–XIX*, ed. Carmen McEvoy and Alejandro Rabinovich (Lima: IEP, 2018), 442.

44 Alberto Ulloa, *Don Nicolás de Piérola: Una época de la historia del Perú* (Lima: Imprenta Santa María, 1949), 296.

45 Ulloa, *Don Nicolás de Piérola*, 297.

46 Basadre, *Historia de la República del Perú*, 11:20.

47 Basadre, *Perú: Problema y posibilidad*, 153.

48 Basadre, *Historia de la República del Perú*, 10:118.

49 Partido Demócrata, *Declaración*, 31.

50 Carlos Contreras and Marcos Cueto, "Caminos, ciencia y estado en el Perú, 1850–1930," *História, Ciências, Saúde-Manguinhos* 15, no. 3 (2008): 635–55.

51 José Luis Rénique, *La batalla por Puno: Conflicto agrario y nación en los Andes peruanos* (Lima: IEP, Sur y Cepes, 2004), 43.

52 Jorge Basadre, *Elecciones y centralismo en el Perú: Apuntes para un esquema histórico* (Lima: Centro de Investigación de la Universidad del Pacífico, 1980), 37–40; Gabriella Chiaramonte, "La redefinición de los actores y de la geografía política en el Perú a finales del siglo XIX," *Historia* 2, no. 42 (2009): 329–70.

53 Pablo Quintanilla Perez-Wicht, "La recepción del positivismo en Latinoamérica," *Logos Latinoamericano* 1, no. 6 (2006): 65–76.

54 Sinesio López, "El estado oligárquico en el Perú: Un ensayo de interpretación," *Revista Mexicana de Sociología* 40, no. 3 (1978): 991–1007.

55 Javier Prado y Ugarteche, *El estado social del Perú durante la dominación española (estudio histórico-sociológico)* (Lima: Imprenta de El Diario Judicial, 1894). See also Víctor Samuel Rivera, "Dios, patria y rey: José de la Riva-Agüero y Javier Prado (1904–1905)," *Araucaria* 12, no. 24 (2010): 218–38.

56 González Prada, "Vigil," in *Pájinas Libres*.

57 José Luis Rénique, *Incendiar la pradera: Un ensayo sobre la revolución en el Perú*, 2nd ed. (Lima: La Siniestra Ensayos, 2018), chaps. 2 and 3.

58 Pedro Dávalos y Lissón, *Diez años de historia contemporánea del Perú, 1899–1908: Gobiernos de Piérola, Romaña, Candamo, Calderón y Pardo* (Lima: Librería e Imprenta Gil S.A., 1930), 205.

59 Jorge Basadre, "Para la historia de los partidos: El desplazamiento de los Demócratas por el civilismo," *Documenta* 4 (1965): 298.

60 Iván Millones Maríñez, "Los caceristas de la República Aristocrática: Composición social, intereses y principios del Partido Constitucional (1895–1919)," *Histórica* 28, no. 2 (2004): 137–72.

61 Justo Tovar Mendoza, "Círculos viciosos de la democracia como antesala de la dictadura: Constitución, dinámica y quiebre del régimen democrático en el Perú: 1895–1919" (PhD dissertation, FLACSO, 2003), 160.

62 Basadre, *Elecciones y centralismo en el Perú*, 65.

63 Basadre, *Elecciones y centralismo en el Perú*, 65.

64 López, "El estado oligárquico en el Perú," 996.

65   Fernando de Trazegnies, *La idea del derecho en el Perú republicano del siglo XIX* (Lima: Fondo Editorial PUCP, 1980).

66   Pedro Planas, *La república autocrática* (Lima: Fundación Friedrich Ebert, 1994), 28.

67   Juan Pedro Paz-Soldán, *Diccionario biográfico de peruanos contemporáneos* (Lima: Librería e Imprenta Gil, 1921), 250.

68   Wilber Alejandro Obregón Hilario, "El porvenir de las razas: El racialismo en el Perú entre los siglos XIX y XX," *Revista Análisis* 51, no. 94 (2019): 81–100.

69   Quoted in Carlos Contreras, *Maestros, mistis y campesinos en el Perú rural del siglo XX* (Lima: IEP, 1996), 3–4.

70   Jorge Alberto Ccahuana Córdova, "¿Educar al indígena? El Partido Civil y los jóvenes reformistas a inicios de la República Aristocrática," *Histórica* 38, no. 1 (2014): 85–127.

71   Manuel Vicente Villarán, "Condición legal de las comunidades indígenas [1907]," in *Páginas escogidas* (Lima: Talleres Gráficos P. L. Villanueva, 1962), 17.

72   Manuel Vicente Villarán, "El factor económico en la educación nacional," in *Estudios sobre educación nacional* (Lima: Librería e Imprenta Gil, 1922).

73   Katya M. Rodríguez Valencia, "Joaquín Capelo: La obra de un ingeniero, sociólogo y luchador social," unpublished manuscript, 2011.

74   Basadre, *Historia de la República del Perú*, 13:49.

75   McEvoy, *La utopía republicana*, 383.

76   Dávalos y Lissón, *Diez años de historia*, 205.

77   Basadre, *Historia de la República del Perú*, 13:51.

78   Paz-Soldán, *Diccionario biográfico*, 27.

79   Augusto B. Leguía, *Un año de gobierno, 1908–1909* (Lima: Imprenta La Actualidad, 1909), 6.

80   Basadre, *Historia de la República del Perú*, 12:214.

81   Juan Pedro Paz-Soldán, *El golpe de estado del 29 de mayo* (Lima: Talleres Tipográficos de "La Revista," 1909), 20.

82   José Carlos Marín, "Origen del Partido Civil Independiente (1912)," *Boletín del Instituto Riva-Agüero* 29 (2002): 561–75.

83   Sergio González Miranda, "Guillermo Billinghurst Angulo: Una biografía regional," *Revista de Ciencias Sociales* 9, no. 10 (2000): 4–22.

84   Osmar Gonzales, *Billinghurst, combatiente del desierto salitrero* (Lima: Fondo Editorial de la UNMSM, 2017), 17.

85   Guillermo E. Billinghurst, *La irrigación en Tarapacá* (Santiago de Chile: Imprenta y Librería Ercilla, 1893).

86   Alejandro Salinas Sánchez, *La época del "pan grande": Billinghurst presidente, 1912–1914* (Lima: Seminario de Historia Rural Andina, Fondo Editorial de la UNMSM, 2014), 8.

87   Paz-Soldán, *Diccionario biográfico*, 30.

88   Michael Gonzalez, *Plantation Agriculture and Social Control in Northern Peru, 1875–1933* (Austin: University of Texas Press, 1985), chap. 3.

89 Rory Miller, "La oligarquía costeña y la República Aristocrática en el Perú, 1895–1919," *Revista de Indias* 48, nos. 182–83 (1988): 551–66. Antero Aspillaga, *Programa de gobierno presentado a la consideración del país por Ántero Aspíllaga, candidato proclamado a la Presidencia de la República por la Asamblea General Extraordinaria del Partido Civil* (Lima: Tipografica "El Lucero," 1911), 9.

90 Aspíllaga, *Programa de gobierno*, 9, 10, 12

91 Aspíllaga, *Programa de gobierno*, 12–14.

92 Luis Torrejón, *Rebeldes republicanos: La turba urbana de 1912* (Lima: Fondo Editorial PUCP, Fondo Editorial de la Universidad del Pacífico, and IEP, 2010), 153–54.

93 Gonzales, *Billinghurst, combatiente del desierto salitrero*, 145.

94 Peter F. Klarén, *Formación de las haciendas azucareras y orígenes del APRA* (Lima: IEP, 1976): 84; Alberto Flores Galindo, *Los mineros de la Cerro de Pasco, 1900–1930* (Lima: Fondo Editorial PUCP, 1974), 56–57.

95 Joaquín Díaz A., *Luchas sindicales en el valle de Chicama* (Trujillo: Librería Star, 1978), 30–31.

96 Basadre, *Elecciones y centralismo en el Perú*, 55.

97 Víctor Andrés Belaúnde, *Trayectoria y destino: Memorias* (Lima: Ediciones de Ediventas, S. A., 1967), 1:87.

98 *La opinión pública del Perú y el movimiento del 4 de febrero de 1914* (Lima: Imprenta Americana, 1916), 6, 19.

99 Víctor Peralta, "Un científico en la política peruana: Mariano H. Cornejo, la República Aristocrática y la patria nueva, 1895–1920," *Revista Complutense de Historia de América* 27 (2001): 163–89.

100 *La opinión pública del Perú y el movimiento del 4 de febrero de 1914*, 16–17.

101 *Variedades* 316 (1914): 4.

102 *Variedades* 316 (1914): 9.

103 *Variedades* 316 (1914): 11.

104 *Variedades* 316 (1914): 17.

105 Klarén, *Nación y sociedad en la historia del Perú*, 280.

106 *Mensaje del ex presidente constitucional del Perú, Guillermo Billinghurst a la nación, Arica, 31 de octubre de 1914* (Santiago de Chile: La Imprenta Diener, 1915), 76.

107 *Mensaje del ex presidente*, 7.

108 *Mensaje del ex presidente*, 66.

109 *Mensaje del ex presidente*, 281.

110 Francisco García Calderón, *El Perú contemporáneo* (Lima: Fondo Editorial del Congreso del Perú, 2001).

111 Belaúnde, *Trayectoria y destino*, 2:458–59.

112 Belaúnde, *Trayectoria y destino*, 1:402.

113 Belaúnde, *Trayectoria y destino*, 2:403.

114 Pedro Planas, *El 900: Balance y recuperación* (Lima: CITDEC, 1994).

115 Luis Loayza, *Sobre el novecientos* (Lima: Hueso Húmero Ediciones, 1990).

116 Basadre, *Historia de la República del Perú*, 13:182.

117 José Pardo, "Memoria de José Pardo" (manuscript). I am grateful to Carmen McEvoy for giving me access to this important document.

118 Eva María Valero Juan, "El grupo Colónida y la 'herejía antinovecentista,'" *Arrabal*, nos. 5–6 (2007); *Variedades* 428 (1916): 616–48.

119 *Variedades* 428 (1916): 616–48. On the spread of an "opium culture" in early nineteenth-century Lima, see Fanni Muñoz, *Diversiones públicas en Lima, 1890–1920: La experiencia de la modernidad* (Lima: Red para el desarrollo de las Ciencias Sociales en el Perú, 2001), 154ff.

120 David S. Parker, "Discursos, identidades y la invención histórica de la clase media peruana," *Debates en Sociología* 22 (1997): 99–112.

121 José Deustua and José Luis Rénique, *Intelectuales, indigenismo y descentralismo en el Perú, 1987–1931* (Cuzco: Centro de Estudios Rurales Andinos Bartolomé de las Casas, 1984), chap. 1.

122 José Luis Rénique, *Imaginar la nación: Viajes en busca del verdadero Perú (1881–1932)* (Lima: IEP, 2019), chap. 6.

123 José Luis Rénique, "De literati a socialista: El caso de Juan Croniquer," in *El hombre y los Andes: Homenaje a Franklin Pease G.Y.*, vol. 1, ed. Javier Flores and Rafael Varón (Lima: Fondo Editorial PUCP, 2002).

124 *Variedades* 570 (1919): 78.

125 *Variedades* 570 (1919): 77–78.

126 Basadre, *Historia de la República del Perú*, 14:15.

127 Quiroz, *Historia de la corrupción en el Perú*, 164.

128 *Variedades* 531 (1918): 417.

129 *Variedades* 516 (1918): 51.

130 *Variedades* 518 (1918): 110.

Fictitious Progress?

Mass Politics and "Integration" in Peru (1919–1968)

In 1919 Peru was a sparsely populated and largely agrarian society. The population of Peru—relatively large country, though its borders were far from being clearly defined—stood at no more than 4 million people. The biggest city, the capital, Lima, had only 172,000 inhabitants. Other major cities, such as Arequipa, Cuzco, and Trujillo, had populations of 35,000, 18,500, and 10,000, respectively. A minority of the population, therefore, lived and worked in urban environments. Of those, a small proportion worked in industrial establishments or workshops. Most worked in nonindustrial sectors, in particular women, who made a living as domestic servants, market sellers, or washerwomen. Outside the cities, wage work (and forms of semi-coercive labor, such as *enganche* [debt peonage]) was concentrated in various export-oriented industries, such as mining and wool production in the highlands and, on the coast, sugar and cotton, which typically were grown on haciendas of significant size, including the giant Casa Grande estate in La Libertad. In the far north, near the border with Ecuador, a fledgling oil industry employed a small workforce. In the Amazon jungle, an important rubber production industry, though much diminished since the collapse of rubber prices in 1910, concentrated a workforce that depended in most cases on debt peonage and in some cases on the enslavement of Indigenous populations.[1] However, the majority of the population did not work in cities, in mines, or on sugar estates but rather on land that they owned, often collectively, or rented: They were subsistence farmers.

In 1968, when Juan Velasco Alvarado initiated his "peculiar" revolution, the Revolutionary Government of the Armed Forces, Peru was very different.[2] Two major demographic processes shaped the intervening period: a demographic transition and mass rural-to-urban migration. By 1968, the national population had tripled to circa 12–13 million thanks to significant drops in child mortality and expanded life expectancy. The country maintained a large agricultural sector, but because of several decades of sustained rural-to-urban migration and lower mortality rates in the cities, particularly among children, more people now lived in cities than in the countryside (circa 7.5 million versus 5.5 million in 1970). By 1972, the population of Lima now stood at 800,000. Moreover, Peru's population no longer was as intimately tied to agricultural labor as in the past, with a growing proportion of the population employed in new industries, such as the rapidly expanding fish meal industry on the coast, or in the service sector (both private and public), where women had become an important part of the workforce. By 1970, slightly less than half of the population was employed in agriculture. In short, in terms of both where people lived and the sort of work they did, during the period covered in this chapter Peru ceased to be a primarily agrarian society and became a primarily if not exclusively urban society.

Politically, too, the country changed dramatically. In 1919, the population that was politically enfranchised was tiny and consisted exclusively of men of property who could read and write. Fewer than 200,000 people, all male, participated in the 1919 elections. By contrast, over 2 million people, or ten times as many (the overall population only increased by a factor of three), took part in the 1962 and 1963 elections. The fact that women gained the right to vote in 1956 accounts for much of this increase. Still, a large proportion of the population, primarily rural and Indigenous, remained disenfranchised because of the literacy requirement. Equally dramatic was the change in the nature of politics, from elite to mass. The 1919 elections, which witnessed the emergence of popular sectors, particularly urban workers, as key political actors, marked the end of the so-called Aristocratic Republic, when the oligarchic Partido Civil dominated politics.[3] Although President Augusto B. Leguía eventually repressed the popular politics that swelled up in the 1910s and 1920s and helped him to power in 1919, by the 1930s Peruvian politics entered a new phase. The 1931 elections brought to the fore new political forces, in particular the Alianza Popular Revolucionaria Americana (APRA, American Popular Revolutionary Alliance) and the Unión Revolucionaria (UR), which sought to represent the country's urban working and middle classes and, to a lesser extent, rural actors. The rest of the period, historians agree, would be marked by attempts by both the oligarchy and the military to contain these forces. However, as I suggest in this chapter, this is not the whole story.

In 1923, José Carlos Mariátegui, Peru's foremost intellectual of the twentieth century, noted: "The new generation feels and knows that the progress of Peru will be fictitious, or at least it will not be Peruvian, as long as it is not driven by and does not mean the well-being of the Peruvian masses, which are four-fifths Indigenous and peasant."[4] This is a central theme of this chapter. Between 1919 and 1968, how to match national progress with the well-being of Peru's Indigenous peasantry became a key concern. Both authoritarian and democratic governments (and right-wing and left-wing intellectuals) promoted various forms of *indigenismo*, broadly understood as projects of cultural and economic uplift and, more generally, "integration," to address the perceived backwardness of "the Indian" in order to increase his (less often her) contribution to the nation—or, as some military reformers saw it, to reduce the threat that he could pose to it. These projects conflated the well-being of the Indigenous peasantry with its "de-indigenization" or *mestizaje*. The useful Indian was the Indian who had become a mestizo. These were economic and cultural but also *racial* projects. To some extent, these policies had their desired effect, with, for example, both military conscription and the expansion of primary education increasing the proportion of the population who spoke Spanish. But these changes were driven primarily by the demographic and economic forces that transformed Peru from an agrarian society into a post-agrarian one.

As this suggests, Mariátegui understood—or, at least, chose to define— "progress" in a manner that contradicted dominant interpretations, which foregrounded economic growth and a particular type of social development that implied the overcoming of the Indigenous character of Peru. In order to account for the extent to which these interpretations were reconciled, it is necessary to study Peru in this period in the context of broader transnational or global changes that reshaped the world. To that end, I have underscored where possible in this chapter the influence of global forces on processes that, often, are considered in isolation because of what is sometimes called "methodological nationalism."[5] Between 1919 and 1968, Peru was swept by a series of waves of global change, marked by the rise of the United States and the Soviet Union and the relative decline of Europe following the First World War, by the Great Depression of the 1930s, by European fascism and corporatism but also Roosevelt's New Deal and the Good Neighbor Policy, by the Second World War and post-war decolonization in Africa, Asia, and the Caribbean (and the concomitant further relative decline of Europe), and ultimately by the Cold War. Alone, these waves of global change do not explain the historical processes that reshaped Peru in this period. But looked at together with—or more precisely, in *their interaction* with—local dynamics, they shed light on the nature of change in the economic, social, political, and cultural spheres.

The *Patria Nueva*

The First World War marked a major point of inflection in twentieth-century world history. It represented the beginning of a shift of power away from Western Europe toward the United States but also, after 1917, the rise of a new global power, the Soviet Union. In Peru, these shifts were registered in several ways.[6] These global repercussions of the First World War began to undermine the authority of the Partido Civil, an alliance of coastal planters and highland hacendados that had formed in the late nineteenth century to contest the grip of military caudillos on power. Weakened by the war with Chile, the alliance regained power after the civil war in 1895, relinquishing it briefly during the Guillermo Billinghurst government (1912–14), but otherwise succeeded in establishing an export-oriented economy and an exclusionary political and social order. However, the "Aristocratic Republic" began to unravel in the wake of the war. In 1918–19, Peru was caught in the "Red wave" that swept the world. Inflation, together with the impact of the global "Spanish" flu pandemic, led to labor unrest as well as growing social unease among the middle class, which the previous year had been shaken by the winds of university reform emanating from the Argentine city of Córdoba. Faced with popular unrest, President José Pardo felt compelled to react with measures such as an eight-hour-day law and food price controls. At least initially, as I discuss below, the government of Augusto B. Leguía (1919–30), established with the support of the military after the new president claimed that the Partido Civil tried to steal the 1919 election, sought to channel these forces, both discursively, by presenting itself as championing the interests of the working class, and through the implementation of limited social reforms.[7]

At the same time, the rise of the United States as a major political and economic power was reflected in Peru in the growing importance of US investment, particularly in mining, with the giant Cerro de Pasco Corporation in the central highlands, but also in the sugar industry, where the W. R. Grace Company became increasingly dominant, and the oil sector, where the International Petroleum Company, a subsidiary of Standard Oil, edged out smaller competitors. This expansion of US capital pushed out local capitalists, leading to a denationalization of key economic sectors. The United States also emerged as an increasingly important market for Peruvian exports and as a source of manufactured imports. These developments displaced European countries and particularly Britain as Peru's main trading partners. The United States also displaced Britain as Peru's main source of capital, a process that began at the turn of the century but accelerated in the 1920s as the Leguía regime took advantage of the "Dance of the Millions," a period of cheap international credit, to raise loans on Wall Street. However, the United States' growing importance to Peru was not only economic: As its geopolitical power grew in the so-called Wilsonian moment, the United States became the undisputed regional diplomatic arbiter. This proved to be the case in the resolution of border disputes with Chile over the provinces of Tacna and Arica in 1929, an unresolved legacy of the War of the Pacific (1879–83). This shift had begun as early as the 1900s, and in the 1920s it accelerated markedly.

Some historians paint Leguía as the expression of a particular sector of the elite, more oriented toward financial or industrial capital than traditional landholding.[8] But such distinctions are difficult to sustain. Although he presented himself as an alternative to the landed elites represented by the divided and weakened Partido Civil, Leguía did not fundamentally challenge their economic power.[9] Some of the policies that he pursued, such as road building and irrigation projects, as well as public health policies (such as the yellow fever eradication campaigns on the northern coast that made possible the mass migration of workers from the highlands of Cajamarca to the sugar haciendas of La Libertad), were of benefit to their business interests. Such measures, of course, were often deployed selectively, with the goal of obtaining consent and compliance.[10] More generally, the distinction between landowning and industrial elites is complicated by the fact that major landowners, such as the Pardo and Aspíllaga families, often boasted a diversified portfolio of investments that ranged from agriculture to finance and industry. True, some members of the business elite, such as the Prado family or immigrant family business groups concentrated in Lima, particularly Italian and German in origin (the Brescia and Wiese families, for example), had no real base in agriculture—their investments were focused in banking, insurance, and services, as well as manufacturing and commerce. But this did not make them an industrial elite, let alone a bourgeoisie that challenged the landed elite.

In the south, a collapsing wool economy weakened the landowning and commercial elites. Some, seeking diversification of their assets, invested in manufacturing. But, again, these elites were far from constituting an industrial class.[11] The Chuquibambilla *granja modelo* in Puno, a state-backed initiative promoted by the British-owned Peruvian Corporation to improve the productivity of the wool industry, was established in 1921. However, the Chuquibambilla farm found limited support from the southern elites, including local landowners, who were disappointed to find that state support was aimed at the foreign company rather than at them, and particularly the commercial elites based in Arequipa, who viewed the modernization of the wool industry as conceived by the Peruvian Corporation as a threat to their interests.[12] As this suggests, Leguía's conception of "progress" did not necessarily align with that of the landed elites, but this does not mean that he acted in favor of the interests of an industrial bourgeoisie against landowners. In short, in his second term as president, known as the Oncenio, Leguía acted to protect his interests, not those of his class, and hollowed out the *civilista* political order (he had few qualms about imprisoning or exiling its leaders) while not fundamentally challenging the economic or social order.

It is tempting to view Leguía's rise to power as mirroring that of Hipólito Yrigoyen in Argentina and Arturo Alessandri in Chile, who represented the rise of mesocratic and popular sectors against recalcitrant elites. But Leguía did not seek to base his legitimacy in the urban middle and working classes. Though they grew in size and influence in this period, they remained weaker than their Argentine and Chilean counterparts. The passage of Law 4916, the Law of the *Empleado*, in 1924 extended some protection to white-collar workers (in cases of dismissal, death, and illness or injury), but it also reinforced paternalistic relations in the workplace. *Empleados* may have felt some degree of gratitude toward Leguía for the passage of the law. But its significance owes more to how it codified in law differences between *empleados* and *obreros* that, as David Parker argues, reflected deep-seated notions of status. These were notions shaped by the idea of decency that, in the Peruvian context, was deeply racialized. In Peru, white- and blue-collar workers were not simply different types of workers; they were different types of human being.[13] Rather than build a base of support among white- and blue-collar workers, the effect of Leguía's Law of the Empleado was to sharpen the division that already existed between the middle and the working classes, arguably blunting rather than sharpening the potential of these subaltern classes to present a challenge to the social order.

As this suggests, Leguía's autocratic rule relied on his ability to co-opt and neutralize the urban working and middle classes (and, for that matter, the elite), by force if necessary. The reorganization in 1922 of the Guardia Civil, or police force, trained by a Spanish mission, extended the coercive capacity of the state (while undermining the power of the army, which Leguía distrusted). This was true in urban contexts, where it could be used against "common" criminals as well as political ones, and in rural contexts, where "bandits" like Eleodoro Benel, who shot himself to avoid capture by government troops in 1927 in the northern *departamento* of Cajamarca, challenged the state's monopoly of violence.[14] At the same time, Leguía engaged in a type of performative politics as a national redeemer fully engaged in the modernization of the country. The celebrations of the 1921 and 1924 centenaries of independence from Spain provided a perfect opportunity to put this modernization on display for national and international audiences alike. This was particularly the case in Lima, where new monuments (including the monument to José de San Martín), buildings (the national stadium), museums (the Museo Bolivariano, the Museum of Italian Art, and the Museum of Peruvian Culture with its neo-Incan architecture), and avenues (Leguía, Unión, and Progreso) were inaugurated, while new rituals of patriotic significance, such as the creation of the Orden del Sol, awarded for service to the *patria*, were introduced.[15]

More generally, Leguía's performative politics translated into a significant expansion in state investment largely funded by international credit. Debt-financed investment in infrastructure (roads, major irrigation projects, new railways, and aviation), public health (new hospitals, yellow fever campaigns on the northern coast undertaken by the Rockefeller Foundation, and urban sanitation—including the creation of a red-light district in Lima in 1928, intended to support the campaign to limit the spread of venereal disease by medically policing prostitutes), and education (though with limited results) increased significantly in this period. So did the urban growth and modernization of Lima, as the city expanded along new avenues toward the *balnearios* of Miraflores, Barranco, and Chorrillos, resulting in the establishment of new urbanizations, like Santa Beatriz, to house the middle classes. The creation of La Victoria as a new, primarily working-class district in 1920 also corresponded to these urban reforms. These changes occurred in the context of a process of centralization that shifted power from local and regional elites to the central government (with a respective ballooning of the central state bureaucracy). Centralization created extensive discontent in places like Cuzco, Arequipa, and Trujillo, as well as Iquitos, where growing regionalist anger over neglect from Lima in the context of the collapse of the rubber economy and at the start of negotiations with Colombia over the border at Leticia—which resulted in the Salomón-Lozano Treaty—led to a brief federalist rebellion in 1921.[16]

As part of his performative politics of refounding the nation as a *patria nueva* and redirecting it toward a new path of modernization, Leguía embraced, at least discursively, the social politics that came to define many regimes in this period, from Weimar Germany to Callista Mexico, that sought to address to a lesser or greater extent the limits of capitalist industrialization and the social conflict they generated. Peru's 1920 constitution, which drew inspiration from Mexico's 1917 constitution, included a series of provisions that signaled a new social contract. Its "social guarantees" recognized formally the "Indigenous community" as a legal entity and established the state's responsibility to "protect the Indigenous race." At the same time, it created a new normative order that sought to protect labor in the workplace and position the state as the arbiter between labor and capital. The measures extended to granting the state a role in the well-being of the "popular classes." These constitutional innovations created a new legal and institutional framework that both workers and Indigenous people could turn to in their disputes with employers and local power holders. As such, they endowed the state, qua bureaucracy but also qua idea, with new power, which was both concrete and symbolic. The expansion of the state bureaucracy in this period, moreover, created employment for the emerging middle class, in Lima primarily but also elsewhere in the country.

The new social politics—with its claims of social justice enshrined in the constitutional changes and in new state institutions such as the Indigenous Affairs Section and the Labor Section in the Ministry of Development (*fomento*), created to mediate conflicts between Indigenous communities and landowners, on the one hand, and between workers and capitalists, on the other, and the Patronato de la Raza Indígena, a foundation headed by the archbishop of Lima, Monsignor Emilio Lisson, intended to oversee the moral uplift of the Indian—promised more than it delivered, even when, at least initially, they were spearheaded by progressives such as Hildebrando Castro Pozo, a prominent *indigenista*, and Erasmo Roca, an erstwhile anarchist.[17] But the new social politics created new, state-sanctioned mechanisms for contestation that in practice could just as well contain social conflict as inflame it.[18] In the southern highlands for much of the early 1920s, the expectations generated by the rise of Leguía, together with the weakening of local elites that his rise represented, in a context of growing tension sharpened by the collapse of wool prices in 1920 led to a series of peasant uprisings, such as at Tocroyocc and Huancané.[19] Workers, too, took advantage of the new order created by what I have called the "labor state" to organize themselves in unions, and later national union confederations—such as the Federación Obrera Regional del Perú (Peruvian Regional Workers' Federation), modeled on the Argentine Regional Workers' Federation (FORA)—and to use the system of state-supported collective bargaining to bring employers to the negotiation table.[20] Although initially led by anarchists, such as the bakery workers Manuel Carracciolo Levano and Delfín Levano, who rejected any dealings with the state, the small labor movement moved toward more conciliatory anarcho-syndicalist positions by the 1920s.

In the cities, and particularly in Lima, the social politics of the Leguía government reflected an attempt to rein in and "improve" urban cultures. Since the early twentieth century, increasing working-class mobilization for improved wages and living conditions had become, for the elite, a particularly concerning aspect of an otherwise welcome process of urbanization. Reformers viewed with suspicion various locations and forms of socialization associated with the urban poor, such as the *callejón* (the tenement alleyway) and the *fonda* (a type of eatery that typically served alcohol), as well as the *casa de cita* (brothel) and the opium den (which, together with attempts to regulate Chinese medicine and the increasingly popular Chinese restaurants or *chifas*, tapped into strong anti-Chinese racism among the elite and the working class)—and diverse cultural expressions, including the *vals criollo* and the *jarana*, carnival celebrations, religious festivities such as the procession of the Señor de los Milagros, and sports, in particular football. Felipe Pinglo's *vals* "El Plebeyo" expressed in its final verse the social tensions of the time: "Sir, why are people not of equal worth?." In Lima, moreover, these cultural expressions were linked strongly with Afro-Peruvian culture, invariably perceived by reformers as backward. Under Leguía, repression of certain forms of popular socialization went hand in hand with the top-down "modernization" of the city. Contracted out to a US firm, the Foundation Company, this new urbanizing drive expanded the city out to new middle-class neighborhoods along wide boulevards, as already noted. At the same time, the promotion of new forms of socialization in new locations, including public squares marked by a new "monumentality," and the encouragement of new leisure practices, such as the *turf* (horse racing), was intended to contribute to the social uplift of the urban population.[21]

Beyond Lima, and equally central to the new social politics, Leguía's embrace of a sort of "official *indigenismo*" amounted to a philosophical acknowledgment, with limited political effects, that economic and social structures and their representatives, the exploitative *gamonales*, rather than any innate characteristics had "relegated" the "Indian." This position marked a departure from the racial pessimism of some intellectuals of the Aristocratic Republic, who viewed Indigenous people as irredeemable and who still held out the hope that mass European migration could turn Peru into a "California of South America." The new framing of the Indigenous question allowed for the introduction of measures in areas such as education, public health, infrastructure (particularly roads but also aviation), and labor policy, as well as a new penal code (1924) that could rescue the Indigenous population from its backwardness and make it useful to the nation, in ways that echoed similar measures in revolutionary Mexico.[22] The *indigenista* project of the Leguía period, focused on the Indigenous people of the sierra (the Indigenous people of the Amazon continued to be seen as savage and irredeemable), is illustrated, literally and figuratively, in a series of paintings that the artist Camilo Blas prepared for the Dirección de Enseñanza Indígena of the Ministerio de Instrucción in 1930. It is unclear whether these paintings, which were obviously intended to be turned into posters that would be distributed widely, were actually used. However, their very existence is instructive. Consisting of panels that in all but one case show a before and an after, with text in Spanish, Quechua, and Aymara, they depict ideas about how changes in behavior would result in the improvement of the Indian family.

One of Blas's paintings includes an upper panel that depicts an Indigenous family sitting on the ground in front of a rustic house with a thatched roof. The caption reads: "I must not live in a single hut that serves as living quarters for my family and my animals." The lower panel depicts the same family, with other family members, in front of a much larger house, with a tiled roof and an animal pen to the right of the house. The caption reads: "An educated and aspiring Indian has at least one room to sleep in, one room to eat in, and one room to store his crops." In another two-panel painting, the upper panel shows an Indigenous man and woman sitting on the floor eating a meal with their hands. In the lower panel, a group of men and women are represented sitting at a table eating with cutlery. The caption reads: "This is how we should eat to be equal with our *misti* [white] brothers and sisters." A single-panel painting shows an Indigenous man bathing in a waterfall. The caption reads: "The Indian who bathes is strong and agile for work. It is necessary to bathe!" Another painting evokes the infamous Ley de Conscripción Vial, which compelled Indigenous men to provide labor for public works, in particular road building. In the upper panel it depicts an Indigenous couple walking behind three llamas and a donkey. The caption reads: "If we don't build roads, we have to carry the products of our agriculture ourselves, like llamas and donkeys." The lower panel depicts a road with two trucks carrying several people. The caption reads: "Let's build roads! Let's pool our money and buy a truck for the Ayllu [Indigenous community]—let's gladly comply with the Ley Vial."

Leguía's "official" *indigenismo*, as expressed in Blas's paintings, found particular support in one field of knowledge and practice: archaeology. Under the leadership of Julio C. Tello, the Oncenio saw the development of a new nationalist and *indigenista* archaeology, which, as it did in revolutionary Mexico at the same time, though to a lesser extent, served to construct a new sense of national self-worth. Supported financially by Leguía, Tello, who had studied in the United States and Europe, began to promote a type of engagement with the past that celebrated Peru's Indigenous cultures. Indeed, he celebrated his own identity as an Indian, calling himself "the Indian Tello." When he opened Peru's first museum of archaeology in 1924, Tello "emphasized the importance of guarding 'the sacred ashes of our fathers' and of understanding a country of 'children of Indigenous mothers.'"[23] At the same time, as a member of Congress, Tello tried to pass legislation to "improve" Peru's Indigenous population, promoting literacy and targeting alcoholism—a program clearly in line with the *indigenismo* expressed in Camilo Blas's posters. We see reflected in Tello the tensions at the heart of much *indigenista* rhetoric and practice: a celebration of an idealized past and a view of the Indigenous present as a problem to be overcome. This was an idea at the center of several creole national projects in the nineteenth and twentieth centuries, projects that reflected a view of the Indian's role in the nation that historian Cecilia Méndez compellingly conveys in the phrase "Incas sí, indios no."[24]

In practice, the *indigenista* measures that the Leguía regime introduced did little to challenge the social order in the highlands or the Amazon, or the relegated status of "the Indian." But, together with the discursive shift they represented, they created a space in which a more radical form of

No debo vivir en una sola choza. que sirve de habitación a mi familia y a mis animales.

Mana allinmi juc chchucllallapi liyay, alccohuan, michi-
huan, ccoe, huallpahuan, millay tantanascca.

Jahniwa ma utana utjañati, wankuh, phihssi
anukara chica iqiñalaqi.

Un indio educado y aspirante tiene cuando menos: una habitación para dormir, otra para comer, y otra para almacenar sus cosechas.

Allin, chchuya causayniyocc runacca, sapace qquilipin puñuna huasin, sapas
pin tacquen mijuna runata, sapaccpitacomi huayckuna cckoncha huasin.

Kehllkahña yatqisa uca jahkehja, mayjama jahkaña munjehja: ma uta iqiñalaqi, ma
uta mankahnalaqi, iskahula phayañalaqi, ma jahchula, yapuchatanaca imañalaqi.

Figure 4.1 Camilo Blas, poster design promoting upgraded housing for the Directorate of Indigenous Education of the Ministry of Education, 1930. Source: Museo
de Arte de Lima.

Figure 4.2 Camilo Blas, poster design promoting the use of cutlery for the Directorate of Indigenous Education of the Ministry of Education, 1930. Source: Museo de Arte de Lima.

Figure 4.3 Camilo Blas, poster design promoting bathing for the Directorate of Indigenous Education of the Ministry of Education, 1930. Source: Museo de Arte de Lima.

Si no hacemos caminos carreteros tenemos que cargar nosotros mismos, como burros y llamas, los productos de nuestra agricultura.

Millay ñancuna cajetinmi, huyhua quiquillan qquepinchis orccon ckkasanta alpaspa.

Jahnilī thāhqi maqina sarañatāqi lurcañani ucaja, jihwas quipca asnu, kjaura chica kjehpiscañani yapuchatanacasa.

Hagamos caminos carreteros! Juntemos nuestro dinero y compremos un camión para el Ayllu.— Cumplamos con gusto la Ley Vial.

"Vial" nisca camachicuyta cusi sonceo juntasun.—Chaypachan allin ñancuna caclin, "camión" nisccapi purisun checcac ccjapac runa jina.

Aywthahpthahsjañani kohllkjeh tantāsiñatāqi, ucampi "camiona" alasisina kjusa thahqina sarnakahñasatāqi.—Acatāqi "Vial" Jihliri churksitu ucaja lurañawa.

Figure 4.4 Camilo Blas, poster design promoting roads and motorized transportation for the Directorate of Indigenous Education of the Ministry of Education, 1930. Source: Museo de Arte de Lima.

indigenismo could develop. This radical *indigenismo* could be top-down and intellectual, centered on urban contexts such as Lima, Cuzco, and Puno, where groups such as the Asociación Pro Derecho Indígena, led by Pedro Zulen and Dora Mayer (who, drawing inspiration from Manuel González Prada's own proselytizing *indigenismo*, denounced the exploitation of Indians by companies like the Cerro de Pasco Corporation), intellectuals such as Luis Valcarcel and José Uriel García, artists such as the painters José Sabogal and Julia Codesido and the photographer Martín Chambi, and publications such as *Boletín Titikaka*, *La Sierra*, and others celebrated a new idealized but dignifying notion of the Indian. See, for example, Sabogal's 1925 painting of the Varayoc of Chinchero, which presents the subject of the painting in a dignified manner. At the same time, these groups called for measures to redeem the Indian that, in practice, echoed the regime's rhetoric.[25]

This radical *indigenismo*, on the other hand, could also be more bottom-up and largely rural, as occurred with the establishment of the Comité Pro-Derecho Indígena (CPDI) and its many subcommittees spread out across the southern highlands. Though initially supported by Leguía, the CPDI evolved into a social movement of Indigenous leaders that used the new constitutional and legal framework to challenge local power holders such as *gamonales* and the church, as well as agents of the state, such as the organizers of the *leva* (forced military conscription) and the Conscripción Vial.[26] In the central Amazon, moreover, the collapse of the rubber economy in the 1910s had already resulted in overt, and often violent, challenges to the (equally violent) social order imposed by white colonists and missionaries from Indigenous groups such as the Asháninkas and Piros, who mobilized to end their oppression and to bring about a new era.[27]

If Leguía's "official" *indigenismo* had to contend with the challenge posed by more radical forms of *indigenismo*, his social politics as a whole came up against the challenge of two major figures and movements: José Carlos Mariátegui and socialism, on the one hand, and Víctor Raúl Haya de la Torre and APRA, on the other. A troublesome but brilliant bohemian journalist exiled in 1919 by Leguía, Mariátegui returned to Peru in 1923 after four years in France and Italy principally, where he saw up close the growth of the Italian labor movement and the Italian Communist Party (he attended the founding conference in Livorno in 1921) as well as the rise of fascism. In Peru, Mariátegui returned to his journalistic labors, writing regularly on a broad range of topics for magazines, such as *Variedades* and *Mundial*, that targeted the small upper class and the growing middle class, and quickly established himself as Peru's major intellectual figure of the left. At the same time, he created strong links with the country's small urban labor movement (and, in the later 1920s, with the miners of the central highlands) thanks initially to his stewardship of the Universidades Populares González Prada (a program of night classes for workers set up by the Federation of Peruvian Students in 1921), where he gave a series of talks on the situation in Europe. These links were deepened following the creation of *Labor*, a periodical aimed at workers, and also through personal connections with key figures in the labor movement, such as Julio Portocarrero, a textile worker.

Through the avant-garde cultural magazine *Amauta*, established in 1926, Mariátegui created a unique, and arguably unmatched, space for political and cultural debate in Latin America.[28] His work for *Amauta* not only contributed to his original reinterpretation of Marxism, which he viewed as adaptable to different national circumstances rather than rigid doctrine, but also fed into his materialist understanding of the "Indian question" and more generally into a broader project of establishing a political party of the left that would represent the interests of workers and peasants—the Partido Socialista del Perú was created under his auspices in 1928. These positions resulted in tensions with the Communist International (Comintern), which viewed Mariátegui's heterodoxy with suspicion and disapproval.[29] Although he engaged in correspondence with many key intellectual figures around the world and received visits from workers and Indigenous people in his home in Lima, because of his physical disability (he became a wheelchair user in 1924 after his right leg was amputated), Mariátegui focused his political activism in the capital and particularly on the organization of a new workers' confederation that would overcome what he viewed as the limitations of the older anarcho-syndicalist organizations. Together with a handful of workers, he helped to establish the Confederación General de Trabajadores del Perú (CGTP, General Labor Confederation of Peruvian Workers) in 1930. It would become a key actor in the conflictive labor relations of the early 1930s.

Like Mariátegui, Haya de la Torre originally drew inspiration from Marxism in developing his project of continental *indoamericanismo*, even though he had little to say about, or much to offer to, Peru's Indigenous populations.[30] A middle-class student leader from the northern city of Trujillo, and the key figure of a new generation of provincial intellectuals, including the avant-garde poet César Vallejo, that was beginning to shake up Peruvian cultural life, Haya de la Torre moved to San Marcos University in Lima, where he rose to lead the Federation of Peruvian Students in the wake of the Córdoba university reform movement of 1918. Through his role in the establishment of the Universidades Populares González Prada in Lima and in the nearby textile town of Vitarte, Haya de la Torre became a key link between the student movement and Peru's emerging labor movement, a link that would endure. Initially close to Mariátegui, he arrived at very different conclusions about how to adapt Marxism to Peru and Latin America more generally. Famously, Haya de la Torre viewed imperialism not as the last stage of capitalism, as Lenin argued, but as its first stage. This interpretation, and the implication that Latin America needed to transition to the next stage of capitalism by taking advantage of technological advances while organizing around an anti-imperialist (which is to say anti–United States) platform, owed perhaps to his experience growing up in the northern region of La Libertad, where foreign, and particularly US, capital had gradually displaced local capital in the sugar industry.[31]

Exiled by Leguía in 1923 following his participation in protests against attempts by the president to consecrate Peru to the Sacred Heart of Jesus (a bid to gain the support of the church for his 1924 reelection bid), Haya de la Torre spent the rest of the 1920s traveling in Latin America, the United States, and Europe, where together with several other exiles peppered across cities in the Americas and Europe he built a strong network of "action-led intellectuals." To foreign observers, his stature as a statesman was clear. Carleton Beals, the US journalist, noted "since the death of the great patriot Sandino, [Haya de la Torre] is undoubtedly the outstanding popular figure of Latin America."[32] Haya de la Torre became convinced that little could be expected of the Soviets and that Peru was not ready for socialism. Foregrounding both anti-imperialism and nationalism in his political platform (scholars have noted the influence of the Chinese nationalist party, the Guomindang, in this position) and favoring the construction of a strong interventionist state, Haya de la Torre envisaged the formation of a multiclass movement of workers, peasants, and the middle class, with the middle class at the helm, to lead not only Peru but "Indoamérica" itself into a new phase of economic and political development. The establishment of APRA in 1924 as a hemispheric political movement was intended to be the vehicle of that transformation.

For all that these challenges—the radical forms of *indigenismo*, on the one hand, and Mariátegui and Haya de la Torre, on the other—represented in terms of their political and intellectual innovation, the end of the Leguía regime, which was precipitated by his deeply unpopular attempt at a second reelection in 1929, was prosaic. Like other caudillos before him, Leguía was deposed by a military coup led by a mid-ranking officer, Colonel Luis M. Sánchez Cerro, a mestizo from the northern department of Piura, who had recently returned to Peru after a period spent in Europe in exile for his involvement in coup plots against Leguía in the early 1920s and who headed the Arequipa garrison. Mired in corruption scandals (some of which involved his playboy son Juan), with an economy in free fall because of the Wall Street crash, with regional elites (particularly in the south of the country) increasingly critical of his centralization policies, and having turned the army against him because of the resolution to the Tacna-Arica dispute (and because this branch of the military felt that it had been neglected as Leguía strengthened the Guardia Civil and channeled money and resources into the navy), by the end of his regime Leguía had few friends and supporters.[33] As happened to most caudillos throughout the nineteenth and twentieth centuries, when the end came there was no one there to defend him. A military junta, headed by Sánchez Cerro, overthrew Leguía on August 22, 1930.

Shut out of power for a decade, the traditional elites saw the coup as an opportunity to regain their positions of political influence. But the country had changed in ways that made the forms of rule they had enjoyed in the Aristocratic Republic impossible. The extent to which Peru changed during the Oncenio is a matter for debate. Some historians see a great deal of continuity in the economy while recognizing the growth not only in the size of the state but also in its symbolic presence. Some institutional changes were cosmetic, but others, such as the establishment of the Sección del Trabajo and the Sección de Asuntos Indígenas, marked a point of inflection in how the state interacted with both labor and the Indigenous population, as we have seen. Equally important was the establishment in 1922 of the Banco de Reserva or central bank, modeled on the US Federal Reserve, which became solely responsible for the issuance of fiduciary money (thus ending the issuance of notes by private banks), and the expansion of the role of the Caja Nacional de Depósitos y Consignaciones in 1927, which became solely responsible for levying taxes. Both institutions were decisive for both monetary and fiscal policy and would have lasting influence.[34]

The growth in power of foreign companies such as the Cerro de Pasco Corporation was a particular legacy of the Leguía years. The following decades would be characterized by the growing importance of foreign capital in the Peruvian economy, but it was arguably in Cerro de Pasco that this particular type of foreign investment, deemed essential for economic development, had the most transformative impact at the local level. After poisonous smoke from its smelter at La Oroya all but destroyed agriculture and sheep and cattle production in the neighboring valleys, after 1922 the US company bought up some 200,000 hectares of land cheaply, establishing one of the largest agricultural concerns in Peru, the Division Ganadera.[35] This is one of several examples, yet to be sufficiently studied, of how capitalist growth and environmental devastation have often gone hand in hand in Peruvian history. But the changes of the Leguía years were not only economic; they were political and societal too. *Indigenismo*, both official and radical, placed the "Indian question" on the table, creating the conditions for the sort of progress that Mariátegui envisaged. In Peru, as elsewhere in Latin America and indeed in the world, the 1930s, marked by the impact of the Great Depression on economies and societies, would open, or broaden, the political sphere in ways that marked the end of the elite politics of old and inaugurated a new phase of mass politics.

The Great Depression and Mass Politics

If the 1920s were shaped by the waves that washed over all the world initiated by the ascendancy of the United States following the First World War and by the Russian Revolution of 1917, the 1930s were a decade marked by waves started by the 1929 implosion of Wall Street and the political fallout that the Great Depression created throughout the world. What historian Jorge Basadre parochially if influentially described as the "third militarism" is better understood as part of a global reaction to these new forces shaping the world.[36] At the time, observers read the Great Depression as a crisis of capitalism, perhaps even as its final crisis, which led to the implementation of radical measures in order to save both capitalism and liberalism, as happened with the New Deal in the United States under Franklin D. Roosevelt. At the same time, this sense of systemic crisis created fertile ground for alternative visions of how to organize society and the economy, which both the Soviet Union (and its international agent, the Comintern) and European fascism, as well as Japanese militarism, were quick to exploit. In colonial contexts in Africa and Asia, meanwhile, the economically and politically destabilizing effects of the Great Depression strengthened nationalist and anticolonial movements.

In Latin America, such forces, and particularly European fascism, found eager consumers. Mussolini's blackshirts, Hitler's brownshirts, and

Franco's Falangists were the inspiration to numerous shirted creole fascists: greenshirts in Brazil, goldshirts in Mexico, and even some blackshirts in Peru. In addition to leaving a sartorial imprint, fascism in Peru found willing ambassadors in intellectuals such as the historian and erstwhile mayor of Lima José de la Riva Agüero, described by the US journalist Carleton Beals as an odious and bigoted reactionary, and engendered a fascist party, the Unión Revolucionaria, established by Sánchez Cerro but led from 1933 onward by Luis A. Flores.[37] However, in Peru the deeper impact of these waves was registered not so much in the political triumph of fascism, as happened in much of Europe, but rather in a shift not only in the nature of politics, from elite to mass, but also in the conception of state-society relations, which resulted in a further and arguably more rapid expansion of the symbolic weight of the state, if not always in its actual capacity.[38] And yet, despite the mass disruption of the Great Depression, the basic structure of the Peruvian economy, and therefore the mainstay of its ruling classes, remained little changed, even as the trends that had started to become increasingly visible in the 1920s became clearer still, with the growth of foreign, and particularly US, capital in key export sectors (mining, oil, coastal agriculture) and the further weakening of the economy in the south as wool prices fell.

The Great Depression hit Peru through a balance-of-payments crisis. As prices for Peru's exports collapsed and the loans from US capital markets dried up following the Wall Street crash, Peru found itself unable to service its debt, a situation made worse by capital outflows resulting from US and European investors repatriating their money. In 1931, like much of the world, Peru defaulted and, the following year, left the gold standard (in which Peru had fixed its currency, the Peruvian pound, to gold). This measure bought the country some room for maneuver but also made external financing impossible. Peru's most important bank, the Banco del Perú y Londres, was one of the most visible casualties of the slump. Its collapse impacted the availability of capital for local businesses, particularly for the agro-export sector. Many businesses either went bankrupt or chose to shut down and weather the economic storm. Unemployment in the cities and in the export sectors increased significantly. In some cases, such as at the US-owned Cerro de Pasco Corporation in the central highlands, workers were fired and then rehired at lower wages. In the mines, as on the sugar estates in the north and, particularly, in the industrial and service sectors in the major cities, processes of proletarianization underway since the late nineteenth century meant that in contrast to earlier crises, workers could not easily be reabsorbed into the rural sector.

Fortunately, the Peruvian economy rebounded from the crisis relatively quickly. In contrast to countries more reliant on single export products, such as Chile (copper) and Cuba (sugar), where the slump was deeper and longer, Peru's diversified export sector helped its recovery. Improving prices for exports of cotton and access to cheap fertilizer in the form of guano provided by the Compañía Administradora del Guano (the state monopoly that managed the country's guano reserves) helped the agro-exporters on the coast (with some sugar producers in the central coast switching production to cotton). Meanwhile, growing international demand for minerals such as lead, zinc, and gold, and strong oil exports, also contributed to the recovery.[39] Cotton, in particular, had a positive effect on employment, accounting, according to some estimates, for half of all new employment on the coast.[40] The disruption to imports created by the slump created opportunities for some import substitution in light industries such as textiles, shoes, soap, pharmaceuticals, hats, and paints, and this may have helped employment recover in the cities.[41] Still, despite the relatively quick rebound from the slump, the general economic disruption, both in Peru and globally, created a context that favored social and political unrest.

Faced with worsening working conditions and rising unemployment, workers in several industries resorted to direct action. A series of strikes in the central highlands in late 1930, which affected the mining industry (and which alarmed the US managers of the Cerro de Pasco Corporation, who demanded that the authorities repress the strikers), numerous sectoral strikes in Lima (textiles, bakeries, telephone operators, printers, etc.), and a general strike in Lima in May 1931, which began as a strike of the *colectivos* or taxis, created a sense of unprecedented political tension as attempts at collective bargaining and conciliation through the mechanisms established by the 1920 constitution failed. Believing that the climate of social conflict was a prelude to a revolutionary crisis, the Peruvian Communist Party (PCP), now under the leadership of Eudocio Ravines (who took over after Mariátegui's death in April 1930), sought to turn the labor unrest—through the CGTP, which it controlled—into a political crisis that, in line with Comintern directives, would bring about a mass uprising of workers and peasants. This strategy backfired disastrously. The police and military easily repressed the strikers, and the PCP's leadership was arrested and jailed or exiled. Consequently, the links between the communists and labor, which Mariátegui had carefully developed in the 1920s, were all but broken.[42]

In this context, and despite serious repression after the 1931 elections that eventually drove it underground, APRA was able to make major inroads in the Peruvian labor movement, particularly in Lima and on the northern coast. It adopted what I have called a tactic of "creole anticommunism" to denounce the "adventurism" of the PCP and its attempts to take over, rather than represent, the labor movement.[43] Under the leadership of Arturo Sabroso, a textile worker, the labor wing of APRA developed a strategy toward the labor movement based on relative autonomy for unions with regard to the party. This strategy, which the party newspaper *La Tribuna*—which reached significant circulation numbers, challenging traditional papers such as *El Comercio*—and its worker-journalists did much to publicize, succeeded in establishing a strong and long-lasting connection between organized labor and APRA. Attempts to establish a new *aprista* labor confederation in 1934 proved unsuccessful because of growing repression, but the sense that APRA rather than the communists represented the Peruvian labor movement began to take hold. In the far north, meanwhile, where both the PCP and APRA had a limited presence, the relatively minor and non-insurrectionist Socialist Party of Luciano Castillo gained the support of the oil workers and sharecroppers (*yanaconas*), whom it helped organize into unions. It would be able to count on their support for much of the twentieth century.

Though they may not have brought about a revolution as the communists hoped, the wave of strikes from late 1930 to mid-1931 set the political tone for much of the early 1930s. At least initially, Sánchez Cerro enjoyed some popularity, which he sought to extend by introducing measures that targeted the unpopular Leguía and his supporters, including establishing a Tribunal de Sanción Nacional, which investigated the crimes and corruption of the Leguía period.[44] Imprisoned on the island of San Lorenzo off Callao and later in the Lima Penitenciaría, Leguía died shortly after the coup. Clearly intending to hold on to power, Sánchez Cerro began to antagonize political opponents, in particular members of APRA and the PCP as well as the organized labor movement. However, the other members of the ruling military junta forced Sánchez Cerro to resign the presidency in March 1931. He was replaced by a new junta led by a civilian, David Samanez Ocampo, a landowner from Cuzco. The new government's main task was to prepare for the October 1931 elections. It introduced important electoral reforms such as the secret vote, shifted oversight of elections from provincial to departmental authorities (reducing the capacity of local power holders to stuff ballot boxes), and lifted property qualifications—thus expanding the franchise from about 200,000 persons to about 323,000, even though it was still restricted to literate men. Despite these restrictions to the franchise, the elections produced a type of political mobilization spearheaded by the Partido Aprista Peruano (founded in 1930) and Sánchez Cerro's hastily put-together party, the UR, that marked a departure in the history of Peruvian politics.[45]

The 1931 electoral campaign was highly polarized. Haya de la Torre regularly used anti-imperialist rhetoric in his speeches while secretly reassuring the US ambassador and US companies of his party's moderation, while the UR accused APRA of being supporters of Leguía and unpatriotic. However, the two parties' programs were not very different; both, in essence, promised greater state involvement in the economy and society in order to address the impact of the slump on the country's middle and working classes. In the end, Sánchez Cerro, who had the support of Peru's elites, won the election with 50 percent of the vote. While APRA did well in its northern heartlands and among organized workers and the middle class, Sánchez Cerro was able to capture much of the vote from poorer urban sectors—thanks, in part, to the work of numerous *sanchez-cerrista* electoral clubs that mushroomed in the run-up to the elections—and from much of Peru's southern highland regions as well as his home department, Piura. Although far less charismatic and not as effective an orator as Haya de la Torre—who, in his electoral speech in Lima's bullring, famously declared, "Only APRA can save Peru!"—Sánchez Cerro, nicknamed "El Mocho," proved popular among a large sector of the electorate who saw him as the architect of the downfall of the Leguía dictatorship and its corruption—and of its unpopular policies such as the Ley de Conscripción Vial—and who also identified ethnically with him. APRA, however, claimed that there had been electoral fraud and refused to accept the result. Further polarization resulted. After he took power, in a context of acute political polarization, Sánchez Cerro introduced measures that curtailed freedoms. Meanwhile, convinced that it had been denied power, APRA adopted a putschist strategy, seeking to provoke sectors of the military sympathetic to its cause to depose Sánchez Cerro.

The establishment of a Constituent Assembly, to replace Leguía's 1920 constitution, became one of the key political battlegrounds. Despite acrimonious debate between the majority UR and minority APRA members, and the failure to extend the franchise to the illiterate population, some progressive measures did make it into the 1933 constitution. The social measures of the 1920 constitution pertaining to workers and Indigenous communities were retained and, in some ways, extended.[46] The 1933 constitution, moreover, introduced civil marriage and divorce, though it did not extend the franchise to women. Contra its original position in favor of granting women the vote, APRA now feared that doing so would strengthen the conservative vote, and thus opposed it.[47] The constitution proclaimed Roman Catholicism the official religion but recognized other faiths. With the Catholic Church already concerned about secularization and growing competition from Protestants in parts of the Andes—and, increasingly, by the rise of what it saw as godless Marxism—the constitution jolted the church into playing a more active political role.[48] The 1933 charter had a strong corporatist character, reflective of the corporatist ideas that prevailed in APRA as in the UR and indeed globally in the wake of the Great Depression. It envisaged the establishment of a senate that would represent corporate sectors, such as capitalists and workers, a proposal that APRA had included in its 1931 electoral program. This measure, which chimed with the social politics that the Leguía regime had introduced, was intended to reduce class conflict and encourage national reconciliation, though it was never implemented.

The debate over the extension of the franchise to women reflected the growing political activism of women and the influence, admittedly limited, of feminism in Peruvian political debate in this period. In the first few decades of the twentieth century, women became increasingly politically visible despite a prevailing patriarchal order that worked to domesticate them, as Mariemma Mannarelli has aptly put it.[49] Elite and middle-class women entered the public sphere—as novelists and journalists primarily, or taking on philanthropic causes—to promote the interests of women like themselves, who were trying to leave the home to study and work, and women they viewed as inferior to themselves and whom they sought to redeem, such as the urban poor and prostitutes.[50] In some cases, they did so with a conservative agenda, promoting a maternalist feminism that called for political rights but did not aim to fundamentally disrupt the social order. This was the case of the early feminism of Zoila Aurora Cáceres and María Jesús Alvarado.[51] Others pushed for a more radical agenda, as in the case of the *aprista* Magda Portal and the communist Ángela Ramos, whose demands extended to economic and social rights for women. However, these elite and middle-class women were not alone in shaping gender politics or politics tout court.[52] Mestiza, Indigenous, and Afro-Peruvian women participated actively in shaping the social politics of this period. Historians have examined some key episodes, such as the strikes in Huacho in 1917, when police killed several women protesters, and the extensive participation of women in the protests against the rise in food prices in 1919.[53] But the political participation of lower-class women remains understudied.

Despite introducing some progressive legislative innovation, even if the more radical proposals of Socialist Party and APRA members were watered down, the Constituent Assembly was characterized by a political polarization that mirrored the growing political conflict in the country. Article 53 of the new constitution banned "political parties of international organization," a measure that clearly targeted APRA (and the PCP). In early 1932, Sánchez Cerro forced through an emergency law that in effect gave his government extensive powers to repress political opponents and the labor movement. The twenty-three *aprista* members of the Assembly were arrested and exiled. A few months later, in July, the navy and air force violently put down an improvised armed uprising in Trujillo, led by local APRA militants in expectation of generating a mass national uprising supported by sectors of the military sympathetic to APRA. This event, the "Trujillo Revolution" or "Trujillo Massacre," would become a defining moment in twentieth-century Peruvian history and, as historian Iñigo García-Bryce has argued, in APRA's politics of memory.[54] It proved key to a long-lasting antagonism between APRA and the military hierarchy (APRA would continue to find support from sectors of the armed forces, particularly mid- to low-ranking officers, in the following decades). A little under a year later, on April 30, 1933, a young *aprista* militant assassinated Sánchez Cerro during a military event held at the Santa Beatriz racetrack in Lima.

The choice of General Óscar Benavides, one of the most senior military figures at the time, a military hero from a brief border conflict with Colombia in 1911 and president in 1914–15 (when he overthrew Guillermo Billinghurst), to complete Sánchez Cerro's presidential term following the assassination owed as much to the idea that he was a relatively safe pair of hands as to the threat of all-out war with Colombia that hung over the country. Dissatisfied with the 1922 Salomón-Lozano Treaty, which had handed a trapezoid-shaped portion of the department of Loreto to Colombia, locals from the departmental capital, Iquitos, had taken over the riverine port of Leticia. This had led to a series of skirmishes between the two militaries, including the aerial bombing of Peruvian positions by

Colombian planes.[55] Although some in the Peruvian armed forces were spoiling for a fight, perhaps wisely Benavides chose to pursue peace and convinced Colombian president Alfonso López Pumarejo to sign peace accords in Rio de Janeiro that ratified the 1922 treaty. At home too, at least initially, Benavides opted to pursue a policy of "peace and concord," leading him to free imprisoned *apristas*, including Haya de la Torre, and to name Jorge Prado y Ugarteche, a moderate and member of the powerful Prado family, as his prime minister.

This opening toward APRA was short-lived, however. It exposed Benavides to intense criticism from the right. Both the UR, which, under its new leader, the blackshirt Luis A. Flores, became more overtly fascist in its iconography and discourse, and *El Comercio*, the newspaper owned by the right-wing Miro Quesada family, put pressure on the president to reverse his policy of *apertura*. The replacement of the moderate prime minister Jorge Prado with the fascist sympathizer José de la Riva Agüero in November 1933 did little to appease these voices. Persecution of APRA soon intensified, leading Haya de la Torre, arrested in 1932 but released in 1933, to go into hiding (he would not reemerge until 1945). In any event, APRA soon reverted to its putschist strategy in late 1934 following the cancellation of promised congressional elections, though all its uprisings, in Ayacucho, Huancavelica, Cuzco, and Arequipa, were easily suppressed. A plot that roped in the Bolivian president, David Toro, was also aborted. The assassination of Antonio Miro Quesada, the editor of *El Comercio*, and his wife by an *aprista* militant in May 1935 contributed to a climate of increasing and seemingly irreversible polarization. When it looked like the candidate backed by APRA, Luis Antonio Eguiguren, a former mayor of Lima, would win the 1936 elections, Benavides canceled the elections and dissolved the Assembly—in effect, establishing a dictatorship.

In this context, APRA entered its "catacombs" period, continuing to operate underground, particularly in Lima, while many of its leaders were in exile. But it was far from inactive. There is a tendency in some of the older scholarship to see the sierra—and even more so the Amazon—in this period as outside of history, bypassed by the political processes taking place elsewhere. However, as several historians have shown, in the 1930s APRA gained a significant foothold outside Lima—in the provincial (*departamental*) capitals but also in smaller towns and even villages. For provincial elites and middle-class sectors, and even for some peasants, APRA's messages of social justice, agrarian reform, and decentralization resonated with their own aspirations for changing what they saw as corrupt and unaccountable local and national orders controlled by elites whose time was up. From Cajamarca and Chachapoyas, in the north, to Tarma, in the central highlands, to Ayacucho, in the south, historians have traced the ways in which provincial and local politics were reconfigured by the presence of APRA in this decade, albeit local versions of APRA with a significant degree of autonomy with regard to the leadership in Lima or exile.[56] Cuzco had a strong communist presence in the 1920s; its influence waned in the 1930s but was not fully extinguished and would resurface in later decades.[57] In Piura, the Socialist Party of Luciano Castillo and Hildebrando Castro Pozo played a similar role among the *yanaconas* of that *departamento's* highlands.[58] Far from the sierra being bypassed by the political developments occurring in Lima and the coast, new forms of political contestation and projects of social change profoundly reshaped the Peruvian sierra in this period in ways that had long-lasting consequences.

Benavides took power at a time when the worst effects of the Great Depression were beginning to wane. In late 1930, the US economist Edwin W. Kemmerer, who became an advisor to several Latin American countries in the wake of the slump, arrived in Peru to advise the Samanez Ocampo junta. Although governments in the 1930s largely followed orthodox economic policies in line with Kemmerer's recommendations, they also deviated (for example, on the gold standard) and innovated to some extent.[59] To address the lack of access to international credit, the Samanez Ocampo junta created an Agricultural Bank to provide credit to agro-exporters, particularly cotton planters, and this placed the planters in a strong position when international cotton prices improved. Benavides extended this policy of state support by creating an Industrial Bank to assist the manufacturing sector, which experienced some moderate growth (tariffs on Japanese imports helped the Peruvian textile industry). Like his predecessors, he did not hesitate to repress strikes, which increased in frequency in 1934—a major strike on the Southern Railway that year shook much of the south of the country. At the same time, Benavides continued and extended policies that aimed to address the impact of the slump on workers, in part to undermine the appeal of APRA among this sector of the population but also as an expression of the idea that workers could be positive agents of industrial progress.[60]

At the height of the slump, the Samanez Ocampo junta created an unemployment tax to support the large number of unemployed workers. The funds raised, administered by local Juntas Pro Desocupados (Unemployment Commissions), were used to create employment through public works in different parts of the country. Road building, in particular, increased significantly during the Benavides government: the Pan-American Highway to the north was completed, and the Central Highway linked Lima to La Oroya and from there to Ayacucho, Huancavelica, and Andahuaylas. Other measures implemented in this period included the establishment of "barrios obreros" (worker districts) in Lima, which were intended to address the terrible living conditions that workers often faced. Four worker districts were built, though in the end they provided housing for only a small proportion of the urban workforce. The creation of "restaurantes populares"—state-run eateries—similarly sought to address the perceived poor nutrition of workers. Most importantly, Benavides oversaw the establishment of the 1936 Worker Social Security Law, a system of social insurance that provided workers with free hospitalization and old-age pensions, among other benefits. In 1940, a Workers' Hospital opened in Lima. The growing importance of the "social question," and the growing perception that the state had a role to play in addressing it, was crystallized in the creation of the Ministry of Public Health, Labor, and Social Foresight in 1935, which gave the issue a new status and visibility.

By contrast, the Benavides regime, like the Sánchez Cerro regime before it, devoted far less attention to Peru's Indigenous population. The working and living conditions of Peru's Indigenous people attracted the attention of the International Labor Organization (ILO), resulting in a wide-ranging study published in 1938 by the Chilean labor lawyer Moisés Poblete Troncoso that reproduced *indigenista* ideas about the negative effects of alcoholism and coca leaf consumption while calling for greater "integration" of the Indigenous population into the social, economic, and political life of the country in a manner that would take greater advantage of the human capital that the Indigenous population represented.[61] But the Peruvian regimes of the 1930s did little to enact these recommendations beyond promoting road building as a means of national integration and employment, as we have seen. Benavides created a Superior Council of Indigenous Affairs, modeled on Leguía's Patronato de la Raza Indígena and just as toothless. Finally, toward the end of his government, Benavides legislated in favor of Indigenous education, increasing resources for rural schools and teacher training while promoting the establishment of Brigadas de Culturización Indígena (Brigades of Indigenous Cultural Improvement), which would provide education in Indigenous languages. But, overall, these were limited gestures that did little to advance the "progress" that Mariátegui had in mind.

Some measures, nevertheless, had important effects. The new Civil Code of 1936 restated some of the provisions of the 1933 constitution but added that Indigenous communities were required to seek formal recognition through registration. For the communities this created opportunities for formal recognition, which, already since the 1920 constitution, they had actively pursued. But the requirement to register the communities also created new challenges that resulted from the need to procure documents and maps that would make the community legible to the state.[62] This was a process that sometimes resulted in significant intercommunity conflict over the delimitations or boundaries, as occurred between the communities of San Juan de Ocros and Pampas in Ayacucho, where a boundary dispute lasted over three decades.[63] In other cases, it gave new form to conflicts between communities and neighboring haciendas, as happened between the community of Huasicancha and the Tucle hacienda near Huancayo.[64] It also exposed the communities further to the arbitrary power of local *tinterillos* (pettifoggers) as well as the local representatives of the state, such as justices of the peace and *gobernadores* and more generally the *gamonales*. Denounced equally by presidents like Leguía and by *indigenistas*, and later by the generals who took power in 1968, as the exploiters of the Indian, the *gamonales*, who could occupy a variety of formal roles, operated in practice as the local representatives of the state and certainly as the form of the state, in its arbitrariness and often violence, that Indigenous people typically experienced.[65]

There is little doubt that the 1930s were a pivotal decade. True, the impact of the Great Depression was milder in Peru than in other countries such as Chile or Cuba and relatively short-lived. In contrast to Argentina or Brazil, it did not bring about a major reorientation of the economy. It did not mark a shift from "export-led" to "inward-led" development, to use jargon favored by economists. After all, the economic recovery was largely export-led, as we have seen. State intervention did result in some policy innovation, with the creation of "development" banks to support agriculture and industry in a context in which international credit was unavailable, and with new taxes to address unemployment (indeed, overall taxation became more progressive in this period, as income taxes increased even though most revenue continued to come from trade taxes), and, for that matter, public works such as road building. However, overall, the role of the state in the economy remained modest, and total government spending hardly rose at all, even when the 1933 constitution, like the 1920 one, prescribed a more interventionist role for the state in the economy. In this decade, "progress," both in the sense of economic growth and in the sense envisaged by Mariátegui, was limited. But as happened in other countries, the Great Depression, viewed as a crisis of capitalism, shifted the terms of the political debate and the nature of political conflict as well as the perceived role of the state.

The rise of mass political parties of the left and the right, APRA and the UR, changed the nature of politics in the country. It introduced a new style and political discourse as well as new ideas about how to organize the economy and society, and about the role the state should play. These changes drew on global influences, such as European fascism and corporatism as well as communism, but also reflected local social dynamics and developments in political thought, from Mariátegui's heterodox Marxism to APRA's *indoamericanismo*. Though the PCP was relatively small and ineffectual, its very existence inserted Peru into a new, global political reality, even if Latin America remained a region of limited interest to the Communist International. Still, shaped by transnational forces like European fascism, concerns by US companies about labor militancy, and the labor strategies of APRA, anticommunism was beginning to emerge as a political force that brought together the elite, the military, and the church. In this context, although the *indigenista* sensibilities of the 1920s were not entirely abandoned and projects of Indigenous redemption continued to inform social policy, the nature of political debate shifted focus to the middle class and particularly the numerically small but politically and symbolically important working class. In the next three decades, even as major demographic and economic processes altered the structure of Peruvian society, attention gradually shifted back to Peru's Indigenous population, as we will see.

The Second World War and Limited Democratization

Sensing growing dissent regarding his hold on power—a failed coup in early 1939 appears to have rattled him—Benavides called elections for late 1939. These were easily won by his chosen successor, Manuel Prado, son of Mariano Ignacio Prado (president at the start of the War of the Pacific) and brother of Jorge Prado, who had served briefly as Benavides's prime minister.[66] Prado led a broad coalition that included the Communist Party acting in accordance with Soviet directives to support all antifascist fronts. In a context shaped by the Second World War, Prado's presidency was marked by a relatively favorable economic and political context. In contrast to the First World War, the export sector did not do as well. For various reasons, including the Prado government's reliance on export taxes of sugar and cotton and low international prices (because of Allied price controls), the increase in agricultural exports did not translate into major gains in revenue. Oil and copper, largely controlled by foreign capital, similarly did not experience much of a war dividend, despite an increase in export volumes. By contrast, the war did result in new investment in gold, zinc, and lead, which, as noted, had played a role in the recovery from the Great Depression. This owed, in part, to the establishment of the Mining Bank in 1941, which extended cheap credit to miners. The expansion of investment by Peruvian entrepreneurs in these minerals, as in cotton, reversed briefly the earlier trend marked by the expansion of foreign, particularly US, capital in the export sector.

As happened during the Great Depression, the disruption of the Second World War created incentives for expanding industrial production, but growth was modest. With limited tariff protection, Peruvian manufacturers proved unable to take advantage of the fall in imports—in fact, the opportunity was seized by other Latin American countries, such as Brazil and Argentina, which had begun their own import-substitution strategies and started to export manufactures to Peru. Absent an industrial elite in Peru, there was little pressure on the Prado government to create a policy framework that promoted their interests. Nevertheless, the period did see some diversification in industrial production into new sectors, as well as some minor policy innovation, with the passage of the Industrial Promotion Law; the establishment, as noted, of the Mining Bank in 1941; and plans for the development of a steel industry in Chimbote (linked to a hydroelectric plant on the Santa River in Ancash).[67] Prado was slightly more interventionist in the non-export agriculture sector, eager to avoid food shortages that would fuel urban discontent. Although there was some substitution of export crops for food crops (such as rice), overall the policy instruments used (such as price controls and compulsory land allocation) proved counterproductive, or benefited one sector of the population (urban consumers) by hurting another (rural producers). By the end of the Prado government, food price inflation and reliance on food imports had become a major problem.

Prado's attempts to keep food prices under control in a context of war-induced inflation reflected the growing political weight of the urban middle and working classes in this period, and consequently of APRA, which claimed to represent them. In reality, the war and the global struggle against fascism had created a temporary rapprochement between APRA and the elites represented by Prado, while marking the political end of the UR. In this context, Haya de la Torre toned down his anti-US rhetoric. Though APRA remained proscribed, it was allowed to operate without much hindrance. This change in tone, and indeed in APRA policy toward "Yankee imperialism," coincided with Roosevelt's Good Neighbor Policy, a shift in US policy toward Latin America—away from military interventions of the "Dollar Diplomacy" period (such as in Nicaragua during the Sandino rebellion) and toward mutual cooperation. Initially a hemispheric corollary to the domestic New Deal policy that sought to lift the United States out of the depths of the Great Depression, the Good Neighbor Policy was intended to create new opportunities for exports and investment in Latin America for US companies. With the start of the war, the Good Neighbor Policy was enrolled in the war effort, developing a cultural dimension—which famously involved Hollywood and particularly the Walt Disney Company—that sought to strengthen alliances with Latin American governments and improve the perception of the United States among the people of Latin America.[68]

Prado supported the US war effort in several ways, not least by agreeing to price controls on strategic raw material exports and breaking diplomatic relations with the Axis powers in January 1942. He allowed the construction of a US airbase near Talara in the far north to be used to defend the oil fields in the zone and the Panama Canal. Perhaps most importantly, like other governments in the region, Prado cracked down on nationals of Axis countries. As happened in most other countries in Latin America, Prado's government confiscated the property of Germans and Japanese (though not of Italians). But he went further than most in helping US officials round up immigrant Japanese families, as well as second- and third-generation Japanese Peruvians, and deported them to concentration camps in the United States. As Benavides did when he introduced a law requiring firms to employ a workforce that was 80 percent Peruvian nationals (a measure that implicitly targeted Japanese businesses and Japanese workers), Prado was able to exploit the climate of anti-Japanese xenophobia that had developed in the 1930s, fueled by both the UR and APRA, which escalated into anti-Japanese riots in Lima in May 1940. Among those deported were prominent businessmen, such as the landowner Nikomatsu Okada, who had become an important planter in the valley of Huaral, where he bought up most of the haciendas during the

1920s and 1930s. The Prado government seized the assets of the deported and distributed them to cronies. After the war, few of these war prisoners returned to Peru, instead settling in the United States.[69]

One of the consequences of Peru's close alignment with the United States during the Second World War was the prohibition of its coca leaf and cocaine industries.[70] Developed at the end of the nineteenth century, Peru's legal coca leaf and cocaine industries had played an important role in regional economies in Huánuco and Trujillo, and to a lesser extent Cuzco, supplying both the pharmaceutical sector and, of course, the Coca-Cola company. It was also a source of tax revenue for the state and came to represent a small but not negligible export sector. After the 1910s, competition from coca produced in Indonesia and Japan undercut Peruvian exports. But the industry's demise came about because of growing prohibitionist trends that built up in the 1920s and 1930s. These were present nationally where anxieties about the effects of coca leaf chewing on Peru's Indigenous population merged with *indigenista* projects of racial uplift. But they were also present globally: The United States, responding to its own anxieties about the effects of narcotics on its population (particularly in wartime), used its growing weight to push through an international prohibitionist regime. Although Peru responded to these challenges initially by creating a coca state monopoly (the Empresa Nacional de la Coca) to protect the industry, growing US pressure led to the full criminalization of cocaine production by the end of the 1940s, thus inaugurating a new age of illicit cocaine production and the making of the global drug trade.

Although Peru was indirectly involved in the Second World War, and only declared war on the Axis in 1945, it became directly involved in a war with Ecuador in 1941. The war arose ostensibly over the unclear demarcation of territory between the two countries. Peru had made inroads in demarcating its southern borders, particularly with Bolivia and to a lesser extent with Brazil, during the early decades of the twentieth century, and in particular during both Leguía governments (1908–12, 1919–30) thanks to the expansion of its engineering and geographic knowledge and capacity.[71] The short war with Colombia in 1932–33 had settled the dispute over Leticia. But the northern border with Ecuador remained in dispute. Ecuadorian territorial claims, which harked back to the 1830s, would have given the northern country access to extensive natural resources in the Amazon and to the Amazon River. Attempts to resolve the dispute in the mid-1920s had failed. Border skirmishes led to all-out war in July 1941, which the superior Peruvian forces won easily, occupying some

Ecuadorian provinces such as El Oro. This was a significant personal and political boost for Prado, whose father was accused of having betrayed Peru during the war with Chile, and it brought him great political capital. Because it coincided with the Second World War, the United States was keen for a quick resolution to the conflict. Together with Argentina, Brazil, and Chile, the United States pushed for a peaceful settlement, which came with the Rio Protocol signed in January 1942. The settlement was favorable to Peru, but it left some parts of the border un-demarcated, and this would become a matter of contention between the two countries for several decades.[72]

Planned during the Benavides regime but carried out at the start of the Prado administration, the 1940 national census, the first since 1876, merits attention. It is of interest both because of what it reveals about the Peruvian population, which was estimated at over six million, and because of what it represents in terms of the development of the Peruvian state. As Mara Loveman argues, censuses are expressions, but also technologies, of elites' political and cultural projects of nation- and state-building, which are informed by racial thought.[73] Already in the 1930s, and even more clearly in the 1940s, earlier notions that Peru's population could only be "improved" through European immigration had largely given way to *indigenista* projects of racial and cultural uplift through education, public health, and labor policy: Peru's Indigenous population could be integrated into the nation and could contribute to its success if the right policies were adopted. This was an approach that drew on the broader "inter-American" *indigenista* movement that emerged from the Pátzcuaro *indigenista* conference in 1940 and that, in Peru, was represented by the journal *Perú Indígena*, edited by Luis Valcarcel. With its capacity to indicate where policies needed to be targeted, the census was integral to such projects. A poster promoting the census (figure 4.5), designed by the artist Camilo Blas, asked: "How many schools does Peru need? The census will tell."

The use of racial classifications in the census and the decision to group whites and mestizos—52 percent of the total population, compared to 46 percent Indigenous, 0.68 percent "yellow," and 0.47 percent Black— reflected the aspiration that such policies were already having the desired effect of, in effect, deindigenizing the population (by eliminating its negative, Indigenous traits) and creating the desired mestizo nation. These racial classifications resonated with increasingly influential racial thinking in the 1940s that foregrounded *mestizaje* as a solution to Peru's racial heterogeneity. This idea was put forward by conservative intellectuals such as

Figure 4.5 Camilo Blas, national census poster, 1940. Source: Museo de Arte de Lima.

Víctor Andrés Belaúnde, who trumpeted the notion of a "living synthesis" (*síntesis viviente*) that represented the solution to, indeed a denial of, Peru's racial conflict.[74] This was a formulation in keeping with similar narratives that emerged elsewhere in Latin America, particularly Mexico, with José Vasconcelos's notion of the "cosmic race," and Brazil, where Gilberto Freyre developed the ideas that later came to be known as "racial democracy." This discursive *mestizaje* did in some ways reflect broader changes registered by the census, such as the beginning of Peru's demographic transition, an effect of the drop in mortality that the limited public health policies of the first few decades of the century had helped bring about, and the process of urbanization, facilitated by the growing connectivity that road building in particular had made possible, and which would increase significantly in later decades.

One of the issues that the census made visible was the very high levels of illiteracy in Peru, over 60 percent. According to David Werlich: "For every 1,000 Peruvians over five years of age, only 247 had attended primary school, 31 of these advanced to the secondary level, 3 received training at a vocational school, and 6 persons entered a university."[75] This negative general picture was complicated further by the facts that girls were far less likely than boys to attend school and that levels of literacy in the sierra were much lower than on the coast. The issue of Indigenous education had surfaced during the Leguía period. One of Camilo Blas's posters depicted the issue in this way: the upper panel, in monochromatic somber dark green, depicted an Indigenous man in a poncho, with eyes closed. The caption read: "The Indian who doesn't know how to read is a miserable blind man with eyes." The lower panel depicted the same person, now wearing a light-blue suit and a white shirt, surrounded by other people, reading a book. The caption read: "By contrast, he who knows how to read secures his happiness and knows how to protect his family, his land and his livestock." The transformation was represented not only by the ability to read but also by the clothes—the suit and shirt suggesting that the subject was no longer an Indian but a mestizo. Of the people surrounding the man, only the woman maintained her "traditional" Indigenous dress and braids, as if to suggest that the transformation of women through education was not a priority and that, as Marisol de la Cadena has argued, women are perceived as being "more Indian."[76]

The 1940 census served to confirm the failure of education policies that dated back to the *civilista* period and instead gave impetus to what Carlos Contreras calls *indigenista* education policies.[77] Under Prado, the

Figure 4.6 Camilo Blas, poster design promoting literacy for the Directorate of Indigenous Education of the Ministry of Education, 1930. Source: Museo de Arte de Lima.

budget of the Ministry of Education (created in 1936 by Benavides) increased by 338 percent and an additional four thousand primary schools were built. Twenty-seven normal schools, or teacher-training schools, were created. Particular efforts were made to address the high levels of illiteracy in the sierra, including a national literacy campaign.[78] Together with the significant growth in state employees in this period, the expansion in education created jobs for the urban middle classes. These policies were enhanced during the government of José Luis Bustamante (1945–48), when an overtly *indigenista* education project targeting illiteracy among Indigenous people took hold and was given new impetus by the noted anthropologist Luis Válcarcel, who became minister of education, and José Antonio Encinas, a prominent education specialist. This drive for *indigenista* education found an echo in *indigenista* public health policies promoted by the physician Manuel Nuñez Butrón, who established so-called sanitary brigades in southern Peru in the 1930s to attempt to contain typhus and smallpox epidemics and promote hygienic practices in Indigenous communities. Although the success of these campaigns was limited, they anticipated a growing attention to public health beyond the coast that started to take shape in the 1940s as national disease eradication campaigns were established to tackle infectious diseases such as plague, yellow fever, malaria, tuberculosis, and syphilis.[79]

The end of the Prado administration coincided with the end of the Second World War, a peculiar conjuncture that favored a brief flourishing of procedural democracy in much of Latin America. It created the conditions for an election that brought to power not the candidate of the elite, General Eloy Ureta, a hero of the war with Ecuador, but a lawyer from Arequipa, José Luis Bustamante. His party, the Frente Democrático Nacional (FDN), swept to power with the support of APRA, which had been legalized at the end of the Prado government. Importantly, the FDN also had the support of former dictator Óscar Benavides, who returned to Peru after serving as ambassador in Buenos Aires and was one of the party's founders but died shortly after the election (had he lived, perhaps he would have served as a counterweight to APRA in the party). Bustamante's election represented a shift to the center-left and resulted in gains for labor—a high proportion of new unions were formed during this period, including the Confederación Campesina del Perú (Peasant Confederation of Peru) in 1947, while workers were able to make significant wage gains—and a continuation and extension of the social policies pursued by earlier regimes, particularly in education and public health. Overall, government spending grew 4.6 times between 1939 and 1948.[80] But Bustamante's government was hampered by a quickly worsening economy, marred by inflation, and a rapidly deteriorating relationship with APRA. The party controlled Congress and in effect tried to govern from the legislative, bypassing the executive, but produced few effective laws that benefited its supporters (a law regulating *yanaconaje*, sharecropping, passed in 1947 is a notable exception). Moreover, APRA succeeded in taking control of the recently established labor confederation, the Central de Trabajadores del Perú (CTP), set up at the end of the Prado government and originally communist-controlled. With this control of organized labor, APRA gained another front on which to attack Bustamante.

A climate of intense political polarization developed following the conflict between Bustamante and APRA. In addition to overt conflict with the Communist Party, which often resulted in street battles, APRA itself was increasingly divided in this period. Many within the party felt unease at Haya de la Torre's increasing rapprochement with the United States—for example, his alignment of the CTP with the US-backed Inter-American Workers' Federation, an anticommunist hemispheric labor confederation, and his support for the granting of exploration rights to the International Petroleum Company, a subsidiary of Standard Oil. Critical of Haya de la Torre's apparent abandonment of the more radical aspects of the APRA platform, several prominent *apristas*, including Magda Portal, left the party. Faced with limited congressional representation, the right used its media platforms, *El Comercio* (run by the Miro Quesada family) and *La Prensa*, to attack the government and its interventionist economic and social policies as well as APRA. The assassination of Francisco Graña, the owner of *La Prensa*, in January 1947 by a suspected *aprista* heightened the sense of crisis. Bustamante responded by removing three APRA ministers and named General Manuel Odría, a hero from the war with Ecuador, minister of government and police. In October 1948, an insurrection that began when sectors of the navy sympathetic to APRA took over the naval installations in the port of Callao was easily put down after the APRA leadership chose not to support the uprising. Nevertheless, Bustamante once again outlawed the party, which had returned to legality in 1945. Using this as an excuse, Odría, who had been planning to overthrow the government, made his move and deposed Bustamante.

The Odría coup marked the end of a period that had begun in the wake of the Great Depression and that to some extent was in motion already during the Oncenio, in which there was a shift away from the politics of the *civilista* governments and their economic policies, premised on a minimal "night watchman" state. Influenced by transnational forces, including communism as well as fascism and corporatism, in the 1930s and the democratizing winds that came with the end of the Second World War, new political movements emerged on the left and the right that changed the tone of political debate and the nature of political competition, which now expanded to new sectors, in particular the urban middle and working classes. The military regimes of Sánchez Cerro and Benavides and subsequently the Prado and Bustamante governments prevented these new political movements—APRA and the PCP on the left, the UR on the right—from ruling outright. But they had a profound effect on the policies that those governments pursued. Though they did not fundamentally change the structure of the Peruvian economy and its dependence on agricultural and mineral exports, the governments of the 1930s and 1940s did use policy measures, albeit modestly in comparison with some other Latin American countries, to promote industrialization while extending state intervention and expanding government spending in areas such as infrastructure, education, and public health, which increasingly focused on populations in the highlands and to a lesser extent the Amazon. These measures, as I will discuss later on, set in motion, or perhaps gave further traction to, demographic and social processes that would radically change the character of Peruvian society.

Dictatorship and Cold War

Historians have tended to view the dictatorship of Manuel Odría (1948–56) and the second democratic government of Manuel Prado (1956–62) as marking a return to oligarchic politics and to the economic liberalism of the pre–Great Depression years. As Rosemary Thorp and Geoffrey Bertram suggest, Peru became, in this period, "the example *par excellence* of the dream of orthodox development economists."[81] Yet both governments continued and indeed extended some of the policies of the 1930s and 1940s, combining selective repression of the opposition with developmentalist measures that sought to dampen popular unrest. A broader outlook is needed, however, to understand the dynamics that shaped this period, and this requires paying attention to two major global processes. On the one hand, both regimes need to be viewed in the context of the onset of the Cold War, and by key events that marked that onset, such as the Chinese revolution of 1949, the Korean War (1950–53), the Sino-Soviet split in 1956, and, perhaps most importantly, the Cuban Revolution of 1959. Summarizing recent scholarship that stresses the local dynamics of the Latin American Cold War, historian Odd Arne Westad is correct to claim that "the Cold War in Latin America was more internal than external." However, these international events had concrete local repercussions.[82] On the other hand, but not unrelated, the emergence of the nonaligned movement and the "Third World"; decolonization in Africa, Asia, and the Caribbean; and, more locally, the 1952 revolution in Bolivia and the rise of a new, influential, "third-way" regional actor, Peronism, all contributed to shaping key developments in Peru in this period.

In this period, more than a simple return to economic orthodoxy, what Peru experienced was an economy that could blow hot or cold depending on export prices but that overall had begun to stall. Neither the business elite nor the governments of Odría or Prado had any real answers to this situation, though they did support investment in the export sector and in infrastructure (irrigation, roads, etc.) and sought to diversify the economy by promoting industrialization. Under pressure from the exporter lobby, represented by Pedro Beltrán (editor of *La Prensa* and a figurehead of the Peruvian elite), whom he appointed head of the Central Bank, Odría tore down Bustamante's interventionist measures shortly after coming to power: He eliminated exchange controls, resumed debt service, and, generally, established a business environment that favored export-led growth. But this reorientation of the economy was not without costs. Because of both local and global factors, the structure of exports changed. Agricultural exports lost ground, fish products experienced a boom (but a boom that turned into a spectacular bust in the early 1970s), oil exports collapsed, and minerals, particularly copper, iron, and lead, grew to account for about half of export earnings. Consequently, the Peruvian economy became increasingly reliant on mineral exports, which were under the growing control of foreign capital. The denationalization of the Peruvian economy in this period, equally visible in manufacturing and banking, produced new political tensions, which both the Odría and Prado governments were forced to manage.

Both governments passed a series of laws that promoted investment in the export sector. Together with favorable external conditions, this policy framework ensured that Peru experienced renewed export-led growth. The 1950 Mining Code, in particular, established favorable tax conditions and helped attract foreign direct investment. The influx of foreign capital made possible new, giant projects, such as the open-cast mines at Toque-pala (copper) and Marcona (iron), which local capitalists were unwill-ing, or unable, to take up. In the 1960s, however, faced with unfavorable international prices and less favorable tax conditions during the govern-ment of Fernando Belaúnde (1963–68), the mining companies postponed investment—a decision that, given the growing weight of mineral exports in export earnings, handicapped the Peruvian economy. In the oil sector, a petroleum law passed in 1952 incentivized private investment and created a favorable legal framework for oil exploration. It produced an oil rush in the Sechura Desert, in the north of the country, as well as offshore and in parts of the Amazon. In contrast to mining, Peruvian capitalists did par-ticipate in these ventures. However, the oil rush—some $20 million was invested—proved a mirage. Oil had been Peru's main export earlier in the century. Now Peru became increasingly dependent on its limited supplies, largely controlled by the International Petroleum Company, for domestic consumption. Perhaps inevitably, the relationship between the company and the Peruvian government began to sour. In both sectors, though for somewhat different reasons, foreign control of resources created tensions that mobilized nationalist sentiments.

Investment in irrigation under Odría (irrigated land increased by close to 20 percent from 1952 to 1962) supported a significant expansion of sugar and particularly cotton production in the 1950s, though the pace of growth of irrigation did not extend into the 1960s. Favorable external shocks, effects of the global Cold War, supported the expansion of these sectors. The Korean War (1950–53) increased demand for cotton (and min-erals), while fallout from the 1959 Cuban Revolution led to a reallocation of the US sugar quota in a way that favored Peruvian exporters. This boom in agricultural exports had differentiated effects. In the case of cotton, which remained relatively labor-intensive, there were positive income effects, though global oversupply in the 1960s, protectionism in the US market, and rising competition from synthetic alternatives led to a drop in the rate of growth. In the case of sugar, the picture was mixed. New investment by com-panies such as the US-owned W. R. Grace, which used byproducts from its Cartavio and Paramonga sugar estates to diversify into new industrial production in paper and chemicals, produced new employment. However, overall, investment in mechanization in sugar production, while increas-ing productivity, could do little in the face of growing competition from sugar beet producers on the world market. Moreover, mechanization resulted in the shedding of labor and in increasingly tense labor relations in a sector where APRA had historically had a strong footprint.

The most remarkable boom and bust story in this period was in the fisheries sector. Taking advantage of (1) the rich anchoveta stocks of the Humboldt Current in waters that Peru had claimed after the proclamation, in 1947, of an exclusive economic zone extending 200 miles from its coast, (2) the collapse of the California sardine industry, and (3) growing world demand for pork and chicken (fed on fish meal), an industry centered on the fishing town of Chimbote, but extending to Supe and Tambo de Mora, developed almost overnight. First focused on canned tuna exports and later on fish meal (used first as fertilizer and later as animal feed), the industry attracted investment from national entrepreneurs—such as the notorious Luis Banchero, who succeeded in establishing a cartel to fix prices and resist regulation—and grew by adopting and adapting technology such as fishing boats and processing plants from California and elsewhere as well as sonar and nylon nets. By the mid-1960s, this sector accounted for 25–30 percent of export earnings, while Peru became the world's leading fishing nation in terms of volume, supplying 40 percent of the world's total supply of fish meal. The rapid growth of the sector and the failure to effectively regulate it eventually led to the collapse of fish stocks as well as a collapse of the bird populations on the Peruvian coast, producing an environmental disaster that bankrupted the fisheries in 1972 (an El Niño year). It was nationalized in 1973 by the Velasco government.[83]

As the author and anthropologist José María Arguedas captured in his novel *El zorro de arriba y el zorro de abajo*, the growth of the anchoveta industry relied on the growing mobility of labor that characterized this period. Tens of thousands of migrants found their way to Chimbote, attracted by the relatively high wages paid on the boats, in the processing plants, and in other allied sectors (including boat building). This migrant workforce was only a small proportion of a much larger migratory wave that radically transformed the character of Peruvian society.[84] A comparison between the 1940 and 1961 censuses provides an overview of these demographic shifts, marked by an overall increase in the rate of growth of the population, fed by a reduction in infant mortality (from 175 to 149 per 1,000) and a growth in life expectancy (from forty to forty-six years). Although in 1961 the largest share of the population still resided in the sierra (44 percent, though down from 65 percent in 1940), the rates of population growth on the coast (3.8 percent) and in the Amazon

(3.6 percent) outstripped that in the highlands (1.2 percent). These shifts also reflected a process of deindigenization. Although the overall number of Quechua speakers in Lima increased in this period, nationwide the proportion of people who spoke Quechua fell from 47 to 33 percent, while the proportion of the population who spoke Spanish increased from 65 to 80 percent.[85] These changes owed both to the expansion of education to the sierra (which tended to lead to hispanicization) and to migration but also to differentiated population growth.

Internal migration, driven by structural factors, such as growing demographic pressure on land (which resulted at least in part from an earlier process of hacienda expansion), but also by more conjunctural ones, such as crop failures and droughts, shifted the demographic profile of the country. In many cases, primarily temporary patterns of migration (which reflected seasonal demand for labor in coastal agriculture) became permanent ones. In 1961, the majority of the population still worked in agriculture, and some migration flows, particularly from the sierra to the Amazon, were rural to rural, as *colonos* driven out of the highland regions sought new agricultural land. But most migration was rural to urban, including within highland regions (the three main cities in the sierra, Arequipa, Cuzco, and Huancayo, doubled in size in this period). As a consequence, the urban population grew rapidly, increasing from 35 percent in 1940 to 47 percent in 1961. Cities on the Peruvian coast, from Tumbes in the north to Tacna in the south, all grew significantly in the period, and at a much faster pace than those in the highlands, though none as much as Chimbote (which posted a 13.4 percent yearly growth rate). In the Amazon, better communications infrastructure, in particular roads and airports, and economic support schemes coordinated by the Corporación Peruana del Amazonas contributed to the growth of cities like Pucallpa and Tingo María (12.2 and 10.3 percent, respectively).[86] But it was Lima that experienced the most important growth: its population grew from 660,000 in 1940 to 1.9 million in 1961.

Although traditional working-class districts such as Barrios Altos, Rímac, and La Victoria absorbed much of the migration to Lima, the development that has come to define this period was the establishment of new urban settlements or *barriadas* (shantytowns). Some predate the Odría regime, but the *barriadas* have come to be associated closely with the dictator. Odría facilitated their growth by allowing "invaders" to take over state-owned land. But he also actively courted the support of the new inhabitants of these *barriadas*.[87] Far from being a simple puppet of the "oligarchy," Odría pursued a form of politics that sociologist Gonzalo

Portocarrero called "liberal populism," which, perhaps contradictorily, combined paternalism and institutionalization. It was an approach that clearly borrowed from Argentina's Juan Domingo Perón (and, arguably, from Marcos Pérez Jiménez and Gustavo Rojas Pinilla in Venezuela and Colombia) but that also continued in the tradition of Leguía and Benavides. Odría's wife set up a foundation for charitable work that mirrored Eva Perón's foundation. The creation of an Employee Social Security Law in 1948, meanwhile, gave white-collar workers what Benavides had given blue-collar workers with the Worker Social Security Law in 1936. Major public works (including several new buildings for ministries), though focused on Lima, created employment for blue-collar workers, while an exchange rate policy that resisted devaluation (thus keeping food imports affordable) combined with price controls for locally produced foodstuffs were clearly aimed at garnering working- and middle-class support while undermining APRA's grip on these sectors. These measures, however, also had the effect of pitting Odría against the interests of the elites.

The growth of Lima and its demographic transformation were reflected in the emergence of new urban cultures, visible in the expansion of the public sphere. Alongside traditional newspapers like *El Comercio* and *La Prensa* that represented the interests of the elite, popular newspapers like *Última Hora* and mesocratic magazines like *Caretas* were established in this period.[88] Responding to new readerships, these new outlets innovated in form as well as style. *Última Hora*, in particular, became well known for its comic strips, or *chistes*, which were very popular, but more generally for its somewhat irreverent and "populist" style. These urban cultures also found expression in new literature, represented by authors such as Enrique Congrains, Julio Ramón Ribeyro, and, in the 1960s, Mario Vargas Llosa, that departed from the *indigenista* tradition and developed a new "urban realism," while in the art world *indigenismo* made way for abstraction, a movement perhaps best represented by Fernando de Szyszlo. In music, too, the 1950s saw a very rapid growth in the popularity of *música criolla*, mostly *valses* and *marineras*, and of Afro-Peruvian music.[89] Performers like Chabuca Granda, Los Embajadores Criollos, Los Morochucos, and Nicomedes Santa Cruz took advantage of new recording technologies to reach new audiences as well as, perhaps more importantly, the growth in transistor radio ownership and the expansion of radio stations. By 1961, there were almost half a million transistor radios in Peru (and only 72,000 televisions). *Música criolla* dominated the airwaves, though *radionovelas* (radio soap operas) also became very popular.[90]

Alongside this creole urban culture, migrant communities from the Andes and, to a lesser extent, the selva also began to carve out spaces of cultural expression and social interaction in "*departamental* and provincial clubs" and other venues, such as *coliseos folklóricos* (Andean music venues).[91] Although their visibility would expand much more in later decades—a process that, for some observers, would amount to the emergence of a new social stratum and cultural actor, the *cholo*—already in the 1950s these new cultures produced an evident backlash.[92] Cultural products like the comic strips in *Última Hora* developed characters such as Boquellanta (an Afro-Peruvian boy), Serrucho (an Indigenous migrant in Lima), and Sampietri (a white creole Limeño) that were identifiably Peruvian in their characterization as racial or cultural stereotypes. Intended as alternatives to US comic strips that had been featured predominantly in Peruvian newspapers, these characters were an expression of a new, bolder, cultural nationalism. But they also clearly expressed and reproduced Peruvian creole racism. Serrucho in particular, with its overtly racist depiction of an Andean migrant, reflected creole anxieties about the transformation of Lima.[93] The celebration and reaffirmation of creole culture in this period, somewhat paradoxically, at times embraced or perhaps incorporated Afro-Peruvian music and culture into the sphere of *lo criollo* (understood broadly as an expression of white and coastal culture) while, as the racist depictions of the character Boquellanta demonstrate, hardly altering the dominant anti-Black racism of creole society. But this affirmation of *lo criollo* can also be seen as an expression of a broader attempt to culturally forestall or even arrest the evident transformation, or andeanization, of Limeño society—as well as, by extension, Peruvian society—that the demographic forces that I have discussed had unleashed.

Shifting back to the political: Odría's coup in 1948 was intended to keep APRA out of power, and initially this made him an ally of the Peruvian elite. His *revolución restauradora* introduced a new level of repression toward political opponents, particularly members of APRA and the Communist Party.[94] Both parties were banned (as was the APRA-controlled labor confederation, the CTP), a measure that Odría was careful to frame as an element in the Cold War struggle against international communism in order to gain support for his government from the United States; US military assistance increased from $100,000 in 1952 to $9.1 million by 1956. Odría increased the military budget by 45 percent (a measure intended to neutralize discontent with his regime within the armed forces) and gave free rein to the police and to his shady interior minister Alejandro Esparza Zañartu to establish a system of political surveillance. The Internal Security Law of July 1949 formalized this repression, which resulted in the detention and exile of thousands. Mario Vargas Llosa's novel *Conversación en la catedral* captures this climate of repression particularly well. Famously, in 1949 the APRA leader Haya de la Torre sought refuge in the Colombian embassy and would remain there for five years, after the regime denied him safe-conduct to leave the country. Sensing that he needed to legitimize his rule through the ballot box, and facing growing opposition from sectors of the oligarchy, Odría called elections in 1950. He ran unopposed after he arrested his main opponent, General Ernesto Montagne, the representative of the hastily assembled Liga Democrática Nacional, whom he accused of plotting with APRA and of being behind an uprising in Arequipa.

While his economic policy broadly aligned with the economic liberalism of the elite—a policy that the 1949 economic mission led by the Harvard economist Julius Klein had recommended for the country—Odría pursued a degree of state intervention in the economy. This put him at odds with the elite, and in particular with Pedro Beltrán, who resigned from his position as head of the central bank in March 1950. The elite sided with Odría in the 1950 election, but tensions had begun to emerge. As I have noted, deviating from economic liberalism, and fearful of the impact that inflation would have on the popular sectors (including organized labor) he was courting, Odría resisted demands from exporters to remove all exchange controls. Although broadly supportive of the idea of export-led growth, he pursued a policy of industrial promotion and state-supported programs (in irrigation and hydroelectricity, and in steel manufacturing), albeit on a much more modest scale than other Latin American countries; moreover, as Thorp and Bertram argue, rather than substitute for imports, industrial growth in this period increased dependence on imports, since parts had to be imported. At the same time, Odría continued several of the social policies of the Benavides and Bustamante years, increasing investment in education and public health. Education minister Juan Mendoza oversaw an expansion and improvement of the country's education system, while in public health the Servicio Cooperativo de Salud Pública—which drew on US expertise—did likewise.

By the time of the 1956 elections, relations between Odría and the elite were at a low ebb. The economy took a hit from the end of the Korean War, as demand for Peruvian exports fell, and it proved difficult for the regime to maintain its social spending. Accusations of corruption became widespread. Even within the military, particularly but not exclusively among sectors connected to the Centro de Altos Estudios Militares (CAEM, Center for Advanced Military Studies, established in 1950), support for Odría, who was increasingly viewed as venal, began to wane. A new conception of national security, one that extended to economic and social development, was beginning to form at CAEM, as discussed below. Meanwhile, Pedro Beltrán, more out of concern for the elite's economic interests than because of any firm commitment to democracy, called for the suspension of the Internal Security Law from his pulpit at *La Prensa* as a way to undermine the dictator. A mass uprising in Arequipa in late 1955 demanding a return to democracy and the removal of Interior Minister Esparza Zañartu heaped more pressure on the regime. In this context, with Odría weakened, new political forces were quickly established to present candidacies for the scheduled elections. The elite threw its weight behind former president Manuel Prado, who maintained some popular support and was able to secure the support of APRA, which saw him as the political leader most likely to legalize the party. Prado defeated Fernando Belaúnde, an architect from an influential Arequipa family who ran on a reformist platform (and whom Odría tried to bar from running), and Hernando de Lavalle, a lawyer.

The importance of the 1956 elections owes not so much to the fact that, with Prado, the elite again took power, or that it did so, improbably, with the support of APRA. Rather, it owes, first, to the fact that it was the first general election in which women voted and were elected to office. From their elected positions, women such as Senator Irene Silva de Santolalla introduced new issues into the political sphere.[95] The enfranchisement of women contributed to a major expansion in the voting population (from 7.1 percent of the total population in 1931 to 22.4 percent in 1956), though the franchise still did not extend to those deemed illiterate, thus excluding a large proportion of Peru's Indigenous population. Second, it owes to the issues—and, arguably, the political style—that gained traction in the election. Belaúnde's reformist campaign gained support from middle-class voters disillusioned with both APRA and the Communist Party. Crucially, in his campaign Belaúnde targeted the provinces, traveling to as many as twenty provincial cities and focusing on their populations' concerns, claiming, "I . . . have crossed the cordilleras ten times during this campaign, in search not of cheering crowds, but of inspiration and ideas."[96] The provinces were underrepresented by virtue of the fact that those able to vote were primarily concentrated in Lima—42 percent of the electorate in 1956 lived in the capital. Similarly, the Partido Demócrata-Cristiano (Christian Democratic Party), with its base in Arequipa, did not field a presidential candidate but won a majority of congressional seats. Its electoral platform denounced social injustice in terms that evoked the growing social mission of the Latin American Catholic Church, represented in Peru by the progressive archbishop of Lima, Juan Landázuri Ricketts.

In short, the 1956 presidential campaign saw new political actors raise issues of national integration and provincial interests, which challenged the growing power of the elite and foreign capital, whose interests were increasingly concentrated on the coast (and mining satellites) and in Lima. These actors also raised the issue of economic and social justice in a manner that mobilized a growing sector of the population. They could do so because APRA had moved so far to the right that it appeared to have turned its back on its founding principles. Abandoning its earlier anti-imperialism, APRA, and Haya de la Torre in particular, now presented themselves as anticommunist allies of the United States. As had happened during the Bustamante period, some militants left the party and went on to form APRA Rebelde (which later evolved into the insurgent Castroite party Movimiento de Izquierda Revolucionaria—MIR, Revolutionary Left Movement—one of two guerrilla movements that took up arms in 1965). Despite considerable parliamentary strength, the politics of *convivencia* (coexistence) that APRA embraced gave the Prado government something of a free pass, leading to accusations that *convivencia* had degenerated into *connivencia* (connivance). This extended to reining in the labor movement, over which it continued to hold sway through the CTP. Once it overcame the economic crisis of 1957–58 and entered a new phase of economic expansion (helped by better export prices and the US sugar quota), and after it neutralized attacks from the right by appointing Pedro Beltrán prime minister, the Prado government, unchallenged on the left and the right, appeared to observers to be doing very little to resolve the country's problems.

True, Prado continued with Odría's investment plans in education and public health: the historian Jorge Basadre was named education minister and particular attention was placed on universities, with their number increasing significantly, from seven to twenty-one, in this period. Problems, however, were mounting. Discontent among precisely the sort of voters who had voted for Belaúnde in 1956 came to the fore during a visit by US Vice President Richard Nixon in 1958, when students prevented him from speaking at San Marcos University and pelted him with stones (he got a better reception at the Pontifical Catholic University of Peru). The growing economic and cultural but also military influence of the United States in Peru in this period (military aid increased by $70 million between 1956 and 1962) was feeding into a nationalist reaction, which Belaúnde tried to capitalize on with his rhetoric of "the conquest of Peru by Peruvians." In the highlands, growing tensions over land led to open conflict between peasants and landowners. A wave of invasions of haciendas swept the sierra. In the central highlands, the peasant community of Rancas took over land claimed by the Cerro de Pasco Corporation, a struggle that the author Manuel Scorza retold in his popular novel *Redoble por Rancas* (1970). In the area of La Convención, Cuzco, where *arrendires* (tenants) and *allegados* (peons) had begun to organize in unions to resist what they considered the illegitimate demands for labor services from landowners, a young Trotskyist, Hugo Blanco, with support from a Trotskyist party, the Frente de Izquierda Revolucionaria (FIR, Revolutionary Left Front), and students from the university in Cuzco, organized peasant takeovers of haciendas.[97]

The Prado government was not entirely oblivious to these problems. By the late 1950s, even *La Prensa* and *El Comercio*, and the Sociedad Nacional Agraria (National Agrarian Society), the agro-exporters' lobby, acknowledged the need for agrarian reform, particularly in the sierra—in part to stop and hopefully reverse migration to Lima, but also because promises of agrarian reform translated into votes. The principle of agrarian reform even had the support of the United States, which, during the Dwight D. Eisenhower and particularly the John F. Kennedy administrations—in the context of the Alliance for Progress strategy—came to view rural development in Latin America as integral to its broader anticommunist struggle. The United States had supported agrarian reform in Bolivia, a cornerstone of the 1952 Bolivian revolution, by providing grants to aid agricultural modernization—though, of course, it violently opposed the agrarian reform of Jacobo Arbenz in Guatemala, where the interests of the United Fruit Company were at stake. Projects like Vicos, a highland hacienda in the *departamento* of Ancash purchased by Cornell University in 1952 with the aim of introducing modern agricultural practices to the Andes, or the Programa Puno Tambopata, supported by the Andean Mission of the ILO, which, in typical *indigenista* fashion, sought to teach Indigenous peasants, and particularly Indigenous women, to overcome their backwardness, point to the ways in which some continued to understand, as had been the case since the 1920s, the "land problem" as primarily technical rather than political and the "Indian problem" as arising from an underutilization of human capital.[98] In 1956, Prado created a commission to study land reform, which was headed by Pedro Beltrán; with only limited support from the government and with extensive representation of landed interests, little came of it.

The Peruvian military also shared the idea that agrarian reform and, indeed, broader structural reforms were needed. Military officers, including those who trained at CAEM and some who did not, such as Juan Velasco Alvarado, increasingly believed that the failure to address social inequality, for which unequal land distribution was largely to blame, was a source of political instability and therefore a threat to national security. The Cuban Revolution and the 1965 guerrilla insurgencies in Peru seemed to confirm this view, but this perspective was not simply the product of new Cold War rationalities. Starting in the early twentieth century, the Peruvian army had viewed itself as a "civilizing force," a reflection of the influence of French military missions and the ideas of colonial strategists like Hubert Lyautey. Military officers viewed military conscription and the two-year military service obligation as a transformative influence on Indigenous recruits, in ways that echoed *indigenista* ideas of cultural uplift. A progressive tradition had formed among midranking officers in the army, represented most clearly by the Comité Revolucionario de Oficiales del Ejercito (Revolutionary Committee of Army Officers), led by Major Víctor Villanueva, which was closely aligned with APRA in the 1940s. But support for structural change was not limited to these radical officers, and by the 1950s, the military increasingly viewed its function in a developmentalist mode that placed the "integration" of "the Indian" at the heart of its objectives. The political elites' failure to address Peru's structural problems, along with the threat of subversion from APRA and, by the 1960s, from the Castroite left, convinced many that the armed forces would need to take responsibility for bringing about the necessary changes.[99]

In the early 1950s, during the high point of the Odría dictatorship, a young Argentine doctor named Ernesto Guevara de la Serna passed through Peru twice, first in 1952 and again in 1953, on his way to becoming "El Che."[100] He jotted down some impressions of the country in his diaries. He was little impressed by Lima and did not think much of the evident US influence on the country: "I think that for Peru Yankee domination has not even meant that fictitious economic prosperity which can be seen in Venezuela, for example." Guevara was more interested in Peru's Indigenous peoples. He wrote about them with an equal measure of fascination and condescension, but he clearly viewed them as victims of an unjust order. Like others at the time, he concluded that Peru "has not developed beyond the feudal condition of a colony. It still awaits the blood of a truly emancipating revolution." Between 1948 and 1962, a combination of repression, commodity export booms fueled by the Korean War, US sugar quotas and the fish meal windfall, economic and military support from the United States, and APRA's policy of *convivencia* helped reestablish and maintain a certain status quo that favored the country's elite and forestalled meaningful change. But pressure for change, as Guevara had sensed, was mounting. When APRA, supported by Odría, won the 1962 elections, defeating the reformist Belaúnde, the military intervened to prevent what it feared would be a shift to the right and a further postponement of needed reforms.

Reform and Revolution

It is ironic that the military officers who led the 1962 coup were motivated, to some extent, by the belief that if APRA took power it would prevent passage of the types of reforms that APRA itself had promoted since 1931. However, by this time Haya de la Torre had become, in the words of US journalist John Gunther, "a confused reactionary." By contrast, the Peruvian armed forces had, in his view, acquired clear "Nasserist tendencies," by which he meant an embrace of relative autonomy with regard to the country's elites but also a developmental vision.[101] This invocation of one of the key figures of the nonaligned movement and of "Third Worldism" points to the sort of new global connections that were beginning to emerge in this period between Latin America and the emerging "global south."[102] The generals conceived of the coup as an "institutional coup" and of their regime as a caretaker government. But they initiated several reforms, including establishing a national planning institution (the Instituto Nacional de Planificación, or National Planning Institute), and enacted a limited agrarian reform in La Convención to forestall further uprisings. Although the regime was described as a *dictablanda* (a soft dictatorship), and for the most part was less repressive than the Odría regime had been, it responded with *mano dura* (a firm hand—i.e., repression) to labor agitation in the central highlands and the northern sugar plantations and did not refrain from arresting *apristas* and communists. Still, as it had promised it would do, it organized elections that Belaúnde—

who by this time the elite, and perhaps more importantly the military, had come to view as a safe bet—won in 1963.

The Belaúnde government from 1963 to the military coup of October 1968 was as underwhelming as the rise of Belaúnde in the 1950s had been a source of excitement. The "architect of hope" was a better political campaigner than he was a president. His ideas of how to modernize Peru, and in particular his showcase project, the Marginal Highway, were certainly ambitious. Running up the spine of the eastern side of the Andes, this new road was intended to open up the Amazon, connect it to the rest of the country, and make it—and those who would flock to its now accessible lands—productive by bringing "progress" to the Amazon. But his projects promised more than they delivered. To his credit, Belaúnde's government continued and expanded the efforts to address the shortcomings in education and public health. He put particular emphasis on university education, and the number of students increased from 41,000 in 1962 to 94,000 in 1968. He also reinstated municipal elections, which his party, in alliance with the Christian Democrats, won easily. But Belaúnde proved less successful in pushing through other reforms. In particular, the timid agrarian reform law passed by his government only benefited a very small proportion of the peasantry and did little to improve the productivity of the sierra or break the power of the sierra landowners (it left the coastal elite's properties untouched). It is true that the APRA-Odría alliance, or *coalición*, in Congress and the agro-exporters did their best to undermine it. Ironically, APRA—a party whose origins can be traced to opposition to the expansion of sugar haciendas on the coast—opposed the breakup of the sugar estates on the grounds that it would produce social conflict.

In the end, the Belaúnde government fell ostensibly because of its mismanagement of the International Petroleum Company crisis. Resisting calls for nationalization from both the left and from *El Comercio*, and under pressure from an increasingly hostile United States, Belaúnde negotiated a more favorable contract with the US-owned company, which held a monopoly on oil production in the country and a very favorable tax position.[103] However, a scandal ensued when one page of the contract, page 11, went missing. This scandal prompted the coup of 1968. But the reasons for the coup were broader. In the latter part of Belaúnde's administration, the economy went into free fall, with soaring public debt (contracted to cover public spending), creeping inflation, and a steep drop in export earnings. Encouraged by a promise of agrarian reform but frustrated by the limited progress made by the government, peasants throughout the highlands began to take over land from haciendas, bringing forward a de facto if not de jure process of land redistribution.[104] In this context, in 1965, two small Cuban-inspired guerrilla insurgencies led by the MIR of Luis de la Puente and Guillermo Lobatón (focused on Cuzco and the central highlands and selva, respectively) and the Ejército de Liberación Nacional (ELN, National Liberation Army) of Héctor Béjar (focused on Ayacucho) created a significant crisis for the Belaúnde government.[105]

These groups were a product of the growing splintering of the Peruvian left following the Sino-Soviet split of 1956 and the Cuban Revolution, which had resulted in the emergence of several small Maoist, Trotskyist, and Castroite parties. Although highly sectarian, they shared the view that the pro-Soviet Communist Party, and APRA for that matter, were incapable of bringing about revolutionary change. They corresponded to a broader development in the global left in this period, which saw the rise of "New Left" movements and parties, often linked to student movements, in Europe, in the United States, and across Latin America. The 1965 guerrillas had received training and inspiration from Cuba, but they proved poorly prepared. Using new counterinsurgency strategies (such as the use of napalm to clear out jungle cover), which impacted civilian populations, including Asháninka communities in the central Amazon who initially supported the MIR, the Peruvian armed forces, aided by US military advisors, easily defeated the insurgents.[106] But these insurgencies spooked the CAEM-trained officers, who saw in the peasant land invasions, in the guerrillas, and more generally in the Peruvian "New Left"—and in their perceived backers in Havana, Moscow, and Beijing—further evidence that unless measures were taken to address the underlying causes of social and political unrest, the Peruvian Andes would become a new Sierra Maestra, a new Cuba. When General Juan Velasco Alvarado took power on October 3, 1968, it was clear to him and his colleagues in the military junta that Peru needed to change radically.

The sense that the situation Peru faced was explosive and that fundamental change was urgent can also be detected in the cultural realm. In 1965, the novelist and anthropologist José María Arguedas published "The *Pongo's* Dream," a *cuento* that, in allegorical form, exposed the violence that characterized the relation between the *misti* (white) world, represented by a hacendado, and the Indigenous peasantry, represented by a *pongo* (or serf). Ultimately, the *cuento* prophesied the coming of a world upside down, a *pachakuti*—an Andean concept that refers to the inversion of order—where the abuses of the hacendado would be met with divine (but also, by implication, earthly) retribution.[107] Whether intentionally or not, the *cuento* encapsulated a growing sense that the social order was fundamentally unjust and unsustainable, a perception that likely drew not only on what was observable in Peru but also on the processes of decolonization taking place around the world at the time (as well as the Vietnam War, for that matter), which challenged both the social and, crucially, the *racial* order of things. "The *Pongo*'s Dream" reflected, arguably, a changing national as well as global mood, and could be read as a threat or a warning. In contrast to *indigenista* narratives, which, as we have seen, imagined Indigenous redemption as a process of deindigenization, in "The *Pongo*'s Dream" redemption comes about through the reversal of roles—a new hierarchy legitimized by just retribution for past wrongs. A similar diagnosis of a world in need of being turned upside down is discernible in Sebastián Salazar Bondy's essay "Lima la horrible," published in 1964, a fierce critique of the ideological underpinnings of creole—that is, Limeño and white—domination over Peru.

Conclusion

Notwithstanding these critiques, Peru had changed since 1919. Far more people had access to education, at the primary, secondary, and university levels, and to public health facilities. Improvements in health meant that fewer children died and that people lived longer, though Peru still fared a lot worse than most Latin American countries in this regard. Although most of the Indigenous peasantry was still disenfranchised, by virtue of literacy requirements, far more people, including women, could vote and political representation was broader. It was now a far more urban country. Investment in transport infrastructure, roads and airports in particular, meant that people were more mobile than before, moving both temporarily and, increasingly, permanently in search of work and better living conditions. For a privileged minority and for foreign visitors, this improved transport infrastructure also meant the opportunity to engage in tourism and leisure travel.[108] Peru was a better-connected country, though whether it was more integrated, as Belaúnde and others before him had hoped, is open to question. For many observers of the time, what characterized Peru was a dual economy, with a sector, concentrated on the coast and in the mines, that was highly modern and capital-intensive and another, concentrated in the highlands, that evoked feudalism. This duality underpinned a highly unequal social order and a potentially explosive political situation. Some questioned this duality and pointed to the development of new processes, such as *cholificación*, the emergence of a new social stratum based on the recently urbanizing population.[109] However, whether *cholificación* sharpened or blunted the explosive political order remained a matter for debate.[110]

Returning, then, to Mariátegui and to the question posed at the start of this chapter: Had Peru's "progress" between 1919 and 1968 brought about the "well-being of the Peruvian masses, which are four-fifths Indigenous and peasant"? In some ways, by virtue of the fact that education, health, and other policies that targeted the Indigenous population had brought about improvements in indicators that measure, say, literacy and life expectancy, we could say that it had. Similarly, the greater levels of connection and mobility achieved by the 1950s thanks to investment in infrastructure allowed sectors of the Indigenous peasantry to seek out better opportunities in the coastal cities and, to a lesser extent, in the areas of agricultural colonization in the Amazon. But overall, as Velasco and the generals concluded in 1968, these changes were insufficient to forestall a political explosion—they needed accelerating. The generals claimed to be breaking with the past, and with the wide-ranging agrarian reform implemented in 1969, it could be argued that they did. But, ultimately, they shared the view that progress entailed overcoming indigeneity, deindigenizing Peru. Their overt reframing of the land question as a peasant or class issue rather than an Indigenous issue was the most evident expression of this.[111] But beyond this discursive reframing, the project of the Revolutionary Government of the Armed Forces did little to challenge the idea that underpinned the *indigenista* policies of the period discussed in this chapter: the idea that Peru's future was necessarily a future without "Indians."

Notes

I am grateful to Carlos Aguirre, Jelke Boesten, Mercedes Crisóstomo, Adrián Lerner, Martín Monsalve, Javier Puente; to students and faculty at the University of Chicago, Stanford University, Universidad de San Andrés, and University College London, where I presented earlier versions of this chapter; and to the coauthors of this volume, for their comments and suggestions. In writing this chapter, I was fortunate to be able to draw on several key texts, including Carlos Contreras and Marcos Cueto, *Historia del Perú contemporáneo: Desde las luchas por la independencia hasta el presente* (Lima: IEP, 2013); Marcos Cueto, *Perú: Mirando hacia adentro*, vol. 4, *1930–1960* (Barcelona: Taurus, 2015); Peter F. Klarén, *Peru: Society and Nationhood in the Andes* (Oxford: Oxford University Press, 2000); Nelson Manrique, *Historia de la república* (Lima: Fondo Editorial de Cofide, 1995); Henry Pease García and Gonzalo Romero Sommer, *La política en el Perú del siglo XX* (Lima: Fondo Editorial PUCP, 2013); Rosemary Thorp and Geoffrey Bertram, *Peru 1890–1977: Growth and Policy in an Open Economy* (London: Macmillan, 1978), David P. Werlich, *Peru: A Short History* (Carbondale: Southern Illinois University Press, 1978).

1   On the development of these regional export economies, see Paulo Drinot, "Peru, 1884–1930: A Beggar Sitting on a Bench of Gold?," in *An Economic History of Twentieth-Century Latin America*, vol. 1, *The Export Age: The Latin American Economies in the Late Nineteenth and Early Twentieth Centuries*, ed. Enrique Cárdenas, José Antonio Ocampo, and Rosemary Thorp (London: Palgrave Macmillan, 2000).

2   See Carlos Aguirre and Paulo Drinot, eds., *The Peculiar Revolution: Rethinking the Peruvian Experiment Under Military Rule* (Austin: University of Texas Press, 2017).

3   The 1912 elections, which brought Guillermo Billinghust to power, were a preamble to this irruption of popular politics. See Luis Torrejón M., *Rebeldes republicanos: La turba urbana de 1912* (Lima: Red para el Desarrollo de las Ciencias Sociales en el Perú, 2010); Peter Blanchard, "A Populist Precursor: Guillermo Billinghurst," *Journal of Latin American Studies* 9, no. 2 (November 1977): 251–73; José Luis Huiza, "From the República Aristocrática to Pan Grande: Guillermo Billinghurst and Populist Politics in Early Twentieth Century Peru" (PhD dissertation, University of Miami, 1998).

4   José Carlos Mariátegui, "El progreso nacional y el capital humano," *Mundial*, October 9, 1923.

5   "Methodological nationalism" refers to the tendency to assume that the nation-state is the natural subject of historical and scientific analysis, which leads to ignoring the transnational or global connections and interdependencies that influence "national history."

6   On the impact of the war in Latin America, see Stefan Rinke, *Latin America and the First World War* (Cambridge: Cambridge University Press, 2017).

7   On the Leguía regime, see Paulo Drinot, ed., *La patria nueva: Economía, sociedad y cultura en el Perú, 1919–1930* (Raleigh, NC: A Contracorriente, 2018); and Paulo Drinot, *Los años de Leguía, 1919–1930* (Lima: Instituto de Estudios Peruanos, 2024).

8   Baltazar Caravedo Molinari, *Clases, lucha política y gobierno en el Perú, 1919–1933* (Lima: Retama, 1977); Julio Cotler, *Clases, estado y nación en el Perú* (Lima: Instituto de Estudios Peruanos, 1977).

9   On the divisions in the Partido Civil, see Rory Miller, "The Coastal Elite and Peruvian Politics, 1895–1919," *Journal of Latin American Studies* 14,

no. 1 (1982): 97–120; and Carmen McEvoy, *La utopía republicana: Ideales y realidades en la formación de la cultura política peruana, 1871–1919* (Lima: Fondo Editorial PUCP, 1997).

10   On yellow fever, see Marcos Cueto, *El regreso de las epidemias: Salud y sociedad en el Perú del siglo XX* (Lima: Instituto de Estudios Peruanos, 2020).

11   See Dennis L. Gilbert, *La oligarquía peruana: Historia de tres familias* (Lima: Editorial Horizonte, 1982); Francisco Durand, *El poder incierto: Trayectoria económica y política del empresariado peruano* (Lima: Fondo Editorial del Congreso del Perú, 2004); Martín Monsalve Zanatti, "Evolución de la gran empresa familiar peruana 1890–2012," in *Familias empresarias y grandes empresas familiares en América Latina y España: Una visión de largo plazo* (Bilbao: Fundación BBVA, n.d.); and Felipe Portocarrero S., *El imperio Prado, 1890–1970* (Lima: Universidad del Pacífico, 1995).

12   Following the 1890 Grace contract with the British bondholders, the Peruvian Corporation was created to manage the Central and Southern Railway. About the *granja modelo*, see Geoffrey Bertram, "Modernización y cambio en la industria lanera en el sur del Perú, 1919–1930: Un caso frustrado de desarrollo," *Apuntes* 6 (1977): 3–22.

13   D. S. Parker, *Idea of the Middle Class: White-Collar Workers and Peruvian Society, 1900–1950* (University Park: Penn State University Press, 2010).

14   On banditry, see Lewis Taylor, *Bandits and Politics in Peru: Landlord and Peasant Violence in Hualgayoc, 1900–30* (Cambridge: Centre of Latin American Studies, University of Cambridge, 1987); and Carlos Aguirre and Charles Walker, eds., *Bandoleros, abigeos y montoneros: Criminalidad y violencia en el Perú, siglos XVIII–XX* (Lima: Instituto de Apoyo Agrario, 1990). On the repression of criminality, see Carlos Aguirre, *The Criminals of Lima and Their Worlds: The Prison Experience, 1850–1935* (Durham, NC: Duke University Press, 2005).

15   Carlota Casalino Sen, *Centenario: Las celebraciones de la independencia 1921–1924* (Lima: Municipalidad de Lima, 2017); Pablo Ortemberg, "Los centenarios de 1921 y 1924, desde Lima hacia el mundo: Ciudad capital, experiencias compartidas y política regional," in *La independencia peruana como representación: Historiografía, conmemoración y escultura pública*, ed. Alex Loayza Pérez (Lima: Instituto de Estudios Peruanos, 2016).

16   On centralization and regional discontent, see José Deustua and José Luis Rénique, *Intelectuales, indigenismo y descentralismo en el Perú, 1897–1931* (Cuzco: Centro de Estudios Rurales Andinos "Bartolomé de las Casas," 1984). On the Iquitos rebellion, see Fernando Santos Granero and Frederica Barclay, *Tamed Frontiers: Economy, Society, and Civil Rights in Upper Amazonia* (Boulder, CO: Westview Press, 2000).

17   Thomas M. Davies, *Indian Integration in Peru: A Half Century of Experience, 1900–1948* (Lincoln: University of Nebraska Press, 1974); Jorge Alberto Ccahuana Córdova, "Buscando una ciudadanía propia: Indígenas y estado durante el Oncenio (1919–1930)" (master's thesis, Pontificia Universidad Católica del Perú, 2017).

18 On *indigenismo*, see, among others, Marisol de la Cadena, *Indigenous Mestizos: The Politics of Race and Culture in Cuzco, Peru, 1919–1991* (Durham, NC: Duke University Press, 2000); Jorge Coronado, *The Andes Imagined: Indigenismo, Society, and Modernity* (Pittsburgh: University of Pittsburgh Press, 2009); and Efraín Kristal, *The Andes Viewed from the City: Literary and Political Discourse on the Indian in Peru, 1848–1930* (New York: P. Lang, 1987).

19 See Manuel Burga, "Los profetas de la rebelión (1920–1923)," in *Estados y naciones en los Andes*, ed. J. P. Deler and Yves Saint-Geours, vol. 2 (Lima: Instituto de Estudios Peruanos / Instituto Francés de Estudios Andinos, 1986). See also José Tamayo Herrera, *Historia social e indigenismo en el altiplano* (Lima: Ediciones treintaitrés, 1982); Nils Jacobsen, *Mirages of Transition: The Peruvian Altiplano, 1780–1930* (Berkeley: University of California Press, 1993); and José Luis Rénique, *La batalla por Puno: Conflicto agrario y nación en los Andes peruanos* (Lima: Instituto de Estudios Peruanos/SUR, 2004).

20 Paulo Drinot, *The Allure of Labor: Workers, Race, and the Making of the Peruvian State* (Durham, NC: Duke University Press, 2011).

21 See Fred Rohner, *La guardia vieja: El vals criollo y la formación de la ciudadanía en las clases populares: Estrategias de representación y de negociación en la consolidación del vals popular limeño (1885–1930)* (Lima: Instituto de Etnomusicología de la PUCP, 2018); Steve Stein, ed., *Lima obrera, 1900–1930* (Lima: Ediciones El Virrey, 1986); Augusto Ruiz Zevallos, *La multitud, las subsistencias y el trabajo: Lima de 1890 a 1920* (Lima: Fondo Editorial PUCP, 2001); Alicia del Aguila Peralta, *Callejones y mansiones: Espacios de opinión pública y redes sociales y políticas en la Lima del 900* (Lima: Fondo Editorial PUCP, 1997); Johanna Hamann, *Leguía, el centenario y sus monumentos: Lima: 1919–1930* (Lima: Fondo Editorial PUCP, 2015); Fanni Muñoz Cabrejo, *Diversiones públicas en Lima: 1890–1920, la experiencia de la modernidad* (Lima: Universidad del Pacífico, 2001); Aldo Panfichi and Felipe Portocarrero S., eds., *Mundos interiores: Lima 1850–1950* (Lima: Universidad del Pacífico, 1998); and Carlos Aguirre and Aldo Panfichi, *Lima, siglo XX: Cultura, comunicación y cambio* (Lima: Fondo Editorial PUCP, 2013).

22 The penal code, for example, introduced a new category of Indigenous criminality that factored in the conditions that had led to their "semi-civilized" status and which judges were required to take into account. See Deborah Poole, "Ciencia, peligrosidad y represión en la criminología indigenista peruana," in *Bandoleros, abigeos y montoneros: Criminalidad y violencia en el Perú, siglos XVIII–XX*, ed. Carlos Aguirre and Charles Walker (Lima: Instituto de Apoyo Agrario, 1990); and Lior Ben David, "Modernización y colonialismo en la 'patria nueva': La perspectiva de los delincuentes indígenas semi-civilizados," in *La patria nueva: Economía, sociedad y cultura en el Perú, 1919–1930*, ed. Paulo Drinot (Raleigh, NC: A Contracorriente, 2018), 115–38. On the development of aviation under Leguía, see

Willie Hiatt, *The Rarified Air of the Modern: Airplanes and Technological Modernity in the Andes* (Oxford: Oxford University Press, 2016).

23 Christopher Heaney, "Seeing Like an Inca: Julio C. Tello, Indigenous Archaeology, and Pre-Columbian Trepanation in Peru," in *Indigenous Visions: Rediscovering the World of Franz Boas*, ed. Ned Blackhawk and Isaiah Lorado Wilner (New Haven, CT: Yale University Press, 2018).

24 Cecilia Méndez G., "Incas Sí, Indios No: Notes on Peruvian Creole Nationalism and Its Contemporary Crisis," *Journal of Latin American Studies* 28, no. 1 (1996): 197–225.

25 De la Cadena, *Indigenous Mestizos*; Deborah Poole, *Vision, Race, and Modernity: A Visual Economy of the Andean Image World* (Princeton, NJ: Princeton University Press, 1997).

26 See chapters by Heilman and Wilson in Drinot, *La patria nueva*. On *gamonales*, see Deborah Poole, ed., *Unruly Order: Violence, Power, and Cultural Identity in the High Provinces of Southern Peru* (Boulder, CO: Westview Press, 1994).

27 Fernando Santos Granero, *Slavery and Utopia: The Wars and Dreams of an Amazonian World Transformer* (Austin: University of Texas Press, 2018).

28 Beverly Adams and Natalia Majluf, eds., *Redes de vanguardia: Amauta y América Latina, 1926–1930* (Lima: Asociación Museo de Arte de Lima–MALI, 2019).

29 Alberto Flores Galindo, *La agonía de Mariátegui: La polémica con la Komintern* (Lima: DESCO, 1980); Gerardo Leibner, *El mito del socialismo indígena en Mariátegui* (Lima: Fondo Editorial PUCP, 1999).

30 For recent studies, see Martín Bergel, *La desmesura revolucionaria: Cultura y política en los orígenes del APRA* (Lima: La Siniestra Ensayos, 2019); Geneviève Dorais, *Journey to Indo-América: APRA and the Transnational Politics of Exile, Persecution, and Solidarity, 1918–1945* (Cambridge: Cambridge University Press, 2021); and Iñigo García-Bryce, *Haya de la Torre and the Pursuit of Power in Twentieth-Century Peru and Latin America* (Chapel Hill: University of North Carolina Press, 2018).

31 Peter F. Klarén, *Modernization, Dislocation, and Aprismo: Origins of the Peruvian Aprista Party, 1870–1932* (Austin: University of Texas Press, 1973).

32 Carleton Beals, *Fire on the Andes* (Philadelphia: J. B. Lippincott, 1934), 421.

33 On corruption in the Leguía regime, see Alfonso Quiroz, *Historia de la corrupción en el Perú* (Lima: Instituto de Estudios Peruanos, 2013). On the Tacna and Arica dispute, which was resolved by a treaty that gave Chile sovereignty over Arica while Tacna was returned to Peru, see William E. Skuban, *Lines in the Sand: Nationalism and Identity on the Peruvian-Chilean Frontier* (Albuquerque: University of New Mexico Press, 2007).

34 Carlos Contreras, *Historia económica del Perú: Desde la conquista española hasta el presente* (Lima: Instituto de Estudios Peruanos, 2021), chap. 11.

35 See Nelson Manrique, *Mercado interno y región: La sierra central, 1820–1930* (Lima: DESCO, 1987). See also Florencia E. Mallon, *The Defense of Community in Peru's Central Highlands: Peasant Struggle and Capi-*

talist Transition, 1860–1940 (Princeton, NJ: Princeton University Press, 1983); Federico Helfgott, "Transformations in Labor, Land and Community: Mining and Society in Pasco, Peru, 20th Century to the Present" (PhD dissertation, University of Michigan, 2013); and Barbara Roberta Galindo Rodrigues Marcos, "Vidas huérfanas, ciudades torturadas y derechos humanos ecosociales: Representaciones culturales del terror minero en los Andes" (PhD dissertation, UCLA, 2021).

36 The first militarism occurred in the immediate post independence period, and the second militarism followed Peru's defeat in the war with Chile and lasted until 1895.

37 Beals, *Fire on the Andes*, 418.

38 On the UR, see Tirso Anibal Molinari Morales, *El fascismo en el Perú: La Unión Revolucionaria 1931–1936* (Lima: Fondo Editorial de la Facultad de Ciencias Sociales de la UNMSM, 2006).

39 Gregory T. Cushman, *Guano and the Opening of the Pacific World: A Global Ecological History* (Cambridge: Cambridge University Press, 2013).

40 Thorp and Bertram, *Peru 1890–1977*, 173.

41 Thorp and Bertram, *Peru 1890–1977*, 195.

42 A former close confidant of Haya de la Torre, and later in life a staunch anti-communist, Ravines took over the Peruvian Socialist Party following the death of Mariátegui in April 1930, renaming it the Peruvian Communist Party and aligning it with the Comintern. On these processes, see Ádám Anderle, *Los movimientos políticos en el Perú entre las dos guerras mundiales: Ensayo* (Havana: Casa de las Américas, 1985).

43 Paulo Drinot, "Creole Anti-Communism: Labor, the Peruvian Communist Party, and APRA, 1930–1934," *Hispanic American Historical Review* 92, no. 4 (2012): 703–36.

44 Quiroz, *Historia de la corrupción*.

45 Steve Stein, *Populism in Peru: The Emergence of the Masses and the Politics of Social Control* (Madison: University of Wisconsin Press, 1980); Robert S. Jansen, *Revolutionizing Repertoires: The Rise of Populist Mobilization in Peru* (Chicago: University of Chicago Press, 2017).

46 Thomas M. Davies, *Indian Integration in Peru: A Half Century of Experience, 1900–1948* (Lincoln: University of Nebraska Press, 1974).

47 Carmen Rosa Balbi and Laura Madalengoitia, *Parlamento y lucha política, Peru 1932* (Lima: DESCO, 1980).

48 The Union Popular, a Catholic political party, was short-lived, but Catholic lay organizations were established to promote social Catholicism among labor and Indigenous populations. See Ricardo Cubas Ramacciotti, *The Politics of Religion and the Rise of Social Catholicism in Peru (1884–1935): Faith, Workers, and Race Before Liberation Theology* (Leiden: Brill, 2018); and Jeffrey L. Klaiber, *La iglesia en el Perú* (Lima: Pontificia Universidad Católica del Perú, 1988).

49 Mariemma Mannarelli, *La domesticación de las mujeres: Patriarcado y género en la historia peruana* (Lima: La Siniestra Ensayos, 2018).

50 On feminism and prostitution, see Paulo Drinot, *The Sexual Question: A History of Prostitution in Peru, 1850s–1950s* (Cambridge: Cambridge University Press, 2020).

51 Margarita Zegarra Flórez, *María Jesús Alvarado: La construcción de una intelectual feminista en Lima (1878–1915)* (Lima: Fondo Editorial del Congreso del Perú, 2016).

52 Myrna Ivonne Wallace Fuentes, *Most Scandalous Woman: Magda Portal and the Dream of Revolution in Peru* (Norman: University of Oklahoma Press, 2017).

53 Carolina Carlessi, *Mujeres en el origen del movimiento sindical: Crónica de una lucha Huacho 1916–1917* (Lima: TAREA, 1976).

54 Iñigo García-Bryce, "A Revolution Remembered, a Revolution Forgotten: The 1932 Aprista Insurrection in Trujillo, Peru," *A Contracorriente* 7, no. 3 (2010): 277–322; Margarita Giesecke, *La insurrección de Trujillo: Jueves 7 de julio de 1932* (Lima: Fondo Editorial del Congreso del Perú, 2010).

55 Carlos Camacho Arango, *El conflicto de Leticia (1932–1933) y los ejércitos de Perú y Colombia* (Bogotá: Universidad Externado de Colombia, 2017).

56 See Luis Miguel Glave and Jaime Urrutia, "Radicalismo político en élites regionales: Ayacucho, 1930–1956," *Debate Agrario*, no. 31 (2020): 1–37; Jaymie Heilman, *Before the Shining Path: Politics in Rural Ayacucho, 1895–1980* (Stanford, CA: Stanford University Press, 2010); David Nugent, *Modernity at the Edge of Empire: State, Individual, and Nation in the Northern Peruvian Andes, 1885–1935* (Stanford, CA: Stanford University Press, 1997); Lewis Taylor, "The Origins of APRA in Cajamarca, 1928–1935," *Bulletin of Latin American Research* 19, no. 4 (2000): 437–59; and F. Wilson, *Citizenship and Political Violence in Peru: An Andean Town, 1870s–1970s* (New York: Palgrave Macmillan, 2013).

57 Julio G. Gutiérrez L., *Así nació el Cuzco rojo: Contribución a su historia política, 1924–1934* (Cuzco: Empresa Editora Humboldt, 1986); José Luis Rénique, *Los sueños de la sierra: Cusco en el siglo XX* (Lima: CEPES, 1991).

58 Karin Apel, *De la hacienda a la comunidad: La sierra de Piura 1934–1990* (Lima: Institut Français d'Études Andines, 2014).

59 Paul W. Drake, *The Money Doctor in the Andes: The Kemmerer Missions, 1923–1933* (Durham, NC: Duke University Press, 1989).

60 On the 1934 railway strike, see Paulo Drinot, "The 1934 Southern Railway Strike in Peru," *Bulletin of Latin American Research* 23, no. 1 (2004): 1–29.

61 Juan Carlos Yáñez Andrade, "La Organización Internacional del Trabajo y el problema social indígena: La encuesta en Perú de 1936," *Secuencia* 98 (2017): 130–57.

62 Javier Puente, "De comunero a campesino: El 'corto siglo veinte' en el campo peruano, 1920–1969," *Investigaciones Históricas* 40 (2020): 9–26. See also Javier Puente, *The Rural State: Making Comunidades, Campesinos and Conflict in Peru's Central Sierra* (Austin: University of Texas Press, 2023).

63 Heraclio Bonilla, "La defensa del espacio comunal como fuente de conflicto: San Juan de Ocros vs. Pampas (Ayacucho), 1940–1970," in *El futuro del pasado: Las coordenadas de la configuración de los Andes*, vol. 2 (Lima: Fondo Editorial del Pedagógico San Marcos / Instituto de Ciencias y Humanidades, 2005).

64 Gavin Smith, *Livelihood and Resistance: Peasants and the Politics of Land in Peru* (Berkeley: University of California Press, 1991).

65 Deborah Poole, "Between Threat and Guarantee: Justice and Community in the Margins of the Peruvian State," in *Anthropology in the Margins of the State*, ed. Veena Das and Deborah Poole (Santa Fe, NM: School of American Research Press, 2004), 35–66.

66 On the Prado family, see Dennis L. Gilbert, *La oligarquía peruana: Historia de tres familias* (Lima: Editorial Horizonte, 1982); and Felipe Portocarrero S., *El imperio Prado, 1890–1970* (Lima: Universidad del Pacífico, 1995).

67 Mark Carey, *In the Shadow of Melting Glaciers: Climate Change and Andean Society* (Oxford: Oxford University Press, 2010).

68 Willie Hiatt, "Slapstick Diplomacy: Charlie Chaplin's *The Great Dictator* and Latin American Theatres of War," *Journal of Latin American Studies* 50, no. 4 (2018): 777–803.

69 See, among others, Mary Fukumoto, *Hacia un nuevo sol: Japoneses y sus descendientes en el Perú* (Lima: Asociación Peruano Japonesa del Perú, 1997); Amelia Morimoto, *Los japoneses y sus descendientes en el Perú* (Lima: Fondo Editorial del Congreso del Perú, 1999); Daniel M. Masterson and Sayaka Funada-Classen, *The Japanese in Latin America* (Urbana: University of Illinois Press, 2004); Luis Rocca Torres, *Japoneses bajo el sol de Lambayeque* (Lima: Universidad Nacional Pedro Ruiz Gallo, 1997); and Chikako Yamawaki, *Estrategias de vida de los inmigrantes asiáticos en el Perú* (Lima: Instituto de Estudios Peruanos / Japan Center for Area Studies, 2002).

70 Paul Gootenberg, *Andean Cocaine: The Making of a Global Drug* (Chapel Hill: University of North Carolina Press, 2009).

71 Ombeline Dagicour, "Régénerer la patrie, construire l'état: Savoirs geographiques et production du territoire: Pérou (1900–1930)" (PhD dissertation, Université de Genève / Université Paris 1 Panthéon-Sorbonne, 2017).

72 For a recent study of the war, see François Bignon, "La guerre entre le Pérou et l'Equateur et la nationalisation des frontières andines (1933–1945)" (PhD dissertation, Université de Rennes 2, 2020).

73 Mara Loveman, *National Colors: Racial Classification and the State in Latin America* (Oxford: Oxford University Press, 2014).

74 David Sulmont and Juan Carlos Callirgos, "¿El País de Todas Las Sangres? Race and Ethnicity in Contemporary Peru," in *Pigmentocracies: Ethnicity, Race and Color in Latin America*, ed. Edward Telles (Chapel Hill: University of North Carolina Press, 2014).

75 Werlich, *Peru*, 227.

76 Marisol de la Cadena, "'Women Are More Indian': Ethnicity and Gender in a Community near Cuzco," in *Ethnicity, Markets, and Migration in the Andes: At the Crossroads of History and Anthropology*, ed. Brooke Larson, Olivia Harris, and Enrique Tandeter (Durham, NC: Duke University Press, 1995).

77 Carlos Contreras, *Maestros, mistis y campesinos en el Perú rural del siglo XX* (Lima: Instituto de Estudios Peruanos, 1996).

78 Werlich, *Peru*, 228; Davies, *Indian Integration in Peru*, 1974.

79 Carlos Bustíos Romaní, *La salud pública, la seguridad social y el Perú demoliberal, 1933–1968* (Lima: Concytec, 2005).

80 Thorp and Bertram, *Peru 1890–1977*, 185.

81 Thorp and Bertram, *Peru 1890–1977*, 205.

82 Odd Arne Westad, *The Cold War: A World History* (London: Penguin, 2018), 361.

83 See Cushman, *Guano and the Opening of the Pacific World*, chap. 9.

84 As Matos Mar wrote in his classic study, "It was the 1950s that gave way to the configuration of the central elements that characterize today's society." See José Matos Mar, *Desborde popular y crisis del Estado: El nuevo rostro del Perú en la década de 1980* (Lima: Instituto de Estudios Peruanos, 1984), 30.

85 Alan Durston, *Escritura en quechua y sociedad serrana en transformación: Perú, 1920–1960* (Lima: Instituto Francés de Estudios Andinos, 2019).

86 Fernando Santos Granero and Frederica Barclay, *Selva Central: History, Economy, and Land Use in Peruvian Amazonia* (Washington, DC: Smithsonian Institution Press, 1998); Santos Granero and Barclay, *Tamed Frontiers*.

87 David Collier, *Squatters and Oligarchs: Authoritarian Rule and Policy Change in Peru* (Baltimore: Johns Hopkins University Press, 1976); Jean-Claude Driant, *Las barriadas de Lima: Historia e interpretación* (Lima: Institut Français d'Études Andines, 2015).

88 Juan Gargurevich, *Historia de la prensa peruana, 1594–1990* (Lima: La Voz Ediciones, 1991).

89 Luis Gómez, "Música Criolla: Cultural Practices and National Issues in Modern Peru, the Case of Lima (1920–1960)" (PhD dissertation, Stony Brook University, 2010).

90 Emilio Bustamante, *La radio en el Perú* (Lima: Fondo Editorial de la Universidad de Lima, 2016).

91 José Antonio Llorens Amico, *Música popular en Lima: Criollos y andinos* (Lima: Instituto de Estudios Andinos / Instituto Indigenista Interamericano, 1983).

92 Aníbal Quijano, *Lo cholo y el conflicto cultural en el Perú* (Lima: Mosca Azul, 1980).

93 José Luis Rodríguez Toledo, "El migrante estereotipado: Etnia y humor en serrucho, 1950–1962" (master's thesis, Pontificia Universidad Católica del Perú, 2019).

94   On how the repression of APRA played out at the local level in Chachapoyas, see David Nugent, *The Encrypted State: Delusion and Displacement in the Peruvian Andes* (Stanford, CA: Stanford University Press, 2019).

95   Raúl Necochea López, *A History of Family Planning in Twentieth-Century Peru* (Chapel Hill: University of North Carolina Press, 2014).

96   Quoted in François Bourricaud, *Power and Society in Contemporary Peru* (London: Faber and Faber, 1970), 234.

97   Howard Handelman, *Struggle in the Andes: Peasant Political Mobilization in Peru* (Austin: University of Texas Press, 1975); Rénique, *Los sueños de la sierra*.

98   On Vicos, see William Stein, *Vicisitudes del discurso del desarrollo en el Perú: Una etnografía sobre la modernidad del Proyecto Vicos* (Lima: SUR, 2000). On the Programa Puno Tambopata, see María Emma Mannarelli, "La Misión Andina en Puno, Peru: el estado y lo doméstico," in *El programa indigenista andino, 1951–1973: Las mujeres en los ensambles estatales del desarrollo*, ed. Mercedes Prieto (Quito: FLACSO Ecuador / Instituto de Estudios Peruanos, 2017), 163–234.

99   Daniel M. Masterson, *Militarism and Politics in Latin America: Peru from Sánchez Cerro to Sendero Luminoso* (Westport, CT: Greenwood, 1991).

100   I draw here on my chapter in Paulo Drinot, ed., *Che's Travels: The Making of a Revolutionary in 1950s Latin America* (Durham, NC: Duke University Press, 2010).

101   John Gunther, *Inside South America* (London: Hamish Hamilton, 1967).

102   On this literature, see Thomas C. Field, Stella Krepp, and Vanni Pettinà, *Latin America and the Global Cold War* (Chapel Hill: University of North Carolina Press, 2020).

103   On US-Peru relations, see Richard J. Walter, *Peru and the United States, 1960–1975: How Their Ambassadors Managed Foreign Relations in a Turbulent Era* (University Park: Pennsylvania State University Press, 2010).

104   A de facto process of private land redistribution had begun already in the northern province of Cajamarca, where, Deere shows, landlords, anticipating an inevitable agrarian reform, sold land to peasants. See Carmen Diana Deere, *Household and Class Relations: Peasants and Landlords in Northern Peru* (Berkeley: University of California Press, 1990).

105   An earlier ELN guerrilla *foco*, in 1963, had been quickly defeated, resulting in the death of the young poet Javier Héraud. José Luis Rénique, *Incendiar la pradera: Un ensayo sobre la revolución en el Perú* (Lima: La Siniestra Ensayos, 2015); Jan Lust, *La lucha revolucionaria, Perú 1958–1967* (Barcelona: RBA, 2013).

106   Michael F. Brown and Eduardo Fernández, *War of Shadows: The Struggle for Utopia in the Peruvian Amazon* (Berkeley: University of California Press, 1991).

107   On "The *Pongo's* Dream" as a *pachacuti*, see Alberto Flores Galindo, *Buscando un Inca: Identidad y utopía en los Andes* (Lima: SUR Casa de Estudios del Socialismo, 2005).

108   Mark Rice, *Making Machu Picchu: The Politics of Tourism in Twentieth-Century Peru* (Chapel Hill: University of North Carolina Press, 2018).

109   José Matos Mar, ed., *Perú problema: 5 ensayos* (Lima: Instituto de Estudios Peruanos, 1968).

110   Bourricaud, *Power and Society in Contemporary Peru.*

111   For a recent study of the agrarian reform, see Anna Cant, *Land Without Masters: Agrarian Reform and Political Change Under Peru's Military Government* (Austin: University of Texas Press, 2021).

FIVE / EDUARDO DARGENT BOCANEGRA

From the Baseless Triangle to the Realm of Anti-Politics

Political Inclusion, "Articulation," and Mobilization in Peru (1968–1994)

The period 1968–94 witnessed major changes in terms of political inclusion, mobilization, and "articulation" in Peru.[1] But one peculiarity of this period is that these changes did not constitute a linear process in every dimension. During the 1960s and 1970s, the increasing inclusion of citizens from sectors that were traditionally left out of politics was accompanied by rising mobilization and "articulation" in political parties and civil organizations. However, these linkages and mobilization would fall away in the 1990s and continue to stagnate in the decades that followed. In this chapter, we will see, then, how during those two decades Peru embraced a more inclusive, organized, and mobilized (while not always democratic) politics while, at the same time, paving the way for the political terrain of the 1990s: a country lacking political linkages and with a demobilized citizenry, yet still inclusive in political terms. This chapter has two objectives: first, to narrate four decades of profound changes and dramatic events in Peru, and second, to explore why a period of great political organization and mobilization also sowed the seeds for the country's subsequent depoliticization.

Why focus on political "articulation," inclusion, and mobilization as a narrative foundation for what was to follow? These dimensions, I argue, were at the heart of a political debate that imagined different ways of promoting and combining them for a better society. This focus allows us to better understand the peculiarities of the period in comparison with what went before and what would come later. In the decades prior to the period studied, there was a slight break from the "traditional" political organization that prevailed in the country—from the political system that Julio Cotler described as a "baseless triangle." In this traditional society, elite actors at the top were linked through different actors (state representatives, latifundistas, judges) all the way down to the bottom to advance their common interests, but those at the bottom lacked analogous connections. Then, in the 1960s, organization and mobilization increased at the base, as this once fragmented and excluded space was gradually connected.[2] These trends continued under a military regime that, despite limiting electoral participation and the exercise of political rights, furthered inclusion by mobilizing—and attempting to co-opt—traditionally excluded sectors. Yet the regime ultimately contributed to its own demise, creating the conditions for the emerging popular organizations to overwhelm the state and push the army out of power. In 1979, the constitution recognized the voting rights of the illiterate, thereby enfranchising a sizable sector that had lacked political rights. The early 1980s marked the high point of mobilization and assemblage of political parties and social organizations in the country. The decade began with a democracy featuring parties that, though far from strong in comparative terms, were enjoying their high-water mark in Peruvian history.[3] Contrary to the gloomy forecasts in previous years about Peru's prospects of such democratizing linkages, the politicization came from below.

By the late 1980s and early 1990s, however, what remained was a "disarticulated" and demobilized political system. The political Peru that President Alberto Fujimori (1990–2000) and his allies attempted to dismantle was the mobilized and organized Peru that, according to the anti-movement narrative propagated by conservatives at the turn of the twenty-first century, brought crisis, disorder, and violence to the country. Fujimori represented a new type of authoritarianism—one that, by permitting the electoral participation and political inclusion of new sectors, would disincentivize mobilization and organization. However, he did not do this by force alone. This regime heralded a new kind of authoritarian legitimacy that Carlos Iván Degregori has called "the realm of anti-politics."[4] Many characteristics of this demobilized and disconnected but more politically inclusive Peru outlived *fujimorismo*.[5] Alberto Vergara's chapter in this book further explores this new reality and the extent of the changes that occurred over the Fujimori years.

One apparent explanation for this change is the crisis of legitimacy precipitated by the weak performance of the political parties during the 1980s amid a brutal economic crisis and the violence of the insurgent group Sendero Luminoso (Shining Path). Another is the control and repression that *fujimorismo* exercised over its opponents for ten years. These explanations are relevant when it comes to the immediate causes, but they lose sight of the deeper-rooted processes that affected Peru, and compounded the breaking of linkages and demobilization, during the period. This is not to downplay the errors, corruption, and malpractice of the parties at that time, which undoubtedly played a part in cementing anti-political legitimacy and enabled the actions and measures of the authoritarian regime during the 1990s. But to understand the extent of Peru's political wasteland, this chapter proposes, from a Latin American comparative perspective, that it is necessary to take into consideration the influence of four transformative processes vis-à-vis political "articulation" in Peru: agrarian reform, political violence, hyperinflation, and market reforms. These processes, as we will see, affect the structure of political and social organizations as well as the resources to which they have access, hampering the sustainability of existing organizations and the emergence of new ones.[6] Several Latin American countries have experienced one or more similar processes. But what makes Peru distinctive is that it underwent all these processes and each had profound consequences. Some authors have explored the effects of one or more of these processes in an attempt to understand the current "disarticulation" in Peru.[7] This chapter builds on these studies but contributes by highlighting the joint and sequential effects of these four seismic processes, two of which unfolded simultaneously.

Why begin the period with 1968 and end with 1994? Although—as Paulo Drinot shows in this book—there had been a good deal of political mobilization and organization beginning in the 1950s, while major demographic and social change was already underway, the military government that took power in 1968 is key to understanding the "democratizing" changes, even if the regime in itself was not democratic. The actions of the military government help to understand the weakening of conservative actors who had limited the participation and organization of popular social actors as well as the promotion (at times involuntary) of other actors from the base. The chapter ends in 1994 because, more than Fujimori's self-coup of 1992—a plebiscitary symbol of anti-politics—or the 1993 constitution, *fujimorismo* and the narrative of demobilization were ultimately legitimized by the economic leap of that year and the sharp decline in Sendero Luminoso's activity starting from the previous one.[8] This legitimacy was evident in Fujimori's emphatic reelection in 1995, when his party won enough seats in Congress to afford the regime a more autocratic turn.

Social Democratization, Conservative Politics, and the Reformist Coup (1968–1980)

What do Peru's politics of the decades prior to Juan Velasco Alvarado's coup of 1968 teach us? Authors such as François Bourricaud, Giorgio Alberti and Fernando Fuenzalida, and Julio Cotler have described a major economic and landowning power that spanned the country and represented the interests of the upper classes in national politics; at the apex of this system were sectors interlinked with the world economy and others associated with traditional economic activities throughout the country.[9] These elites involved themselves in society through local operators, among them public officials whose appointment and continuity in post depended on the local powers. This was a tacit alliance for control of politics from above. It was this conservative order that Cotler termed the "baseless triangle," as the union of the elites and their go-betweens contrasted with the lack of linkages of the actors at the base of the triangle due to the actions of that same elite.[10] Although the Partido Aprista Peruana (APRA), the left, and other groups had sought to build a distinctive political representation, until the 1950s the traditional order proved robust. In general terms, the armed forces had been instrumental in maintaining this state of affairs. Bourricaud describes this political order as "an oligarchy that does not feel identified with the society it directs from a distance; middle classes both insurgent and prudent; a 'submerged' mass who escape their condition by organizing to defend specific, narrow interests, and who abandon themselves to brief bouts of violence whose political exploitation until now no one has been able to take advantage of."[11]

More recently, this conceptualization has been called into question. As Alejandro Diez argued some years ago, in reality the elites were not quite so united and the base not so disorganized.[12] The chapter by Paulo Drinot, which precedes this one, explores some of these very nuances. However, in general, the image is one of a hierarchical political system, closed off to subaltern groups. To be sure, all this reveals a country where—unlike others in the region with more inclusive systems or more channels of participation—these differences still characterized and marked politics. The notion of the baseless triangle may have proven hyperbolic but, from a comparative perspective, it is still useful for the purposes of the analysis I seek to present in this chapter.

Moreover, the state was weak and highly dependent on the interests of the business elite and its international partners. Regulation and control of banking, agricultural, and mining activities were limited. In comparative terms, the Peruvian state was still tied to a model characterized by export promotion and little distinction between the interests of business actors: a clear case of an enclave economy in Latin America.[13] The state had undergone fewer transformations than others in the region, many of which had established professional bureaucracies with greater autonomy from these business interests. Many of the recommendations disseminated globally by international agencies about the need for state action to plan and promote development or tackle the problem of concentrated agricultural ownership had reached Peru during the governments of Manuel Prado (1956–62) and Fernando Belaúnde (1963–68), but their political uptake was timid and their impact limited. That is, the developmentalist wave swept over Peru without leaving much of an impression.

In the 1950s, major political and social shifts affected the system. The end of the Odría dictatorship in 1956 left a country in flux, with considerable demographic changes and mass rural-urban migrations. Acción Popular (Popular Action) emerged in those years as a mesocratic and regional party-political force. Though by now approaching its most conservative incarnation, APRA also retained strong support despite the numerous elite and military vetoes against its political participation in the previous decades. And an event in 1962 is key to understanding the subsequent military reformism of Velasco's Revolutionary Government of the Armed Forces, starting in 1968. That year, land seizures in the Valle de La Convención in Cuzco threatened prevailing land usage and working conditions in the valley.[14] Although this mobilization was ruthlessly suppressed by the state, it coincided with a shift in the army's perspective on the mobilization of popular sectors. One sector of the military, reacting in part to the triumph of the Cuban Revolution, feared that a malaise was brewing in Peruvian society that threatened to spread throughout the country. Thus, a military reformist thought developed, especially at the Center for Advanced Military Studies (CAEM), which advocated channeling mobilization through the armed forces—which saw itself as the only institution capable of at once preventing revolutionary violence and leading the country to development. In contrast to what happened in the Southern Cone countries, in Peru the military sought the inclusion of the excluded rather than their repression. Of course, in Peru too there were restrictions on political participation and the exercise of rights, but in broad terms the military pursued inclusion and participation. There were also calls for the inclusion of sectors that had previously been marginalized, such as Indigenous people, who were now renamed "campesinos" in the government's rhetoric.[15]

These antecedents give some insight into the peculiarities of the military government, especially in its first phase under Juan Velasco Alvarado (1968–75). Velasco's "revolution from above," as Ellen Kay Trimberger called it, shook the country with its reforms.[16] The coup d'état of October 3, 1968, that unseated Fernando Belaúnde Terry only months before the 1969 general election was much more than a traditional coup. The pretext was political tension, economic crisis, and, in particular, the renewal of the oil exploitation contract between the Peruvian state and the International Petroleum Company (IPC). The army, like so many other times in its history, had toppled the president. But this time its plans were different: it was not just a case of "restoring order" and going back to the barracks. The army had a project for change.

The army and its civilian allies sought to undermine the established order, replace it with another, and build a new state that would implement reforms inspired by nationalist and developmentalist diagnoses of Peru's condition. As early as October 9, the military government made its mark by expropriating the IPC—then a potent symbol of foreign power in Peru—and signaled a shift in the relationship between the elite and foreign investment in the country. As Velasco stated on the first anniversary of the coup: "This revolution was initiated in order to lift Peru from its stagnation and its backwardness. It was done to radically alter the traditional structure of our society. . . . The implacable adversaries of our movement will always be those whose interests and privileges come under threat: the oligarchy."[17]

These words were no exaggeration: Those years ushered in major changes in the Peruvian state and in its relationship with society. The government strengthened and expanded the bureaucracy by broadening its functions and objectives. It also increased the number of ministries. The state took on planning responsibilities and became highly active in the business sphere. As well as the IPC, other foreign and certain national privately owned companies were nationalized so that new state-run firms could exploit the country's resources or provide services considered strategic in the mining, fishing, oil, and communications industries, among others; examples included Centromin (mining), Pescaperú (fisheries), Petroperú (oil), Aeroperú (aviation), and the Compañía Peruana de Teléfonos (telecommunications).[18] In a few short years, the liberal economic model that had prevailed until then, focused on the export of raw materials, was replaced by one in which the state was far more active, with broad developmentalist aims, though the economic structure was only marginally altered.

The military government pursued a different international path for the country: a third way in a bipolar world. In those Cold War years, the government presented itself to the world as an alternative to both capitalism and communism. It proposed a nationalism that would strengthen Peruvian-owned private enterprise, alongside public enterprises, and the exploitation of natural resources to achieve development. The government bolstered relations with the Soviet bloc while distancing itself somewhat from its close ally the United States, though the two countries remained on open and relatively cordial terms.[19]

Thus, the military government, at least during its first phase, represented much more than just an authoritarian chapter in the history of Peru. This was a developmentalist and national integration project that understood change through different dimensions. In addition to implementing agrarian reform, industrial policies, and the nationalization of foreign companies, the Velasco government demonstrated its broad-based approach by fostering change on several other fronts. It sponsored educational, cultural, and sports policies, made efforts to establish organizational links with popular associations, and took an interest in building a new national history and developing tourism, among other endeavors.[20] The extent of those changes can be ascertained in the video sequence of the national anthem that Peru's state television channel broadcast in the 1970s and early 1980s. In the video, the government's recognition of *mestizaje* and indigeneity as part of the nation, the exploitation of natural resources, the development of industry and science, and other aspects of the national revolutionary project are all clearly represented.[21]

It is not possible to dwell here on each of these reforms, but, given its significance and its impact on political "articulation," we will focus on the agrarian reform. The purpose of this reform was to tackle Peru's vast concentration of land, improve distribution, and promote greater productivity. On June 24, 1969, the reform process began with the expropriation of sugar plantation owners in the north. The Agrarian Reform Law adopted the most extreme positions in the debates that had been taking place over how to implement reform: limits of 50 hectares were placed on plantations, and not only were unproductive latifundios in the Andes expropriated, but so too were agro-industrial complexes on the coast. The Peruvian agrarian reform was the most far-reaching of its kind in Latin America after Cuba's, and it fundamentally shifted the balance of agrarian power.[22] It was complemented, in the following years, by popular participation measures channeled through the National Support System for Social Mobilization (SINAMOS), which aimed to strengthen relations between the state and the campesinos—albeit, as Anna Cant shows, with significant variation from region to region.[23] The Spanish acronym represented the government's ideal of a new society without masters (*sin amos*), although co-optation, not just mobilization, was also one of the policy's main aims.

Although land redistribution was extensive (some 369,000 families benefited), critics argued that it privileged campesinos who worked the haciendas on a regular basis and not the many others whose work was more occasional. Other criticisms were leveled against the reform's negative impact on production and on modern areas of agriculture in which there was greater potential for development. But as we will see, its impact in terms of weakening landowning interests and their influence on politics was considerable.

In the educational sphere, the military junta strove to build a more inclusive national community that recognized its campesino roots, while promoting a new narrative about what it meant to be Peruvian. The government increased educational spending and furthered the access of the rural and urban poor to education. It built educational infrastructure throughout the country and introduced new forms of technical education amid the drive to industrialize. Moreover, it added new content to the national

Figure 5.1 General Juan Velasco Alvarado headed a peculiarly authoritarian government by the armed forces which nevertheless sought to democratize social relations
in a country that was highly exclusionary.

curriculum and introduced a single school uniform as a symbol of equality. The teaching of Quechua and pre-military instruction became part of
regular school courses. Other government measures included turning public universities into more inclusive spaces that would contribute to national
development through training and research. The profound yet contentious
reforms continued until 1974, just one year before Velasco's removal. That
year, the government brought mass media under state control and pledged
that it would serve the *pueblo organizado*, the organized people.

There is a contentious debate about the legacy of this period, especially as concerns the agrarian reform and other measures that impacted
the country's economy. The reform had a highly negative impact on Peru's
nascent agroindustry; many of the nationalization experiments were onerous (foreign companies were expropriated at high prices), and the nationalized companies clearly underperformed. A developmentalist model was
vigorously pursued when the serious limitations and drawbacks of many
of the associated policies were already apparent from the experiences of
other countries. It is clear that these ambitious plans were beyond what
a weak state was able to successfully implement, giving rise to a series of
inefficiencies and spiraling costs.[24] Many of these inefficiencies would

continue to plague the state into the 1980s. But it is also unquestionable that the seven years of the Velasco government brought about necessary social changes in society. The democratization process now gathering pace shook Peru's social and political structures. Moreover, the state expanded and developed its territorial presence while distancing itself from the business world and pursuing greater inclusion of the people.

When it comes to political inclusion, "articulation," and mobilization, which is the focal point of this chapter's narrative and analytical approach, the first phase of the military government entailed processes in which inclusion and participation were incentivized through ties with the state. As noted earlier, in its promotion of participation, *velasquismo* was very different from other Latin American military regimes of the era that opposed participation and even harshly suppressed popular organizations. Alfred Stepan has classified contemporaneous military governments in the region as either "inclusive corporatist" or "exclusive corporatist," depending on their relations with popular organizations.[25] The Peruvian regime resembled other military corporatisms in the region in that it took power to launch a national development plan and privileged a corporate relationship with society. But in this case, the regime's diagnosis was that the best way of avoiding a revolution was to channel popular malaise and interests—not suppress or marginalize them in the manner of the exclusive corporatisms of the Southern Cone.

The military government's measures aimed to manage the growing mobilization, reduce the influence of political parties and other organizations such as labor unions, and build its own support base.[26] Evelyne Huber shows how the reforms aimed at fostering the industrial community and establishing new labor relations served to protect and promote unions and strengthen the left, which continued to grow over these years.[27] The assumption was that these state-promoted organizations could be part of a base of support for the reforms, but in reality they exploited the sympathetic new legislation and remained close to established leftist organizations. Organizations that did so included the Campesino Confederation of Peru (with 250,000 members in 1978) and various unions, such as the General Union of Peruvian Education Workers (SUTEP) and the General Workers' Union of Peru (CGTP). According to Julio Cotler, this failure is also explained in part by the competition between different factions of the military, which ended up diluting any joint effort.[28]

The best-known program to this end was SINAMOS, but similar forms of organizational promotion were also deployed in other associations, such as the National Agrarian Confederation and the Workers' Union of the Peruvian Revolution. However, this effort failed and these organized popular actors achieved considerable autonomy from the state.[29] Thus, it was mobilization that ultimately had a hand in toppling the government and precipitating a return to democracy, with many of these organizations, defined as classist (which meant that they were intended to further the class interests of their members), demanding the army's departure from power through mass mobilizations in 1976 and 1977. This classism was not just strategic or symbolic; it had very important implications for these organizations' relations with the state, the types of demands channeled, and their conception of democracy. The simultaneous economic slowdown due to international conditions accompanying this moment kindled social protest and weakened the government.

However, the left that grew stronger over this period was highly fragmented. Far from building a united front based on their similarities, its constituent groups were divided by their differing views about the appropriate route for revolutionary political action, their links to various economic activities, or their adherence to leftist governments around the world. Though fragmentation was not atypical of Latin American left-wing politics, in the Peruvian case it was particularly severe, with no dominant group capable of linking (and subordinating) the rest. The different factions included those with close links to the Soviet Union, who espoused strategies centered on the urban unions as a basis for political action; Maoists, who pursued linkages with the countryside and used universities and rural associations as their platforms; and minority strands ranging from Trotskyists to eccentric extremists who followed the Albanian route.[30] As Paula Muñoz has proposed, the need to appear more radical than a nationalist and developmentalist government likely pushed several of these actors to even further extremes on the spectrum, which not only exacerbated fragmentation but also produced differing degrees of ideological radicalism—a trend that would continue into the 1980s.[31]

In August 1975, General Francisco Morales Bermúdez (1975–80) staged an internal coup against Velasco amid increasing political instability. Velasco, seriously ill since the previous year, had lost control of the armed forces, and his reform project was on the wane.[32] A negative economic situation along with the enormous costs to the treasury of the ongoing reforms took their toll on his government. The military faction that took over was more conservative and halted the reform processes, even if it did retain elements of the revolutionary rhetoric and the economic model. Yet the economic measures with which this new faction proposed to tackle the economic crisis left it more vulnerable to criticism from political parties, business owners, and the mobilized population.

As noted earlier, the military government negotiated its return to the barracks under pressure from mass mobilizations against the austerity measures. A new, organized society, more vociferous in its redistributive demands than in the past, marked the transition. And the traditional political parties also added their voices to the demands for democratization. The mass protests and general strikes of 1976 and 1977 paved the way for a constituent assembly. When it came, the Constituent Assembly of 1978 marked the return of APRA to national politics, with the party returning thirty-seven members out of one hundred. It was followed by a coalition of the left (thirty-two members), divided among six groups, and the Partido Popular Cristiano, PPC (twenty-five members), a more economically liberal right-wing party that emerged from the split within Christian democracy. Acción Popular opted not to participate, to signal its rejection of the military government, while other leftist parties also opted out given their objection to bourgeois electoral politics.

The outcome of this assembly was the 1979 constitution, which prefaced a new democratic regime. The constitution made few changes to the economic model, though it did extend the franchise to those who could not read or write, which translated into the formal inclusion of all adult citizens in the country. In the 1980 election—the first in which all adults participated—the president and party overthrown in the coup of 1968, Fernando Belaúnde and Acción Popular, obtained resounding triumphs in the presidential and congressional contests. Belaúnde's party finished ahead of APRA, PPC, and, again, several leftist groups. In this way, the military government came to an end.

The new government did more than simply accelerate social changes that were already underway. Yes, there were ongoing transformations: brewing rural discontent over the land question, the emergence of new industrial actors, and mass migrations from the countryside to the cities. However, the intensification of many of these processes can only be understood, for better or for worse, in light of the actions of Velasco's Revolutionary Government. Velasco's administration created a different state, bolstered the organization and the relevance of the business class, and altered relations between state and society in a fundamental way. Moreover, he left a vast legacy to explore in terms of cultural change and national self-perception, from soccer to the emergence of national television. These years witnessed the composition of the patriotic songs Peruvians still sing, more than four decades on, when they watch their national soccer team play. This was an image of "being Peruvian" that truly cut through.

Before concluding this section, it is worth noting the other side of political "articulation" and participation that will contribute to understanding the Peru that would emerge in the following decades. Just as forms of social organization continued to grow in a democratizing and participative sense, in this period state action also influenced other forms of political organization that, elsewhere in the region, have sustained right-wing political parties and conservative organizations in general: specifically, elite agricultural powers were weakened and broke down in rural areas as a result of the agrarian reform. These actors have remained more active over time in countries that did not undergo an agrarian reform as profound as Peru's. Though it would be an exaggeration to suggest (as propagandists of the regime did) that the agrarian reform "broke the back of the oligarchy"—a series of changes in previous years had already paved the way for a less oligarchic country, while other economic actors remained operational during the military government—the process certainly broke the back of powerful agrarian interests. Local political actors and associations, as well as the then-influential National Agrarian Society, lost power and resources.[33] The *gamonales*, or hacienda landlords, faded as actors who could articulate national politics throughout the country. And, overall, a more centralized state, with more functions and agencies that exerted greater territorial presence, came to replace the previous state and the traditional local powers.

Toward the end of the military government, the weakening of these old actors was already apparent; no similar conservative agrarian actors would emerge in the politics of the 1980s and 1990s. By contrast, in other Latin American countries these conservative actors continue to organize politics to this day. In Colombia, for example, the National Front governments (1956–74) did not make fundamental changes to the land ownership structure and, partly as a result, the Liberal and Conservative Parties kept their rural bases in the 2000s even as these parties faded at the national level.[34] Or, in the case of Argentina, right-wing party politics continued to organize throughout the country through elite agrarian interests. The power afforded by land ownership in areas far from the seat of central government remains important to the analysis of political order in these societies. But this is not true of Peru, which, still today, has forms of large-scale agricultural property that differ from those in countries where landowning elites still enjoy a prominent voice in elections and considerable lobbying power. In Peru, the influence of these conservative actors has diminished.

It is also worth stressing, in order to understand what ensued in subsequent years, that the collapse of conservative power was not followed by the emergence of strong party elites in these regional spaces. The agrarian reform may have left a power vacuum but, given that the post-coup military government lasted twelve years, it was not filled by a new regional political elite linked to political parties. There was no consolidation of a more progressive political elite tied to the liberal professions represented by Acción Popular, Christian democracy, and some leftist groups—to which might have been added a still-stronger APRA at the local level, especially in the north.[35] For twelve years, the military government either fended off or co-opted regional political powers, preventing them from growing stronger and curbing their "training" in electoral politics and state administration. And though these actors reemerged once the military regime came to an end, they did so amid trying economic conditions and political conditions that were not conducive to the development of such capabilities. And so we come to the 1980s.

The 1980s: Greater Popular Political "Articulation" During the Worst Crisis in Peruvian History

The democracy that arose in the 1980s had some characteristics that were more auspicious for the development of political parties and social movements. The debilitation of the conservative framework did not mean that the country became disorganized politically. On the contrary, the late 1970s saw broad sectors of the population included by way of the party system, which appeared to be leading to a more inclusive politics structured into ideological blocs. The traditional parties returned to the fold together with a new electoral left looking to represent many of the new actors that were bolstered during the military government. These groups faced the challenge, following the return to democracy, of building new, stable relations to represent a very different population than that which existed in the 1970s. As we have seen, the collapse of the military regime attested to widespread social mobilization, led by labor unions and associations that became more prominent and fueled the Peruvian left during those years.[36] Other traditional parties, such as APRA and Acción Popular, also sought new forms of connecting to the expanded and diverse electorate.

The period began with Acción Popular and Fernando Belaúnde back in government (1980–85), though the party was further to the right than its previous incarnation. Belaúnde's first cabinet was led by Manuel Ulloa, a veteran from the right of the party. Alongside his dynamic team of technocrats in the Ministry of the Economy, Ulloa attempted to spearhead a series of reforms aimed at overhauling the economic system inherited from *velasquismo* through privatizations, elimination of price controls and subsidies, greater commercial openness, attraction of foreign investment to the mining sector, and other liberal measures. But Ulloa quickly encountered resistance—not only from APRA and the left but also from figures within his own party who saw the reforms as inimical to their own political and electoral interests. Belaúnde himself, an avid builder of infrastructure, contested the limits that his minister attempted to place on his projects. By comparison to the market reforms of the 1990s, these measures—especially those that were ultimately approved—were relatively modest, and this provides an insight into the predominant conceptions in Peruvian politics during those years. Belaúnde ended his term with more pragmatic cabinets but also facing an economic crisis and inflation—caused in part by the efforts of the United States to control its own interest rates—that was reaching worrying levels. The performance of the Acción Popular candidate in the 1985 election (who obtained just 7 percent of the vote) is revealing of a party that had failed to capitalize on its time in government.

We will say a lot more about the first Alan García government (1985–90) when we explore the concurrent economic crisis, but for now let's consider what Peru's first-ever APRA electoral victory, in 1985, meant for the country. García, who was just thirty-six years old, was able to exploit his position as a member of Congress to project a centrist discourse in a country polarized between left and right. He also managed to strike agreements with regional actors in order to win the candidacy and sideline an entire generation of APRA figures who, during the years of military dictatorship, had been awaiting their turn. García ended up winning 53 percent of the votes cast, well ahead of the left's candidate, Alfonso Barrantes, who mustered just 25 percent. The García government evinced a more protectionist and developmentalist profile, but it combined this formula with a series of measures intended to benefit party activists. As we will discuss later, this had the hallmarks of a typical populist party template to develop a base of activism and social support, but it was deployed during a global crisis in which, as we are more fully aware today, there was less space for such measures. Just as the military government had belatedly embraced developmentalism, García and APRA bet on expansionary measures at the worst possible moment. Political expediency appeared to have predisposed APRA and García toward audacious, heterodox ideas aimed at overcoming the crisis and avoiding the constraints of orthodox prescriptions. The government betrayed not only irresponsibility but also a belief that the crisis could be escaped without swallowing the bitter pill of economic orthodoxy.

To return to the theme of political "articulation" and mobilization, several domestic and comparative studies from that period have highlighted the changes that occurred in these dimensions. Those who read these descriptions from the vantage point of the politically fragmented Peru of today will be surprised by what they learn about the country's political life at the time.[37] Among the popular sectors, there was enthusiasm for the transformational potential of social movements, trade unions, and new forms of social organization.[38] The traditional parties returned to successfully contest democratic elections at the national and regional levels, and were joined by other new ones—especially from the left. A more democratic society, political sectors that represented it, and demands channeled through parties and social movements create the impression that, when it came to organizational strength, Peru's situation was somewhat positive: The political system was finally including marginalized sectors and, in so doing, recognized a series of interests beyond the "baseless triangle." This emerging modernity was auspicious for social democratization and inclusion.[39]

It would be an overstatement to suggest that all studies in those years displayed similar optimism about the transformational potential of social movements or the nascent party system. Moreover, the optimism on the part of various authors was not a product of similar expectations about the type of political regime that might arise from these changes; proposals ranged from classist positions, with their upbeat forecasts of a people's government, to others closer to a pluralist democratic conception. But the common basis of the prevailing optimism, beyond the differing degrees and positions, was the belief that—following the debilitation of the traditional conservative forces who opposed inclusion—a less hierarchical political society could emerge alongside a better state capable of responding to democratic demands and interests. Elsewhere, the cautious optimism was echoed in a continent undergoing transformation, including in some countries that a little earlier were governed by extremely repressive dictatorships. On the negative side, however, the Cold War was warming up, while authoritarianisms in Central America hardened.

Figure 5.2 Alfonso Barrantes at a rally during the electoral campaign for the office of mayor of Lima, 1983. Source: Archivo La República.

In Peru, the political party structure enjoyed success in local and general elections throughout the decade. In stark contrast to what we see today, local elections were won by candidates (most of them men but, very occasionally, some women) representing parties. Independent mayors were the exception. The left won the Lima mayoralty in 1983 when, under the leadership of Alfonso Barrantes, the Izquierda Unida (United Left) electoral alliance succeeded in representing a broad leftist coalition, as figure 5.2 shows. This alliance illustrated the advantages of joint action—and its prospects of winning—but there were also drawbacks to a coalition between political groups that had many differences, even if these were often difficult to understand from the outside. The Izquierda Unida lacked a centralized organizational structure that would enable the construction of common messages or policies. And the unanimity required for agreements precluded a rapid and strategic response to the challenges of electoral politics. These assorted advantages and limitations were demonstrated in the 1985 election.[40]

This greater political participation was explained, in part, by more clientelistic policies by the political parties. Given the type of state that

Peru had in those years, there were many spaces in public companies and offices that were occupied by party members, as well as mechanisms for incentives and subsidies that helped in the building of political links with different sectors. Overall, if one studies the Peruvian case at the start of the 1980s and consults the academic literature, one will be left with the impression of a country on its way to stronger political organization under democratic conditions—perhaps still not at very high levels, but beyond anything achieved in previous decades. There is no hint of the country's dramatic debilitation.

As we will see later when we take a more detailed look at the political violence and economic crisis of this decade, political parties old and new lost credibility to such an extent that the problem still endures today. Throughout most of Latin America, the decade did not bring good news in terms of political "articulation": partocracy (government by political parties) became synonymous with bad governance and corruption. This, in part, can be understood in light of the region's generally poor economic performance, which damaged the reputation of governing parties and their allies. The international economic crisis—precipitated, to an extent, by the rise in oil prices—paved the way for the so-called lost decade that hit the region as a whole and led to abrupt cuts in international credit as well as problems in servicing the international debt, which had been mounting in previous years. The crisis took its toll on the region's governing parties, which were left discredited by their poor handling of the economy and the reduction in public spending due to the external shock. But all parties within the system sustained heavy damage to their legitimacy. In Peru, however, the impact was much greater. As we will see, this loss of credibility is key to understanding the emergence of a popular outsider in the 1990 election, and the ability of that outsider, once in power, to make political capital by attacking the partocracy.

The economic crisis, but also the political violence, had severe repercussions for political organizations as well as society. The parties that governed during this period, which had been the country's strongest at the start of the decade—Acción Popular (1980–85) and APRA (1985–90)—suffered a loss of standing. To be sure, this was partly due to serious errors and corruption scandals (especially in the case of APRA) coming on top of a multiplicity of shortcomings. The failed administrations of these traditional parties contributed to the delegitimization of the party system as a whole. Added to this was the delegitimization of the electoral left, which saw its links with voters weaken for a host of reasons. Several of these groups had murky links to the ensuing violence, especially at the start of the decade, while fragmentation weakened their capacity for organization and concerted political action. Moreover, they were considered as representing more of the same in some other regards, and were criticized for supporting measures similar to those adopted by the APRA government—such as the nationalization of banking in 1987—which came to be associated with the economic crisis.

Two processes were especially relevant to this trajectory of delegitimization and organizational weakening: the political violence and the economic crisis. We will explore these processes separately, albeit bearing in mind that they unfolded simultaneously. Moreover, the two processes were intertwined with the escalation of the cocaine trade in those years: a phenomenon that catalyzed the weakening of the state and the growth of corruption.

Political Violence

Political violence broke out in 1980, when Sendero Luminoso made real the long-standing threat wielded by several revolutionary groups of initiating armed violence. The timing, of course, was not down to chance: The group's arrival on the scene coincided with the elections, which they acknowledged by symbolically burning ballot papers in the Ayacucho countryside. This juncture is critical for the delimitation of different leftist groups in terms of their actions vis-à-vis democracy. Among the various strands of left-wing groups that arose during the military government, it was the Maoists who saw ample scope for revolutionary action in the countryside. Sendero Luminoso broke from much of the left—from the reformists who sought to participate in elections with a greater or lesser degree of conviction and from those factions that looked to remain on the fringes of bourgeois democracy but without turning to armed struggle.[41] This group, officially known as the Partido Comunista del Perú (PCP, Communist Party of Peru), was one of the groups that utilized public universities as a springboard for the development and launch of their campaign of violence.[42] Many of their leading figures came from the Universidad de Huamanga in Ayacucho and were attracted to the movement by the promise of social change and the empowerment of traditionally excluded sectors.[43]

Despite the centrality of Sendero and the group's development during the early 1980s, it would be mistaken to explain away the violence as a purely external phenomenon in which students' minds were poisoned, as if their preexisting social conditions and contexts did not matter. Rather, it is necessary to understand the conditions that led, during these early stages, to Sendero Luminoso taking root in certain areas and social sectors, as well as the reasons the group appealed to some sectors while it was resisted by many others and, ultimately, was confronted by a broad mobilization of the communities it claimed to be representing and liberating.[44] Sendero Luminoso is part of a long history of land conflicts, prior trajectories linked to state actions, the differential impact of agrarian reform, and other factors that created fertile ground for the group's emergence while also delineating its limitations.[45] This finer-grained history of the conflict is still being written, and will permit a more nuanced understanding of what happened after the violence started.

As the final report of the Truth and Reconciliation Commission has documented, both the totalitarian ideology of Sendero Luminoso and the tactics that the armed forces employed to confront it—inspired by anti-insurgency models that assumed that the enemy was lurking among the civilian population—had an extremely high human cost.[46] The impact on rural areas—which were among the main theaters of the conflict—was devastating, albeit with important variations that can be partly explained by the history of political mobilization and prior state processes in different areas. The differences between Ayacucho, Cuzco, and Puno, for example, were considerable, in terms of both magnitude and types of violence. These differences went beyond the country's history of conflict; the cocaine trade, which was beginning to take off in those years, overlapped with the conflict in different parts of the Amazonian region, and combined to turn these territories into cauldrons of heavy violence.

Human rights violations in Latin America tend to be linked with authoritarian governments, but Peru shows how the rights of thousands of citizens can be violated in democratic regimes too. Toward the end of the decade, the armed forces revised their strategy and came to see the population as an ally in their struggle against Sendero. Moreover, unlike insurgent groups in other countries that are responsible for fewer deaths than the state, partly due to their desire to enlist the support of the population and popular organizations, Sendero Luminoso killed thousands of its "enemies," among them both state and nonstate actors.[47] It was necessary, in the group's view, to raze everything that went against its vision of Peru, including popular sectors classed as the lumpenproletariat or those allied to the forces of reaction. According to the Truth and Reconciliation

Figure 5.3 Aftermath of a Shining Path attack in Lima's Plaza de Armas, June 1985.
Source: Archivo La República.

Commission, Sendero was the actor that caused most deaths during the period of violence.[48]

Though not on the same level as Sendero Luminoso, the Movimiento Revolucionario Túpac Amaru (MRTA, Túpac Amaru Revolutionary Movement) also perpetrated violent acts in the 1980s. This was a *gueva-rista* guerrilla group whose characteristics were more comparable with those of other groups in national and regional history. It was active primarily in central Amazonia and the cities, and though its methods were less bloody than those of Sendero vis-à-vis the wider population, it too committed assassinations and kidnappings.

Another group that became involved in the national political violence, albeit one that did not have much of a presence until some years later, were the so-called self-defense committees, otherwise known as *rondas campesinas* (rural patrols). The *rondas* operated a system of surveillance and punishment in certain rural areas and became the primary form of local self-organization that confronted the insurgent groups. The state was reluctant to support these groups, in part due to doctrines that warned of the dangers of arming the population for fear that they might support the insurrection. But a change of strategy in 1989 prompted active collaboration between the army and the *rondas* in order to corner Sendero.[49]

The legacies of those years of violence are numerous.[50] For instance, it is worth pausing to reflect on the consequences of the displacement of tens of thousands of people, seeking refuge from the terror, to safer areas, resulting in urban growth. Or we might ponder the degradation or outright collapse of a series of state services, such as education, healthcare, and public utilities, which facilitated and legitimized the adoption of market and privatization solutions. The legitimization of President Alberto Fujimori is also explained by the state's return to different spaces from which violence had expelled the public bureaucracy. Moreover, let us consider the effects of violence and state repression on a series of countercultural activities that emerged in those years, even if they were not related to the insurgent groups. As Shane Greene has described in one of the best books about Peru in the 1980s, Peru's punk subculture was inhibited and repressed due to its links, real or imagined, with these groups.[51] Following this chapter's main argument, in what remains we will focus on the impact of the violence on the political parties and the various civil organizations—which, overall, was far more extensive.

The process of violence contributed to the collapse of the party system by weakening these groups organizationally and discrediting them as ineffective at combating the insurgent groups. The violence also left its mark on social organizations. To begin with, it directly affected the territorial networks of national political parties. The parties suffered heavy losses among their activists and regional leaders. The violence likewise hit a series of social organizations that had a presence in both rural and urban areas. The assassination of María Elena Moyano, a leftist leader in Villa El Salvador, for instance, exemplifies Sendero's violence against social actors whom it saw as competing with its interests. The repressive actions of the state and Sendero Luminoso heightened the risks to local leaders, which weakened the social organizations they led. According to the Truth and Reconciliation Commission, 2,267 leaders were killed or disappeared. Some 21 percent of the victims attributed to Sendero, equating to 1,680 people, were local and social leaders. Their deaths broke the intermediation networks in the system of parties and other organizations: "It is evident that an entire generation of political representatives and intermediaries has been deliberately eliminated by PCP-SL [Sendero Luminoso] as part of its strategy of creating a power vacuum that could be subsequently filled by its own figures."[52]

The violence affected the fortunes of Izquierda Unida, the political grouping that came in second in the 1985 election. On the one hand, this electoral alliance's reputation among the population was tarnished due to both the radical posturing of its constituent groups and activists and the attacks by political opponents who branded the entire alliance as extremists. This difficulty in distancing itself from the political violence is a critical factor in understanding why Peru did not have a strong left in the 2000s, unlike most other countries in the region.[53] Differences in how to conceptualize Sendero Luminoso's violence drove a wedge between radical and moderate sectors of the left, creating a split.[54] At the same time, the violence weakened these groups organizationally, since leftist grassroots organizers contested control and influence over rural and associative spaces with Sendero, and, consequently, suffered Sendero violence firsthand.[55]

The breakdown of these political and social bonds had a clear impact on the post-conflict country. Deborah Yashar has highlighted the impact of violence on the Indigenous and campesino organizations of Peru. For this author, the violence explains why in Peru, unlike Bolivia and Ecuador, no pro-Indigenous national political parties were formed in the 1990s.[56] Conversely, in Bolivia, a national party emerged from these very rural and campesino organizations after the collapse of the party system in the 1980s. In Peru, the popular rural networks built by the left (such as Vanguardia Revolucionaria, or Revolutionary Vanguard) and agrarian labor unionism ended up heavily damaged in those years by Sendero Luminoso's attacks.

The violence, then, was a process that marked the Peruvian political system in several of its dimensions. It severed ties between the rural and urban worlds, intensified the party crisis, ravaged social organizations and their resources, and discredited other organizations. And this situation persisted—albeit with considerable variations in the levels of violence— until 1992, when Abimael Guzmán, the head of Sendero Luminoso, was captured, and the state, in alliance with the *rondas campesinas*, succeeded in progressively defeating the insurgent groups.

But the violence did much more than just that. It occurred during a time of highly polarized political debate. Ideological maximalisms clashed against the backdrop of a country in ruins. These political attitudes, an inability to successfully counter the challenge of violence, and a preference for squabbling amid an unfolding crisis damaged the quarreling political parties. The legitimization gained by *fujimorismo* in the 1990s, despite its authoritarian abuses and media manipulation, was also based on this negative perception of the parties and their irresponsible behavior at a time when Peruvians were killing one another.

Figure 5.4 Throughout the 1980s, Peru's women's volleyball team won a series of victories, becoming one of the country's few sources of joy and national pride. The team returned from the 1988 Seoul Olympics to a massive reception as silver medalists. Source: Archivo El Comercio.

To fully understand the processes linked to violence, we cannot disregard another phenomenon that gathered pace during the 1980s: *narcotráfico*. During the decade, the cocaine trade underwent exponential growth in Peru, in both territorial and economic terms. To give an example of its impact on violence, organizations involved in coca cultivation, processing, and exportation funneled resources into the insurgent groups in the coca-producing valleys where they operated. These ties ensured the insurgents' access not only to money but also to arms. Relations were not always harmonious but, in general, in the early years such resources boosted the firepower and the territorial control of both Sendero and the MRTA. In the end, it was pragmatism on the part of the armed forces that enabled negotiation with the illegal coca actors to stop these resources from reaching the insurgent groups.

As if a conflict of this type and magnitude wasn't already devastating enough for the country, economic crisis and hyperinflation escalated the situation to another level. In the final years of the decade, the country was mired in multiple and intractable problems. Perhaps Peru's only positive memory of collective triumph during those years is its silver medal for women's volleyball during the 1988 Seoul Olympics. Indeed, the 1980s were tarnished by a dual crisis in the memory of Peruvians. The violence imposed energy blackouts and fear; the economic crisis, desperation and precarity.

Economic Crisis and Hyperinflation

Centering on the worst years of the 1980s can obscure an entire decade of economic difficulties. It is the memory of the final years that endures because that was when the actual economic collapse occurred. But to understand the severity of those later years, it is necessary to stress the hardship of the previous years, when problems were incubated and later compounded by the arrival of hyperinflation and the intensification of the economic crisis. Belaúnde's government did not manage to address certain basic deficiencies in the Peruvian model that became more pressing with a challenging international context: high deficits due to expenditure by public enterprises, as well as deficits and inflated public works budgets. Although the government introduced a few reforms in an attempt to tackle these issues, in the main it was overcome by the serious problems of economic performance that saw its five-year term end with spiraling inflation.

Today we may be guilty of overlooking this poor economic governance given the shock of what followed. In 1988 inflation reached 1,722 percent, and in 1990 it was 7,649 percent. These were dramatic years for Latin America. The international crisis left countries in the region without international credit and heavily indebted to their creditors. Peru's case was especially ruinous, not just because of the hyperinflation it faced but also because the impact of that inflation on employment, production, and the state itself was greater. The poor decisions of the García government coupled with the cataclysmic international backdrop gave rise to the worst economic performance in Peruvian history. Rather than facing the crisis through prudent policymaking, García forged ahead with a series of heterodox measures that served only to worsen the deficit, trigger hyperinflation, and deepen the problems. Inflation, and the consequent increase in food prices, had a serious impact on the poorest sectors. The cities, which had long attracted many migrants in search of a better future, saw an increase in hardship. The following summary by Jo-Marie Burt reveals the extent of the economic impact and its social costs:

GDP per capita fell by 20 percent between 1988 and 1989. In 1989, real earnings were half of what they were in 1979. Labor unrest broke out in

Figure 5.5 Passengers queued at Jorge Chávez Airport in Lima during the economic crisis of the 1980s. Source: Archivo La República.

response to the reduction of purchasing power due to inflation and food shortages. There was a tenfold increase in hours lost to strikes, including a two-month strike in the mining sector—the main source of foreign exchange—which intensified the currency crisis and pushed up inflation even further. The percentage of people unemployed or underemployed increased from 50 percent in 1985 to 75 percent in 1990.[57]

Moreover, there was an even greater increase in internal migration to the cities due to political violence. However, just as some fled to the cities from the inferno that had consumed much of the country's rural areas, others, with more resources and contacts, migrated abroad. Indeed, during these years, hundreds of thousands of Peruvians, most of them from the middle and upper classes, left the country to escape the crisis. According to an old joke, a poster on display at Jorge Chávez Airport read: "The last person to leave turns out the light" (see figure 5.5). These tendencies anticipated what would become, leading out of the crisis, a more widespread pattern of international migration and the increasing importance of remittances.

The profound economic crisis aggravated the low legitimacy of politics in the eyes of the population. While everything was going under, the press reported acts of corruption and abuses by political parties, which were also paralyzed by an ideological polarization that forestalled agreement on sensible economic measures. This and the cocaine trade added to a sense that there was no way out of the crisis. Press exposés of political corruption linked to *narcotráfico* likewise became more common.

The economic crisis also had a major impact on the resources available to parties, unions, and other organizations. On the one hand, the political parties had to operate within a broken state. Many party members, after twelve years of military government, looked toward the state as a potential source of employment. It was also a way in which political groups could access resources to strengthen and facilitate political participation. But with a state in crisis, it was more difficult to recruit party members to public positions or to leverage fiscal policy to establish territorial or associational benefits that would contribute to strengthening political links on the ground. State-run companies—from which it was common to recruit party members—in the mining, fishing, and public service sectors found themselves in the red. These party members, as we have noted, had been waiting patiently and insistently for access to public positions. The crisis also hit the labor unions, causing their numbers to plummet while driving up forms of informal work. Maxwell Cameron has documented the various ways in which these unions became weaker, and how this especially affected the parties of the left.[58] The drop in the number of strikes and in worker participation was particularly abrupt toward the end of the decade.[59]

A key feature of those years was the erosion of formal employment and the attendant rise in informal options—a legacy that endures into the present. *Ser obrero es algo relativo*, a highly influential study by Jorge Parodi, aimed to challenge the limitations of the classist reading of Peruvian labor unionism by pitting it against the harsh reality of a workforce that sought to "escape" formal employment in search of better possibilities in the informal sector.[60] This reality was accentuated during those years of unemployment and underemployment, when many workers had to leave their jobs and seek a living on the streets—as the historian Jesús Cosamalón illustrates in an ambitious study on the life of traveling vendors in Lima. According to Cosamalón, itinerant selling or street peddling, which increased exponentially during the crisis, also affected the more affluent sectors in Lima, with the middle classes venturing out to sell their belongings in the streets of Miraflores.[61] Though filmed some years later, the documentary *Metal y melancolía*, by Dutch director Heddy Honigmann, collected the testimonies of taxi drivers who describe the harsh reality of work made

Figure 5.6 Because of hyperinflation and the consequent devaluation of Peru's currency, people crowded into informal centers such as this one on Ocoña Street in downtown Lima to exchange foreign currency. Source: Archivo La República.

Figure 5.7 Endless queues in markets and at grocery stores were common in the Peru of the 1980s. Source: Archivo La República.

precarious by the economic crisis.[62] Speaking about legacies, this informal Peru was here to stay; to this day, Peru's vast informal economy exceeds those of other countries in the region. Years later, the political discourse of certain right-wing groups would cite the example of the entrepreneur as a model of progress. Yet the hardship of informal precarity and well the cost of lack of access to basic social services provide a more pessimistic, but more accurate, characterization of the phenomenon.

Though the crisis had international roots and, as stated earlier, the Belaúnde government's economic mismanagement had a hand in increasing inflation, one cannot downplay the role of APRA and President Alan García in its intensification. The García administration was responsible for measures that ran counter to the economic prudence required during those years—and which other Latin American countries had abandoned as inefficient and costly—such as complex differentiated exchange rate regimes for the US dollar and price controls. In the international sphere, the government boldly announced that it would restrict external debt payments to the equivalent of 10 percent of the value of exports—a measure that had to be reversed toward the end of the decade when Peru was forced to seek external credit to address its collapsing economy. (Incidentally, in yet another example of symbolism, the debt payments had never previously reached that magnitude at any point.)

Moreover, APRA pressed for, and in many cases obtained, jobs that increased the volume of public employment but weakened the state. The effects were felt on the country's most bureaucratically robust institutions, such as the Central Bank and Petroperú, the state oil company. Meanwhile, political corruption blighted these years of increasingly scarce public resources.[63] A weak state, without a proper civil service, proved unable to resist the incursions of a leader and his party who exploited it for their own ends during this fiscally critical period. They behaved irresponsibly at the worst possible time.

The period left a state on its knees, unable to fulfill its most basic functions. In the words of Sinesio López:

The state's traditionally precarious relations with society and the citizenry had been broken. Education and healthcare services operated at an infinitesimal level. Some, such as housing and infrastructure investment, had vanished. Others, such as public security, ran at half throttle, despite the reality of terrorist violence. For society, the state was missing when it was most needed.[64]

The state's territorial presence and its ability to apply the law receded, and the legacy of weakened bureaucracy remained.

As we have seen, García and his party attempted a kind of political incorporation using the developmentalist manual of the 1960s and 1970s, turning to onerous mechanisms—some of them already discredited in the region—at the worst possible moment, when violence and hyperinflation left little room for such bloated spending. As a result, the state collapsed. This perception of an inefficient and corrupt state, and distrust of the politicians in charge, helps us understand why, in the following decade, there was little resistance to the dismantling of this state as well as creeping antipolitical sentiment.

By the end of the decade, the party system was in crisis. In part, this was due to the poor performance of the parties in confronting the political violence and the economic crisis. Those in government governed poorly, while the left, though not in power, suffered the consequences of a polarized politics and of their support for measures—such as the nationalization of banking—that were associated with the meltdown. The most immediate causes of the decline, such as the aforementioned economic performance and the promotion of clientelism at a time of crisis, are central to understanding the steady emergence of an antipolitical legitimacy.[65]

However, the foremost causes of Peru's political wasteland in the years that followed are associated with the ruptures in the parties' economic and organizational resources during the 1980s. These help us understand the extent of the slump as well as the difficulties in constructing new parties after the existing ones collapsed. At the end of the 1980s and into the 1990s, it was not just a party system that collapsed; deep-lying connections went too, making new forms of "articulation" difficult. Violence shook the countryside and broke down the organizational forms that filled these spaces following the collapse of conservative power. Labor unions were diminished and lost members. State clientelism was left unable to develop, while ties eroded between parties and their activist bases.

A comparative perspective can help us understand the impact. In other countries that underwent inflationary processes, such as Argentina and Bolivia, parties lost legitimacy, and in the latter country the system also collapsed eventually. However, in both cases multiple organizations survived the crisis, and neither country experienced the kind of violence that shook Peru. The Peruvian case illustrates not only the weak legitimacy of its political organizations but also breakdowns in society's organizational bases that would prove very difficult to rebuild. With this situation of profound yet invisible corrosion we reach the 1990s, when political organization was beset by fresh challenges.

First Years of Fujimori and Market Reforms: A New Political Order

The crisis combined with the low levels of party legitimacy to deliver the surprise election of Alberto Fujimori, a political outsider who also happened to be an unknown—unlike other outsiders who enter the political arena to harness popularity acquired in other fields. For his part, Fujimori was a rector of a public university, and the extent of his prior contact with the public had been a low-key show about agriculture on national television. An engineer by profession, Fujimori ran an austere candidacy that played off his Japanese background and that country's reputation as an emerging power. He presented himself as someone who could bring work and technology to Peru, though his discourse was divested of ideological references: One was left with a clearer idea of what he was *not* than of what he *was*.[66]

In his list of candidates for Congress, Fujimori included members of Protestant churches who helped spread the word about his presidential campaign; during those years, these groups began to emerge as more important actors in Peruvian politics. Despite Fujimori's frequent appeals to his Japanese identity, the population started referring to him using a term commonly applied to all Asian Peruvians: "El Chino." Few in the summer of 1990 could have imagined that a candidate who turned up at his campaign rallies on a tractor would be a central actor in Peruvian politics for the next three decades.

But in the final three weeks of the election campaign a groundswell of anti-party feeling propelled the Fujimori "tsunami" to second place (27.1 percent) in the first round, just a few points behind the solid favorite, the novelist Mario Vargas Llosa of Frente Democrático (FREDEMO), who received 32.6 percent. FREDEMO was an alliance made up of traditional rightist parties (Acción Popular and the Partido Popular Cristiano) along with Movimiento Libertad, founded by Vargas Llosa himself in opposition to the nationalization of banking. In the second round, Fujimori capitalized on the vote against Vargas Llosa and his market reform proposals, taking 62.3 percent to his opponent's 37.6 percent—barely five percentage points higher than the FREDEMO candidate's first-round tally.

Figure 5.8 Mario Vargas Llosa during a FREDEMO rally for the presidential 1990 election campaign. Source: Archivo La República.

Vargas Llosa also had to reckon with a relentless dirty campaign by APRA and the outgoing president, García, aimed at preventing the right from taking power. For instance, APRA released a video warning of the potential impact of the economic shock with which Vargas Llosa proposed to halt inflation. Borrowing images from the Pink Floyd film *The Wall*, it depicted a warlike apocalypse that would do away with Peru's poor. Moreover, as Vargas Llosa himself recounts in his memoir *El pez en el agua*, the right's campaign was onerous and unwieldy, with its congressional candidates competing against one another in what was perceived as a squandering of resources and an act of hubris by the representatives of Lima's upper classes.

While many APRA and leftist voters lent their support to Fujimori as an alternative to the market reforms promoted by the right, these years saw a rise in votes for independent candidates. For instance, in 1989 the television presenter Ricardo Belmont won the Lima mayoralty. In general, a significant number of Peruvians who no longer felt represented by the existing parties preferred to put faith in someone from outside the system, leaving the country and the international community bemused at the speed of Fujimori's ascent and how little voters knew about him. The electorate, then, backed an unknown. All that was clear was that the victor was not Vargas Llosa or his proposed liberal reforms, then considered extreme. However, the defeat of Vargas Llosa did not equate to the triumph of APRA or the left. They too were enfeebled, as APRA rounded up a little over 20 percent of the vote and the parties of the fractured left mustered barely 15 percent between them.

Once in power, Fujimori converted to the scripture of market reforms, changed his team of advisors, and forged links with international financial institutions. Rather than acting out of neoliberal reformist conviction, Fujimori was following a path constrained by the enormous restrictions all around him. Still, he embarked upon profound neoliberal reforms comparable in the region only with those that were unfolding in Argentina and Bolivia at the same time.

What is interesting is that the volte-face did not carry the political costs that might have been expected given that Fujimori drew enormous support from the opposition to Vargas Llosa and his liberal reform proposals. Much of the population did not protest against the market reforms, initiated, it should be recalled, before the coup of April 1992, when the regime opted to move toward authoritarianism with the support of the armed forces. After the coup, the reforms gathered pace and were cheered on by business actors and international agencies. This support was crucial to establishing and deepening a government authoritarianism that had been creeping for over a decade. While other countries in Latin America democratized, Peru provided a glimpse of a type of government that would later become more common in the region: electoral authoritarianism, whereby governments win elections in somewhat competitive processes in which the balance is clearly weighted against the opposition.

Alberto Vergara's chapter, which follows this one, delves deeper into the Fujimori government, the ways in which it constructed an authoritarian regime, and how it managed to stay in power for ten years. However, here it is worth stressing two points that are related to the argument presented in this chapter and allow us to close with reference to what we noted at the outset: In the 1990s, Peru veered into a political wasteland that contrasted with its earlier mobilization and organization. On the one hand, *fujimorismo* was a regime that built its support and legitimacy on disenchantment and anti-politics, predicated on the idea that promises of political organization and participation brought about a disaster. And as the disaster was all too real in the 1980s, the organization and mobilization that marked the politics of the 1960s became dirty words.[67] To sum up the effect of market reforms on organized politics, it placed one more brick in the bulwark against the prospects of political "articulation."

In the first place, unlike elsewhere, disenchantment with political parties did not give rise to new organizations. In Peru, disaffection ushered in a president who capitalized on the ill-feeling and the discredited party system. Fujimori and his allies built a narrative that laid the blame for the crisis at the door of the parties and their own petty interests. He, in turn, presented himself as a pragmatist intent on fixing the country's problems. The new president's outsider status prompted him to seek alliances with senior military figures and businessmen and prioritize a direct link to the population at the expense of the established parties.

The coup of April 5, 1992, was a decisive moment that allowed Fujimori to capitalize on the rejection of the political representatives in Congress. This popularity handed him a majority in the Constitutional Congress that drafted the 1993 constitution, a text that incorporated a series of measures and regulations in accordance with the newly implemented economic model (which was approved by a very small margin in a referendum as a result of the population's rejection of several of the reforms). However, the fundamental shift toward the delegitimization of the old politics and the consolidation of Fujimori's power came when two of the country's biggest problems were resolved: The economic crisis abated and Sendero Luminoso was decimated. On the one hand, the capture of Abimael Guzmán on September 11, 1992, triggered the group's sharp descent. With its leader and several other senior figures seized, and its militants under siege from the armed forces and the *rondas campesinas*, Sendero disappeared in short order. The MRTA, for its part, was also defeated following the capture of its leaders (though it reemerged some years later when it attacked the residence of the Japanese ambassador in Lima during an official event and held several of the ambassador's guests hostage for over four months, an event that attracted international attention). In parallel, the economy stabilized and inflation was brought under control. The contrast in the social and economic order with that of the final years of the APRA government was stark.

To understand what these changes meant for the national mood, it is important to stress the public perception of a crisis in which the country had long been caught up. Though a series of blows had been struck in the countryside and the city against Sendero Luminoso, violence was still part of the everyday experience—especially in Lima—right up until the capture of Abimael Guzmán. For instance, the brutal bomb attack on Calle Tarata in Lima took place on July 16, 1992, less than two months before

Guzmán was apprehended. And though the economy had been improving, it was still by no means out of the woods. Thus, the perception was of a country very slow to emerge from its dual crisis (and some doubted whether the situation was resolvable at all).

The apocalyptic mindset is illustrated in an article by Mark Malloch Brown, political consultant to Mario Vargas Llosa, in a special issue of *Granta* magazine on Peru's election campaign (June 1991). Malloch states: "Today Fujimori is grappling to apply Mario's economic programme of stabilization, with the inevitable economic dislocation and pain that Mario warned of and that Fujimori pretended could be avoided. Charges of betrayal are rife. Sendero Luminoso and other terrorist groups have stepped up their violence and the country seems to be sliding towards breakdown. . . . Within months the country's only viable export will probably be cocaine. . . . The presidential palace may be Fujimori's now but Peru's real choices remain what they were before the election: Vargas Llosa's bourgeois reform or Sendero's revolution. The odds favor Sendero."[68]

And, all of a sudden, the two crises came to an end. Fujimori capitalized upon the aggregate successes, which came after his self-coup, to compound his authoritarian legitimacy. Yet there are more precise (and complex) explanations for the resolution of both crises that, without overlooking the influence of the government and its decisions, detract from the notion of the president's leading role. For instance, the capture of Abimael Guzmán and his lieutenants owed more to the work of police intelligence carried out over a period of years, with which Fujimori's National Intelligence Service had little to do. Moreover, the military victories over Sendero can be traced back to 1989, when the army changed its strategy for pursuing the group. Nor should we downplay the improving condition of the global economy and its impact on Latin America at the time.

However, the perception of the president's "success" in resolving the problems caused by "irresponsible politicians" exacerbated the reputational damage to the parties, allowing Fujimori to win the 1995 election with a formidable 65 percent, far ahead of Javier Pérez de Cuellar (21 percent), the former secretary-general of the United Nations. The once-unknown Fujimori had now vanquished Peru's two most distinguished public figures: the renowned author and the international leader. Fujimori would utilize this electoral majority to enhance his power and consolidate the authoritarian regime. It was this success, then, and not just the authoritarian turn that enabled the construction of a collective anti-party and anti-mobilization feeling.

The government not only delegitimized the parties with its actions but also competed unfairly with them and attacked them by authoritarian means. For example, Fujimori concentrated state aid and rebuilt relations with social actors, bringing them into his orbit. A special state fund known as the Cooperation Fund for Social Development (FONCODES) and the Ministry of the Presidency were used to focus national spending and the delivery of public works throughout the country. This spending, as Norbert Schady has shown, had a clear political orientation.[69] Though Fujimori's authoritarian grip tightened after the 1995 election, the government was active in harrying and persecuting the opposition before that point. His regime took steps to disincentivize political organization and mobilization using a fear-mongering technique known as *terruqueo*—a derivation of the Peruvian neologism *terruco*, meaning "terrorist"— whereby those who expressed critical or anti-establishment views were denounced as apologists for terrorism. This strategy in its worst version included the use of death squads and political violence against social and political actors. *Fujimorismo*, in turn, catalyzed organizational debilitation through its use of the state for its own ends. Its moves against the opposition and social organizations, especially in the second part of the decade, were aimed at curbing political linkages that might threaten its own power. The state became visible again, restoring and even expanding its presence throughout the decade. However, relations with society differed from those witnessed in the 1970s and 1980s: Gone was the state that encouraged organization or mobilization.[70] What should be stressed here is that this was not simply down to a change of mood or values within the population vis-à-vis politics or mobilization, or to *fujimorista* authoritarian action. The changes that occurred in the pre-Fujimori years rendered political organization more difficult by breaking bonds and depleting the resources required for mobilization. That is, Peruvians did not simply depoliticize as a consequence of collective psychological change or repression. Thus, repoliticization down the line would prove difficult.

Moreover, this period witnessed another process that further diminished the prospects of rebuilding political linkages and forming organizations capable of mobilizing: market reforms. Across Latin America, market reforms affected the availability of resources to governments and changed the functions of the state. The privatization and deficit reduction measures that accompanied economic shock programs left limited scope for public spending. The earlier developmentalist states possessed better tools with which to promote different forms of intermediation between

Figure 5.9 Alberto Fujimori greeting voters during his 1990 presidential campaign. Source: Archivo La República.

state and society throughout the national territory. In all the region, development banks, territorial fiscal benefits, zones of economic interest, and other measures had all allowed links to be forged between the political system and society. But it is not just economic crises that affect the resources parties can access. The "cure" to these crises, in the form of drastic reductions to budgets and state functions, can have a similar effect.[71] Kenneth Greene, for instance, has shown how in Mexico the Partido Revolucionario Institucional lost its considerable power partly due to neoliberal reforms, which curbed the party's resource availability as well as its capacity to confer employment within the state, to establish corporate links with associations, and to provide subsidies to interest groups.[72]

The market reforms had these effects on political organization in Peru. On the one hand, the reforms limited the opportunities for parties to use the state to establish a stable activist base. A reduction in the clientelistic distribution of resources is not a negative, of course, especially when one recalls the costs and inefficiencies of the Peruvian state in the 1980s. But the point worth stressing is that these changes break bonds that might have served for reconstructing organizations, and that, moreover, a phenomenon that is positive in some regards can have negative consequences in others. In the present case, market reforms made it more difficult for parties to use the state to construct (or reconstruct) their activist bases.

And a *fujimorismo* with a high anti-party content, with the armed forces as its political backbone, did not concern itself with party reconstruction. Rather, it created a new party political vehicle for each election.

In the Peruvian case, these "disarticulation" effects extended further than in other countries given the aforementioned processes and how they unfolded. The market reforms were so extensive not just because of the reformers' convictions but also because they met with little social or organized resistance. In other countries in which market reforms were introduced, the existence of clientelistic political actors, especially in subnational spaces, was key to compelling the central government to continue providing other types of resources that could be used for clientelistic ends. Edward Gibson, for example, has discussed how regional clientelistic actors in Argentina and Mexico became allies of government by implementing market reforms through social spending or public works, through which they succeeded in displacing other groups—such as labor unions or associations of state employees, whose ties were more corporative—in the developmentalist state.[73] In Colombia, the market reforms did not fundamentally affect clientelistic groups on the ground; these groups were able to continue negotiating resources with the government. Conversely, in Peru, the weakness of territorial actors, unions, and parties—a product of the processes explored here—made it easier for *fujimorismo* to implement reforms without having to strike bargains. The immediate material benefit for the very poor of ending hyperinflation and violence gave the government a social base of support that was unmatched by groups affected by the reforms. Not only was Alberto Fujimori's style antithetical to dialogue and agreements, but the political context gave him considerable latitude in which to act and propose profound reforms that would alter the Peruvian state.

Thus, with political organizations now weakened, the reforms caused still more damage to political linkages. There were no actors capable of obtaining or negotiating new resources with which to sustain their networks and construct new forms of organization. The political parties grew weaker still during those years, though it was the labor unions and associations of public employees that were most seriously affected. The reforms did away with a series of regulations designed to promote and protect trade unionism. Fujimori's neoliberal program reduced the incentives for these forms of organization, and the diminished actors concerned no longer had the capacity to resist. Unions of state employees vanished amid the privatizations.[74] For its part, *fujimorismo* did not channel resources into establishing a party political organization beyond "articulating" a replacement political class for each congressional election, drawing support from the armed forces and the state apparatus, and building relations with local leaders, often through parties whose names changed throughout the decade. To reiterate, this is not to say that these processes were inherently negative. Reducing clientelism and the discretionary use of resources has much to commend it. But the analytical point to be made here is that these processes were facilitated by organizational debilitation and, in turn, exacerbated the phenomenon. Thus this debilitation had negative effects.

Viewed in this way, the relatively peaceful acceptance of the government reforms, whether the economic measures or the 1993 constitution, is, in general, a characteristic of those first years of the Fujimori regime that, in part, can be explained by the now established political organizational weakness. Fujimori's self-coup of April 5, 1992, may have been popular and certainly laid the foundations for a more repressive and authoritarian state while discouraging criticism and participation, but all this happened in a disjointed, delegitimized polity with weakened organizations. Indeed, the fact that many of the reforms were adopted before the self-coup would have come as a surprise to those who, in the 1970s and 1980s, felt that mobilized popular interests would fend off any such agenda. As discussed earlier, during the early years of the second Belaúnde government, swaths of civil society and the political opposition rejected reform proposals that were far more timid. But as it was, in 1990, the economic regime adopted in 1968 was reformed and the population, exhausted from so much instability, was not a critical opponent of these changes and even supported a repressive government. An important contributing factor to this outcome was the organizational weakness already present in society.

Conclusion: From the Old Order to a Future That Is Not What It Used to Be

To conclude, in the late 1980s and early 1990s, the Peruvian party system went into free fall alongside several other organizational forms. Though this system was never as strong as in other countries in the region, it was still more organized and mobilized than it is at present. By the end of the decade, the "disarticulation" was considerable. There were no strong agrarian networks, whether conservative or popular. Clientelistic networks had been depleted by the economic crisis. What is more, the organizations from which it might have been possible to build future parties were weakened, and conditions for maintaining those in existence were difficult. It was in this context that market reforms occurred, cutting off other sources of organization. The impact of these reforms on political "articulation" was compounded by preexisting weakness: There were no actors capable of negotiating with central government for access to resources that would have allowed the reconstruction of old links or the creation of new ones. From those early years onward the Fujimori regime governed over a disarticulated society, and this facilitated its subsequent concentration of power.

This brought to an end a trajectory that took Peru from a position of considerable political inclusion and mobilization to a disarticulated and demobilized system. In the present chapter I have tried to present the reasons behind this trajectory. I have sought to stress the errors made by political actors, as well as the enormous barriers they came up against in their attempts to mobilize and represent. Moreover, I have discussed the major factors that have undermined organization and the possibility of reconstructing it.

This organizational wasteland has similarities with the traditional system in terms of its "disarticulation" from below and its demobilization. However, in earlier times, the population was forcibly excluded by a highly closed system that precluded participation and that, every so often, suppressed mobilization when it generated an excess of social demands. In the late 1980s, the scenario of an exclusionary authoritarian regime was feared by some Peruvian authors who, in those years, saw Pinochet's Chile as the most potent example of such authoritarian danger. They feared that Peru's enormous crisis would be "resolved" through a military coup, which would usher in a return to authoritarian exclusion. Alberto Flores Galindo, after describing two other possibilities then open to the country (estate-led reformism or social revolution), characterized this authoritarian threat as follows: "For this same reason, neither of the previous alternatives cancels out the persistent threat of a repressive solution to the crisis: reestablishing the principle of authority, whose absence has been lamented by business owners for quite some time, by resorting to large-scale impositions and sanctions on the entire country, turning each city into a barracks."[75]

What emerged during the crisis, however, was something different: a regime that was increasingly authoritarian and reliant on the armed forces but in which there was still inclusion, effective (albeit intermittent) political participation, and support from a large section of the population for much of the regime. *Fujimorismo* was not an authoritarianism like those of the past—but this is not to deny its repressive character. It was, moreover, popular among sectors that were supposedly excluded from politics. For much of the 1990s, acceptance coexisted with control and repression.

This organizational weakness at the base did not mean, of course, that different actors at the summit did not organize and that they did not work to defend their own interests. In the 1990s, this organizational weakness led to an increase in the relative power of business actors who benefited from the market reforms, for example. However, this power was unlike the old conservative power with a dominant presence across the country. This time there would be no channels of transmission; as a result, it became difficult for these economic actors to establish a stable presence through a rightist party. Although these powers have international economic ties that are redolent of the old order, they lack more stable links and do not control territorial spaces as they did before—not even with the different forms of business activity that arise in these spaces. Thus, they frequently see their interests undermined by different powers that are less consequential at the national level but which have local presence and capacity.

The developments that this chapter has explored help to understand the current situation. This state of affairs has persisted largely unchanged over time, even though an authoritarian power like *fujimorismo* no longer exists. Peru has normalized the absence of social and territorial linkages and political demobilization despite better conditions for competition and participation. The weakness of Peru's political parties has seen the country styled (perhaps with a degree of exaggeration) as a "democracy without parties."[76] Peruvians have become used to their parties being volatile and gaining little to no ground in local elections, but the phenomenon cuts deeper and transcends electoral politics. This concerns not only a lack of parties but also the absence of civil society organizations or interest groups that can form associative links throughout the territory, be they conservative or progressive. Such weakness in the social fabric also hinders the "articulation" of sectors that fail to establish national agendas despite similar agendas or interests.[77] Although there are moments of mobilization, in contrast to other countries, these protests tend to be more limited, lacking linkages throughout the territory, and limited over time. The roots of many of the present-day weaknesses lie in the events and processes undergone in the tumultuous years that changed Peru. If Peruvian society ended the 1960s as a hierarchical triangle without a base, it ended the 1990s as a society where the traditional hierarchy had ended, but without any triangle or shape to envision change.

Notes

1 The term *articular* is used in this chapter's original Spanish version to denote linking, connecting, putting together, or organizing different parts in one structure—in this case, linking politically different actors and groups. The English translation *articulation* does not capture this meaning and may confuse the English reader. For clarity, I have replaced the term with some synonyms throughout the text (*organize, connect, link*) and signaled with quotation marks when I kept the original.

2 Julio Cotler, "La mecánica de la dominación interna y del cambio social," in *Perú problema: 5 ensayos*, ed. Augusto Salazar, Alberto Escobar, and Jorge Bravo (Lima: Instituto de Estudios Peruanos, 1968).

3 Mainwaring and Scully show that despite their relative strength, Peruvian parties of the 1980s were still some way behind their counterparts elsewhere in Latin America. Scott Mainwaring and Timothy Scully, "Introduction," in *Building Democratic Institutions: Party Systems in Latin America*, ed. Scott Mainwaring and Timothy Scully (Stanford, CA: Stanford University Press, 1995), 1–35.

4 Carlos Iván Degregori, *La década de la antipolítica* (Lima: Instituto de Estudios Peruanos, 2000).

5 Other characterizations of the political wasteland of the 1990s can be found in Jo-Marie Burt, *Silencing Civil Society: Political Violence and the Authoritarian State in Peru* (New York: Palgrave Macmillan, 2007); and Maxwell Cameron, "From Oligarchic Domination to Neoliberal Governance: The Shining Path and the Transformation of Peru's Constitutional Order," in *Politics After Violence: Legacies of the Shining Path Conflict*, ed. Hillel Soifer and Alberto Vergara (Austin: University of Texas Press, 2019).

6 Disarticulation is not only a phenomenon at the national level. The groups that were set up to compete in local and regional elections are not robust either. That is, the breakdown is evident at all levels. Mauricio Zavaleta, *Coaliciones de independientes: Las reglas no escritas de la política electoral* (Lima: Instituto de Estudios Peruanos, 2014); Paula Muñoz and Andrea García, "Tendencias, particularidades y perfil de los candidatos más exitosos," *Perú Debate: El Nuevo Poder en las Regiones* 1, no. 1 (2011): 8–17.

7 Jo-Marie Burt, "Contesting the Terrain of Politics: State-Society Relations in Urban Peru, 1950–2000," in *State and Society in Conflict: Comparative Perspectives on Andean Crises*, ed. Paul Drake and Eric Hershberg (Pittsburgh: University of Pittsburgh Press, 2006); Maxwell Cameron, *Democracy and Authoritarianism in Peru: Political Coalitions and Social Change* (New York: St. Martin's Press, 1994); Steven Levitsky and Mauricio Zavaleta, "Why No Party-Building in Peru?," in *Challenges of Party-Building in Latin America*, ed. Steven Levitsky et al. (Cambridge: Cambridge University Press, 2016); Jana Morgan, *Bankrupt Representation and Party System Collapse* (University Park: Penn State University

Press, 2012); Paula Muñoz, "Estado, clientelismo y partidos políticos: Una perspectiva comparada," in *Incertidumbres y distancias: El controvertido protagonismo del estado en el Perú*, ed. Romeo Grompone (Lima: Instituto de Estudios Peruanos, 2016); Alberto Vergara, *La danza hostil: Poderes subnacionales y estado central en Bolivia y Perú (1952–2012)* (Lima: Instituto de Estudios Peruanos, 2015).

8 But, as will hopefully be obvious, I make no claim that the events of these decades fully explain Peru's current political disarticulation. Other aspects, long predating and postdating this period, should also be taken into account. As authors such as Vergara have proposed, Peru's economic centralization—which precedes the processes studied here—makes it difficult to politicize regional agendas and construct local organizations that can influence the national debate. Vergara, *La danza hostil*. The actions that *fujimorismo* and its allies took against political parties in the 1990s, as well as the decentralization process initiated in 2002, are also factors that would affect political articulation. See, for example, Jana Morgan, "Decentralization and Party System Decay," *Latin American Research Review* 53, no. 1 (2018): 1–18; Muñoz, "Estado, clientelismo y partidos políticos"; and Alberto Vergara, "United by Discord, Divided by Consensus: National and Sub-National Articulation in Bolivia and Peru, 2000–2010," *Journal of Politics in Latin America* 3, no. 3 (2011): 65–93.

9 François Bourricaud, "Structure and Function of the Peruvian Oligarchy," *Studies in Comparative International Development* 2, no. 2 (1966): 17–31; François Bourricaud, *Poder y sociedad en el Perú contemporáneo* (Lima: Instituto de Estudios Peruanos, 1984); Giorgio Alberti and Fernando Fuenzalida, "Pluralismo, dominación y personalidad," in *Dominación y cambios en el Perú rural* (Lima: Instituto de Estudios Peruanos, 1969), 285–324; Cotler, "Mecánica de la dominación interna."

10 Cotler, "Mecánica de la dominación interna."

11 Bourricaud, *Poder y sociedad en el Perú*, 193. In the original Spanish the passage reads: "Una oligarquía que no se siente identificada con la sociedad a la que dirige a distancia; clases medias a la vez insurgentes y prudentes; una masa de 'sumergidos' que escapan a su condición organizándose para defender intereses específicos, estrechos, para abandonarse a breves accesos de violencia cuya explotación política hasta ahora nadie ha podido aprovechar."

12 Alejandro Diez, "Organizaciones de base y gobiernos locales rurales: Mundos de vida, ciudadanía y clientelismo," in *Repensando la política en el Perú*, ed. Elsa Bardales, Martín Tanaka, and Antonio Zapata (Lima: Red para el Estudio de las Ciencias Sociales, 1999).

13 Dennis Gilbert, *The Oligarchy and the Old Regime in Latin America, 1880–1970* (Lanham, MD: Rowman and Littlefield, 2017).

14 Wesley Craig, "El movimiento campesino en La Convención, Perú: La dinámica de una organización compleja," *Serie Documentos Teóricos* 11 (January 1968).

15 Javier Puente, "The Military Grammar of Agrarian Reform in Peru: Campesinos and Rural Capitalism," *Radical History Review* 133 (January 2019): 78–101.

16 Ellen Kay Trimberger, *Revolution from Above: Military Bureaucrats and Development in Japan, Turkey, Egypt, and Peru* (New Brunswick, NJ: Transaction Books, 1977).

17 Message to the nation delivered by Divisional General Juan Velasco Alvarado, president of the Republic of Peru, on the first anniversary of the revolution, October 3, 1969.

18 Carlos Contreras and Marcos Cueto, *Historia del Perú contemporáneo*, 4th ed. (Lima: Instituto de Estudios Peruanos, 2009), 331–32.

19 Richard Walter, *Peru and the United States, 1960–1975: How Their Ambassadors Managed Foreign Relations in a Turbulent Era* (State College: Penn State University Press, 2010).

20 Abraham Lowenthal and Cynthia McClintock, *The Peruvian Experiment: Continuity and Change Under Military Rule* (Princeton, NJ: Princeton University Press, 1983); Carlos Aguirre and Paulo Drinot, eds., *The Peculiar Revolution: Rethinking the Peruvian Experiment Under Military Rule* (Austin: University of Texas Press, 2017).

21 "Himno del Perú en los 70s HD (stereo)," YouTube, posted by Recuerdos3000, July 28, 2014, https://www.youtube.com/watch?v=kFykTjEQAvM.

22 Michael Albertus, *Autocracy and Redistribution* (Cambridge: Cambridge University Press, 2015).

23 Anna Cant, "Promoting the Revolution: SINAMOS in Three Different Regions of Peru," in Aguirre and Drinot, *The Peculiar Revolution*.

24 For an evaluation of the "peculiar revolution," see Abraham Lowenthal, *The Peruvian Experiment: Continuity and Change Under Military Rule* (Princeton, NJ: Princeton University Press, 1975); Lowenthal and McClintock, *The Peruvian Experiment*; and Aguirre and Drinot, *The Peculiar Revolution*.

25 Alfred Stepan, *The State and Society: Peru in Comparative Perspective* (Princeton, NJ: Princeton University Press, 1978).

26 Cynthia McClintock, "Velasco, Officers, and Citizens: The Politics of Stealth," in *The Peruvian Experiment Reconsidered*, ed. Cynthia McClintock and Abraham F. Lowenthal (Princeton, NJ: Princeton University Press, 1983).

27 Evelyne Huber, "The Peruvian Military Government, Labor Mobilization and the Political Strength of the Left," *Latin American Research Review* 18, no. 2 (1983): 57–93.

28 Julio Cotler, "Military Interventions and 'Transfer of Power to Civilians' in Peru," in *Transitions from Authoritarian Rule: Latin America*, ed. Guillermo O'Donnell, Philippe Schmitter, and Laurence Whitehead (Baltimore: Johns Hopkins University Press, 1986).

29 Cotler, "Military Interventions"; Burt, "Contesting the Terrain of Politics."

30 José Luis Rénique, *Incendiar la pradera: Un ensayo sobre la revolución en el Perú* (Lima: La Siniestra, 2018); José Luis Rénique and Adrián Lerner, "Shining Path: The Last Peasant War in the Andes," in Soifer and Vergara, *Politics After Violence*; Jaymie Heilman, *Before the Shining Path: Politics in Rural Ayacucho, 1895–1980* (Stanford, CA: Stanford University Press, 2010).

31 Paula Muñoz, "Political Violence and the Defeat of the Left," in Soifer and Vergara, *Politics After Violence.*

32 Henry Pease, *El ocaso del poder oligárquico: Lucha política en la escena oficial, 1968–1975*, 2nd ed. (Lima: DESCO, 1979).

33 Sinesio López Jiménez, *Ciudadanos reales e imaginarios: Concepciones, desarrollo y mapas de la ciudadanía en el Perú* (Lima: Instituto para el Desarrollo y Sostenibilidad, 1997), 268–69.

34 This conservative agrarian power also played an important yet tragic role in the creation of paramilitary groups in the 1980s and 1990s in a bid to keep control of the land and counter guerrilla activity.

35 Alberto Vergara, "The Fujimori Regime Through Tocqueville's Lens: Centralism, Regime Change, and Peripheral Elites in Contemporary Peru," in *Peru in Theory*, ed. Paulo Drinot (London: Palgrave Macmillan, 2014), 19–47.

36 Huber, "Peruvian Military Government"; Julio Cotler, *Democracia e integración nacional* (Lima: Instituto de Estudios Peruanos, 1980).

37 Huber, "Peruvian Military Government"; Susan Stokes, "Politics and Latin America's Urban Poor: Reflections from a Lima Shantytown," *Latin American Research Review* 26, no. 2 (1991): 75–101; Carol Graham, "The APRA Government and the Urban Poor: The Pait Programme in Lima's *Pueblos Jóvenes*," *Journal of Latin American Studies* 23, no. 1 (1991): 91–130.

38 Carlos Iván Degregori, Cecilia Blondet, and Nicolás Lynch, *Conquistadores de un nuevo mundo: De invasores a ciudadanos* (Lima: Instituto de Estudios Peruanos, 1986); Carmen Rosa Balbi, *Identidad clasista en el sindicalismo: Su impacto en las fábricas* (Lima: DESCO, 1989); Eduardo Ballón, *Movimientos sociales y democracia: La fundación de un nuevo orden* (Lima: Centro de Estudios y Promoción del Desarrollo, 1986).

39 Carlos Franco, "Exploraciones en 'otra modernidad': De la migración a la plebe urbana," in *Imágenes de la sociedad peruana: La otra modernidad* (Lima: Centro de Estudios para el Desarrollo y la Participación, 1991), 15–56.

40 Gonzales presents a thorough review of the reasons the left, despite its opportunities, did not achieve the sort of unity it needed in order to operate effectively in the political arena. Osmar Gonzales, "La izquierda peruana: Una estructura ausente," in *Apogeo y crisis de la izquierda peruana: Hablan sus protagonistas*, ed. Alberto Adrianzén (Lima: IDEA Internacional, Universidad Antonio Ruiz de Montoya, 2011).

41 Iván Hinojosa, "On Poor Relations and the Nouveau Riche: Shining Path and the Radical Peruvian Left," in *Shining and Other Paths: War and*

Society in Peru, 1980–1995, ed. Steve Stern (Durham, NC: Duke University Press, 1980); Rénique and Lerner, "Shining Path," 21–22.

42 Carlos Iván Degregori, *El surgimiento de Sendero Luminoso: Ayacucho 1969–1979* (Lima: Instituto de Estudios Peruanos, 1990); Heilman, *Before the Shining Path.*

43 Carlos Iván Degregori, "La revolución de los manuales: La expansión del marxismo leninismo en las ciencias sociales y la génesis de Sendero Luminoso," *Revista Peruana de Ciencias Sociales* 3, no. 2 (1990): 103–24.

44 Carlos Iván Degregori, *Las rondas campesinas y la derrota de Sendero Luminoso* (Lima: Instituto de Estudios Peruanos, 1996).

45 Ponciano Del Pino, *En nombre del gobierno: El Perú y Uchuraccay: Un siglo de política campesina* (Lima: La Siniestra Ensayos, 2017); Heilman, *Before the Shining Path*; Miguel Laserna, *The Corner of the Living: Ayacucho on the Eve of the Shining Path Insurgency* (Chapel Hill: University of North Carolina Press, 2012); María Eugenia Ulfe and Ximena Malága, *Reparando mundos: Víctimas y estado en los Andes peruanos* (Lima: Fondo Editorial PUCP, 2021).

46 Comisión de la Verdad y Reconciliación, *Informe final* (Lima: Comisión de la Verdad y Reconciliación, 2003).

47 Valérie Robin Azevedo, *Los silencios de la guerra: Memorias y conflicto armado en Ayacucho-Perú* (Lima: La Siniestra, 2021), 123–90.

48 Comisión de la Verdad y Reconciliación, *Informe final.*

49 Degregori, *Las rondas campesinas.*

50 On the impact of the violence and its legacies, see Soifer and Vergara, *Politics After Violence.*

51 Shane Greene, *Punk and Revolution: Seven More Interpretations of Peruvian Reality* (Durham, NC: Duke University Press, 2016).

52 Comisión de la Verdad y Reconciliación, *Informe final*, 169.

53 Maxwell Cameron, "Peru: The Left Turn That Wasn't," in *The Resurgence of the Latin American Left*, ed. Steven Levitsky and Kenneth Roberts (Baltimore: Johns Hopkins University Press, 2011), 375–98; Muñoz, "Political Violence."

54 Burt, "Contesting the Terrain of Politics."

55 José Luis Rénique, *La batalla por Puno: Conflicto agrario y nación en los Andes peruanos* (Lima: Instituto de Estudios Peruanos, SUR, Centro Peruano de Estudios Sociales, 2004).

56 Deborah Yashar, *Contesting Citizenship in Latin America: The Rise of Indigenous Movements and the Postliberal Challenge* (New York: Cambridge University Press, 2005).

57 Jo-Marie Burt, *Violencia y autoritarismo en el Perú: Bajo la sombra de Sendero y la dictadura de Fujimori* (Lima: Instituto de Estudios Peruanos, 2011), 89.

58 Cameron, *Democracy and Authoritarianism in Peru.*

59 Martín Tanaka, *La dinámica de los actores regionales y el proceso de descentralización: ¿El despertar del letargo?* (Lima: Instituto de Estudios Peruanos, 2002).

60 Jorge Parodi, *Ser obrero es algo relativo: Obreros, clasismo y política* (Lima: Instituto de Estudios Peruanos, 1986).

61 Jesús Cosamalón, *El apocalipsis a la vuelta de la esquina: Lima, la crisis y sus supervivientes (1980–2000)* (Lima: Fondo Editorial PUCP, 2018).

62 *Metal y melancolía*, directed by Heddy Honigmann (Cologne: Ariel Films, 1994).

63 John Crabtree, *Alan García en el poder: Perú: 1985–1990* (Lima: PEISA, 2005).

64 López, *Ciudadanos reales e imaginarios*, 286.

65 Martín Tanaka, *Los espejismos de la democracia: El colapso de un sistema de partidos en el Perú, 1980–1995, en perspectiva comparada* (Lima: Instituto de Estudios Peruanos, 1998); Nicolás Lynch, *Una tragedia sin héroes: La derrota de los partidos y el origen de los independientes: Perú, 1980–1992* (Lima: Fondo Editorial de la UNMSM, 1999); Jason Seawright, *Party-System Collapse: The Roots of Crisis in Peru and Venezuela* (Stanford, CA: Stanford University Press, 2012).

66 Luis Jochamowitz, *Ciudadano Fujimori: La construcción de un político* (Lima: PEISA, 1997); José Alejandro Godoy, *El último dictador: Vida y gobierno de Alberto Fujimori* (Lima: Penguin Random House, 2021).

67 Degregori, *La década de la antipolítica*.

68 Mark Malloch, "The Consultant," *Granta*, June 27, 1991.

69 Norbert Schady, "The Political Economy of Expenditures by the Peruvian Social Fund (FONCODES), 1991–95," *American Political Science Review* 94, no. 2 (2000): 289–304.

70 Burt, *Violencia y autoritarismo en el Perú*.

71 Muñoz, "Estado, clientelismo y partidos políticos."

72 Kenneth Greene, *Why Dominant Parties Lose: Mexico's Democratization in Comparative Perspective* (Cambridge: Cambridge University Press, 2007).

73 Edward Gibson, "The Populist Road to Market Reform: Policy and Electoral Coalitions in Mexico and Argentina," *World Politics* 49, no. 3 (1997): 339–70.

74 It is also worth thinking about the ways in which the economic model affects possibilities for organization. Marcus Kurtz has discussed how, in Chile, the agri-export promotion reforms adopted as part of Augusto Pinochet's neoliberal reforms constituted barriers to the organization of agricultural unions. There were no incentives nor facilities to this end, as the worker-employer relationship was privatized and individualized. Something similar can be observed in Peru, where the reforms put up more barriers to organization in new economic activities or privatized sectors. Marcus J. Kurtz, *Free Market Democracy and the Chilean and Mexican Countryside* (Cambridge: Cambridge University Press, 2009).

75 Alberto Flores Galindo, *La tradición autoritaria: Violencia y democracia en el Perú* (Lima: SUR, 1999).

76 Steven Levitsky, "Peru: The Challenges of a Democracy Without Parties," in *Constructing Democratic Governance in Latin America*, ed. Jorge

Dominguez and Michael Shifter (Baltimore: Johns Hopkins University Press, 2013); Steven Levitsky and Maxwell Cameron, "Democracy Without Parties? Political Parties and Regime Change in Fujimori's Peru," *Latin American Politics and Society* 45, no. 3 (2003): 1–33; Martín Tanaka, *Perú 2000–2005: Democracia sin partidos: Los problemas de representación y las propuestas de reforma política* (Lima: Instituto de Estudios Peruanos, 2005).

77   Carlos Meléndez, *La soledad de la política: Transformaciones estructurales, intermediación política y conflictos sociales en el Perú (2000–2012)* (Lima: Mitin Editores, 2012).

Shut Up and Shop!

Representation and Governance in Contemporary Peru (1992–2021)

"How did you go bankrupt? . . . Gradually and then suddenly."
—ERNEST HEMINGWAY, *THE SUN ALSO RISES* (1926)

The brief juncture between the Fujimori self-coup of April 5, 1992, and the approval of the 1993 constitution ushered in a distinctive period in Peruvian history. Books, scholars, and even a collective national understanding have established as much. This short period closed an era and opened a new one: "contemporary" Peru. But the character of this contemporaneity is less clear. Throughout post-1992 Peru there was a perception of an atmosphere in common, but we have yet to identify which precise traits single it out. In this chapter I attempt this endeavor. My argument is as follows: The pre-1992 political Peru can be characterized as a country built around a desire for representation, whereas post-1992 it was founded on a yearning for effective governance.

To flesh out this argument, I will start with a quick glance at Peruvian political life from 1930 to 1990. Over that period, most political organizations sought, despite their differences, to represent the country's different social sectors. What emerged after the 1992 coup and its institutional offshoot, the 1993 constitution, altered this horizon of political action.

This is what I address in the second part of the chapter: Peruvians, saturated by crisis, started demanding effective governance. They did not call for rights or inclusion by way of a representative; they asked for *order*. Note, for instance, how an Izquierda Unida member of the regional assembly for the Inka region greeted Fujimori's dissolution of regional government:[1] "On April 5 [1992] the people clapped like seals! Everyone felt that the regional question was unmanageable. It was unmanageable by a country that was generally falling apart, but also because of the assembly formula that had been adopted [for regional government]."[2] Before President Alberto Fujimori's self-coup, then, the members of the *representative* organ of the Peruvian south—traditionally the most rebellious region, whose seat was the combative city of Cuzco—"clapped like seals" for their own dissolution. The representatives were cheering the fact that someone, at long last, was taking responsibility for the regional and national chaos. That is, 1992 gave rise to a situation in which representation and governance appeared to be antithetical objectives. Too much assembly and too little government would have to be remedied through government without assemblies.

This exchange (more government and less representation) is what gives contemporary Peru its political character. The third section of the chapter studies how this formula survived the collapse of Fujimori's authoritarian government in 2000 and how it adapted to the new democratic circumstances. It was not for nothing that the 1993 constitution—the institutional structure that embodied the premise of "government without assemblies"—endured despite constant fierce critiques and the electoral success of different political platforms that called for its replacement in these last two decades. In other words, political practice and political institution were not divorced. The deliberation associated with representation remained silenced by the effectiveness of an executive operating by decree.

What has it meant to govern efficiently in contemporary Peru? With the defeat of Shining Path and the Túpac Amaru Revolutionary Movement, it came to mean the promotion of a drive toward national economic growth. Gross domestic product (GDP) was no longer a mere indicator but became a mark of success in itself. It was a long time coming, but Peru had finally accomplished what the sociologist Daniel Bell observed in the 1950s of developed countries: Economic growth had become the secular religion of society. And to fatten GDP, prudent management of the nation's finances was needed. Such prudence was to be found not in the people and their representatives but in the technocrats. This was prime time for the minister of the economy, and the formula bore fruit for several years. We will explore this dynamic in the fourth part of the chapter. Between 2001 and 2014 the Peruvian economy doubled in size, poverty plummeted from

54.8 percent to 22.7 percent, and consumption patterns as vibrant as they were unexpected electrified a country that earlier had feared its future was, as in the bolero, *sombras, nada más* (nothing but shadows).

This economic success consolidated the exchange of representation for governance. In essence, Peruvians were urged to shut up and shop. And they did as they were told. The market expanded and millions were lifted from poverty while concerns about political, institutional, and social frailties were swept aside.

But this is not how democracy works. The inherent contradictions of such an exchange were compounded over time, precipitating its eventual implosion. In a democracy, the government improves by responding to the demands of society. If democracy has proven the best (or the least bad) of the political systems, it is because it is the only one in which the government *responds* to its citizens. It does not govern better because it obviates the public but because, as in Robert Dahl's classic definition, its primary characteristic is the government's "continued responsiveness" to the preferences of the citizens.[3] Or, to borrow the analogy that the US philosopher John Dewey used to explain the relationship between government and representation in a democracy: The cobbler can repair a shoe, but only the wearer can say where it pinches.[4] Thus, a democratic system in which representation is deferred in the name of good government will end up giving rise to poor government.

Peru would come to discover this starting in 2014, when it fell into a period of decay from which it has yet to emerge. Since then, the government formula of fattening up the GDP has been exhausted: Economic performance has dwindled, the ideological consensus has crumbled, political practices have changed, institutional reforms are still put off, several criminal economies have grown out of control, and the perennial corruption of political and economic elites is plain to see. In addition to these developments, the coronavirus pandemic exacerbated the country's weaknesses as the nation faced up to collective failure. Modern Peru's most prosperous days ground to a halt, with the country resembling a mass grave. This stage of national breakdown fostered the election of 2021. This election and what it has produced—the brief government of Pedro Castillo and that of Dina Boluarte—shows that the democratic consensus is broken in Peru. It is a democracy emptied of all content and increasingly assaulted by interests on the margins of the law, which survives by inertia. At the end of the period surveyed in this chapter, Peru is neither represented nor governed. An era has ended, and nobody can tell what will come next.

The trajectory that I have just traced out does not constitute a dynamic that is purely Peruvian. As Paulo Drinot has noted in his chapter in this volume, Peru's modernizing attempts were generally smaller parcels of global modernization projects. Something similar can be glimpsed in what concerns us here. The principal thesis regarding the exchange of representation for governance mirrors, for example, Pierre Rosanvallon's analyses of contemporary democracies, where he argues that the center of gravity has shifted from representative bodies—parliaments—to executives that remain "authorized" electorally to govern as they see fit.[5] Confidence in consumption resonates as an important feature of citizen well-being and evaluation.[6] And we can cite global phenomena such as the lack of programmatic variety,[7] public life marked by the emergence of the individual at the expense of the collective,[8] a democracy restricted to what is permitted by technocratic reason,[9] a representation marked by the collapse of class-based and worker parties,[10] the recent rise of anti-elite populisms,[11] the dynamics of democratic backsliding,[12] and the increased collusion of state institutions and crime,[13] among many other worldwide processes. Peru is not alone. With its own idiosyncrasies, it is part of broader international developments.

The Twentieth Century: Representation Above Governance

> I am a politician, I am not a manager hired for a crisis.
> —ALAN GARCÍA (1987)

What do we mean when we speak about representation? Without plunging into theoretical depths, we are referring to the stable connection between representative and represented, between political authority and citizen. As we saw in John Dewey's metaphor, the authority in a democracy must resolve problems by responding to society. The institution that makes this possible has always been political parties. They must ensure that the ultimate objective of democracy—that is, that politicians reflect the will of the citizenry—is fulfilled.

The link between parties and citizens can hinge on varying factors (clientelism, ideology, loyalty to the leader), but here we do not need to concern ourselves with these complexities. Suffice it to say that in a representative democracy, parties ensure that citizens participate in the system. Therefore, I do not allude here to the relationship between dictatorial governments and the population. Under such regimes there may be benefits for the population, but these stem not so much from the channeling of their demands as, ultimately, from the will of a ruler who is not responsive to the citizens—who does not *respond* to them. I do not consider, for example, the governments of Óscar Benavides, Manuel Odría, and Juan Velasco Alvarado to have been representative in the democratic sense. When I speak about representation, I refer to the involvement of citizens in the affairs of the republic—especially but not solely via the electoral route.[14]

In Peru, unlike other Latin American countries, a party system never congealed.[15] However, there is a crucial difference between *effective* representation and representative *aspiration*. The country may never have had institutionalized systemic or partisan representation, but the aspiration of representation has long appeared on the horizon of republican Peru.

Since the beginnings of the republic, Congress has had special relevance in national representation even though the country opted for a presidential system.[16] In the second half of the nineteenth century emerged the Partido Civil, led by Manuel Pardo, setting in motion an important representative link in ideological, organizational, and representative terms. As Carmen McEvoy has shown, leaders and citizens with an interest in reviving the republican ideals of the citizen, respect for the law, and education converged on the party.[17] The party's ideological adhesive was its relaunch of the promises associated with Peru's emancipatory moment (which had unfolded five decades earlier), thus putting an end to political life dominated by the military. This mission was pushed by a pluri-class coalition and expanded throughout the country, entangling with a vast network of organizations that we would today call civil society. Thus in the final decades of the nineteenth century, representative ambition shone through a party that would endure for many years.

Into the twentieth century, the main flag bearer of this representative ideal was the Alianza Popular Revolucionaria Americana (APRA), a mass party the likes of which had never been seen before in Peru. APRA exploded onto the scene of the 1931 elections, the year zero of Peru's political modernity.[18] The speech that the party's leader, Víctor Raúl Haya de la Torre, delivered at Lima's Plaza de Acho bullring during that election campaign lent Peruvian politics a series of coordinates that would orient it for decades.

It signaled a robust vision, a colossal leader, and an unprecedented mass organization. Against oligarchy and imperialism emerged the representative roar: "the party of the people." This has been APRA's slogan from the outset. The party bolstered its inclusive and Latin Americanist sermon with fabulous organization. Operational cells emerged—*aprista* groupings of lawyers, employees, artisans, and even newspaper vendors, as Martín Bergel has noted.[19] At the same time, the party articulated a discourse about and for the new middle class, who were demanding new rights.[20] As various historical studies show, beyond the party's strength in the Peruvian north since its foundation,[21] APRA would very quickly come to represent, in different regions of the country, distinct forms of an anti-oligarchy ethos.[22] If we ponder the history of republican Peru, Víctor Raúl Haya de la Torre stands out as the exceptional figure who, "in a country of occasional centralizations and eternal fragmentations" (to use the words of Moisés Leimlij),[23] constructed the body and soul of a modern political organization with an influence like none other in the twentieth century and part of the twenty-first.[24]

During the twentieth century, Haya de la Torre was not alone in articulating this desire for representation. Acción Popular (AP) and its leader, Fernando Belaúnde, arose in Peruvian politics when APRA's reformist flames were extinguished in the convulsions of the 1950s. Acción Popular was a party that combined, in its own way, a developmentalist agenda typical of the mid-twentieth century with a discourse that invoked vague precolonial notions while giving unprecedented space to the provinces. For the first time, the Andean and Amazonian regions featured not as a problem but as a possibility ("I have crossed the cordillera not in pursuit of homages, but in search of inspiration and ideas," announced Fernando Belaúnde).[25]

AP made the agrarian reform flag its own and gave political representation to a host of rural demands that had been expressed for decades through *indigenista* intellectual groups and multiple campesino movements. "Wiracocha Belaúnde," they called this leader in the south of Peru, after the Inca creator deity. Moreover, when Belaúnde assumed the presidency for the first time (1963–68), one of his first steps, in 1964, was to introduce municipal elections. In sum, AP and Fernando Belaúnde shaped a reformist agenda that rested on middle-class professionals and urban youth (Belaúnde was a university professor) but in which rural and Andean demands played a central role.[26]

There were other twentieth-century political parties that established and sustained specific doctrines and relations with certain sectors and regions of the country. Christian democracy, as in the rest of the continent, grouped together reformist and democratic elites that in Peru's case had a notable presence in the south.[27] The Partido Popular Cristiano (PPC), a conservative splinter of Christian democracy led by Luis Bedoya, established a prolonged link with traditional sectors of Lima and Callao that endured for decades.[28] The Frente Nacional de Trabajadores y Campesinos (FRENATRACA) gave voice to new campesino interests in the south, where the transformation of relations between the urban and rural sectors was gathering pace.[29] And in the 1980s, a union between a multiplicity of leftist groups gave rise to Izquierda Unida, which became particularly relevant at the municipal level.[30]

As this abbreviated account shows, Peru's political twentieth century was marked by representative will. This will was manifested through both citizen demands and the appearance of certain organizations that established links with these sectors. It did not, however, consolidate in the form of a lasting party system. Multiple coups d'état, political violence, state weakness, and economic crises, among other factors, poured cold water on this possibility. Above all, the administrative inefficiency of these parties encumbered the task. Several democratic governments were caught up in squabbles between state powers (Bustamante y Rivero in 1948, Belaúnde in 1968), often amid severe economic crises (Belaúnde in 1968 and 1985, García in 1990).

This dynamic of a representative politics with serious governance shortcomings reached its most critical point in the 1980s. During that decade the historical representative parties plunged the country into misgovernment. They had no idea how to control the economy or Sendero Luminoso's violence. The economy suffered recessions of close to 10 percent of GDP in 1983, 1988, and 1989. Between 1980 and 1989, GDP per capita contracted by 22 percent, while average inflation exceeded 500 percent and, in 1990, reached its historic peak of 7,649 percent.[31] Poverty soared from 53 percent in 1973 to 60 percent in 1986.[32] Seventy-five percent of the total death toll in Peru's internal armed conflict occurred in the ten-year period between 1980 and 1990.[33]

During the 1980s, the parties that for decades had given form to Peruvian political life governed the country at different levels (national, regional, municipal). Amid the disarray, the party system went into meltdown. Perhaps the first alarm bell was the election of Ricardo Belmont as mayor of Lima in 1989. Hailing from radio and television, Belmont trialed a political category that would put down roots: that of the outsider. And with this, public fury against politicians would begin to mount. As Martín Tanaka judged, in the 1980s the party system collapsed more from deficiencies in governance than from inadequacies in representation.[34]

The Great Transformation: Governance Above Representation

I'd prefer to open a school than a party venue.

—ALBERTO FUJIMORI

Alberto Fujimori closed a political cycle marked by desire for representation. But before closing it, he rose to power by its rules. His campaign slogan was paradoxical: "A president like you." The campaign spots boasted repeatedly of "a president who is like you, who thinks the same as you, who feels like you." The elementary representative impetus could not be more stark. More than governing the country or righting its course during its hour of need—as rival candidate Mario Vargas Llosa had proposed to do—Fujimori campaigned in 1990 by pledging the most basic representation of Peruvians' sentiments and customs. But once in power, he detected a country exasperated with warfare, ravaged economically, and ruined morally. As expressed by the Izquierda Unida regional assembly member quoted early in this chapter, a longing for order hung over Peru. Fujimori betrayed his mandate to represent when he instituted economic policies that ran counter to those he had championed during his campaign. He launched the "Fujishock," a series of orthodox economic policies. Vargas Llosa's program ended up in the hands of a partyless outsider. But more than being paradoxical, this policy was a foretaste of what would become a custom. Inflation was brought under control and the economy was revived. No matter that the policy was founded on non-representativeness, thought the majority. The link between representative and represented collapsed. After the self-coup of April 5, 1992, and, above all, the capture that September of Sendero Luminoso leader Abimael Guzmán, it gave way to a link between governor and governed. And the jubilation began.[35]

Let us elaborate. What was celebrated was not the mere constitutional rupture but rather its ultimate consequences. Between 1987 and 1992, the country hit rock bottom: GDP shrank by 23.29 percent; annual inflation topped 7,000 percent; a cholera epidemic killed 2,909 people and infected almost 400,000 in 1990 alone; and Sendero Luminoso caused thousands of deaths and financial losses in the millions. The situation was so grave that when Francis Fukuyama published his ultra-optimistic *The End of History and the Last Man* (1992), in which he heralded the global and unstoppable triumph of liberal democracy, he name-checked Peru as

Figure 6.1 Alberto Fujimori's self-coup on April 5, 1992, initiating a civilian-military regime. Source: Archivo La República.

a crisis-wrought exception where democracy would not arrive and some form of dictatorship would likely come in its place.[36] Thus, Peru bucked global trends, applauding authoritarian government and the expulsion of "freeloading" members of Congress.[37] But that was not all. The population's passive and enthusiastic—no contradiction—support was paired with active backing by the military. Thus, a civilian-military regime was constructed to solve problems that had looked to be never-ending: those of political violence and the collapsing economy. Of course, more than problems of governance, these were problems of statehood—that is, of a state that could not fulfill the most basic of functions.[38] And this was corrected in the first years of the Fujimori government.[39]

However, effectiveness without democracy, comes with strings attached. From October 1991, an old contingent of army officers with expertise in the art of "search-interrogate-execute-bury" was revived.[40] This was the squad originally called Escorpio when it was established in the 1980s but which later came to be known as the Grupo Colina. The group's revival owed to a new counterinsurgency strategy set out in an armed forces manual approved at the end of the 1980s in which indiscriminate killing was expressly forbidden and intelligence actions were to be honed in order to "neutralize or destroy subversive elements."[41] As a result, selective extrajudicial executions multiplied.[42] There were dozens of assassinations, and some became emblematic cases of human rights violations. The massacres of Barrios Altos (fifteen fatalities, including one child), Cantuta (nine university students and one professor killed), and Pativilca (nine deaths), among others, revealed the dictatorial tendencies of a regime that, taking recourse to its popularity, acted outside the most elementary laws of democratic coexistence.[43]

Beyond the scandalization of certain print outlets and the denunciations by human rights organizations, most of the country was unperturbed by these developments. What emerged and was consolidated at the junction between dictatorship and effectiveness is the apogee of anti-republicanism: a providential figurehead, the military, and government by decree. Self-governance, deliberation, due process, the separation of powers—everything, in short, that constitutes the basis of a dignified republic—was sacrificed at the altar of efficiency. Fujimori was applauded when he announced at the Annual Conference of Executives, a business lobby summit, in 1991 that "it would be preferable to install an emperor and give him at least ten years to solve our problems."[44] Irrespective of social class, the predominant impression was of a docile Peru satisfied with its savior. The country appeared to be regretful of its *movementist* excesses in the preceding decades. And Fujimori did not disappoint: The bicameral Congress was closed, regional assemblies and governments dissolved, municipal governments postponed—steps all couched in an aggressive rhetoric against the *partidocracia*, partocracy. In sum, this was a blitzkrieg against all the institutions of representation. When these institutions returned in 1993—more because of international pressure than national demand—they were fewer in number, smaller, and diminished in their ability to check the executive. The national legislature, whose two chambers had grouped together 240 legislators, reappeared in unicameral form with half as many representatives. Moreover, they were to be elected in a single-district bloc, which effectively left the country's provinces without representation since the concentration of the population in Lima made it very difficult to elect a representative from anywhere else. The regional authorities were replaced by Temporary Regional Administration Councils appointed by the executive (which remained "temporary" for ten years). Of course, these and many other transformations that the Fujimori government introduced were facilitated by the prior debilitation of social, regional, and economic actors that now were either too weak to counterbalance the process or nonexistent.[45]

The new institutional structure of diminished representation coexisted with political discourse and actions of the same tenor. In the Democratic Constituent Congress of 1993, the bulk of the parties and representatives that had been in Congress during the 1980s were no longer present.[46] Just two of the ten parties predated 1990: the PPC and FRENATRACA, which amassed just 13 percent of the seats between them. In the municipal elections of 1993, 76 percent of the district mayors elected nationwide were "independent." Ricardo Belmont was reelected mayor of Lima. In short, politics ceased to be what it once was. Without ideologies, without organizations, without loyalties, Belmont's electoral vehicle bore a name that encapsulated the new times: Obras (Works). That is to say: Don't represent me, govern me.

This change of political era was also enshrined in the 1993 constitution. As Maxwell Cameron has noted, the outgoing constitution of 1979 began with "We, the representatives of the Constituent Assembly . . . in exercise of the sovereign power that the people of Peru have conferred upon us . . ."[47] The preamble to the 1993 magna carta, on the other hand, established that the Democratic Constituent Congress, "obeying the mandate of the people," "has resolved to provide the following constitution." The tone is the reverse of the 1979 document. As Cameron stressed, it makes reference to neither "popular sovereignty" nor to members of Congress being "representatives" of the nation.

But it was not only politics that was transformed; the economic order was also turned on its head. The essence of the new constitution lurked in its economic chapter (articles 58 to 89). This section, in short, establishes the subsidiary role of the state, limiting—and in practice eliminating—the prospect of an entrepreneurial state, dismissing the notion of strategic economic activities or sectors, and granting constitutional assurances to private actors. The weight and responsibility of economic activity, prosperity, and planning would be transferred to the private sector, as in much of Latin America.[48] The old state was retired.

These constitutional principles translated into a vast network of changes at the level of organizations and public policies. Now the state was interested in attracting investment: 228 public companies were privatized. The plethora of regulatory agencies created amply attests to the orientation of the new model; they included the Supervisory Agency for

Private Investment in Telecommunications (OSIPTEL), the Supervisory Agency for Investment in Transportation Infrastructure for Public Use (OSITRAN), the Supervisory Agency for Investment in Energy (OSIN-ERG, since 2007 OSINERGMIN), the National Superintendency for Sanitation Services (SUNASS), and the National Institute for the Defense of Competition and Protection of Intellectual Property (INDECOPI). To promote local and foreign investment, interest rates were allowed to float, tariffs were reduced, and restrictions on the circulation of foreign currency were removed.

At the fiscal level, the Central Reserve Bank of Peru (BCRP) was afforded greater autonomy. Public financing was eliminated in order to forestall inflation, while multiple exchange rates were prohibited. On the taxation front, the National Superintendency of Customs and Tax Administration (SUNAT) was restructured, and emphasis was placed on removal of exemptions and expansion of the tax base. Finally, labor rights were curtailed and reconceptualized as costs. The measures introduced facilitated temporary and outsourced hiring, made firing easier, flexibilized working conditions, and weakened labor unions.

Fujimori's zenith came in 1995. That year he was reelected with 64 percent of the vote and achieved an absolute majority in Congress. The opposition's complaints about the lack of a level playing field fell on deaf ears. In this election, the collapse of the old organizations was evident: Izquierda Unida disappeared; AP and PPC (representing the center-right) dropped from 55 percent of the vote in 1980 to 1.6 percent in 1995; APRA, which had managed 22.5 percent of the vote in 1990 after its disastrous term of government, now mustered just 4.1 percent. That same year, promoted by the fujimorista benches, a general amnesty law was approved for armed forces and military personnel who had committed any crime linked to the counterinsurgency strategy. That is, the law blocked the prospect of judicially prosecuting human rights violations. With this anti-constitutional measure, redolent of the worst traditions of Latin American dictatorships, Fujimori and his electoral vehicle sealed an alliance with the armed forces that would bind them judicially for decades.

However, if the prevailing public mood was supportive of the government, it would be incorrect to suggest that this spirit was unanimous. On the political fringes, opposition candidate Javier Pérez de Cuéllar took 21.8 percent of the vote in 1995, paving the way for a minority but combative legislative opposition in Congress. However, Peruvian civil society, which between the 1950s and 1980s had been among the most organized

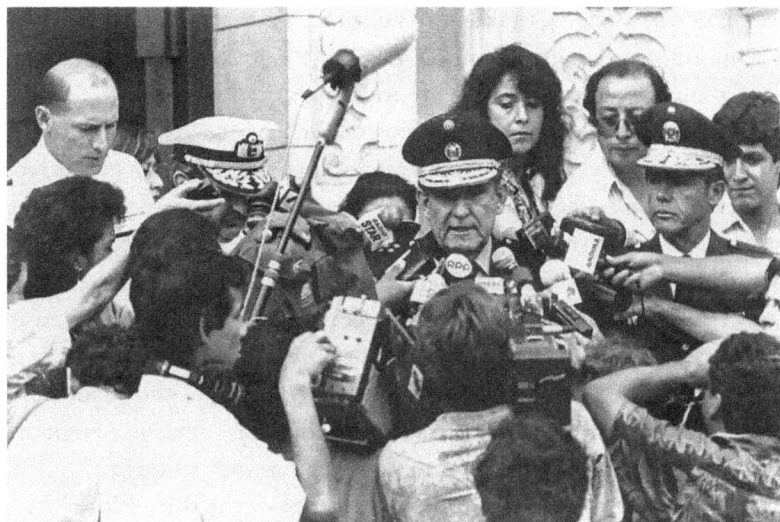

Figure 6.2 The commander general of the Peruvian army (1992–98), Nicolás de Bari Hermoza Ríos, faces the press. Fujimori's government granted general amnesty to members of the police and armed forces who had committed crimes in the context of the antisubversive struggle. Source: Archivo La República.

and mobilized in Latin America, was left without any real means of counteracting the government's effectiveness.[49] On the one hand, over a decade of internal armed strife and uncontrolled violence had weakened the country's social fabric and left civil society leaders running scared.[50] On the other hand, the economic reforms, particularly on the labor front, depleted the density and activity of union organizations. The result was a decrease in the average number of strikes per year from 699 in the 1980s to 184 in the 1990s.[51] In sum, a politics that for decades had been highly "movementist" was ultimately demobilized.[52] Or, in the vocabulary of *fujimorismo*, the country had been "pacified." This was also true of Peruvian cultural life. Peru's urban rock scene of the 1980s, for example, in which the original "underground punk" or *subte* movement had emerged, lost its vitality along with the rest of Peruvian society.[53] Indeed, to signal the social and political transformation of Fujimori's Peru, it is almost sufficient to note that members of Narcosis, the emblematic *subte* band of the 1980s, played in the pop bands Mar de Copas and La Liga del Sueño the following decade. Pacified.

The second half of the 1990s confirmed classical liberal convictions: Power unchecked leads to corruption and abuses. The role of Vladimiro Montesinos as Alberto Fujimori's main advisor became evident as the two set about orchestrating the country's institutional demolition. In terms of corruption, according to Alfonso Quiroz, the Fujimori-Montesinos dyad likely went beyond anything else in Peruvian history.[54] These practices were financed through the misappropriation of public money, the siphoning of military funds, illegal commissions on imports, overvaluation of state acquisitions, arms trafficking, links to the cocaine trade, and so on.[55] This was all perpetuated by a network composed of public officials, servicemembers, business actors, bankers, and the media. The editorial lines of the major television channels, as well as showbiz personalities and talk show hosts themselves, were bought off, while so-called *chicha*, or tabloid, newspapers were funded using public money and deployed to attack the opposition. Control of the media was such that, according to Montesinos, Fujimori gave instructions about the type of headlines that were to appear.[56]

These measures resulted in the destruction of the rule of law. Montesinos took control of the judiciary by stuffing it with provisional judges whom he managed according to his whims. Yet Fujimori's made-to-measure constitution soon became a hindrance to his reelection ambitions for 2000. As a result, its provisions were altered illegally, and, most egregiously of all, the prohibition on a third consecutive term in office was subject to an "authentic interpretation" by the *fujimorista* majority in Congress. Subsequently, when the Constitutional Court objected to such juridical barbarism, the *fujimorista* majority reacted by defenestrating the three magistrates who had voted to annul the new provision. That is, the legislature did not fulfill its role of representing but limited itself to endorsing what Fujimori and Montesinos ordered it to do. One could fill an entire article with examples of what proved to be an institutional massacre. Because of this corrupt and despotic behavior, the government's legitimacy gradually waned in the second half of the 1990s.

And as a result of this process Peru's economy stalled. This was only natural, as the priorities of the corrupt and authoritarian *fujimorista* project were placed above the national economy. It was no coincidence that the Ministry of the Economy and Finances (MEF), led at that time by Jorge Camet, thwarted initiatives from political actors who could potentially overshadow Alberto Fujimori. Thus, a sizable World Bank loan to the municipality of Lima, which at that time was led by Alberto Andrade, was sabotaged by the MEF. Along similar lines, Víctor Joy Way, a politician without any training in economics, was appointed to this ministry to pave the way for Fujimori's illegal third election. Following this subjugation of the economy to political priorities (as well as the impact of the Asian financial crisis), between 1998 and 2001 the Peruvian economy grew by an annual average of just 1 percent.

Along with the institutional, political, and economic transformations, Peruvian society also underwent changes that are worth mentioning. Informal economic activity (informality) had taken off in the 1980s and, although intellectuals discussed these developments and President Fujimori sought counsel from the guru on the matter, Hernando de Soto, president of the Institute for Liberty and Democracy, nobody held back the expansion of this sector. As part of this trend, labor union membership among the economically active population tumbled at great speed: from 42.1 percent in 1990 to 15.3 percent in 1998. At the same time, the number of micro and small enterprises mushroomed. Beyond the sphere of labor economics, many public services were deregulated rendering informality far more of a "social bond" than a mere economic characteristic.[57] At the level of both public policy and the public imaginary, the transformation in the realm of public transport was perhaps most profound and revealing of all. In the 1990s, Peru's roads and highways were taken over by combi vans, Daewoo Ticos, minibuses, and *mototaxis* (motorized tricycles) that very quickly became something other than mere modes of transport: They were the metaphors of choice when alluding to the chaotic manner in which the country operated. Beginning in 1991, anyone could be a public transport operator. In that year alone, the country imported 5,000 combi vans (a fourfold increase over the previous year) and 604 buses.[58] By 1997, there were more than 800 registered operators, of which scarcely 200 were authorized to provide a service.[59] Interestingly, despite being a bearer of many of the country's ills, informality was treated as a virtue: Far from being conceptualized as the absence of law, it was painted as a manifestation of the free market, spontaneous and creative. This new virtue was dubbed "entrepreneurialism" and its urban hero the "entrepreneur."

As we end this section, we will turn to national television to sum up the 1990s and the decisive shifts in the country's economic, political, and societal coordinates during the decade. *Los de arriba y los de abajo* (The ones from above and the ones from below), a *telenovela* written by Eduardo Adrianzén and directed by Michel Gómez, was a huge hit when it was first screened in 1994 and 1995. Viewing an episode or two on YouTube today, one realizes that, more than a television show, it held up a mirror to Peru in the first half of the 1990s. The show portrayed almost all the transformations of the era with a key distinction: Those from below really were from below, and its characters, such as the beloved Chamochumbi, were genuinely revolutionary for Peruvian television, which was always disinclined to depict the country's underbelly. More important than the specific plotlines was the climate it captured—something akin to a country that was blowing off steam. As Eduardo Adrianzén put it: "The show reflects the *animus jocandi* [lighthearted humor] of the time."[60] And something of this spirit could also be discerned in its opening sequence, which became a classic of Peruvian television. This was a clip that showcased succulent early 1990s Peruvianness to the rhythm of "Triciclo Perú" by the fusion band Los Mojarras. What appears is a country screwed but less bleak, as vigorous and amusing as it is informal: one where soccer violence and the *barra brava* ultras have replaced political violence, and where politicians are synonymous with disrepute and nonsense. In short, despite everything, there we were, wheeling along "a moving tricycle called Peru."

But the mood of the country soon turned sour, and the follow-up television project of Adrianzén and Gómez captured this too. Debuting in 1997, *Todo se compra, todo se vende* was a tale of moral transgression: the countenance of a country destroying its institutions by way of informality, greed, and disregard for others. The main character is no longer the endearing Chamochumbi but one Rafael Muro, who gets his start with a burglary and then makes a fortune selling used cars in the southern region of Tacna and investing the proceeds in the casino business. In contrast to the highs and lows of its early 1990s predecessor, this *telenovela* depicted pure gloom.[61]

Despite this trajectory, the imaginary around the Fujimori government would remain far more bound to the start of the decade than to the end: to the moment when the air returned to the country and not to when it was asphyxiated all over again. Thus, the idea took hold that Peru prospered when someone—an effective leader who was disinterested in representation—took charge of its destiny. The country flourished as the people kept quiet. And this revealing anti-republican portrait would outlast the collapse of the Fujimori regime.

Modernizing Democracy

> Modernization is, let's say, a computerized yet immobile society.
> —CARLOS MONSIVÁIS

The downfall of the corrupt and authoritarian government of Alberto Fujimori sparked an important shift: The breakneck process of deinstitutionalization was halted. The judiciary, formerly controlled by Montesinos, regained its independence; the Constitutional Court, once dismembered, was reassembled; elections and the institutions overseeing them became credible again; Congress recovered a plurality that had vanished through majorities built on bribes; more than two hundred officials close to the Fujimori regime were convicted of crimes; and Alberto Fujimori and Vladimiro Montesinos themselves ended up behind bars for their graft and their human rights violations. Throughout its history Peru had endured multiple dictatorships, but what made the aftermath of this one unusual was that many of those responsible for the crimes committed were brought to justice. The collapse of the regime and the restoration of democracy, therefore, constituted a major transformation.[62]

But history knows few total changes. And this was no exception. The most toxic elements of the Fujimori regime may not have survived into the new millennium, but other vestiges of the 1990s did. For starters, the two pillars that, in my view, tie together the entire period covered by this chapter—the "government for representation" exchange and the constitution of 1993—outlived the vices of authoritarianism by adapting to the new democratic context. Furthermore, and somewhat paradoxically, their status was secured by this new context and its unprecedented economic growth. If the Fujimori government's legitimacy in the 1990s owed largely to the removal of the country from the cauldron of violence and the inflationary spiral, in the 2000s the perception of good government rested on the economy and, in particular, the growth of GDP and consumption. Meanwhile, representation continued to decline. The role reserved for politics and society was confined to noninterference in the fattening up of GDP. That is, Peruvians were still being urged to shut up and shop.

From the 2000s onward, what was imposed was a renewed project of modernization by economic means. However, it should be noted that this did not occur from the very outset. Rather, at the start of the decade, the main impetus was political (democratizing) and not economic (modernizing). The authoritarian and corrupt excesses of the Fujimori regime were followed by a *democratic* transition. That is, the hope for change lay in the sphere of the institutions that guarantee political liberty and popular sovereignty. It was no surprise that this transition was spearheaded by Cuzco native Valentín Paniagua, a long-standing leader of Acción Popular who had started out as a member of the Partido Demócrata Cristiano. When he was sworn in as transitional president amid the chaotic implosion of the Fujimori regime, Paniagua established an agenda of republican priorities based on representation, elections, and the fight against corruption.[63] Much of the hope was prolonged following the election of Alejandro Toledo in 2001. It was Toledo, after all, who had led the resistance to the illegal reelection of Fujimori in 2000.

However, Toledo had no way of keeping alive the republican flame that the transitional government had managed to install. He was, above all, a scoundrel, lacking in both stature and capability. And fifteen years later serious signs would emerge that he was a thief to boot. All the same, institutional life changed. Elections could be trusted again. The authorities reflected popular will processed through a legitimate electoral system. A Truth and Reconciliation Commission was appointed to produce a report that went on to become pivotal to furthering knowledge about the internal armed conflict. Congress, for its part, reprised a less submissive role vis-à-vis the executive (in 2002, for instance, a minister was censured and forced out of office due to the legislature's actions).[64] Added to the renewed—albeit still modest—importance of the legislature was a series of reforms intended to undo the *fujimorista* vices of clientelist and authoritarian centralism, with the hope of designing what I at one point called "a regime symmetrically opposed to the *fujimorato* [the Fujimori era]" in acknowledgment of its participatory and decentralized pretensions.[65]

However, beyond these political throws of the dice, what really defined the Toledo administration and blazed a trail for the following governments lay in the economic realm. The reins of government were taken up by technocratic sectors with an interest in orthodox management of the economy and its openness to the world. Pedro Pablo Kuczynski (popularly known as "PPK")—banker, technocrat, and an old fox of national politics—became, for all practical purposes, the strongman of government, enshrining the MEF as the epicenter of power. During the Fujimori government, this role had been shared with the Ministry of the Presidency, a politically managed dependency that was dismantled as part of the transition. With the advent of democracy, power was transferred to the MEF, an "island of efficiency" of the new regime.[66]

In these circumstances, representative political life continued to be treated with disdain. Congress became subordinate to the executive; this was not the well-oiled genuflection of the 1990s but rather resulted from the fact that politicians had little to offer the executive technocrats who set the agenda of the country. And though a constitutional separation of powers returned, party political contestation did not. On the other hand, as Catherine Conaghan noted with near clairvoyant anticipation, the economic regime inherited from the 1993 constitution had no difficulty surviving the demise of Fujimori despite the lack of parties.[67] Quite so. A model of modernizing development was structured along economic lines.

PPK, his technocrats, and big business, then, pushed orthodox economic management and commercial openness to the world. Moreover, the planks for development were infrastructural megaprojects; the great actor for progress, private capital; and the sectors privileged, mining and coastal agrobusiness. In 2003, the mining and hydrocarbon sector grew by 4 percent; in 2004, 6 percent; and in 2005, 10.3 percent. When Alan García took office in 2006 for the second time, the world had entered a raw materials supercycle. Things were moving hand over fist. And the raw materials fiesta was about to be fleshed out with ideological content. Although the foundations of the modernization project had already been laid, García turned them into articles of faith by projecting a vision of progress in a series of articles published in the newspaper *El Comercio*. The most influential of these was the first, titled "El perro de hortelano" (the dog in the manger), a title that evokes a play by Lope de Vega relating to a dog that will not eat and will not let others eat.[68] It is important to consider this discourse, not because it conjured up a new development project for Peru but because it consolidated one that already existed and was celebrated by the business, technocratic, and media elites who governed the country according to those ideological principles. Take the title of the article: It is an index finger pointed at the traitors to national progress. For García, these were the dog-citizens who were undermining progress. That is, the title alludes to a path of progress that was to be taken *against* the citizenry—essentially, the poorest and most marginalized.

The first paragraph observed that the country's main problem was its abundance of "idle property." The Amazon region and the Andes awaited its major investors. Peru was depicted as a collection of resources to be exploited, triggering clashes with the canine citizens who, poisoned by ideology, conspired against progress. The country's future, wrote the then-president, lay "in bringing to bear the resources we do not use," for this was "the *only thing* that will let us progress" (emphasis added). It is crucial to stress that what García proposed was not an *economic* model but a *development* model, one in which democracy, the rule of law, representation, institutions, anticorruption initiatives, and the citizens would play no part. Rather, the actor of progress would be the major investor; the indicator of success, the GDP figures. Nothing else. And just as the country's elites fifteen years earlier had applauded the prospect of an emperor, this time they celebrated a doctrine that we might term "dog-in-the-mangerism" (*hortelanismo*). This was a project that cast aside all interest in citizenship, institutions, and liberties.[69]

This dog-in-the-mangerism for the new millennium was the Peruvian version of what is known in some of the social sciences as the "modernization theory." This theory usually holds that societies embark upon progress on the basis of economic and social dimensions, and only later—once they have urbanized, grown wealthy, and attained literacy—do they develop inclusive, democratic systems. That is, the political and institutional sphere is a mere derivative of what truly matters: economic progress. Wherever they are espoused, such principles produce disdain for politics, democracy, and citizens. And so it was in Peru of the 2000s, when the economic, technocratic, and media elites adopted them uncritically. To cite another example of this affiliation, it is worth mentioning the formulation "no bourgeoisie, no democracy," which was first proposed by Barrington Moore Jr. and adopted by Jaime de Althaus—surely the Peruvian intellectual most committed to modernization theory.[70] According to this posture, democracy flows from economic and social processes. Such were the country's programmatic horizons: prioritizing economic gain via the route of private investment, with the conviction that it would generate future institutional and political well-being.[71]

Between 2002 and 2020, this modernization pact was, to all intents and purposes, respected by the different actors in Peruvian politics. The "autopilot" approach was a constant throughout the period: no matter who won the elections, the modernizing project would continue apace. Even the anti-system Ollanta Humala—elected in 2011 on a platform styled "the great transformation" that pledged major changes to the country's economic model and sought to scrap the 1993 constitution—ultimately governed against his own campaign. Once again, administration of the modernization project came at the expense of representation. When he assumed the presidency, Humala appointed Luis Miguel Castilla, who had been a deputy minister under Alan García, as minister of the economy. The casting and the script of Peruvian governance were kept unchanged.[72] And throughout the period, Congress did little to keep the executive in check. Neither Toledo nor García nor Humala had legislative majorities, but they were nonetheless able to govern with limited congressional opposition. In sum, politicians—whether presidents or members of Congress—lacked both the resources and the incentives to come up with any alternative to the modernization project. With varying hues, a dynamic inherited from the 1990s was perpetuated in which representation and governance went their separate ways.

The main source of legitimacy underpinning the project was economic success. In this regard, the country made strides. In the period 2002–16, GDP grew from 237 to 502 billion soles,[73] poverty was reduced by a third, and extreme poverty fell by one-fifth.[74] The country's reserves increased from $8.6 billion to $61.7 billion.[75] Average annual inflation was 2.8 percent. These achievements were down to several factors. On the one hand, as noted, they coincided with the commodity-price supercycle, which propelled economic growth throughout Latin America and lifted 66 million people out of poverty across the region between 2002 and 2014.[76]

On the other hand, it was also an outcome of aggressive policy on the part of successive Peruvian governments, which prioritized integration into international markets to the point that seventeen agreements were signed with different countries. Finally, responsible management of national fiscal accounts by the MEF and the BCRP yielded macroeconomic robustness, facilitating growth and accumulation.

All this redounded to the benefit of society, which attained unheard-of purchasing power, while many of Peru's cities awoke to the comforts and habits of a new middle class. Private consumption leapt from 152 to 321 billion soles between 2002 and 2016.[77] In 2002 the country had just three shopping malls; by 2015, this number had increased to seventy-eight.[78] The expansion of sectors that ceased to be poor was resounding: The middle classes, who accounted for 11.9 percent of the population in 2005, totaled 50.6 percent by 2014.[79] The sociologist Danilo Martuccelli summed up this transformation better than anyone else: The new Limeños (though this assessment could be extended to much of urban Peru) could now "treat themselves."[80]

This economic prosperity also enabled the expansion of the state and its social services. Juntos, the conditional cash transfer program, went from a few thousand beneficiaries in 2005 to 750,000 in 2015. Spending on social programs doubled from $282 to $599 per person between 2001 and 2015; in the health sector, it went from $51 to $129; and in education, from $92 to $204. Moreover, the territorial reach of the Peruvian state increased considerably. The network of paved roads, for instance, expanded from 8,500 kilometers in 2000 to almost 20,000 kilometers in 2016.[81]

These transformations, pushed forward by a galloping economy, resulted in unbounded optimism for much of the country. A renewed nationalism was propelled by consumption and encapsulated by the new

"Brand Peru" formula and logo. And as is well known, brands do well when the norms of accounting establish as much. Such was the optimism associated with Brand Peru that it motivated, in 2011, the creation of a documentary spot called "Peru, Nebraska" in which an eponymous town in the US Midwest was invaded by a mission of Peruvians seeking to enlighten their northern namesakes. Central to this mission was something that was also integral to that moment of optimism: gastronomy. Under the undisputed and notable leadership of celebrity chef and restaurateur Gastón Acurio, Peruvian cuisine achieved a world renown that was well suited to the hopeful climate. Meanwhile, the business sector was the most elated of all, as attaining first-world status seemed not only possible but close. This spirit was encapsulated by the graphs and the content that featured in the Annual Conference of Executives (CADE) in 2014: The Peruvian tricycle had become a supersonic train. And much of this same mood could be glimpsed among the public when Machu Picchu was ranked as one of the New Seven Wonders of the World in 2007. What did these scenes of optimism have in common? A confidence that economic growth was bequeathing a noticeably better country. A conviction that this was no mere national mirage: Forecasters abroad were pointing in the same direction, including former US Vice President Al Gore, who insisted that the world would soon recognize "the Peruvian miracle."[82] The national wealth, according to the modernizing plans, seemed to be trickling down to other spheres of social life and improving them. An imaginary of nationalist concord thus took its place alongside economic progress and consumption. Shut up and shop.

But beneath the surface exuberance, social and institutional debts were mounting. First, any initiative that might place the rule of law at the heart of the debate was put off. The anticorruption laws that had motivated Paniagua's transitional government melted away. Moreover, the country's budgetary allocations increased as a product of the overall inertial enrichment, but without responding to a development plan concerned with the quality of public spending, citizens' needs, or corruption.[83] Thus, the budgets of many sectors multiplied many times over, but without culminating in better services for the public. In a few years this would become especially apparent—and tragic—in the domain of health and education. A similar story played out within the national judicial system in which, as a result of economic growth, earnings and resources increased, but without giving rise to a new and legitimate relationship with Peruvian society.

Second, national electoral politics consolidated as a kind of flea market of candidates in which electoral letterheads hyperbolically styled as political parties offered candidacies to the highest bidder. This was a politics of personalities in search, during each electoral cycle, of a platform on which they could surface. At both the national and subnational levels, representatives and society compounded the atrophic relations they inherited from the 1990s. As Steven Levitsky and Mauricio Zavaleta have noted, politics in Peru was reduced to its minimum and indivisible expression: the independent politician.[84] In this sense, it constituted the most severe case of party collapse in Latin America. This representative debacle, devoid of organizations and ruled by opportunists, became an open door for informal and illegal interests to place their own agents in many parliamentary groupings and subnational governments.[85] More than one party has had cadres with links to national and international drug trafficking investigations. According to the researcher Jaime Antezana, in 2014 there were fourteen members of Congress with ties to the cocaine trade.[86] Another investigation found that in the 2014 subnational elections, 124 candidates had this sort of connection.[87]

Female representation, on the other hand, remained largely static despite women accounting for 48 percent of the membership of political organizations.[88] In 2001, just 18 percent of parliamentarians were women. This rose slightly to 23 percent in 2011 but dropped back down to 21 percent in 2016. And after five regional electoral contests, just five women have been elected as governors. In sum, the world of representation had withered and nobody took seriously the task of reforming it.

Third, informality and illegality expanded rapidly.[89] Peru's informal economy remained among the largest in the world, encompassing some 80 percent of the economically active population in 2007, while the rate of union membership dropped from 8.1 percent in 2006 to 5 percent in 2016.[90] Informality could also be perceived in the way in which Peruvian cities expanded. A study by Álvaro Espinoza and Ricardo Fort found that 93 percent of urban growth between 2001 and 2018 was informal.[91] Yes, you read correctly: 93 percent.

Illegal activities followed a similar path. The spike in the international price of gold saw informal and illegal mining spread rapidly throughout the country, such that by 2016 it had taken root in every region. This had a devastating effect on Amazonia and many of its "protected" parks. By 2013, approximately 25 percent of Peru's gold production was of informal or illegal origins.[92] As to *narcotráfico*, for a time Peru became the world's biggest cocaine producer, though Colombia has monopolized this position since 2013.[93] All this would translate into a resounding perception: By 2018, 87 percent of Peruvians thought that illegal economic activity, in whatever form, played an important part in their region's economic growth.[94]

In relation to this, the public endured urban criminality to an increasing degree. Several Peruvian regions began to post indicators of assault and homicide that were up there with those of the most dangerous countries in the world. In Tumbes, for example, the homicide rate in 2017 exceeded that of Guatemala in 2016 (28.8 versus 27.3 homicides per 100,000 inhabitants), while Huaral and Barranca (just two hours from Lima) also approached these percentages. The rate in Madre de Dios rocketed from 16.5 to 46.6 homicides per 100,000 inhabitants between 2012 and 2017—numbers similar to those recorded in El Salvador in 2013.[95] This criminality and decline in law and order also had critical effects on the well-being and security of women. In 2017, the Thomson Reuters Foundation considered Lima to be the fifth-most-dangerous city in the world for women.[96] All in all, Peruvians would discover, like citizens elsewhere in the continent, something that confounded the modernizing prognostications: "more money, more crime."[97]

That is, the economic expansion feeding the fantasies of the national elites also fueled an informality and criminality that met with no resistance from a weak rule of law that had fallen into neglect during the modernizing project. Eduardo Dargent, Andreas Feldmann, and Juan Pablo Luna have identified the paradox of "more state and less stateness."[98] In other words, there was a greater state presence but less enforcement of the law. An example of this dynamic could be seen in the new Interoceanic Highway that connected Brazil and Peru, whose construction began in 2005. This development allowed the state to penetrate previously unconnected territory, but once opened, it became an infrastructure project that served, above all, to invigorate illegal economies such as drug trafficking, illegal deforestation, and unauthorized mining, all of which favored the depredation of Amazonia. That is, the state could expand because the resources were there, but effective law enforcement required much more than money.

To recap: On the one hand, the modernizing democracy generated vast economic growth, as the public was buying while the political, business, and media elites were ebullient. This chimed with the impetus of an urban Peru in which the habits and expectations of middle-class life were burgeoning. On the other hand, a country was taking shape in which the rule of law did not prosper, political representation became increasingly weak, and the economic boom encouraged criminality in various forms. Thus, beyond the enthusiasm of the business community, the period was never one of unanimous satisfaction with Peru's enrichment. Other contemporary developments demonstrated as much.

Alfredo Torres, a specialist in Peruvian public opinion, shrewdly observed that the country was undergoing a stage of "unhappy growth."[99] This could be appreciated in different arenas. For example, from Toledo to PPK, the presidents were unpopular. Humala twice reached the runoff (in 2006 and 2011) with a discourse that exploited national resentment about the manner in which the country was being run.[100] Around that time it became increasingly common to hear talk of "socioenvironmental conflicts." The coming together of major investors and the most overlooked of Peru's citizens in the absence of political parties resulted in deaths in significant quantities.[101] Across the governments of García, Humala, and PPK, a total of 279 deaths were recorded in such conflicts. In 2009, in the Amazonian city of Bagua, unrest sparked by a series of decrees that "facilitated" major private investment in communally held land culminated in the death of thirty-three Peruvians, among them police officers and protesters who viewed the decrees as a threat to their livelihoods and ways of being. This is the problem with the dog-in-the-manger mandate: Progress demands that the dog-citizens be brought to heel. As the researcher Javier Arellano Yanguas has observed, conflicts in Peru were not related to poverty per se but to poor areas in which vast streams of resources suddenly entered.[102] In summary, beneath the whopping macroeconomic figures, ill-feeling simmered undetected.

Finally, let us note another change in the Peruvian social sphere. New conservative sectors had appeared in tandem with the growth of evangelical churches. In 1993, evangelical Christians made up 7.2 percent of the population; in 2017, they totaled 15.6 percent.[103] Part of this expansion allowed conservative social movements to become more visible and stage mass demonstrations under the banner of social-media-driven slogans such as "#ConMisHijosNoTeMetas" (Don't mess with my kids). Targeting a perceived "gender ideology," this movement sought to wreck state secular education policies grounded in the principle of equality among children. In an echo of international trends, this elicited the emergence

Figure 6.3 In the town of Bagua in 2009, a tragic confrontation between citizens and police left thirty-three people dead. The episode became an allegory of the times: a desire to expand private investment, a mistreated citizenry, and a precarious state. Source: Archivo La República.

of a progressive countermovement concerned with the status of women. Little by little, the magnitude of domestic violence against women became evident. Indeed, 63 percent of Peruvian girls and women between the ages of fifteen and forty-nine reported experiencing domestic abuse—and in some regions, such as Apurímac, Cuzco, and Puno, the figure neared 80 percent.[104] Amid a number of horrific cases of gender-based violence, the Ni Una Menos (not one [woman] less) movement—which originated in Argentina—came to Peru, sparking, in 2016, the largest march that the country had seen in the post-Fujimori era.[105]

Three governments on from the fall of Fujimori, the dog-in-the-manger modernization project had achieved much of what it had set out to achieve—a more dynamic economy and a wealthier (or less poor) population—while political and institutional considerations were sidelined at the expense of these priorities. Among Peru's elites, nobody wanted to know that wealth without law is just another form of underdevelopment. But everyone would come to understand this in the years that followed.

The Unraveling of the Modernization Project

> The eclipse was not partial.
> —SODA STEREO

By the midway point of the Ollanta Humala presidency (2011–16), the limitations of Peru's development model had become evident. From the academic realm it was noted that the initial corporate enthusiasm about Peru's economic boom had been mistaken, insofar as the model did not contain "the seed of development."[106] Economic growth rates had slowed. International prices had not remained at pre-2013 levels, and the country had failed to increase its productivity. The graph in figure 6.4 shows that if we look beyond the drop in GDP in 2009, what we are left with is a constant decline in the growth rate from 2008 onward.

Peru's economic decline occurred alongside its political and institutional descent as politicians and political groupings entered a dynamic of aggression without consideration for the country. The bloc that became known by the portmanteau *fujiaprismo*, for the convergence over more than a decade between the interests of APRA and *fujimorismo*, coarsely confronted the Humala government, and then, without remorse, that of PPK (2016–18) and Vizcarra (2018–20). The sad—and interesting—thing about this spiral of political feuding is that it did not revolve around anything of relevance for Peru. At the time, I described this conflictive atmosphere bereft of substance as "tension without crisis" (*crispación sin crisis*).[107]

Today, however, I realize that I was mistaken. There was a huge crisis. But it was unseen. In March 2014, Brazil's judiciary went public on an enormous investigation related to a web of corruption that had drawn in Brazilian businesspeople and politicians as well as dozens of projects in Latin America and Africa. As is now clear, Peruvian politicians were not being nervous and hostile just for the sake of it. They were trying to push back the Brazilian tsunami. Almost the entire ensemble of Peruvian politics was in some way linked with the corruption orchestrated by construction firms such as Odebrecht, Camargo Corrêa, and OAS. Journalistic and fiscal reports revealed that Toledo had received around $20 million in bribes; García was implicated in several illegal operations with Odebrecht; Humala and his wife, Nadine Heredia, were involved in siphoning off the donations they received for the 2006 and 2011 electoral campaigns; Kuczynski had signed contracts with Odebrecht that he concealed during his presidency; Keiko Fujimori, member of Congress, perennial presidential

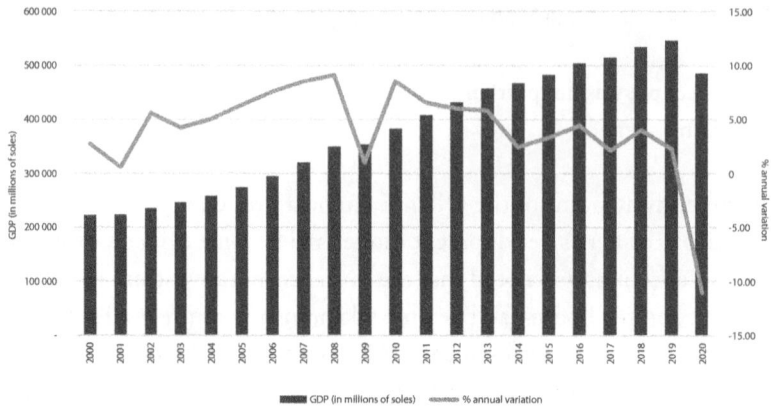

Figure 6.4 Peru's economic growth, 2000–2020. Source: Compiled by author based on data from the BCRP, https://estadisticas.bcrp.gob.pe/estadisticas/series/.

candidate, and daughter of the former president, had received compromising donations; and Luis Castañeda and Susana Villarán, former mayors of Lima, were also tainted by shady deals. In sum, from top to bottom and left to right, almost everyone had been at it. Brazilian corruption found excellent Peruvian partners in both the business and political worlds.[108] That is, more than the dog-citizens that dog-in-the-mangerism had identified as the impediment to progress, it was the elites themselves.

The large-scale corruption of the first two decades of the 2000s is important because to the economic and institutional degradation it added a crop of politicians fearful of imprisonment. The political game became an imposture that concealed a criminal logic.

In this context, the 2016 elections were a box of surprises and paradoxes. PPK scraped through to the second round after a raft of rival candidates were eliminated from the running. There he faced Keiko Fujimori. Without any trace of the left in the runoff and with this faction now a minority in Congress, the country anticipated five years of rightist harmony. However, instead of grasping that the country was submerged in a process of gradual deterioration that called for important reforms, the two faces of the Peruvian right—one technocratic in the executive and the other populist in Congress—compounded the institutional and economic inertia, leaving a colossal mess.

PPK only managed to beat Keiko Fujimori—by the slenderest of margins—because he built a campaign around the defense of democracy, the rule of law, and the fight against corruption—the institutional banners

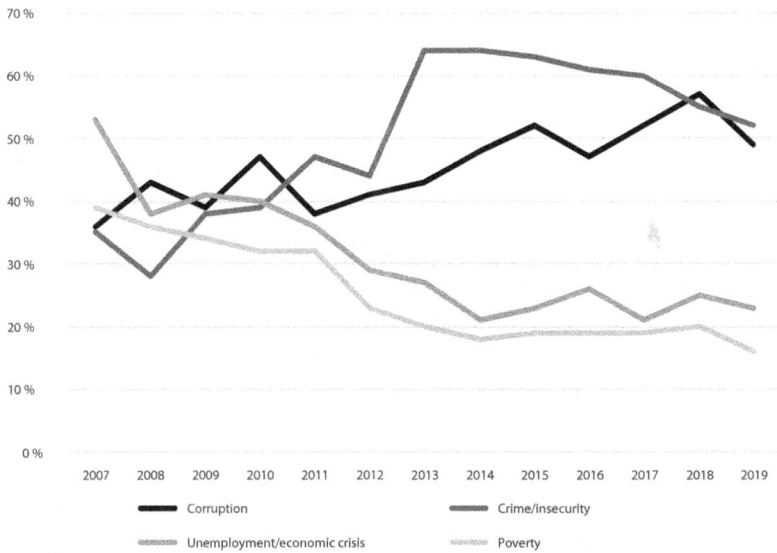

Figure 6.5 Key problems in Peru, 2007–2019. Source: Compiled by author from Ipsos reports (2007–19). Ipsos and El Comercio, *Informe de resultados: Estudio de opinión El Comercio-Ipsos* (Lima: Ipsos and El Comercio, 2020), https://www.ipsos .com/es-pe/la-gestion-publica-octubre-2020-encuesta-de-opinion-el-comercio -ipsos.

long abandoned in the country of economic modernization. But once in power, PPK made it clear that he could not go against his true nature: "The government that I lead is a bet for modernization."[109] Once again, representation was stifled in the name of a government project disinterested in citizens' will. PPK and his people snubbed not only the mandate given to them at the election but also the mood that was captured in the opinion polls. There, citizens clearly established that corruption, crime, and the absence of law and order were the country's main problems (see figure 6.5).

The government of modernization and its managerial experts, of course, were not going to stop to listen to the public. Their priorities were elsewhere. On the one hand, it was decided to aggressively pursue a fiscal deficit at a time when the economy was cooling off. In the end, the government itself recognized that this had been a mistake, but the damage had already been done and GDP growth had slowed more than had been envisioned. On the other hand, they pushed some inconsequential reductions in bureaucratic procedures to assuage the naive belief on the part of the business community that red tape was bogging down economic growth.

The modernizing proposal had been a disaster. Neglecting the public demands and the agendas that had allowed PPK to win the elections came to nothing. Nothing positive, that is. In just a year and a half, the PPK administration oversaw a slowdown in the economy with its ultra-orthodox measures, an increase in the informality that it had promised to curb, and, finally, by the end of 2017, for the first time this millennium, a rise in poverty.[110] The PPKausas—as PPK's followers were generically labeled—perceived themselves not as representatives but as administrators. Yet the trade-off between representation and administration was no longer paying off, and they were not even good administrators. They opted for the well-worn autopilot when not long before, the country had been anxiously wondering: Where is the pilot?

In the legislative sphere Congress had a different appearance, as Fuerza Popular (the *fujimorista* party) took 73 of the 130 seats available. Yet this new look in the Congress was based on the intensification of two representative ills that had been inherited. On the one hand, Congress again featured a conglomeration of "independents": 80 percent of the *fujimorista* legislators were new to the group,[111] having arrived there via the highest-bidder system that we discussed earlier. On the other hand, once elected, many of these independents unmasked themselves as crude agents of particular interests: poor-quality private universities, informal mining, cooperatives suspected of money laundering, the casino business, unlicensed transportation, and a vast et cetera. The representative ills had plumbed new depths. And they dragged the entire country down.

Demonstrating that the political scientist Juan Pablo Luna was correct when he insisted that "a democracy without representation is a government for politicians," the Fuerza Popular lawmakers placed themselves at the disposal of Keiko Fujimori to undermine the PPK government.[112] From the outset, the ministers were summoned to Congress on dozens of occasions without rhyme or reason.[113] Jaime Saavedra, an excellent minister of education, was censured on the most arbitrary of grounds. This all amounted to a vehement attack on an executive that bore representative deficiencies of its own, as in practice it lacked a parliamentary presence with which to defend itself.

One morning in December 2017, after more than a year denying any kind of relationship with Odebrecht, PPK let slip that, yes, now it was coming back to him: He had entered into a contract with Odebrecht. A few days later he added that he might have received "a little bit of money" thereby. Then PPK was spared from a first impeachment attempt thanks to some ignoble horse trading with another member of Congress, Kenji Fuji-mori: If he broke away from the grouping led by his sister Keiko and took a good number of her legislators with him, the president would pardon their father, Alberto Fujimori, who was still serving his twenty-five-year prison sentence for corruption and crimes against human rights. How-ever, in March 2018, PPK was forced to resign when it became evident that the votes were there to oust him in a second attempt. The *viveza criolla*, traditional Peruvian craftiness, was of little use to PPK and Alberto Fuji-mori: The former ended up without his presidency and under house ar-rest, and the other returned to jail with his pardon revoked.

Such was the costly outcome of Keiko Fujimori's designs. She took her revenge on those who had denied her the presidency to which she felt she was entitled, castigating her disloyal brother and send-ing her father—who posed a threat to her now preeminent position in *fujimorismo*—back behind bars.[114] This leader and her parliamentary majority seemed implacable.

It is worth pausing to consider the substance of the story behind the noise of the events. First, let us underline the most striking anomalous characteristic: Congress overcame the executive. Or, to put it another way, politics killed off the managers. The Peru of the 1993 constitution was founded on the primacy of government over politics, but the *fu-jimorista* majority was indifferent to the call to shop and shut up: They made political noise and decapitated, among others, a minister of the economy.[115] Remarkably, Congress had defeated the MEF. This topsy-turvy world could only be explained by the intensification of longer-standing processes. PPK and his technocrats insisted on the exhausted paradigm of modernization through economic means, which gave rise to an unpopular government; the crisis of political representation precipitated a Congress of mercenaries without institutional preoccupations; and the Odebrecht corruption produced the proof needed to make viable the removal of a president. This was a breakdown that was entirely inherited. But this was not a case of pure inertia, as those who took power in 2016 *decided* to intensify—and not alter—these processes.

Let us return to Keiko Fujimori. It is March 2018 and, like an avenger in a Tarantino movie, she has got her way. But the sequel needed to be altogether less toxic. To this end, she contrived to get along with PPK's vice president, Martín Vizcarra, who took over the presidency following PPK's resignation.[116] All this pointed toward government according to the designs of the *fujimorista* majority. But the liaison was short-lived.

Once again, a corruption scandal derailed all the planning: that of the *cuellos blancos del puerto* (white collars from the port). Thousands of leaked audios from a judicial investigation revealed a gigantic criminal network that involved judges, politicians, police officers, businesspeople, and public prosecutors. As Luis Pásara has pointed out, throughout Peruvian history the judiciary had always had limited autonomy vis-à-vis the economic and political powers, but these audios revealed something worse: The judicial institutions had been infiltrated by criminal interests.[117] In one of the audios, a businessman close to *fujimorismo* was conniving with a corrupt judge to arrange an appointment for "Madame K."

It was now or never, Vizcarra must have thought. In his presidential speech on July 28, 2018, Peru's independence day, President Vizcarra ranged his artillery against corruption. He said the audios had prompted him to table a reform of the country's judicial and political systems, while also accusing the *fujimoristas* of blocking these reforms in Congress. The public sided with Vizcarra. This was to be expected: Institutional considerations had long been neglected in favor of economic priorities. Seizing the opportunity to rid himself of the *fujimorista* straitjacket, Vizcarra elected to represent the will of the public rather than deferring, once again, institutional necessities. A referendum was duly scheduled for December 2018, and the proposed reforms of justice and political representation for which Vizcarra campaigned received massive popular backing.[118]

All this marked a new chapter of fierce confrontation between executive and legislature. The *fujiaprista* majority protected the principals implicated in cases of corruption and scuttled the proposed reforms. The political climate was defined by an irresponsible brinkmanship based on the two nuclear buttons of the constitution: Congress threatened to impeach Vizcarra, and Vizcarra threatened to dissolve Congress. This went on until September 30, 2019, when Congress was about to renew in an arbitrary way the Constitutional Court with its own handpicked judges. The prime minister, Salvador del Solar, arrived at the legislature to propose a motion of confidence regarding the procedure used for selecting the judges. When no response was received during a turbulent session, President Vizcarra assumed that the confidence had been de facto denied. As this amounted to a second rejection of confidence in a single term of government (the first was against the premier Fernando Zavala in September 2017), the president was authorized to dissolve Congress. That very afternoon, he did just that.[119]

With Congress dissolved and Vizcarra triumphant, it seemed that political calm had been restored to the country. Once again, we were

Figure 6.6 After thirty-six years, the national football team returned to the World Cup. Qualifying for the 2018 event in Russia after winning the playoff against New Zealand aroused a national uproar. Ricardo Gareca, the coach at the helm of the team's feat, earned admiration and respect that is unlikely to wane.
Source: Ernesto Benavides/AFP.

wrong. In January 2020, a new Congress was elected to see out the term until July 2021. Predictably, with *fujimorismo* discredited, its supermajority fragmented into a sharing of the spoils between twelve parties. This looked set to be a weak Congress pitted against a popular executive. It was impossible to predict that the country was on the brink of an eighteen-month period in which its decline would hasten.

A Republic Left Without Oxygen

> Never, mister secretary of health, was health more mortal.
> —CÉSAR VALLEJO, "NINE MONSTERS" (1939)

At the start of 2020, the world looked on with alarm as the Chinese city of Wuhan, with a population of 11 million, was placed in strict quarantine due to the novel coronavirus SARS-CoV-2 (COVID-19). Soon the new virus would spread around the world. Unimaginable scenes of death and public health collapse unfolded in Italy, Spain, and the United Kingdom. A few days later, the pandemic reached the Americas. Peru's first case was detected on March 6, 2020. This occurred as the country's modernization project was already on the wane: The economy was flatlining, and corruption and political representation—dominated by agents of private interests—plotted against the government. The pandemic aggravated this multifarious calamity, intensifying the conflict between politicians and the powers of state while also unleashing an economic, public health, and social crisis of wartime dimensions just as orthodox economic management vanished. So it was that Peru entered an emergency in which every sphere of the country crumbled. The 2021 general elections and the ill-fated presidencies of Pedro Castillo and Dina Boluarte show that the degradation has not stopped.

Just as health services throughout Europe and Latin America buckled under the strain of the pandemic, it was no surprise that Peru's did too. And given that the entire world went into recession because of the pandemic, that the Peruvian economy was struggling hardly raised eyebrows. But what is difficult to contemplate—and traumatic to verify—is that in terms of both the economy and mortality, the pandemic shook Peru like nowhere else in the world. Figure 6.7 provides a macabre snapshot of Peru's performance in the Latin American context.

The reasons Peru fared worse than anywhere else will be the focus of research for many years to come, and a vast quantity of comparative studies with other countries and regions will be required in order to propose a systematic and robust explanation. Here I will note just a few fragments of the story.

We will begin with reference to the state of the Peruvian health system when the pandemic struck.[120] Here we find a seemingly paradoxical situation that, at this point in the analysis, is hardly paradoxical at all: In the previous fifteen years, Peru's health budget had increased considerably. This is yet another case of what Dargent, Feldman, and Luna would deem "more state without stateness." Despite having more money at its disposal, the sector was very poorly prepared.[121] At the start of the pandemic the country had just 100 intensive care beds: that is, 2.9 ICU beds per 100,000 inhabitants. This was one-sixth the figure for Argentina, Brazil, and Uruguay, and one-third the regional average. The number of doctors per 100,000 inhabitants was almost half that of Chile (1.3 versus 2.5). The number of hospital beds per 100,000 inhabitants was half that of Trinidad and Tobago in the Caribbean (1.6 versus 3). Spending on health

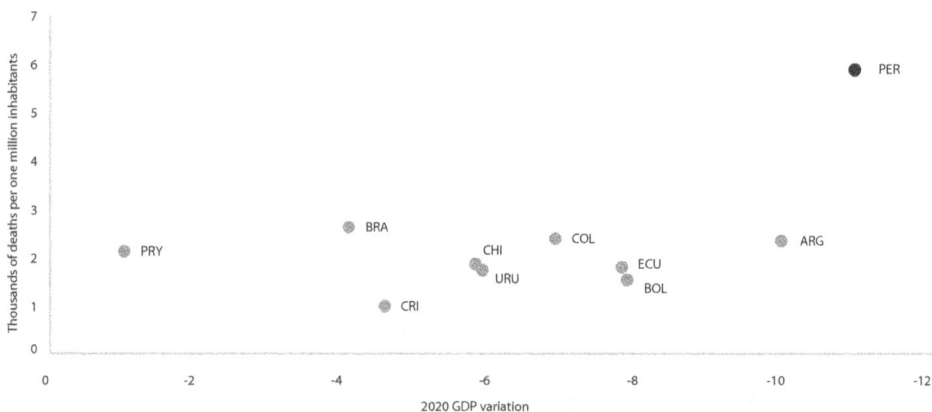

Figure 6.7 Economic and health impact of the 2020 COVID-19 pandemic. The marker at top right refers to Peru. Source: Compiled by author based on Our World in Data (https://ourworldindata.org/coronavirus) and World Bank data (https://data.worldbank.org).

(5.2 percent of GDP in 2018) was below that of other countries in the region (Colombia 7.4 percent, Chile 9.1 percent) and half that of the OECD countries (12.5 percent).[122]

The drastic confinement measures adopted by the government of Martín Vizcarra would have terrible economic consequences. The economy crashed by 40 percent in April 2020; 42 percent of Peruvians stopped earning or were left unemployed; 89 percent reduced their spending; and 80 percent used savings to meet their needs.[123] Moreover, 14 percent of households reported that they were unable to buy food with any protein content. In response, the government decided to distribute a series of monetary payments to alleviate the penury. Happily, the reserves were there to put this into practice. But the capacity to do so effectively was not. The payments arrived late if they arrived at all, and for all practical purposes they failed in the objective of discouraging the population from going out to work. Few examples illustrate so clearly the chasm that had emerged between "macro" and "micro" management of the economy.

This institutional inability was linked to an informal society. Millions of people may have left poverty behind in monetary terms, but they continued to live a precarious life. In 2019, 72.7 percent of Peru's economically active population worked in the informal economy, which points toward a society without bonds and without confidence, one in which everyone fends for themselves. While a third of Peruvians from socioeconomic sector A (the richest, representing 2 percent of the population) hold a private health insurance policy, nobody in sector E (the poorest, representing about 35 percent of the population) does. That is, Peru lacks a common institutional framework with which to overcome crises. The lucky few pay for high-quality services, while many, many more resign themselves to taking what they can get from a depleted and corrupt state. This absence of bonds became apparent when the start of the confinement measures was announced and tens of thousands of Peruvians hailing from the provinces but resident in Lima were forced to set off on foot to their home towns and villages, creating veritable scenes of biblical exodus. They had no means of surviving in the capital. To the best of my knowledge, only India experienced a similar situation.

At the public health, economic, and social levels, the pandemic exposed failings that had been sown decades earlier. Against modernizing predictions, economic growth had not spontaneously led to the construction of the framework of institutions and practices that permit a dignified common life. Amid this national fiasco, Peruvians looked at their country and thought, as in the Bob Dylan song, "Everything went from bad to worse; money never changed a thing."[124]

Now, the fact of being the country with the worst response to the pandemic cannot be explained by institutional legacies alone, for one simple reason: The Peruvian institutions are not the worst in the world. Many of the decisions made by the Vizcarra government intensified Peru's problems. For example, the Ministry of Health opted to distribute and promote ivermectin and hydroxychloroquine, drugs that have no clinical basis for treating COVID-19; at the same time, the state bought millions of inadequate serological (rapid) tests to monitor the virus. Moreover, the Peruvian government was astonishingly slow when it came to buying vaccines on the international market. All this meant that a second wave of infection, between December 2020 and April 2021, was even more devastating than the first (from April to July 2020).[125] As Luis Jochamowitz and Rafaella León have shown, this deficient management was due, in large part, to Vizcarra's isolation during the pandemic alongside a reduced and mediocre group of people.[126]

In eighteen months, the pandemic had claimed the lives of 200,000 Peruvians. To put this toll into national perspective, the Túpac Amaru rebellion caused 100,000 deaths; the war with Chile, 20,000; and the internal armed conflict of the 1980s, around 69,000.[127] More than 3 mil-

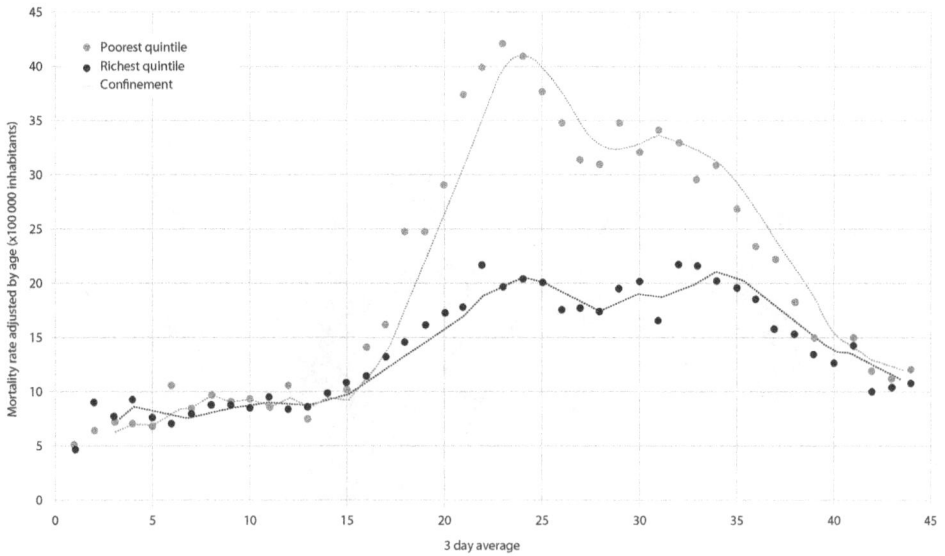

Figure 6.8 Mortality (by district) in the top and bottom wealth quintiles of Lima and Callao. Source: Oscar Mujica and Paul Pachas, "Desigualdades sociales en la mortalidad durante la COVID-19 en Lima y Callao," *Revista Peruana de Medicina Experimental y Salud Pública* 38, no. 1 (2021): 183–84.

lion Peruvians fell into poverty during the pandemic. However, these tolls were not distributed at random throughout Peruvian society; rather, they followed patterns based on historical and more recent inequalities. It is worth citing an example of this segmented impact of the pandemic in Peru. Figure 6.8 relates the number of COVID-19 deaths with the districts of Lima in order of average income. As can be appreciated, we did not all navigate the storm of the pandemic in the same boat.

In sum, the pandemic not only exposed an economic and public health crisis but also unveiled structural faults in the prospects of building a community worthy of that name. Images of Peru's streets and plazas taken over by rows of oxygen bottles attest to an economy hijacked by mafias while many clinics exploited a national tragedy—all of which reflects an every-person-for-themselves society and a state incapable of guaranteeing the most basic provisions.

At the same time, democracy was also left without oxygen. Despite its fragmentation, the newly elected Congress proved just as noxious as the one before. Let us look at just two of its traits. On the one hand, the pandemic saw members of Congress lose all regard for the most basic norms

Figure 6.9 The country literally runs out of oxygen: around 200,000 people died as a result of the COVID-19 pandemic. The consequences of this tragedy will be felt for many years to come. Source: Archivo La República.

of national economic management. The vast majority of Congress went into overdrive and legislated time and time again, breaking the constitutional principle that legislators do not have the "initiative to spend." To make matters worse, many of these new laws were declared unconstitutional, while others that were enacted caused more than one problem in a beleaguered economy. Furthermore, Congress proceeded to intensify its power struggle with the executive. With the country looking increasingly like a field of the fallen, the president of Congress, Manuel Merino of the Acción Popular party, went into cahoots with other benches to oust President Vizcarra based on complaints that may have warranted investigation but did not justify plunging Peru into a new megacrisis. In their second attempt at impeachment, Merino and Congress prevailed. Demonstrating that popularity alone is not enough to protect presidents, Vizcarra, with a public approval rating of 55 percent but without party or parliamentary presence, was expelled from office, and Merino took the presidency.

Even though the adventure lasted for just six days (from November 10 to 15, 2020) amid citizen resistance, Merino and his adherents demonstrated a willingness to resort to practices typical of dictatorships to try to stay in power. They took a swipe at a state television channel to

Figure 6.10 Manuel Merino, then president of Congress, led the campaign against Martín Vizcarra for the vacant legislative position but managed to hold on to the presidency for only six days due to mass rejection by the public. Source: Archivo La República.

stop it from covering marches against the government;[128] took the first steps to deactivate SUNEDU, the university regulator; and, worst of all, backed police repression against citizens.[129] In response to these abuses, the country organized and mobilized, with social media playing a vital role.[130] According to opinion polling, around 3 million citizens took part in various forms of protest, from sonorous *cacerolazos* (a popular form of protest, in Latin America and elsewhere, which involves the banging of pots and pans) to decentralized barrio-level marches and sizable concentrations in the center of the capital. From the first few days it was noted that the police responded with particular brutality, and that plainclothes operatives, dubbed *ternas*, acted outside the law in their arrests. Despite all this evidence, aired domestically and internationally, the premier, Ántero Flores-Aráoz, congratulated the police for their work and reassured them that "in me they will find a champion."[131] With the repression now firmly established, it only escalated on the Friday and Saturday at the end of Merino's short spell in power. As Human Rights Watch verified, the police repeatedly employed excessive force against demonstrators, including tear gas and pellets. On Saturday, November 14, dozens of people were injured and arrested, and two young protesters, Inti Sotelo and Bryan Pintado, were killed. The government of Merino and Flores-Aráoz crumbled, and on Sunday, November 15, Merino resigned.[132]

According to Ipsos figures, 94 percent of the public disapproved of the Merino government, and 84 percent disapproved of his prime minister. Given such resounding public rejection, the new president had to be drawn from the ranks of the nineteen members of Congress who had not endorsed Merino's legislative riot. Thus, Francisco Sagasti became Peru's fourth president in the five-year period between 2016 and 2021. With little political experience and communicative shortcomings, Sagasti headed a government that achieved two major objectives in this turbulent context. In political terms, the government stopped the plotters within and outside Congress from attempting another antidemocratic seizure of state and, in turn, protected the passage to clean general elections for 2021. As far as the pandemic was concerned, the interim administration procured 78.7 million doses of vaccine, safeguarding the immunization program until December 2021. Before Sagasti came to power, it is worth recalling, Peru had not bought a single dose of vaccine under either Vizcarra or Merino.

As ought to be clear, Peru's crisis had spread through cannibalistic politics, death, and penury. But one element still had to be added to this great fresco of collective failure: the 2021 presidential elections. Demoralized, the country had no interest in this process and its competing candidates. The first round produced a fragmentation that the country had never seen before. As little as ten days before the polls opened, seven candidates had a realistic chance of progressing to the second round. Given what had unfolded over the past five years, it was hardly a surprise that no single candidate managed to enthuse the population. In the end, the runoff would be contested by Pedro Castillo, an almost unknown rural schoolteacher representing Perú Libre, who took 19 percent of the vote, and Keiko Fujimori of Fuerza Popular, who obtained 13 percent. Never before had two candidates reached the second round on such a meager share of the vote. And if we take the vote as percentages of the universe of citizens who were eligible to vote, Castillo was backed by just 10.7 percent, and Fujimori by 7.6 percent. The relentless decline of the representative arena continued apace. Yet curiously, in a matter of days, a political offering that had been met with disinterest and fragmentation gave way to polarized activism. Lined up behind Castillo and Fujimori were an array of variables. She, the heir to the corrupt *fujimorista* dictatorship, appeared as the political veteran, representing the coastal upper and middle classes in a campaign against the communist scourge. Pedro Castillo, the teacher and *ronda* patroller from the province of Chota in Cajamarca, representing a Marxist-Leninist party plagued by accusations of corruption, drew massive support from Andean Peru. Both candidates claimed, without any substantiation, electoral fraud against them. This, then, was a joust poisoned by two authoritarian and retrograde options—one from the left and the other from the right—in which the public was invited to a "collective self-immolation event."[133] The seeds of democratic destruction had prospered.

Their germination proved robust when the Peruvian right rejected the election results that handed Pedro Castillo victory by an extremely tight margin of 44,058 votes. Keiko Fujimori's band cast shameful and baseless accusations of fraud in an attempt to derail the results, placing the country in a state of high turbulence. But the electoral institutions did their job and announced Pedro Castillo as the new Peruvian president.

Castillo took power on July 28, 2021. The date was no minor thing: two hundred years after independence. Although it was a historic date, that did not move the country. The indifference revealed more than one historical problem. But Castillo gave it unexpected relevance. A peasant who came from one of the poorest districts in the country had prevailed against the intolerance of coastal Peru. Without anyone planning it, the bicentennial made sense. Castillo placed an excluded part of the nation at the heart of the public sphere. With his constant evocation of "the people," he reintroduced an undeniable representative dimension.

However, beneath the symbology there was nothing. Or nothing good. From day one his government was a mix of corruption, ineptitude, and radical rhetoric (not even radical initiatives). A few weeks after coming to power, a prosecutor found in the office of Castillo's right-hand man in the Government Palace $20,000 in cash that, everything suggests, came from bribes from individuals seeking promotions in the police and armed forces. The president himself was involved in more than one corruption scandal, with clandestine nighttime outings to negotiate public works and other illegal schemes. At the same time, the president and his entourage dedicated themselves to dismantling the precarious Peruvian public institutions. Even in such crucial ministries as health, they appointed ministers who were not at all prepared for the position, solely for partisan reasons. In the fifteen months that Castillo headed the government, seventy-eight ministerial changes were made—about one ministerial change every week. There were five ministers of economy, seven of the interior, five changes of foreign minister. His was a presidency, in short, destined to destroy the efficiency of public institutions. And finally, this combo of corruption and ineptitude came wrapped in radical and vindictive rhetoric aimed at maintaining polarization in the country.

That government came to an end on December 7, 2022. Pedro Castillo thought that evidence of his acts of corruption would become public and decided to carry out a coup d'état. He ordered the dissolution of Congress, called for a curfew, convened a Constituent Assembly, and announced that he would govern by decree, among other measures, all of which were unconstitutional. He didn't have anyone's support. A couple of hours later he was detained when he tried to reach the Mexican embassy to seek asylum. He was immediately arrested and removed from the presidency.

As in previous years, this led to a new presidential change. As in previous years, many people believed that this would calm the country. Once again they were wrong. The presidency passed to his vice president, Dina Boluarte. Although she had also been Castillo's minister of development and social inclusion throughout his administration, except for the last twelve days, she soon became a fierce anti-Castillo figure. Eighty-three percent of the population called for early elections after Castillo's removal, and only 13 percent supported Boluarte completing the presidential term until 2026. However, she insisted that she would stay until the end of the constitutional mandate. Once again, a political ecosystem of opportunistic amateurs led to a power grab that failed to uphold the responsibility of representation.

This worsened during Boluarte's term. Citizen rejection of her government escalated into protests in different parts of the country, especially in southern Peru. In response, Boluarte's government opted for brutal and unacceptable repression. The social protests had elements of vandalism, but the response was disproportionate and violated the country's laws. In just three months, the protests led to dozens of deaths. Local and international investigations by organizations like the *New York Times*, IDL-Reporteros, Human Rights Watch, Amnesty International, and the Inter-American Commission on Human Rights documented that forty-nine of these deaths were caused by projectiles fired by the police and the army. Boluarte's government backed this brutality and stigmatized the protests as if they were the work of hordes of terrorists, drug traffickers, and criminals who deserved to be repressed with the utmost severity. Unlike episodes of violent protest where detentions are the norm and deaths are regrettable accidents, for Boluarte's government the norm was to kill and never have anyone detained. And all of this happened in a context in which racism, which had already grown since Castillo's emergence as a candidate, played a key role. Boluarte's education minister referred to Andean women assaulted by the police as "worse than animals." It is hard to find in any other government of recent decades such an open degree of contempt for citizens as displayed by Boluarte's government.

Both Dina Boluarte and the Congress have single-digit popularity. She is the least popular president in Latin America. The crisis of representation has reached a new low. Both the president and the members of Congress aspire to preserve power while disregarding the laws of democracy and even more so the spirit of democracy. Boluarte clings to power based on a constitutional formality (the law establishes her right to succeed Castillo in the presidency), but her presidency is already devoid of any substance.

Yet she is also incapable of governing; her approach is to subdue. Unlike many authoritarian right-wing governments in Latin America that repressed their citizens and, at the same time, had some sort of national project, Boluarte and her right-wing allies don't even want citizens to shut up and shop; they aspire only to domesticate and frighten them. The government can neither represent nor govern. In other words, it cannot even create the conditions for "shopping." According to recent data, Peru is by far the Latin American country with the most newly poor people since the pandemic. In 2023 Peru fell into economic recession. In other words, the characters in the Peruvian drama may have changed, but the script remains the same, lacking a ruling class able to represent or govern. Boluarte has been not a rupture with Castillo but its degraded continuity. In Peru at this moment neither the right nor the left can boast democratic credentials. The country looks like the eccentric case of a democracy compelled to survive without democrats.

Conclusion

José Carlos Agüero, one of Peru's most profound writers, has argued the following: "Perhaps it is not clearly appreciated, but we are facing a tragedy that, it would seem, will take us to the brink of dissolution as a community."[134]

This is not alarmism. Recent years have sketched out the portrait of a country in which it is difficult to detect a stable rock from which to embark on reconstruction. Peru's gigantic macroeconomy has microfoundations of mud: 96 percent of the country's companies employ fewer than ten people, giving shape to an economy as informal as it is unproductive and creating, in turn, pernicious consequences in different facets of society.[135] The pandemic wreaked havoc with this neglected reality, with the result that, as Carolina Trivelli has noted, "in Peru hunger was no longer a problem and now it is again."[136] In political terms, Peru seems to have entered its own "impossible game."[137] Most of its political forces, on both left and right, display a recurrent inclination toward dismantling the democratic system. As Eduardo Dargent explained, the country's leadership is composed of "precarious democrats" always disposed to break democracy should their immediate interests require as much.[138] And society, from top to bottom, seems to have assumed that the rule of law is nothing more than an arm to twist (or to break) so that it does not stand in the way of all sorts of business. Criminal economies have gotten stronger and infiltrated institutions. Peru lacks the civic, productive, institutional, and moral bonds required to unite it. Such a juncture has meant that 60 percent of the country's youth want to move abroad.[139] This is a country demoralized.

In this chapter we have traveled from the economic depression of 1990 to bicentennial dejection, passing through a period of naive official optimism. But this bipolar itinerary is no invention of contemporary Peru; rather, it feels like the adaptation of an old script. We might sum up by quoting Leonard Cohen: "new skin for the old ceremony."[140] Several of the earlier chapters in this book point, each in its own way, toward processes punctuated by similar highs and lows. The decades that Charles Walker studies are marked by the struggles against viceregal power, the enthusiasm awakened by its collapse, and the dawn of the republic; come the end of his account, the country is the paradigmatic example of post independence Latin American anarchy. Natalia Sobrevilla's analysis reviews the illusion of order, prosperity, and profligacy engendered by guano, which preceded total defeat by Chile. José Luis Rénique describes the postwar resurrection and the ebullience motivated by an Aristocratic Republic that appeared to be combining integrated international capitalism with representative democracy, only to collapse in the Leguía years—paving the way for a twentieth century that Drinot and Dargent, in their respective chapters, describe as marked by ambitious yet ultimately frustrated projects. In a nod to Sisyphus, Peru seems to be doomed to a cycle that involves gathering up its remains, bringing them back to life, and squandering them all over again.

The national history is a cemetery of political projects. The reasons for this are convoluted, and are certainly not peculiar to Peru. Paul Drake has suggested that the history of Latin America is one of confrontation between tyranny and anarchy,[141] while Pablo Gerchunoff and Lucas Llach likened Argentina to a pendulum between hope and disenchantment.[142] Each country in the continent has had its own vicissitudes. Peru's, I would say, are driven by myriad dimensions, but it is worth underlining at least the most notable political factor behind the oscillation between enthusiasm and disappointment, between reconstruction and fresh bankruptcy. Although they differ in content, many of Peru's political projects have been endeavors taken up and pushed by specific, minority interests without the consent—or against the will—of vast sectors of the population. Or, to put it another way, these are projects lacking in the legitimacy that only broad consensus and coalition provide. And the absence of legitimacy is another way of describing the flimsy and fleeting.

It matters not whether we focus on the republic established by San Martín, on the *república práctica* of Pardo, on the *patria nueva* of Leguía, on the liberated man of Velasco, on the so-called new popular democracy of Sendero Luminoso, on the modernizing/consumer project of the 2000s, or on the venture that Pedro Castillo sought to found on the basis of "the people" of Peru. Despite their differences, each of these projects sought to include without failing to exclude. Take the slogan "Only APRA will save Peru": It is a sort of sectarian hope for progress without the legitimacy bestowed by pluralism. Only our projects, each says, can save Peru from the Peruvians. Or from a good part of the Peruvians, that is. If representation often seemed to be beleaguered by government effectiveness, this would also suggest that Peruvians have always had anti-pluralist aspirations of representation. Each is the new and incomplete answer of an incomplete and exhausted project.

Peru of 2024 is no different. It lacks a common project, and each political tribe seems only too delighted to reject the notion of any such thing. And society is demoralized because it shares in this mood: It considers itself complicit. The so-called vaccinegate scandal is very revealing on this point. Amid the pandemic, a banquet of vaccines was arranged for those who had influence and access to the clinical trials carried out by the Universidad Peruana Cayetano Heredia with the Chinese vaccine Sinopharm. The elite scientists at this university and several of their students, the then-president Martín Vizcarra and some of his ministers, well-known lobbyists, ex-ministers, members of Congress, business figures, apostolic nuncios, owners of *chifa* restaurants—in short, people from various walks of life—pulled the stunt of vaccinating themselves surreptitiously against COVID-19 while tens of thousands died. Indeed, we might ponder the

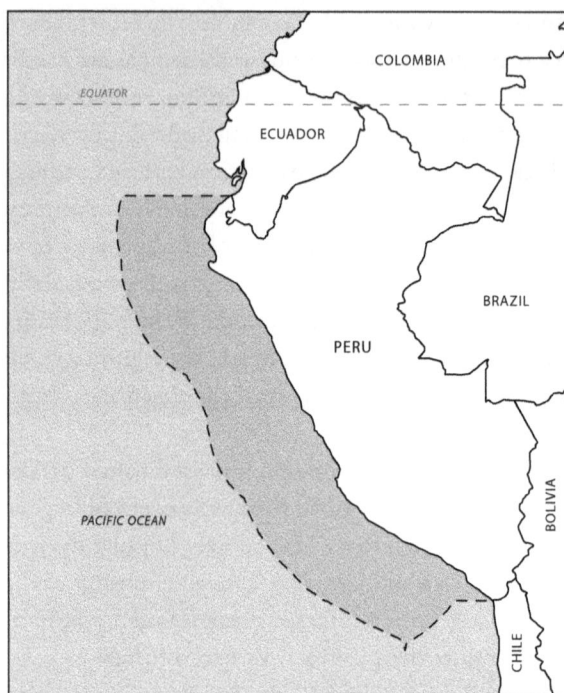

Map 6.1 Map of contemporary Peru, including territorial waters. After the Cenepa conflict in 1995, Peru's territorial borders were finally settled with Chile and Ecuador. Early in the twenty-first century, Peru settled its maritime boundaries with Ecuador by means of a new agreement and, following an International Court of Justice ruling from The Hague, also settled its maritime claims with Chile. Source: Instituto Geográ fico Nacional (2021).

grave implications of this: That absolutely nobody refused to participate in this unseemly carousel shows how ingrained it has become in Peru to take personal advantage of public goods and walk over everyone else. As Dr. Germán Málaga, the clinician in charge of this national disgrace, put it: "It is not a matter of privileges; this is just how things work." And what to say of the open and repulsive racism that Peruvians witnessed once again during and since the 2021 elections? As Carlos Monsiváis noted, "The Latin American bourgeoisie claim descent from Machu Picchu and Chichén Itzá, but not from their builders."[143] Beyond the legitimate resistance there may be to any number of political projects, this classist and racist aversion exposes certain distances and horrors that do not befit a republic.

Thus, we reach a blind spot: If there is no shared idea of what Peruvians wish to construct, there cannot be progress. *Progressing* implies the existence of certain public targets and that we can observe whether they have been reached or not. But this is futile if the goals are just for a minority or a faction. Goals must be accepted by a majority. And this can come about only through deliberation and negotiation. It is not a question of finding the chimerical project with which we all fall in love without exception; it is about achieving a shared substrate through mutual concessions.

A classic proposal by John Rawls holds that an orderly society is one that has a common and public idea of justice. In Peru, however, the prevailing notion of justice is clandestine and sectarian. Therefore, quite logically, many Peruvians feel they are destined for disorder. And so we return to the words of José Carlos Agüero with which we opened these final comments. Agüero did not say that Peru *would* disintegrate as a community; he said that it was *on the brink* of doing so. On the brink, under threat, in uncertainty, out of balance, in suspense—like someone who decides or is forced to build a house in a ravine through which the mudslides pass every year, and all that remains is to keep praying that the next rainy season is not one of the worst.

Notes

Epigraphs: Ernest Hemingway, *The Sun Also Rises* (New York: Charles Scribner's Sons, 1954), 136; Alan García, quoted in Javier Barreda, *1987: Los límites de la voluntad política* (Lima: Mitin Editores, 2012), 11; Alberto Fujimori, quoted in José Alejandro Godoy, *El último dictador: Vida y gobierno de Alberto Fujimori* (Lima: Debate, 2021), 189; Carlos Monsiváis, *Entrada libre: Crónicas de una sociedad que se organiza* (Mexico City: Ediciones Era, 1987), 1; Soda Stereo, "Té para tres," on *Canción animal* (Miami: Discos CBS International, 1990), track 9; César Vallejo, "Nine Monsters," in César Vallejo, *The Complete Posthumous Poetry*, trans. Clayton Eshleman and José Rubia Barcia (Berkeley: University of California Press, 1978), 173.

1   In 1989, the Alan García administration initiated a form of political decentralization that created regional assemblies throughout the country. The so-called Inka region, composed of the departments of Apurímac, Cuzco, and Madre de Dios, was one of them.

2   Alberto Vergara, *La danza hostil: Poderes subnacionales y Estado central en Bolivia y Perú (1952–2012)* (Lima: IEP, 2015), 298.

3 Robert Dahl, *Polyarchy: Participation and Opposition* (New Haven, CT: Yale University Press, 1971).

4 John Dewey, *The Public and Its Problems* (1927; repr., Athens: Ohio University Press, 2016).

5 Pierre Rosanvallon, *La legitimidad democrática: Imparcialidad, reflexividad, proximidad* (Buenos Aires: Manantial, 2009); Pierre Rosanvallon, *El buen gobierno* (Buenos Aires: Manantial, 2015).

6 Andy Baker, *The Market and the Masses in Latin America: Policy Reform and Consumption in Liberalizing Economies* (New York: Cambridge University Press, 2009).

7 Francis Fukuyama, *The End of History and the Last Man* (New York: Free Press, 1992).

8 Danilo Martuccelli, *La condition sociale moderne: L'avenir d'une inquiétude* (Paris: Gallimard, 2017).

9 Miguel Ángel Centeno, *Democracy Within Reason: Technocratic Revolution in Mexico* (University Park: Penn State University Press, 1997).

10 Steven Levitsky, *Transforming Labor-Based Parties in Latin America: Argentine Peronism in Comparative Perspective* (New York: Cambridge University Press, 2003).

11 Jan-Werner Müller, *What Is Populism?* (Philadelphia: University of Pennsylvania Press, 2016).

12 Nancy Bermeo, "On Democratic Backsliding," *Journal of Democracy*, January 2016, 5–19.

13 Javier Auyero and Katherine Sobering, *The Ambivalent State: Police-Criminal Collusion at the Urban Margins* (New York: Oxford University Press, 2019).

14 On civic responsibility and its agency in democracy, see Guillermo O'Donnell, *Democracia, agencia y estado: Teoría con intención comparativa* (Buenos Aires: Prometeo, 2010). On the importance of representation and accountability, see Catalina Smulovitz and Enrique Peruzzotti, "Societal Accountability in Latin America," *Journal of Democracy* 11, no. 4 (2000): 147–58; and Adam Przeworski, Susan C. Stokes, and Bernard Manin, eds., *Democracy, Accountability, and Representation* (Cambridge: Cambridge University Press, 1999).

15 On representation in historical perspective, see Julio Cotler, "Political Parties and the Problems of Democratic Consolidation in Peru," in *Building Democratic Institutions: Party Systems in Latin America*, ed. Scott Mainwaring and Timothy Scully (Stanford, CA: Stanford University Press, 1995); Alicia del Águila, *La ciudadanía corporativa: Política, constituciones y sufragio en el Perú (1821–1896)* (Lima: IEP, 2010); and Cristóbal Aljovín de Losada and Sinesio López, eds., *Historia de las elecciones en el Perú* (Lima: JNE and IEP, 2019).

16 Natalia Sobrevilla Perea, "Power of the Law or Power of the Sword: The Conflictive Relationship Between the Executive and the Legislative in

Nineteenth-Century Peru," *Parliaments, Estates and Representation* 37, no. 2 (2017): 220–34.

17 Carmen McEvoy, *La utopía republicana: Ideales y realidades en la formación de la cultura política peruana (1871–1919)* (Lima: Fondo Editorial PUCP, 1997); Carmen McEvoy, *Homo politicus: Manuel Pardo, la política peruana y sus dilemas, 1871–1878* (Lima: IEP, 2007).

18 On this juncture, see Robert S. Jansen, *Revolutionizing Repertoires: The Rise of Populist Mobilization in Peru* (Chicago: University of Chicago Press, 2017). Jansen incorporates the analysis of Sánchez Cerro and the Revolutionary Union.

19 Martín Bergel, *La desmesura revolucionaria: Cultura y política en los orígenes del APRA* (Lima: La Siniestra Ensayos, 2019).

20 D. S. Parker, *The Idea of the Middle Class: White-Collar Workers and Peruvian Society, 1900–1950* (University Park: Penn State University Press, 1998).

21 Peter F. Klarén, *Modernization, Dislocation, and Aprismo: Origins of the Peruvian Aprista Party, 1870–1932* (Austin: University of Texas Press, 1973).

22 On Chachapoyas, see David Nugent, *Modernity at the Edge of Empire: State, Individual, and Nation in the Northern Peruvian Andes, 1885–1935* (Stanford, CA: Stanford University Press, 1997); on Cajamarca, see Lewis Taylor, "Los orígenes del partido Aprista peruano en Cajamarca, 1928–1935," *Debate Agrario* 31 (2000): 39–62; on Ayacucho, see Jaymie Patricia Heilman, "We Will No Longer Be Servile: Aprismo in 1930s Ayacucho," *Journal of Latin American Studies* 38, no. 3 (2006): 401–518; on Puno, see Nils Jacobsen, *Mirages of Transition: The Peruvian Altiplano, 1780–1930* (Berkeley: University of California Press, 1998).

23 Moisés Lemlij, "El país, desde antes de la conquista, ha sido tierra de conquistas ocasionales y fraccionamientos eternos," in *¿Qué país es este? Contrapuntos en torno al Perú y los peruanos*, ed. Luis Pásara (Lima: Fondo Editorial PUCP, 2016), 191.

24 On Haya de la Torre, see Iñigo García-Bryce, *Haya de la Torre and the Pursuit of Power in Twentieth-Century Peru and Latin America* (Chapel Hill: University of North Carolina Press, 2018).

25 Cited in François Bourricaud, *Power and Society in Contemporary Peru* (London: Faber and Faber, 1970), 234.

26 For an exploration of Acción Popular as an anti-oligarchy vehicle, see Vergara, *La danza hostil.*

27 On Christian Democrats, see Pedro Planas, *Biografía del novimiento social-cristiano en el Perú (1926–1956): Apuntes* (Lima: Facultad de Teología Pontificia y Civil de Lima, 1996).

28 On the PPC, see Harold Forsyth, *La palabra del Tucán: Conversaciones con Luis Bedoya Reyes* (Lima: Planeta, 2016).

29 See José Luis Rénique, *La batalla por Puno: Conflicto agrario y nación en los Andes peruanos 1866–1995* (Lima: IEP and Sur, 2004), chap. 7.

30 On Izquierda Unida, see Paula Muñoz, "Political Violence and the Defeat of the Left," in *Politics After Violence: Legacies of the Shining Path Conflict in Peru*, ed. Hillel Soifer and Alberto Vergara (Austin: University of Texas Press, 2019); and Alberto Adrianzén, ed., *Apogeo y crisis de la izquierda peruana: Hablan sus protagonistas* (Lima: IDEA Internacional and Universidad Antonio Ruiz de Montoya, 2011).

31 BCRP data portal, Central Reserve Bank of Peru, https://estadisticas.bcrp .gob.pe/estadisticas/series/.

32 CEPAL data quoted by Efraín Gonzales de Olarte and Lilian Samamé, *El péndulo peruano: Políticas económicas, gobernabilidad y subdesarrollo, 1963–1990* (Lima: IEP, 1991), 12.

33 According to data published in the Truth and Reconciliation Committee report. Comisión de la Verdad y Reconciliación, *Informe final (Perú 1980–2000)* (Lima: UNMSM and PUCP, 2004). The data can be accessed at Higher National University of San Marcos, Collección Digital, https:// sisbib.unmsm.edu.pe/bibvirtual/libros/sociologia/informe_final/ficha.htm.

34 Martín Tanaka, *Los espejismos de la democracia: El colapso de un sistema de partidos en el Perú* (Lima: IEP, 1998).

35 It is important to note that the transformation of a politician who wins with a political platform only to abandon it once in power became common in Latin America at that time. See Susan C. Stokes, *Mandates and Democracy: Neoliberalism by Surprise in Latin America* (Cambridge: Cambridge University Press, 2001).

36 Fukuyama, *The End of History and the Last Man*, 82.

37 A survey conducted by Apoyo and published by newspapers on April 9, 1992, found that 71 percent of the population was in agreement with the dissolution of Congress, while 89 percent expressed support for the restructuring of the judiciary.

38 Jo-Marie Burt, "State-Making Against Democracy: The Case of Fujimori's Peru," in *Politics in the Andes: Identity, Conflict, Reform*, ed. Jo-Marie Burt and Philip Mauceri (Pittsburgh: University of Pittsburgh Press, 2004).

39 There is a vast bibliography on the Fujimori regime; as a starting point, see Luis Jochamowitz, *Ciudadano Fujimori: La construcción de un político* (Lima: PEISA, 1993); Godoy, *El último dictador*; Yusuke Murakami, *Perú en la era del Chino: La política no institucionalizada y el pueblo en busca de un salvador* (Lima: IEP, 2007); and Catherine Conaghan, *Fujimori's Peru: Deception in the Public Sphere* (Pittsburgh: University of Pittsburgh Press, 2005).

40 Ricardo Uceda, *Muerte en el Pentagonito: Los cementerios secretos del ejército peruano* (Lima: Planeta, 2004), 34.

41 Godoy, *El último dictador*, 72.

42 Two decades later, alluding to this mechanism, the *fujimorista* Jorge Trelles would note for posterity, by way of comparison to the governments of the 1980s, that "nosotros matamos menos" (we killed fewer people).

43   On the Grupo Colina, the mandatory reference is the formidable Ricardo Uceda, *Muerte en el Pentagonito: Los cementerios secretos del Ejército Peruano* (Lima: Planeta, 2004). For an overview of the human rights violations in the counterinsurgency strategy, see Comisión de la Verdad y Reconciliación, *Informe final (Perú: 1980–2000)* (Lima: UNMSM and PUCP, 2004).

44   Quoted in Godoy, *El último dictador*, 103. Translation by Paulo Drinot.

45   On the long-term relations between the central state and the regions, see Eduardo Dargent's chapter in this volume, as well as Vergara, *La danza hostil.*

46   Many parties neglected to participate. On the legislative dynamic of the 1990s, see Carlos Iván Degregori and Carlos Meléndez, *El nacimiento de los otorongos: El Congreso de la República durante los gobiernos de Alberto Fujimori (1990–2000)* (Lima: IEP, 2007).

47   Maxwell Cameron, "From Oligarchic Domination to Neoliberal Governance: The Shining Path and the Transformation of Peru's Constitutional Order," in Soifer and Vergara, *Politics After Violence.*

48   Cameron, "From Oligarchic Domination to Neoliberal Governance."

49   Kenneth Roberts, *Deepening Democracy? The Modern Left and Social Movements in Chile and Peru* (Stanford, CA: Stanford University Press, 1999).

50   On the consequences of the internal armed conflict in contemporary Peru, see Soifer and Vergara, *Politics After Violence.* On the fear within civil society, see Jo-Marie Burt, "'Quien Habla Es Terrorista': The Political Use of Fear in Fujimori's Peru," *Latin American Research Review* 41, no. 3 (2006): 32–62.

51   Data obtained from the Ministry of Labor and Promotion of Employment, Government of Peru, https://www.gob.pe/mtpe.

52   Tanaka, *Los espejismos de la democracia.*

53   Shane Greene, *Punk and Revolution: 7 More Interpretations of Peruvian Reality* (Durham, NC: Duke University Press, 2016).

54   Alfonso Quiroz, *Historia de la corrupción en el Perú* (Lima: IEP, 2014).

55   On the details of the sources of financing of corruption and the networks established under the *fujimorista* regime, see Quiroz, *Historia de la corrupción*, chap. 7.

56   Statements made by Vladimiro Montesinos during the oral hearings on the case of *chicha* newspapers in July 2001. "Alberto Fujimori: Estas son las claves del caso diarios chicha," *El Comercio*, August 16, 2013, https://elcomercio.pe/politica/justicia/alberto-fujimori-son-claves-caso-diarios-chicha-398324-noticia/.

57   Danilo Martuccelli, *Lima y sus arenas: Poderes sociales y jerarquías culturales* (Lima: Cauces Editores, 2015).

58   Data presented in Claudia Bielich Salazar, *La guerra del centavo: Una mirada actual al transporte público en Lima* (Lima: IEP, 2009).

59   Data from the Plan Maestro Lima-Callao 2004, quoted in Salazar, *La guerra del centavo.*

60   Personal interview with the author.

61   I am very grateful to Eduardo Adrianzén for the interview that he gave me and which proved indispensable for this section of the essay. On the history of Peruvian television, see Fernando Vivas, *En vivo y en directo: Una historia de la televisión peruana* (Lima: Fondo Editorial de la Universidad del Pacífico, 2013).

62   On the collapse of the *fujimorista* regime, see Martín Tanaka and Jane Marcus-Delgado, *Lecciones del final del fujimorismo: La legitimidad presidencial y la acción política* (Lima: IEP, 2001); Conaghan, *Fujimori's Peru*, 220–56; Murakami, *Perú en la era del Chino*, chaps. 5 and 6.

63   These were not merely discursive priorities; several legal initiatives against corruption were introduced. For example, the working group for the National Anticorruption Initiative (including civil society organizations) was set up, the National Anticorruption Program was created and assigned clear lines of action, and judicial and comptroller budgets were increased. Of particular note is the drive toward an anticorruption judicial system that permitted the creation of public prosecutor's offices, courts, and specialist anticorruption courts. It was under this system that Alberto Fujimori, Vladimiro Montesinos, and other members of the *fujimorista* network were subsequently processed. On the republicanism of Paniagua, see Alberto Vergara, *Ciudadanos sin república: De la precariedad institucional al descalabro político* (Lima: Planeta, 2018), prologue and introduction.

64   For the changes in the role of Congress between the Fujimori and post-Fujimori periods, see Alberto Vergara and Aaron Watanabe, "Delegative Democracy Revisited: Peru Since Fujimori," *Journal of Democracy* 27, no. 3 (2016): 148–57.

65   See Alberto Vergara, *El choque de los ideales: Reformas institucionales y partidos políticos en el Perú post-fujimorato* (Lima: IDEA Internacional, 2009).

66   See Eduardo Dargent, *Technocracy and Democracy in Latin America: The Experts Running Government* (New York: Cambridge University Press, 2014).

67   Catherine Conaghan, "The Irrelevant Right: Alberto Fujimori and the New Politics of Pragmatic Peru," in *Conservative Parties, the Right and Democracy in Latin America*, ed. Kevin Middlebrook (Baltimore: Johns Hopkins University Press, 2000).

68   Alan García Pérez, "El síndrome del perro del hortelano," *El Comercio*, October 28, 2007, https://elcomercio.pe/185-aniversario/2007-l-el-sindrome-del-perro-del-hortelano-l-bicentenario-noticia/.

69   For an analysis of the *hortelanista* project, see Vergara, *Ciudadanos sin república*. From another perspective, see Paulo Drinot, "Foucault in the Land of the Incas: Sovereignty and Governmentality in Neoliberal Peru," in *Peru in Theory*, ed. Paulo Drinot (New York: Palgrave Macmillan, 2014).

70   Jaime de Althaus, *La promesa de la democracia: Marchas y contramarchas del sistema político en el Perú* (Lima: Planeta, 2011); Jaime de Althaus, *La revolución capitalista en el Perú* (Lima: FCE, 2007).

71 For proposals from the modernization thesis, see Seymour Martin Lipset, "Some Social Requisites of Democracy: Economic Development and Political Legitimacy," *American Political Science Review* 53, no. 1 (1959): 69–105; and Adam Przeworski and Fernando Limongi, "Modernization: Theories and Facts," *World Politics* 49, no. 2 (1997): 155–83. For an analysis of its application in the Peruvian case, see Vergara, *Ciudadanos sin república.*

72 On the Humala government, see Marco Sifuentes, *H & H. Escenas de la vida conyugal de Ollanta Humala y Nadine Heredia* (Lima: Planeta, 2018); Eduardo Dargent and Paula Muñoz, "Perú 2011: Continuidades y cambios en la política sin partidos," *Revista de Ciencia Política (Santiago)* 32, no. 1 (2012): 245–68, https://bit.ly/3I9uhr1; Paula Muñoz and Yamilé Guibert, "Perú: El fin del optimismo," *Revista de Ciencia Política (Santiago)* 36, no. 1 (2016): 313–38, https://bit.ly/3uhzkQl. For an analysis of technocratic continuity, see Alberto Vergara and Daniel Encinas, "Continuity by Surprise: Explaining Institutional Stability in Contemporary Peru," *Latin American Research Review* 51, no. 1 (2016): 159–80.

73 BCRP, Portal de Estadísticas, https://www.bcrp.gob.pe/estadisticas.html.

74 Sistema de Información Estadística del INEI, https://www.gob.pe/inei/.

75 BCRP, Portal de Estadísticas, https://www.bcrp.gob.pe/estadisticas.html.

76 See the report by the Comisión Económica para América Latina y el Caribe (CEPAL), *Panorama Social de América Latina 2019* (Santiago: CEPAL, 2019).

77 BCRP, Portal de Estadísticas, https://www.bcrp.gob.pe/estadisticas.html.

78 Pilar Bermudez, "Una mirada prospectiva de los resultados obtenidos por el retail moderno," GfK, 2016, https://cdn2.hubspot.net/hubfs/2405078/cms-pdfs/fileadmin/user_upload/dyna_content/pe/presentacion_gfk_retail_2016.pdf.

79 Data from the Inter-American Development Bank retrieved from "BID: Unos 328 mil peruanos ingresaron a la clase media," RPP Noticias, https://rpp.pe/economia/economia/bid-unos-328-mil-peruanos-ingresaron-a-la-clase-media-noticia-797249.

80 Martuccelli, *Lima y sus arenas.* On the impact of consumption on Latin American political life, see Andy Baker, *The Market and the Masses in Latin America: Policy Reform and Consumption in Liberalizing Economies* (New York: Cambridge University Press, 2009), 285.

81 This paragraph can be found in its entirety in Alberto Vergara and Aaron Watanabe, "Presidents Without Roots: Understanding the Peruvian Paradox," *Latin American Perspectives* 46, no. 5 (2019): 25–43.

82 "Próximamente el mundo reconocerá 'milagro peruano,' asegura Al Gore," Agencia Peruana de Noticias Andina, October 13, 2010, https://andina.pe/agencia/noticia-proximamente-mundo-reconocera-milagro-peruano-asegura-al-gore-322394.aspx.

83 Álvaro Espinoza and Ricardo Fort, *Inversión sin planificación: La calidad de la inversión pública en los barrios vulnerables de Lima* (Lima: GRADE, 2017).

84 Steven Levitsky and Mauricio Zavaleta, *¿Por qué no hay partidos políticos en el Perú?* (Lima: Planeta, 2019).

85 On the contribution of illegal economies to the election campaigns of political parties, see Denisse Rodríguez, "Partidos pobres, campañas ricas," in *Perú: Elecciones 2016: Un país dividido y un resultado inesperado*, ed. Fernando Tuesta (Lima: Fondo Editorial PUCP, 2017), 65–90.

86 "Jaime Antezana: 'Hay 14 congresistas vinculados al narcotráfico,'" *Perú21*, September 5, 2014, https://peru21.pe/politica/jaime-antezana -hay-14-congresistas-vinculados-narcotrafico-183732-noticia/.

87 Federico Tong, "Elecciones regionales, provinciales y distritales en el VRAEM, ERM 2014," Informes Analíticos (UNODC and Devida, 2014).

88 JNE-Observa Igualdad platform, https://observaigualdad.jne. gob.pe/.

89 On the legal, informal, and illegal economies and how they are inter-linked, see Francisco Durand, "Socioeconomías informales y delictivas," in *Perú hoy: El Perú subterráneo* (Lima: DESCO, 2013), 21–36.

90 For an analysis of the causes of this, see Omar Manky, "Liderazgos precarios: Organización y líderes sindicales en perspectiva comparada," *Latin American Research Review* 54, no. 4 (2019): 877–92.

91 Álvaro Espinoza and Ricardo Fort, *Mapeo y tipología de la expansión urbana en el Perú* (Lima: GRADE and Asociación de Desarrolladores Inmobiliarios, 2020).

92 See Víctor Torres, *Minería ilegal e informal en el Perú: Impacto socioeconómico* (Lima: CooperAcción and Acción Solidaria para el Desarrollo, 2018).

93 UNODC, *Colombia: Monitoreo de territorios afectados por cultivos ilícitos 2017* (Bogotá: SIMCI-UNODC, 2018).

94 Data from the LAPOP 2019 survey, Vanderbilt University, Center for Global Democracy, Americas Barometer 2018/19, https://www .vanderbilt.edu/lapop/ab2018.php.

95 The data on Peruvian cities were obtained from the INEI portal. On Cen-tral American countries, see the World Bank Open Data portal, https:// data.worldbank.org.

96 The ranking only includes megacities.

97 Marcelo Bergman, *More Money, More Crime: Prosperity and Rising Crime in Latin America* (New York: Oxford University Press, 2018).

98 Eduardo Dargent, Andreas Feldmann, and Juan Pablo Luna, "Greater State Capacity, Lesser Stateness: Lessons from the Peruvian Commodity Boom," *Politics and Society* 45, no. 1 (2017): 3–34.

99 Alfredo Torres, "La paradoja del crecimiento infeliz," *El Comercio*, December 2, 2008, https://www.ipsos.com/es-pe/la-paradoja-del -crecimiento-infeliz.

100 Omar Awapara has argued that Peruvian votes from the period have been marked by the winners and losers of the country's economic model. See Omar Awapara, "The Geography of Free Trade: Explaining Variation in Trade Policy in Latin America" (PhD dissertation, University of Texas at Austin, 2018).

101   See Eduardo Dargent et al., eds., *Resource Booms and Institutional Pathways* (Cham, Switzerland: Palgrave Macmillan, 2017); Moisés Arce, *Resource Extraction and Protest in Peru* (Pittsburgh: University of Pittsburgh Press, 2014); and Carlos Meléndez, *La soledad de la política: Transformaciones estructurales, intermediación política y conflictos sociales en el Perú (2000–2012)* (Lima: Mitin Editores, 2012).

102   Javier Arellano Yanguas, "Bonanza minera y conflictos sociales en Perú: Límites de la nueva agenda política para la gestión de los recursos naturales," in *Temas sobre gobernanza y cooperación al desarrollo*, ed. Jokin Alberdi and Miguel Gonzálezin (Bilbao: Hegoa, 2009), 59–68.

103   José Luis Pérez Guadalupe, "Las nuevas formas políticas de representación religiosa," in *Aproximaciones al Perú de hoy desde las ciencias sociales*, ed. Felipe Portocarrero and Alberto Vergara (Lima: Fondo Editorial de la Universidad del Pacífico, 2013).

104   Instituto Nacional de Estadística e Informática, "Perú: Encuesta Demográfica y de Salud Familiar," May 23, 2024, https://www.gob.pe/institucion/inei/informes-publicaciones/5601739-peru-encuesta-demografica-y-de-salud-familiar-endes-2023.

105   In Lima alone, it was estimated that half a million people took part in the march.

106   Piero Ghezzi and José Gallardo, *Qué se puede hacer con el Perú: Ideas para sostener el crecimiento económico en el largo plazo* (Lima: Fondo Editorial PUCP and la Universidad del Pacífico, 2013), 11. Other examples of books that stress the limitations with their own accentuation include John Crabtree, ed., *Construir instituciones: Democracia, desarrollo y desigualdad en el Perú desde 1980* (Lima: Fondo Editorial PUCP, Fondo Editorial de la Universidad del Pacífico, and IEP, 2006); Carlos Ganoza and Andrea Stiglich, *El Perú está calato: El falso milagro de la economía peruana y las trampas que amenazan nuestro progreso* (Lima: Planeta, 2015); and Vergara, *Ciudadanos sin república*.

107   Vergara, *Ciudadanos sin república*, 248.

108   Vital to this point is the report that Congress member Juan Pari Choquecota presented in 2017: Francisco Durand, *Odebrecht, la empresa que capturaba gobiernos* (Lima: Fondo Editorial PUCP, 2019); Malu Gaspar, "Una trama de vale un Perú: Ascenso y caída de Odebrecht en Latinoamérica," *Folha de S. Paulo* 130 (2017); and the journalistic articles of Gustavo Gorriti and Romina Mella for IDL-Reporteros, https://www.idl-reporteros.pe. On the Lava Jato scandal from a Latin American perspective, see Paul Lagunes and Jan Svejnar, eds., *Corruption and the Lava Jato Scandal in Latin America* (London: Routledge, 2020).

109   TV Peru, "Presidente Kuczynski: 'El gobierno que yo lidero apuesta por la modernización,'" September 20, 2016, https://www.tvperu.gob.pe/noticias/politica/presidente-kuczynski-el-gobierno-que-yo-lidero-apuesta-por-la-modernizacion.

110 In 2016, economic growth stood at 4 percent, while come the final quarter of 2017 it had fallen to 2.2 percent. Meanwhile, informality totaled 72 percent in 2016 and rose to 72.5 percent in the final quarter of the following year. In 2017, according to the INEI, poverty increased by a percentage point to 21.7 percent.

111 Mauricio Zavaleta and Paulo Vilca, "Partidos nacionales, políticos locales: Una mirada a las candidaturas parlamentarias desde el sur del Perú," in *Perú: Elecciones 2016: Un país dividido y un resultado inesperado* (Lima: Fondo Editorial de la PUCP, 2017), 309–36.

112 Juan Pablo Luna, "Parallel Universes, Time Compression, and the Collapse of Legitimate Representation" (unpublished manuscript, 2021).

113 According to information provided by the Peruvian Congress, between August 2016 and May 2017 ministers of state attended Congress on 141 occasions.

114 In 2013, Keiko had declared that her "father does not believe in parties. Like a good *caudillo*, he does not like to cede power. And to build a political organization one must cede power." Quoted in Steven Levitsky and Mauricio Zavaleta, "Why No Party-Building in Peru?," in *Challenges of Party-Building in Latin America*, ed. Steven Levitsky, James Loxton, et al. (Cambridge: Cambridge University Press, 2016), 433. In 2017, with a supermajority, the congressional grouping refused to approve an amendment to the penal code that would have permitted Alberto Fujimori's release from prison.

115 The minister of the economy, Alfredo Thorne, was censured in June 2017.

116 See Martin Riepl, *Vizcarra: Una historia de traición y lealtad* (Lima: Planeta, 2019).

117 Luis Pásara, *De Montesinos a los cuellos blancos: La persistente crisis de la justicia peruana* (Lima: Planeta, 2019).

118 Valid votes exceeded 80 percent. Support for constitutional reform of the composition and functions of the National Board of Justice stood at 86.5 percent; support for a reform to regulate part financing, 85.8 percent; and the introduction of non-reelection of Congress members, 85.8 percent. Conversely, a proposal to introduce a second chamber was rejected by 90.5 percent of the voters.

119 In its judgment on January 14, 2019, the Constitutional Tribunal confirmed the legality of the dissolution of Congress.

120 See Camila Gianella, Jasmine Gideon, and Maria José Romero, "What Does COVID-19 Tell Us About the Peruvian Health System?," *Canadian Journal of Development Studies / Revue Canadienne d'Études du Développement* 42, nos. 1–2 (April 3, 2021): 55–67.

121 For further details on this, see Zoila Ponce de Leon, "Healthcare Reform out of Nowhere? Policy Reform and the Lack of Programmatic Commitment in Peru," *Journal of Latin American Studies* 53, no. 3 (2021): 493–519. On the other hand, the Organization for Economic Co-operation and Development (OECD) and the World Bank showed that, in 2010 and

2017, the rise in health spending in Peru was proportional to the growth in GDP. That is, the rise in health spending was inertial. See OECD and World Bank, *Panorama de la salud: Latinoamérica y el Caribe 2020* (Paris: OECD, 2020), https://www.oecd.org/es/publications/panorama-de-la-salud-latinoamerica-y-el-caribe-2020_740f9640-es.html.

122 See OECD and World Bank, *Panorama de la salud.*

123 Data from Ipsos polling conducted in April 2020, https://www.ipsos.com/sites/default/files/ct/news/documents/2020–04/opinion_data_-_22_de_abril_del_2020.pdf.

124 From the song "Up to Me."

125 Miguel Jaramillo and Kristian López, *Políticas para combatir la pandemia del COVID-19* (Lima: GRADE, 2021).

126 Luis Jochamowitz and Rafaella León, *Días contados: Lucha, derrota y resistencia del Perú en pandemia* (Lima: Planeta, 2021).

127 On the Túpac Amaru rebellion, see Charles Walker, *La rebelión de Túpac Amaru* (Lima: IEP, 2014). Peruvian losses in the War of the Pacific are estimated at between 12,000 and 18,000, while Chilean losses are thought to have been no higher than 3,000; see William Sater, *Andean Tragedy: Fighting the War of the Pacific, 1879–1884* (Lincoln: University of Nebraska Press, 2007). For the data on the internal armed conflict, see the final report of the Truth and Reconciliation Commission: Comisión de la Verdad y Reconciliación, *Informe final.*

128 "Comunicado de periodistas de TVPerú," TVPE Noticias, November 13, 2020, https://tvperu.gob.pe/noticias/nacionales/comunicado-de-periodistas-de-tvperu.

129 This was made clear when the prime minister, Ántero Flores-Aráoz, stated with reference to the police force, "In me they will find a champion." "Flores-Aráoz a policías: 'En mí encontrarán un defensor,'" Canal N, November 13, 2020, https://canaln.pe/actualidad/antero-flores-araoz-policias-mi-encontraran-defensor-n427530.

130 Eduardo Villanueva, *Rápido, violento y muy cercano: Las movilizaciones de noviembre de 2020 y el futuro de la política digital* (Lima: Fondo Editorial PUCP, 2021).

131 "Flores-Aráoz a policías: 'En mí encontrarán un defensor.'"

132 On Merino's week in power, see Human Rights Watch, "Perú: Graves abusos policiales contra manifestantes" (2020), https://www.hrw.org/es/news/2020/12/17/peru-graves-abusos-policiales-contra-manifestantes.

133 José Carlos Agüero, *Cómo votan los muertos* (Lima: La Siniestra Ensayos, 2021), 8.

134 Agüero, *Cómo votan los muertos,* 6.

135 Piero Ghezzi, *El estado productivo: Una apuesta para reconstruir la relación entre mercado y estado en el Perú de la pospandemia* (Lima: Planeta, 2021).

136 Javier Prialé, "Carolina Trivelli: "Ahora tenemos una pobreza marcada por el hambre," *Gestión*, November 20, 2022, https://gestion.pe/economia/crolina-trivelli-ahora-tenemos-una-pobreza-marcada-por-el-hambre-noticia/.

137   Guillermo O'Donnell, "Un juego imposible: Competición y coaliciones entre partidos políticos en Argentina, 1955–1966," in *Modernización y autoritarismo* (Buenos Aires: Paidós, 1972).

138   Eduardo Dargent, *Demócratas precarios: Élites y debilidad democrática en el Perú y América Latina* (Lima: IEP, 2009).

139   Laura Amaya, "Volando sin retorno," Instituto de Esudios Peruanos, September 26, 2023.

140   The title of Cohen's fourth studio album.

141   Paul Drake, *Between Tyranny and Anarchy: A History of Democracy in Latin America, 1800–2006* (Stanford, CA: Stanford University Press, 2009).

142   Pablo Gerchunoff and Lucas Llach, *El ciclo de la ilusión y el desencanto: Un siglo de políticas económicas argentinas* (Buenos Aires: Ariel, 1998).

143   Carlos Monsiváis, *Las esencias viajeras: Hacia una crónica cultural del Bicentenario* (Mexico City: FCE, 2012), 65.

SEVEN / CYNTHIA MCCLINTOCK

Peru, the First Two Centuries

Challenges, Failures, and Achievements in Comparative Perspective

From the start, the challenges to nation-building in Peru were formidable. Peru's colonial legacy and its geography were daunting. In the War of the Pacific (1879–83), Peru suffered a major military defeat. Through the country's two centuries, it underwent cycles of economic boom and bust more frequently than other Latin American nations. These painful experiences led to exceptionally severe levels of social mistrust and pessimism, impeding efforts to build political parties and achieve political and social inclusion; until recently, Peru lagged behind its neighbors in political and social inclusion. Yet to Peru's great credit, despite the country's challenges its people have been resilient and resourceful, fashioning unusual experiments that, in the first decades of the twenty-first century in particular, led to considerable achievements. Indeed, arguably, in the metaphor in this book's introduction, Sisyphus pushed the rock farther up the hill than ever before and gained greater understanding of the challenges before him than he had ever had previously.

The Challenges: Peru During the Conquest, Colony, and Nineteenth Century

The Spanish Conquest of the Incas catalyzed Peru's fundamental challenge: building one nation from different peoples, one of whom had ravaged the other and betrayed its leader. The Peru-based Incan Empire was the largest in the hemisphere, holding sway over approximately ten million people—many more than the Aztecs or, before them, the Mayans. It is not surprising that the traumas of the conquest would be more severe and long-standing in Peru than in other Latin American countries and that Peru's political culture—the values and expectations of its citizens—would be marked for centuries by the legacies of brutality and deceit by the Spaniards against Peru's Indigenous peoples. By comparison, the two Latin American countries with the most robust records of inclusion and democracy—Costa Rica and Uruguay—were remote, un-demarcated areas of the Spanish colony, without large Indigenous civilizations, without minerals, and, accordingly, without the cruelty of the colonial labor regime.

Not only was the ethnic divide between white descendants of Europeans and Indigenous peoples wide, but it was also reinforced by geography. Whereas the capital cities of Peru's Andean neighbors are in the mountains, Lima is on the coast, and the mountains between Lima and Peru's Indigenous population centers are exceptionally steep. Accordingly, the distinct ethnic groups in Peru interacted less frequently than the distinct ethnic groups in other Latin American countries.

The immensity of the challenge was clear. As Mario Vargas Llosa wrote, Peru was "an artificial gathering of men from different languages, customs, and traditions whose only common denominator was having been condemned by history to live together without knowing or loving one another."[1] Peru's foremost historian, Jorge Basadre, distinguished the "two Perus"—*Perú oficial*, the Peru of Lima and the state bureaucracy, and *Perú profundo*, the Peru of the *provincias* and Indigenous peoples. Similarly, a foremost sociologist, Gonzalo Portocarrero, argued that two fantasies—among European descendants, the fear of a race war; among Indigenous peoples, the return of the Inca emperor to rescue his people—divided Peruvians.[2]

The deep fear of a race war is cited in this volume by Charles Walker, and it is likely that Peru's elites were less confident in their own project and more fearful of the lower classes than the elites in Peru's Andean neighbors. Yet, rather than seek to accommodate the lower classes, Peru's elites sought to continue their exclusion. As Walker emphasizes, into the middle of the nineteenth century "Peru . . . maintained a rigid class or caste system"; as one example, Walker points out the paucity of discussion of the injustice of slavery in Peru. Slavery was finally abolished in Ecuador in 1822, in Bolivia in 1825, and in Colombia in 1851, but in Peru not until 1854.

Why were Peru's elites more fearful and less confident in their own project? Perhaps one reason was the larger size of Peru's Indigenous population. Perhaps another reason was the experience of the Túpac Amaru rebellion; as Walker notes, it was the largest in Spanish American colonial history, and directly in Peru's heartland. Perhaps another was the extreme precariousness of power in Peru in its early decades; as Walker notes, there were fourteen different presidencies in the twenty years between 1821 and 1841.

Probably, too, both a cause and effect of fear and pessimism among Peru's elites was Peru's devastating defeat by Chile in the War of the Pacific (1879–83). Not only did Peru lose nitrate-rich territory to Chile, but Lima was occupied by the Chileans, who exacted a terrible toll in human life, rape, and destruction of infrastructure. While Bolivia was also defeated in the War of the Pacific (and subsequently in the Chaco War), its capital was not occupied; Paraguay is the only other Latin American nation that has suffered the occupation of its capital by a rival Latin American country (in the War of the Triple Alliance, 1869–70). Nor was the military conflict about the Peru-Bolivia Confederation (1837–39) salutary. Although the Lima-based forces prevailed, Peru's southern sectors were dispirited; further, General Agustín Gamarra (who had become president for a second time) was killed when he tried to take over Bolivia in 1841—as Walker reports, "likely by one of his own troops."

Yet another factor shaping elites' fear and division was likely to have been the volatility of its key exports. Peru's cycles of export booms and busts implied cycles of making fortunes and gaining power but then losing fortunes and losing power. As Natalia Sobrevilla Perea shows, Peru's first economic roller coaster was with guano; guano exports boomed in the early 1840s but collapsed in the early 1870s. In the late nineteenth century, Peru's key exports were silver and wool, originating in the sierra; but by the middle of the twentieth century, its key exports were sugar, cotton, and oil, all originating on the coast, favoring coastal elites.[3] In the 1960s and 1970s, oil was exhausted while silver and copper rebounded. But the most dramatic change was a boom in fish products off Peru's coast—which in turn collapsed in the 1980s.[4] There is no other Latin American country that has undergone such a large number of cycles of export booms and busts. From the 1870s into the 1970s in Brazil, Colombia, and most of Central America, coffee was the key export; in Argentina, Paraguay, and Uruguay, livestock products; in Bolivia, minerals, first silver and then tin. In Chile and Venezuela, a major export of the nineteenth century ended but was succeeded by a steady export in the twentieth: nitrates were followed by copper in Chile, cacao by oil in Venezuela. Changes in the structure of exports have been considerable in Ecuador and Mexico, but not as abrupt as in Peru.[5]

For arguably all these reasons, Peru's elites had tremendous difficulty building enduring political parties—difficulty reaching out to people at the country's grassroots and difficulty maintaining leaders' cooperation. Parties last only when they build popular support that withstands some leadership errors and only when long-standing party leaders are trusted to make way for new leaders. If pessimism prevails and presidents are expected to fail, they are likely to be abandoned by allies at the first crisis and concomitantly lose popular support. Parties fragment and governance is more difficult.

In the history of Peru, only three parties—the Constitutional Party, the Democratic Party, and the Partido Civil (the *civilistas*)—have had elected to the presidency more than one individual from their ranks; the last year that a party did so was 1915. In other words, for more than one hundred years, no Peruvian political party has elected two different presidents. Electing its first president in 1872 and its last in 1915, by most criteria the Partido Civil was the strongest party in Peru's history. But, by the standards of Peru's neighbors, it was short-lived and, as José Luis Rénique shows, governance was problematic and cohesion elusive. Corruption continued (albeit to a lesser degree than under the previous military administrations); the second *civilista* president, Mariano Ignacio Prado, was claimed to have fled Peru just as the War of the Pacific began.[6] The Partido Civil was wracked by internal rivalries: from 1908 to 1912, Augusto B. Leguía was president for the *civilistas*, but then he broke with the party and, amid a fraught election, looked to the military to secure support for his reascension to the presidency in 1919.

This extreme party weakness and volatility were rare in Latin America. In Colombia, Honduras, Paraguay, and Uruguay, parties that were founded in the nineteenth century remained robust at least through the twentieth century. In Peru's neighbors Bolivia, Chile, and Ecuador, parties founded in the nineteenth century remained robust until 1934, 1948, and 1947, respectively.

As Peruvian elites' fear, pessimism, and division continued in the twentieth century, their efforts to impede popular inclusion continued also. For example, just as Peru was behind its neighbors in the abolition of slavery, it was behind most of them in the extension of suffrage to illiterate individuals. Illiterate individuals gained the franchise in Colombia in 1936, Bolivia in 1952, and Chile in 1972, but not until 1979 in Peru (and Ecuador). The only Latin American country where people who could not read or write gained the franchise later was Brazil (in 1985).[7]

The exclusion is evident in the statistics for economic growth, health, and education in Peru as of approximately 1960 relative to its Andean neighbors. (That is chosen as the start year because it marks the onset of popular frustration with export-based economic growth and because it is the first year for which comparative data are readily available.) Whereas Peru's GDP per capita was the highest of the four countries, life expectancy, infant mortality, literacy, and knowledge of the dominant language were worse than in Colombia and Ecuador—better only than in Bolivia, a country with a much lower GDP per capita (see table 7.1). Not only was Peru behind other Andean nations relative to its per capita GDP, but regional inequalities were exceptionally severe. Table 7.2 shows that in the 1960s and 1970s, for per capita farm income, infant mortality, and illiteracy, the disparity between Peru's most advantaged department and its least advantaged department was considerably greater for Peru than for rural Ecuador. Only for potable water was the disparity greater in Ecuador than in Peru—but the absolute percentages without potable water were much lower in Ecuador. Also, in Ecuador, the map of poverty was much more blurred than in Peru; one of Ecuador's poorer departments might fare worse on one indicator than another, whereas in Peru Ayacucho was almost invariably at a nadir.

Peru's rigid social and political hierarchy is emphasized by many analysts. Throughout this volume, Julio Cotler's metaphor of Peruvian society as a "baseless triangle" has been highlighted. Paulo Drinot cites Ernesto "Che" Guevara's conclusion in the early 1950s that Peru "has not developed beyond the feudal condition of a colony." When I was first in Peru, beginning research on Peru's agrarian reform, much was changing in the country, but the hierarchical tradition was yet evident. I was living in an agrarian cooperative near Huancayo when one day the former *patrón*

Table 7.1 The Andean Nations in 1960: Key Economic and Social Indicators

	GDP per Capita (in constant 2010 USD)	Life Expectancy (years from birth)	Infant Mortality Rate (per 1,000 live births)	Literacy (% of population > 15 years)	Population Speaking Dominant Language (% of population > 15 years)
Peru	2,660	48	55	61	53
Colombia	2,339	57	39	73	98
Ecuador	2,238	53	60	68	70
Bolivia	1,005	42	71	no data	37

Source: For GDP per capita, life expectancy, and infant mortality rates, see World Bank, Open Indicators, https://data.worldbank.org/country. For literacy rates, see Kenneth Ruddle and Kathleen Barrows, eds., *Statistical Abstract of Latin America 1972* (Los Angeles: University of California Latin American Center, 1974), 164; for the population speaking the dominant language, see David Scott Palmer, "'Revolution from Above': Military Government and Popular Participation in Peru, 1968–1972" (PhD dissertation, Cornell University, 1973), 7.

returned for a visit. As he strode around what had been his hacienda, the current cooperative members walked dutifully behind him, not beside him. When the former *patrón* spoke with the current cooperative president, the former *patrón* used the pronoun *tú* for the president and added the word *hijo* (for a man in his late twenties, studying for a graduate degree at the local university); by contrast, the cooperative president used the pronoun *usted* for the former *patrón*. Later, when I queried the cooperative president about the exchange, he said, "Well, that's just how things have always been here." In a survey of social and political values in various haciendas in Peru in 1969, more than 65 percent of the residents agreed with the statement "A few are born to command and others to obey."[8]

As Eduardo Dargent describes, it was, uniquely in Latin America, a military government that was the first to strive vigorously, through agrarian reform and educational reform in particular, for national integration and social inclusion. The power of Peru's hacendados was eclipsed and popular participation increased dramatically. Living in the agrarian cooperative near Huancayo and then two others near Trujillo, I had the opportunity to observe firsthand the cooperative members' excitement that the feudal relations of the haciendas had ended and that they were gaining respect and a political voice.[9] In sharp contrast to the 1969 survey

Table 7.2 Inequalities Between Advantaged and Disadvantaged Departments: Peru and Ecuador, 1960s–1970s

	Annual Farm Income per Capita	Life Expectancy (years from birth)	Infant Mortality Rate (per 1,000 live births)	Adult Illiteracy (%)	Without Potable Water (%)
Peru	1961 (in *soles*)	1972	1979 (rural and urban)	1972 (rural and urban)	1972 (rural and urban)
Lima	30,200	57	56	6	44
Ayacucho	3,300	45	128	55	93
Ecuador	1961 (in 1979 USD)	1972	1977 (rural)	1974 (rural)	1974 (rural)
Guayas	553	no data	56	36	13
Most disadvantaged department	201 (Loja)	no data	84 (Cotopaxi)	58 (Chimborazo)	34 (Pichincha)

Sources: For Peru, see Cynthia McClintock, "Why Peasants Rebel: The Case of Peru's Sendero Luminoso," *World Politics* 37, no. 1 (1984): 61, and Cynthia McClintock, *Revolutionary Movements in Latin America: El Salvador's FMLN and Peru's Shining Path* (Washington, DC: US Institute of Peace, 1998), 171. For Ecuador, see Carlos Luzuriaga C. and Clarence Zuvekas Jr., *Income Distribution and Poverty in Rural Ecuador, 1950–1979* (Tempe: Center for Latin American Studies, Arizona State University, 1983), 48, 71, 75, and 80.

about political values cited above, in 1974 only 26 percent of residents in the cooperatives believed the statement "A few are born to command and others to obey"; rather, 69 percent agreed with the statement "A few are not born to command."[10] Meetings among cooperative members were regular; most members attended and many spoke up. Said one member, for example: "At times there's no unity and I don't like the meetings. But in general you can learn what's going on and agree about investments and planting. You vote about what you want."[11]

However, the period of profound reform under General Juan Velasco Alvarado was brief. As Dargent points out, that government's ambitions were huge but the state was weak; also, the contradictions of a military government claiming to call for a "fully participatory social democracy" were severe. Despite cooperative members' happiness with the demise of the haciendas, most were skeptical of the Velasco government.[12] In the early 1980s, the cooperative near Huancayo where I had lived was destroyed by

Sendero Luminoso and the cooperatives near Trujillo dissolved into privately owned land parcels.

Further, despite the advances under the Velasco government, material benefits in Peru's most disadvantaged departments were scant. Very soon, in the early 1980s, the disadvantaged southern highland departments became the political base of the savage Sendero Luminoso insurgency. The explanations for the rise of the Shining Path insurgency include the charisma and shrewdness of the insurgency's leader, Abimael Guzmán; the frustration of young people raised in impoverished Andean communities but gaining an education and then furious at Peru's continuing inequalities; and Peru's 1980s economic plummet, exacerbating poverty and hunger in much of rural Peru despite the agrarian reform.[13] As Sendero Luminoso expanded, human rights abuses by Peru's security forces became egregious, despite Peru's elected governments. As Dargent and Alberto Vergara indicate, the legacy of the violent conflict was to tarnish the legitimacy of democracy and of Peru's left and advantage the authoritarian government of Alberto Fujimori, which tried to claim, however incorrectly, the mantle of success against the insurgency.

Why were the efforts at social inclusion in Peru insufficient in the twentieth century? Why was democracy not sustained for any period of time? Various theoretical perspectives offer helpful explanations.

Theorists of political culture believe that a country's historical experiences shape the norms, expectations, and values that in turn determine their behavior, especially behavior toward authority and in authority. Without social trust, citizens, political allies, and political rivals are quick to doubt that a leader is well-intentioned and quick to withdraw their approval, severely complicating the leader's task and, in a vicious circle, abetting the failure to keep promises that first catalyzed mistrust. In Peru, social trust is perennially elusive. In the 1969 survey of values in Peru's haciendas mentioned above, only 13 percent of residents agreed with the statement "You can trust most people in this place."[14] In annual Latinobarómetro surveys since the 1990s, social trust is low throughout Latin America, but particularly low in Peru, with barely above 10 percent of Peruvian respondents displaying trust, higher only than in Brazil.[15] Concomitantly, for the period 2002–18 in the Latinobarómetro surveys, average approval ratings "of the government led by President [name]" were lower in Peru than in any other country.[16] Although it is logical that average approval ratings would be higher in countries such as Bolivia and Venezuela, governed for much of this period by leftist presidents during commodity price booms, it is not logical that they would be higher in countries such as El Salvador, Honduras, or Mexico, governed largely by presidents to the right, growing slowly, and racked by organized crime.

Dependency theory (which argues that the economic interests of elites in "center" countries shape their country's foreign policy and that economic elites in the "center" countries ally with elites in "periphery" countries to exploit the lower classes) is also helpful. Drinot notes that in the 1920s, the United States was becoming the major political and economic power in Peru. The United States became Peru's most important trading partner and most important investment partner; US capital was predominant in Peru's mining, sugar, and petroleum industries. And US policy usually conformed to the interests of US capital.

First, when the authoritarian Leguía government welcomed US investors, it was embraced by Washington. By contrast, when the reformist government of José Luis Bustamante (1945–48) was struggling to service the country's debt, it found no support from the United States. During the Cold War, the weight of the United States in Peruvian politics increased further. As both Drinot and Dargent highlight, a key catalyst of the 1968 military coup against the democratic Belaúnde government was Peruvians' widespread perception that, succumbing to intense pressures by not only the US-based International Petroleum Company (IPC) but also by the US government, Belaúnde had covertly agreed to a new contract with the company that was insufficiently favorable to Peru. IPC was one of the most important companies in Peru and it had long enjoyed legal and tax privileges. Peruvians' opposition to IPC had mounted, and one of Belaúnde's key campaign promises had been the renegotiation of its contract. Within a week of the coup, the military government expropriated IPC.

As Dargent describes, although relations between the Velasco government and the United States were never broken, Peru established a considerable distance from the United States.[17] In 1967, in a context of increasing tensions between Peru and its neighbors (Chile in particular), Peru had asked to purchase sophisticated weapons from the United States, but the request was denied by the US Congress. Shortly thereafter the Belaúnde government purchased supersonic aircraft from France. More worrisome to the United States, the Velasco government turned to the Soviet Union for fighter bombers and other sophisticated equipment. Peru was only the second Latin American country after Cuba to purchase Soviet armaments. Not surprisingly, when subsequently the Velasco government was struggling to service its debt, the US government was unsympathetic.

Even during the 1980s and 1990s, when sectors of the US government were much more supportive of democracy in Latin America, pro-business sectors remained powerful and the US goal of market reform often trumped democracy. As was the case for many Latin American nations in the 1980s, Peru found that servicing the country's international debt was very difficult, but the Washington-dominated international financial institutions demanded debt service and a difficult transition to market economics despite the devastating impact on popular support for incumbent political parties, which in Peru were Acción Popular and APRA. In the 1990s, the sectors of the US government that supported democracy in Peru faced stiff headwinds from US companies and their political allies, which liked the warm welcome of US investment by Alberto Fujimori's government and looked the other way regarding its authoritarianism and corruption.[18]

Modernization theory is helpful as well. In this perspective, advanced by Seymour Martin Lipset and Adam Przeworski in particular, it is only as countries grow economically that democracy becomes viable. It is argued that, as countries become more urban and industrialized, educated middle classes emerge and demand democracy; it is argued too that as countries become wealthier, state capacity is increased, and with more diverse economic alternatives, the battle for political office becomes less savage. Przeworski found that democracy is likely only when a country's GDP per capita reaches a threshold of $4,115 (measured in 1985 purchasing power parity dollars).[19] Even as late as 1999, Peru's GDP per capita was considerably below this threshold.[20] Although access to education was increasing considerably—from, for example, 35 percent of the relevant age group enrolled in secondary school in 1970 to 70 percent in the early 1990s, a figure well above the regional average—it was also the case that, even so, less than 50 percent of the relevant age group was completing secondary school in the early 1990s.[21]

Not only the level of economic development but the pace of economic growth is important. Przeworski and his colleagues found that if a country's growth rate is negative, a coup is much more likely.[22] The economic crisis in Peru in the 1980s was catastrophic—as Dargent points out, the "worst economic crisis in Peru's history," and very possibly the worst in Latin America at the time. The plummet in Peru's real minimum wage—in 1989, it was only 23 percent of its 1980 level—was the worst among the nineteen Latin American countries for which data were reported.[23] Peru's decline in per capita GDP over the 1970s and 1980s was the most severe in Latin America save for Nicaragua.[24] Between 1981 and 1990, per capita

GDP fell at an annual average rate of -3.2 percent in Peru—much worse than the regional average of -1.1 percent.[25] As noted above, this economic plummet was fundamental to the expansion of Sendero Luminoso and the decline in support for Peru's major political parties.

Political institutions and electoral rules matter too. While an independent judiciary is widely deemed important for transparency and the prevention of corruption, the judiciary in most Latin American countries, including Peru, has been dominated by the executive.[26] Parliamentary systems are widely deemed superior to presidentialism; parliamentary systems are believed to provide valuable flexibility, in particular enabling an unpopular executive to be replaced, and also (because of the fact that the executive must have a legislative majority) making it possible to limit executive-legislative gridlock.[27] But of course presidentialism has been in place in Peru and throughout Latin America; and, as Dargent mentions, one factor in the 1968 military coup was the political paralysis resulting from the relentless opposition to the Acción Popular executive by the APRA-*odriismo* legislative majority. Further, a runoff rule for the election of the president has been shown to be valuable for presidential legitimacy, but in Peru no such rule was in place prior to 1979.[28] Rather, if no candidate won 33.3 percent of the vote, the president was chosen by Peru's Congress; in the 1962 election, the leading candidate fell just shy of this threshold and the ensuing unseemly machinations and likely paucity of presidential legitimacy were important factors catalyzing a coup.[29]

Further, as Dargent and Vergara indicate, although Peru's political parties were more structured in the 1980s than previously and more structured than in the twenty-first century, they were not robust. Acción Popular and APRA governed poorly and, amid the economic crisis and the Shining Path insurgency, all parties suffered a loss of human resources. Further, the paucity of cooperation and trust among party leaders continued. These deficits were especially apparent in the fraught 1990 election that led to the election of Fujimori. Most importantly, although until about a year before the election Izquierda Unida (IU) had appeared poised to win, the coalition divided; in order to win, the IU's leader, Alfonso Barrantes, decided to moderate and run a personalistic campaign, but this shift alienated his colleagues, who believed that Barrantes was disrespecting IU's principles and procedures. The result was a low vote tally for both leftist factions. Further, incumbent President García did not want his leadership of APRA questioned by a strong showing for the APRA candidate and gave support to Fujimori.

Bad luck is a factor too. From the 1930s through the 1960s, Peru's elites refused to accept APRA, the country's first reformist mass political party, as legitimate. Blocked from electoral participation, APRA often behaved in an intransigent and at times violent way—which of course stiffened elites' resolve to repress the party. Elites were successful in their exclusion of APRA in good part because while Peru's army did not entirely and invariably oppose reform, it fiercely opposed APRA; APRA militants' 1932 armed uprising in Trujillo had led to the deaths of numerous army officers, and Peru's military was unforgiving. It is possible that if this uprising and death toll had not occurred, various military coups that sustained elites' power would not have occurred either.

The Achievements: Peru, 2000–2019

In the first nineteen years of the twenty-first century—before the onset of the devastating pandemic in 2020—Peru came a long way. For the first time in its history, Peru maintained democracy and economic growth for more than a decade.[30] Arguably for the first time too, Peruvians saw the possibility of a cohesive nation. Still, Peru was trying to overcome long-standing political and social exclusion, and Peru's advances went only so far.

Peru's first three elections during this period (2001, 2006, and 2011) were exemplary. Charges of irregularities or systemic bias were minimal to none; voter turnout rates were among the highest in Latin America.[31] The 2016 election was not unproblematic—a leading centrist candidate was disqualified for a dubious reason—but was otherwise deemed free and fair, despite a very close result in the runoff. Unusually for Latin America, among the victors in the presidential contests, two were candidates of color (Alejandro Toledo and Ollanta Humala), the first of whom had also been born beyond the capital; in Peru's Congress and cabinets, the representation of women increased remarkably.[32]

As Vergara indicated, economic growth was robust; indeed, in the first decade of the twenty-first century, Peru's GDP per capita increased more than in any other decade since 1920.[33] Between 2002 and 2013, averaging about 5 percent per year, Peru's GDP growth was the best in Latin America save for Panama; between 2014 and 2018, Peru's GDP growth easily surpassed the Latin American average but was not as fast as in several other countries.[34] While minerals continued to account for almost half of Peru's exports, the value of nontraditional exports such as asparagus and tropical fruits increased considerably, and tourism boomed.[35]

A major reason for Peru's economic growth was skyrocketing demand for Peru's minerals from China. China became Peru's most important trade and investment partner.[36] Although the United States remained a major actor, there were now two economic powers in the country, and the dependency relationship with the United States that had circumscribed Peru in the twentieth century attenuated. During most of this period, Peru's corporate tax rate was 30 percent, approximately the Latin American average but somewhat higher than in Chile (a key rival for mining investment).[37] While damage to nearby communities from extractive industry was considerable, Peru sought to attenuate the damage through the *canon* (the payment of 50 percent of a mining company's taxes to the governments of the regions and municipalities where the extractive operations take place) and, since 2016, through "prior consultation," requiring that extractive companies submit their plans to companies for review.

In this context, reductions in poverty and inequality in Peru were well above regional averages. Peru's poverty rate fell from 59 percent in 2004 to 20 percent in 2018—a stunning 48-point improvement.[38] Peru's GINI index for inequality fell from 56 in 1999 to 42 in 2019; Peru's 14-point improvement was similar to that in Ecuador and Bolivia but much greater than the regional average and roughly double that in Colombia and numerous other countries.[39] Peru's infant mortality rate improved from 30 deaths per 1,000 live births in 2000 (a rate about 30 percent higher than in Colombia and Ecuador) to 12 deaths per 1,000 live births in 2016 (a rate almost identical to that in Colombia and Ecuador).[40]

Scholars suggested that, finally, Peru's "baseless triangle" had become a "trapezoid," including a significant middle class.[41] Much of Peru's middle class was educated; Peru's educational gains in the twenty-first century were large. Enrollment in secondary school became universal.[42] Enrollment in tertiary education (beyond high school) jumped from 34 percent of the relevant age group in 2000 to 71 percent in 2015, versus a regional average of 52 percent in 2015.[43]

At the same time, Peru gained international prestige, which in turn fostered pride in the nation—in one Peru, not "two Perus." Machu Picchu was selected as one of the New Seven Wonders of the World; Mario Vargas Llosa won the 2010 Nobel Prize in Literature; and Peru's top chef, Gastón Acurio, won the 2014 Global Gastronomy Award. In this context, international tourism boomed. In a 2014 opinion poll, 55 percent of respondents said that Peru gave them a feeling of "pride"; Machu Picchu and gastronomy competed as the top reasons for pride.[44] Such a large percentage of

Peruvians with pride in their country would have been extremely unlikely in previous decades.

Perhaps most important, icons such as Acurio and singer and rapper Renata Flores became famous by integrating both Quechua and European or North American practices. Whereas Gonzalo Portocarrero had previously argued that two distinct fantasies—a race war and the return of the Inca emperor—divided Peruvians, he now believed that both fantasies were fading.[45]

Yet, as Vergara emphasizes, problematic legacies did in fact endure. Although Peru's elections gave rise to presidents with legitimacy, none of the four elected presidents was backed by a consolidated political party with strong ties to civil society. (By the time of García's reelection in 2006, APRA was a shadow of its former self, dominated by García.) Alberto Fujimori's daughter Keiko led a well-organized party, widely called the *fujimoristas*. But the party was polarizing and, after its narrow loss of the 2016 presidential election, it used its clout in Congress not to advance Peru but—just like APRA in the 1960s—to oppose the executive and paralyze the country. None of the four elected presidents enjoyed robust popular approval. Although it was praiseworthy that, after 2016, prosecutions against the four presidents (for corruption linked to Latin America's construction giant Odebrecht) advanced more than in any Latin American country save for Brazil, the revelations of wrongdoing angered citizens.

While economic growth was not based as much on one or two commodities as in the past, the main engine of growth was still mining, and mining concessions were affecting more than half of Peru's peasant communities and often damaging their land, water, and culture.[46] As mentioned, the *canon* and prior consultation were introduced to improve the lot of the communities, but success was limited.[47]

In this context, poverty and inequality continued. Although the rural poverty rate declined from 83 percent in 2004 to 45 percent in 2015, the rural poverty rate was many times the urban rate of 6 percent.[48] In Cajamarca—home to several of Peru's most lucrative mines—almost 20 percent of the population was in extreme poverty.[49] While public health was improving, the distance to adequate public health was very long.

In March 2020, the pandemic hit Peru with horrific force. The toll in lives was one of the worst in the world; more than double the number of Peruvian lives were lost to the pandemic than to the Sendero Luminoso insurgency. The plummet in Peru's GDP per capita was the deepest in Latin America save for Venezuela; poverty and inequality worsened.[50] In addition, the pandemic intensified global trends toward an international context of each-country-for-itself and toward the expansion of social media, which indulges misinformation.

Yet, while Peru had become a tinderbox and pandemic restrictions remained in place, presidential and congressional elections were held as scheduled in April 2021. The pandemic raised many challenges to these elections; candidates could not campaign, pollsters could not poll, and citizens could not meet to discuss the candidates and strategize their votes in a first-round presidential field fragmented among eighteen candidates. Two polarizing candidates at opposite ends of the spectrum—Pedro Castillo and Keiko Fujimori—reached the runoff, and the victory of the winner, Castillo, was very narrow; after weeks of Fujimori's baseless charges of fraud and then Castillo's appointment of a largely far-left cabinet headed by a very hard-line prime minister, polarization, cynicism, and dismay intensified. In December 2022, the polarization culminated in Castillo's irrational attempt to close the Congress, his immediate impeachment, and massive popular protests that left a tragic toll of more than fifty civilians killed by Peru's security forces. Proposals for early elections had overwhelming support but were dismissed by a Congress that appeared interested only in its own survival. Cynicism and dismay intensified further.

Conclusion

Despite the resounding advances in Peru during the first two decades of the twenty-first century, democracy and inclusion are again in peril. Not only does Peru continue to face the formidable challenges that began with the Spanish Conquest, but it suffered tremendously during the pandemic, and global trends are problematic also.

Still, Peru is resilient, and it is unlikely that Peru's advances in the earlier years of the twenty-first century will be evanescent. Arguably, only about sixty years ago Peru was a feudal country. But now, for more than forty years, every Peruvian has had the right to vote and overwhelming majorities have exercised that right; they will not quickly forget the principle of one person, one vote. Nor will the new roads and communication systems that link Peru's diverse citizens together disappear. It is likely that, with major infrastructure and educational advances, Peruvians will be able to resume the diversification of the country's economy to at least some degree. Further, the pandemic has reinforced the importance of a robust public health system and the importance of integrity and professionalism in public contracts. Amid the current political turbulence, promising proposals for political reforms have gained salience. While the tensions in Peru are severe, they catalyze intensity and, frequently, brilliance.

Notes

1 Mario Vargas Llosa, "Questions of Conquest," *Harper's Magazine*, November 1990, https://harpers.org/archive/1990/12/questions-of -conquest/.

2 Gonzalo Portocarrero, *Desde lejos, lo cercano: Reflexiones sobre el Perú* (Lima: PEISA, 2018).

3 Rosemary Thorp and Maritza Paredes, *Ethnicity and the Persistence of Inequality: The Case of Peru* (New York: Palgrave Macmillan, 2010), 109.

4 Rosemary Thorp and Geoffrey Bertram, *Peru 1890–1977: Growth and Policy in an Open Economy* (New York: Columbia University Press, 1978), 208.

5 See, among other sources, Rex A. Hudson, ed., *Colombia: A Country Study* (Washington, DC: Library of Congress, 2010), 144–52; Rex A. Hudson and Dennis M. Hanratty, eds., *Bolivia: A Country Study* (Washington, DC: Library of Congress, 1989), 152–64; and Dennis Michael Hanratty, ed., *Ecuador: A Country Study* (Washington, DC: Library of Congress, 1989), 143.

6 Alfonso W. Quiroz, *Corrupt Circles: A History of Unbound Graft in Peru* (Baltimore: Johns Hopkins University Press, 2008), 448–49.

7 Marisa Kellam, "Suffrage Extensions and Voting Patterns in Latin America: Is Mobilization a Source of Decay?," *Latin American Politics and Society* 55, no. 4 (2013): 29.

8 Cynthia McClintock, *Peasant Cooperatives and Political Change in Peru* (Princeton, NJ: Princeton University Press, 1981), 179.

9 This argument is also made robustly by Anna Cant, *Land Without Masters: Agrarian Reform and Political Change Under Peru's Military Government* (Austin: University of Texas Press, 2021).

10 McClintock, *Peasant Cooperatives*, 179.

11 Quoted in McClintock, *Peasant Cooperatives*, 133.

12 McClintock, *Peasant Cooperatives*, 287–315.

13 Gustavo Gorriti, *Sendero: Historia de la guerra milenaria en el Perú*, vol. 1 (Lima: Apoyo, 1990); Carlos Iván Degregori, *Sendero Luminoso: Los hondos y mortales desencuentros y lucha armada y utopía autoritaria* (Lima: Instituto de Estudios Peruanos, 1986); Cynthia McClintock, *Revolutionary Movements in Latin America: El Salvador's FMLN and Peru's Shining Path* (Washington, DC: US Institute of Peace Press, 1998), 178–84.

14 McClintock, *Peasant Cooperatives*, 207.

15 See, for example, Marta Lagos, "Latinobarómetro Survey Data 1996–2000," document presented at "Challenges to Democracy in the Americas,"

Carter Center, Atlanta, Georgia, October 16–17, 2000; Corporación Latinobarómetro, *Informe 2018*, 47, www.latinbarómetro.org.

16   Corporación Latinobarómetro, *Informe 2018*, 46.

17   For greater detail on these events, see Cynthia McClintock and Fabián Vallas T., *La democracia negociada: Las relaciones Perú–Estados Unidos (1980–2000)* (Lima: Instituto de Estudios Peruanos), 55–70.

18   McClintock and Vallas, *La democracia negociada.*

19   Adam Przeworski, Michael E. Álvarez, José Antonio Cheibub, and Fernando Limongi, *Democracy and Development: Political Institutions and Well-Being in the World, 1950–1990* (New York: Cambridge University Press, 2000), 92–106.

20   The information, in purchasing power parity dollars, is from World Bank, Open Indicators, https://data.worldbank.org/country, adjusted by the inflation calculator, https://www.usinflationcalculator.com.

21   David Post, "Peruvian Higher Education: Expansions amid Economic Crisis," *Higher Education* 21, no. 1 (1991): 106; World Bank, Open Indicators, https://data.worldbank.org/country.

22   Adam Przeworski, Michael Álvarez, José Antonio Cheibub, and Fernando Limongi, "What Makes Democracies Endure?," *Journal of Democracy* 7, no. 1 (1996): 42.

23   Inter-American Development Bank, *Economic and Social Progress in Latin America: 1990 Report* (Washington, DC: Inter-American Development Bank, 1990), 28.

24   Inter-American Development Bank, *Economic and Social Progress in Latin America: 1992 Report* (Baltimore: Johns Hopkins University Press, 1992), 286.

25   Inter-American Development Bank, *Economic and Social Progress in Latin America: 1992 Report*, 286.

26   Luis Pásara, *La justicia en la región andina: Miradas de cerca a Bolivia, Colombia, Chile, Ecuador y Perú* (Lima: Fondo Editorial PUCP, 2015).

27   Juan J. Linz and Arturo Valenzuela, eds., *The Failure of Presidential Democracy* (Baltimore: Johns Hopkins University Press, 1994).

28   Cynthia McClintock, *Electoral Rules and Democracy in Latin America* (New York: Oxford University Press, 2018).

29   Arnold Payne, *The Peruvian Coup d'Etat of 1962: The Overthrow of Manuel Prado* (Washington, DC: Institute for the Comparative Study of Political Systems, 1968), 48–55.

30   The Aristocratic Republic endured nineteen years but, with only a tiny percentage of the population allowed to vote, cannot be deemed "democratic."

31   McClintock, *Electoral Rules*, 156.

32   Joseph Cerrone and Cynthia McClintock, "The Impact of Runoff on Political Inclusion: Insights from Europe and Latin America," paper presented at the annual meeting of the American Political Science Association (virtual), September 10–13, 2020.

33   Shane Hunt, "Seeking Progress in Twentieth-Century Peru: What the Numbers Show," *ReVista: Harvard Review of Latin America* 14 (2014): 12–15.

34   Economic Commission for Latin America, *Economic Survey of Latin America and the Caribbean 2013* (New York: United Nations, 2013), table A-3; Economic Commission for Latin America, *Economic Survey of Latin America and the Caribbean 2019* (New York: United Nations, 2019), table A-2.

35   Cynthia McClintock, "Peru's Cleavages, Conflict, and Precarious Democracy," in *Oxford Research Encyclopedia of Politics* (New York: Oxford University Press, 2021), 103–22.

36   Alarco Germán, "China-Perú: ¿Una relación comercial y de inversiones del siglo XIX?," *Gestión*, July 13, 2020, https://gestion.pe/blog/herejias-economicas/2020/07/china-peru-una-relacion-comercial-y-de-inversiones-del-siglo-xix.html/.

37   KPMG provides comparative tax figures; see https://home.kpmg/xx/en/home/services/tax/tax-tools-and-resources/tax-rates-online/corporate-tax-rates-table.html.

38   For the poverty threshold set by the particular nation, see World Bank, Open Indicators, https://data.worldbank.org/country; "Latin America and Caribbean Poverty Rate 1981–2024," Macrotrends, https://www.macrotrends.net/countries/LCN/latin-america-caribbean-/poverty-rate.

39   World Bank, Open Indicators, https://data.worldbank.org/country.

40   World Bank, Open Indicators, https://data.worldbank.org/country.

41   Ludwig Huber and Leonor Lamas, *Deconstruyendo el rombo: Consideraciones sobre la nueva clase media en el Perú* (Lima: Instituto de Estudios Peruanos, 2017).

42   World Bank, Open Indicators, https://data.worldbank.org/country.

43   World Bank, Open Indicators, https://data.worldbank.org/country.

44   "Estas son las razones de nuestro orgullo y preocupación," *El Comercio*, May 4, 2014, 12.

45   Portocarrero, *Desde lejos, lo cercano.*

46   See, for example, Fabiana Li, *Unearthing Conflict: Corporate Mining, Activism, and Expertise in Peru* (Durham, NC: Duke University Press, 2015).

47   Gerardo Damonte, Barbara Gobel, Maritza Paredes, Bettina Schorr, and Gerardo Castillo, eds., *¿Una oportunidad perdida? Boom extractivo y cambios institucionales en el Perú* (Lima: Fondo Editorial PUCP, 2021).

48   World Bank Group, "Perú: Systematic Country Diagnostic," Report #112694-PE, 2017, https://documents.worldbank.org/en/publication/documents-reports/documentdetail/919181490109288624/peru-systematic-country-diagnostic.

49   Richard Webb and Graciela Fernández Baca, *Perú en números 2016* (Lima: Cuánto, 2016), 413.

50   World Bank, Open Indicators, https://data.worldbank.org/country.

Contributors

EDUARDO DARGENT BOCANEGRA is a full professor of political science at Pontificia Universidad Católica del Perú. His main teaching and research interests are comparative public policy, political economy of Latin America, and the state in the developing world. He has published in *Comparative Politics*, the *Journal of Latin American Studies*, and the *Journal of Politics in Latin America*. He is the author of *Demócratas precarios* (2009), *Technocracy and Democracy: The Experts Running Government* (2016), and *El páramo reformista* (2021).

PAULO DRINOT is a professor of Latin American history at University College London. He is the author of *The Allure of Labor: Workers, Race, and the Making of the Peruvian State* (2011), *The Sexual Question: A History of Prostitution in Peru, 1850s–1950s* (2020), *José Carlos Mariátegui o el "cojito genial": Historia y discapacidad en el Perú* (2023), and *Los años de Leguía (1919–1930)* (2024) and editor or coeditor of several volumes, including *Che's Travels: The Making of a Revolutionary in 1950s Latin America* (2010), *The Great Depression in Latin America* (with Alan Knight, 2014), and *The Peculiar Revolution: Rethinking the Peruvian Experiment Under Military Rule* (with Carlos Aguirre, 2017). He is currently writing a biography of José Carlos Mariátegui.

CYNTHIA MCCLINTOCK is a professor of political science at George Washington University. She is the author of *Electoral Rules and Democracy in Latin America* (2018), *Revolutionary Movements in Latin America: El Salvador's FMLN and Peru's Shining Path* (1998), and *Peasant Cooperatives and Political Change in Peru* (1981) and the coeditor of *The Peruvian Experiment Reconsidered* (1983). She was the president of the Latin

American Studies Association in 1994–95 and won its Peru Section's Lifetime Achievement Award in 2019.

JOSÉ LUIS RÉNIQUE holds a BA in *letras* from Pontificia Universidad Católica del Perú and a PhD in history from Columbia University. He has been a professor at the City University of New York since 1990. His most recent book is *Imaginar la nación: Viajes en busca del "verdadero Perú," 1881–1933*.

NATALIA SOBREVILLA PEREA was a professor of Latin American history at the University of Kent until 2024. She is currently a researcher at the Instituto Riva Agüero at the Pontificia Universidad Católica del Perú. She obtained her PhD at the University of London and has been a visiting fellow at Yale University, the John Carter Brown Library, and the Freie Universität in Berlin. She has held grants from the British Academy, the British Library, the Leverhulme Trust, and the Alexander von Humboldt Foundation. She has published extensively in both English and Spanish. Her most recent books include *Independence and Nation-Building in Latin America: Race and Identity in the Crucible of War* (2022), coauthored with Scott Eastman; *La nación subyacente: Diez ensayos para pensar la independencia peruana* (2024), and *Ayacucho, 1824: El fin del ciclo revolucionario* (2024).

ALBERTO VERGARA is a professor in the Department of Social and Political Sciences at the Universidad del Pacífico in Lima, Peru. His research has been published in the *Journal of Democracy*, *Latin American Research Review*, *Current History*, and the *Journal of Politics in Latin America*, among others. Among his latest books are *Politics After Violence: Legacies of the Shining Path Conflict in Peru* (coedited with Hillel Soifer, 2019); *Aproximaciones al Perú de hoy desde las ciencias sociales* (coedited with Felipe Portocarrero, 2019); and *Repúblicas defraudadas: ¿Puede América Latina escapar de su atasco?* (2023). His journalism pieces have been compiled in the volume *Ciudadanos sin república* (2013 and 2018 editions).

CHARLES WALKER is a professor of history at the University of California, Davis. He is the author of *Witness to the Age of Revolution: The Odyssey of Juan Bautista Túpac Amaru* (2020); *The Tupac Amaru Rebellion* (2014);

Shaky Colonialism: The 1746 Earthquake-Tsunami in Lima, Peru, and Its Long Aftermath (2008); and *Smoldering Ashes: Cuzco and the Transition from Colony to Republic, 1780–1840* (1999), all translated into Spanish. He has also edited and translated numerous volumes, including *Tu ausencia ha sido causa para todo esto: Cartas de amor y guerra—Túpac Amaru/Micaela Bastidas/Tomasa Tito Condemayta* (2024). He is currently working on a history of youth and the Shining Path.

Index

Arbenz, Jacobo, 188

Arequipa, 14, 20–21, 29, 35, 54, 57, 64, 68, 70, 74, 118–22, 145, 164, 176, 182–87; attack on, 36; as a city, 56, 138; commercial elites of, 143; courts of, 73; people from, 39, 69

Argentina, 54, 62, 71, 77, 94, 105, 167, 169, 172, 217, 234, 237, 242, 278, 286, 297, 314; Chile, and, 35, 63, 143; northern, 32; Perón and, 183; Juan Manuel Rosas and, 36; Sarmiento and, 75

Argentine Confederation, 71

Arguedas, Jose María, 181, 192

Arica, 20, 90, 112, 120. *See also* Tacna-Arica dispute

Aristocratic Republic, 81, 95, 105, 127, 156; and civilismo, 109; democratic aspects of, 327; end of the, 139; intellectuals of the, 147; postwar resurrection of the, 296; social tensions in the, 88; wake of the war and the, 141

Arriaga, Antonio, 14

Asháninkas, 153

Aspíllaga, Ántero, 108, 112–13

Atusparia, Pedro, 94

authoritarianism, 220; and corruption, 320; danger of, 244; exclusion of, 244; authoritarian governments, 140, 224, 268, 295, 318; authoritarian leaders: Alberto Fujimori, 2, 206–7, 227, 237, 239–40, 243–45, 254, 261, 269–70; Agustín Gamarra, 36; Leguía, 319; Velasco Alvarado, 213

autonomy, 35–8, 63, 68, 78, 112, 160, 190; concepts of, 19; degree of, 59, 61, 63, 165; fiscal, 57; greater, 18–9, 209, 264; Indigenous, 41, 60; lack of, 93; limited, 284; local, 16; movements for, 18; and political rights, 18; and power, 55; regional, 54, 68, 77; state, 215

Ayacucho, 27, 57, 69, 94, 98, 164–67, 192, 223–24, 315, 317; as a city, 89. *See also* Battle of Ayacucho

Aymara, 35, 147

Balta, José, 74, 90

Barrantes, Alfonso, 219, 221, 321

barriadas (shanty towns), 182

Barrios Altos, 182, 262

Basadre, Jorge, 4, 47n49, 95, 99, 110, 129; as historian, 31, 43, 53, 91, 157, 187, 312

Bastidas, Micaela, 14–15

Battle of Agua Santa, 56

Battle of Angamos, 90

Battle of Ayacucho, 12, 28

Battle of Carmen Alto, 56

Battle of Caseros, 71

Battle of Chacabuco, 22

Battle of Huaqui, 20

Battle of Ingavi, 36

Battle of Yanacocha, 35

Battle of Yungay, 36

Bautista Lavalle, Juan, 32

Bedoya, Luis, 259

Béjar, Héctor, 192

Belaúnde, Víctor Andrés, 118, 122, 124, 174

Belaunde Terry, Fernando, 186–93, 209–10, 216, 219, 229, 233, 243, 258–59, 319; first government (1963–68), 190–93; 210; second government (1980–85), 216–243

Belmont, Ricardo, 236, 259, 263

Beltrán, Pedro, 179, 185–87, 189

Benavides, Óscar, 163–66, 170, 172, 176, 257

Benel, Eleodoro, 144

Bermúdez, Pablo, 34

Bilbao, Francisco, 63, 67

Billinghurst, Guillermo, 89, 103, 112–22, 126, 130–31, 141, 163

Blanco, Hugo, 188

Blas, Camilo, 147–48

Bolívar, Simón, 19, 22–29, 34–35, 47n48

Bolivia, 12–13, 16, 27, 32–35, 55, 72, 76, 89, 171, 179, 188, 227, 313, 316. *See also* Peru-Bolivia Confederation

Bolognesi, Francisco, 90

by, 231; assemblage of, 206; building of, 311, 314; and civil organizations, 205; clientelistic policies of, 221; convention of, 124; crisis of, 227; criticism from, 216; development of, 218; disenchantment with, 238; government by, 222; incumbent, 320; influence of, 214; performance of, 207; pro-Indigenous national (type of), 227; right-wing (type of), 217; rise of mass, 168; traditional, 216; violence against, 226; twentieth-century context of, 258; weakness of, 242, 245

Pontifical Catholic University of Peru, 188

Portal, Magda, 162

Portales, Diego, 36

post-war reconstruction, 102, 122; civil war, 88, 91, 98; Grace contract, 92–93, 196n12; military rule, 88, 98

Potosí, 1, 12, 15–16, 19–20, 35; mines, 9, 32

power, 12–3, 18, 20, 24, 42; alternated, 33; and autonomy, 55; challenge to, 30; of the church, 17, 31; dictatorial, 26; enormous amount of, 41; eruption of, 55; fought for, 39, 56; hold on, 26, 30, 38; local, 53; loss of, 23; relations of, 36; seizure of, 30; struggle for/over, 56; to take, 29, 56

Prado, family business group, 94, 118, 142

Prado, Jorge, 164, 168

Prado, Mariano Ignacio, 72–76, 92, 89, 98, 161, 168, 314

Prado Ugarteche, Manuel, 115, 168–78, 179, 186–89, 209

Prado y Ugarteche, Javier, 102, 115, 125

Protestantism, 162, 235, 277

Pucallpa, 182

Pumacahua, Mateo, 21

Puno, 21, 36, 57, 101, 127, 143, 153, 224, 278; and Programa Puno Tambopata, 188

Quechua, 14–15, 35–38, 108, 147, 182, 213, 324. *See also* Aymara

Quiroz, Francisco, 56

Quispicanchis, 93

Quito, 26

Racism, 106, 146, 184, 295, 298

Ramírez, Juan, 21

Ramón Ribeyro, Julio, 183

Ramos, Ángela, 162

Real Felipe Fortress, 23

rebellions, 16, 17, 19; in Cuzco, 14–15, 17, 21, 27–28, 39; in Huánuco, 20–21, 28, 30–31. *See also* Amaru, Túpac

Reglamento Interior de las Haciendas de la Costa, 31

representation, 5, 189, 256, 262, 271, 275, 281, 297; accountability and, 300n14; aspiration/desire for, 253, 257–58, 260, 297; congressional, 177; crisis of, 295; decline of, 269; deliberation associated with, 254; democratic system of, 255; democracy without, 282; effective, 257; exchange of, 255–56; expense of, 272; female/women's, 275, 322; and governance, 254–55, 269, 273; inadequacies in, 259; national, 257; partisan, 257; political, 193, 208, 258, 277, 283–84, 286; republican priorities of, 270; responsibility of, 294; trade-off with administration, 282

republican: constitutions, 30, 32; utopia, 53

Restoration Army, 36

Restoration Government, 36

Revolutionary Government of the Armed Forces: agrarian reform, 5, 164, 203n104, 258, 315–18; Agrarian Reform Law, 191, 212; *La Convención*, 190; National Agrarian Society, 188; transformative processes, 207; Military reformism, 101, 140, 210; National Support System for Social Mobilization (SINAMOS). *See also* Velasco Alvarado, Juan